Advances in Cognitive–Behavioral Research and Therapy

Volume 3

Contributors

Robert A. Berley

Michael E. Bernard

Robert Cohen

Martin E. Ford

Neil S. Jacobson

Alan E. Kazdin

Thomas V. Merluzzi

Andrew W. Meyers

Thomas E. Rudy

Advances in
Cognitive–Behavioral
Research and Therapy
Volume 3

Edited by

PHILIP C. KENDALL

Department of Psychology
University of Minnesota
Minneapolis, Minnesota

1984

ACADEMIC PRESS, INC.
(Harcourt Brace Jovanovich, Publishers)
Orlando   San Diego   San Francisco   New York   London
Toronto   Montreal   Sydney   Tokyo   São Paulo

ACADEMIC PRESS, INC.
Orlando, Florida 32887

United Kingdom Edition published by
ACADEMIC PRESS, INC. (LONDON) LTD.
24/28 Oval Road, London NW1 7DX

ISBN 0-12-010603-5

ISSN 0730-5389

This publication is not a periodical and is not
subject to copying under CONTU guidelines.

Contents

Causal Attributions in Intimate Relationships: Toward a Model of Cognitive–Behavioral Marital Therapy

Robert A. Berley and Neil S. Jacobson

Recovering Social-Cognitive Schemata: Descriptions and Applications of Multidimensional Scaling for Clinical Research

Thomas E. Rudy and Thomas V. Merluzzi

Covert Modeling

Alan E. Kazdin

Cognitive–Behavioral Interventions in Educational Settings

Andrew W. Meyers and Robert Cohen

Linking Social-Cognitive Processes with Effective Social Behavior: A Living Systems Approach

Martin E. Ford

Childhood Emotion and Cognitive Behavior Therapy: A Rational–Emotive Perspective

Michael E. Bernard

Contributors

Numbers in parentheses indicate the pages on which the authors' contributions begin.

Robert A. Berley[1] (1), Department of Psychology, University of Washington, Seattle, Washington 98105

Michael E. Bernard (213), Department of Education, University of Melbourne, Parkville, Victoria 3052, Australia

Robert Cohen (131), Department of Psychology, Memphis State University, Memphis, Tennessee 38152

Martin E. Ford (167), School of Education, Stanford University, Stanford, California 94305

Neil S. Jacobson (1), Department of Psychology, University of Washington, Seattle, Washington 98105

Alan E. Kazdin (103), Department of Psychiatry, Western Psychiatric Institute and Clinic, University of Pittsburgh School of Medicine, Pittsburgh, Pennsylvania 15213

Thomas V. Merluzzi (61), Department of Psychology, University of Notre Dame, Notre Dame, Indiana 46556

Andrew W. Meyers (131), Department of Psychology, Memphis State University, Memphis, Tennessee 38152

Thomas E. Rudy[2] (61), Department of Psychology, University of Notre Dame, Notre Dame, Indiana 46556

[1]Present address: 1415 Western Avenue, Seattle, Washington 98101.

[2]Present address: Psychology Service, West Haven Veterans Administration Medical Center, West Haven, Connecticut 06516.

Preface

Although the history of cognitive–behavioral approaches to psycho-therapy is surprisingly short, writers have been active in the attempt to capture the transitions in the field accurately. It is public record that cognitive–behavioral strategies have been labeled a "shotgun wedding," and "oxymoron," and, less pejoratively, a rational integration of procedures with demonstrated efficiencies. The changes in the status of cognitive–behavior therapy have been dramatic: from radical criticisms of its mentalistic and theoretically weak foundations, to its being endorsed as the *second* most dominant theoretical orientation (eclecticism aside) among clinical and counseling psychologists.[1]

In addition to this expanding acceptance, there continue to be increases in the quality and quantity of research and applications pertinent to the integration of cognition and behavior. The growing field requires an outlet for authoritative reviews, critical commentaries, and theoretical treatises, as well as more speculative analyses.

Advances in Cognitive–Behavioral Research and Therapy is broadly conceived to include a diversity of topics relating cognition and behavior. For example, systematic exploration of assessment issues, theoretical analyses, treatment strategies for distinct clinical disorders, basic studies in psychology and psychopathology, and advanced research methodologies are a few of the topics appropriate for inclusion. Drawing on the developments in the study of cognition, behavior therapy, development, learning, personality, and social interaction, and occasionally including dialogues on pertinent issues, this serial publication draws together the advances in diverse areas related to cognitive–behavioral research and application. All contributions are prepared with the academic researcher and practicing clinician in mind.

[1] D. Smith. Trends in counseling and psychotherapy. *American Psychologist*, 1982, **37**, 802–809.

This serial publication is not intended to be only a collection of literature reviews, nor is it designed to serve solely as a display of treatment successes. Rather, each volume will contain a collection of articles that deal with a sample of the numerous content areas that are of interest to researchers and clinicians struggling with the interplay of cognition, emotion, and behavior. There will not be a single theme or mold to each volume. Rather, each contribution will stand by itself. Most important, perhaps, contributors are encouraged to develop their thinking and present these advances in the written product.

The contributions of research and applied psychologists contained in Volume 3 include theoretical and methodological papers that deal with adults, adolescents, and children. Robert A. Berley and Neil S. Jacobson provide an integrative and stimulating review of attributional processes in dyadic relationships with a special focus on theoretical and therapeutic aspects. Thomas E. Rudy and Thomas V. Merluzzi draw from and describe the advanced methodology of multidimensional scaling in their explanation of how to recover social cognitive representations. The literature on covert modeling as a therapeutic strategy is reviewed by Alan E. Kazdin, providing informative analysis of the characteristics of the procedure, the outcome evidence, and the issues in contemporary research. The application of cognitive–behavioral interventions in educational settings is examined and reviewed by Andrew W. Meyers and Robert Cohen. These authors provide an appraisal of the current efforts and offer an organismic conceptualization, emphasizing the organism as an active processor. Social cognitive processes and effective social behavior are linked by Martin E. Ford within a theoretically rich and empirically supported systems model. RET has been a seminal theory. In the final article, Michael E. Bernard advances the rational–emotive theoretical position to the area of childhood problems.

I am grateful to each of the authors for being a part of this venture and to the staff of Academic Press for their expertise and support. I also wish to recognize the competent aid of the staff of my home institution, the University of Minnesota, and the highly valued support of my wife, Sue.

Philip C. Kendall

Contents of Previous Volumes

Causal Attributions in Intimate Relationships: Toward a Model of Cognitive–Behavioral Marital Therapy

ROBERT A. BERLEY[1] AND NEIL S. JACOBSON

Department of Psychology
University of Washington
Seattle, Washington

---

[1]Present address: 1415 Western Avenue, Seattle, Washington.

1

ADVANCES IN COGNITIVE–BEHAVIORAL RESEARCH
AND THERAPY, VOLUME 3

I. INTRODUCTION

The marital therapy literature has proliferated dramatically over the past decade. This rapid growth has included elaborate theories on the origins of marital distress, descriptions of technologies for alleviating marital distress, and research relevant to both theoretical models and the applications of these models. At the forefront of this research have been clinical investigators operating from a behavioral or social learning perspective. A theoretical model of marital distress based on social learning principles has emerged, and, along with this model, a comprehensive approach to the treatment of marital distress has been developed, a model that we shall refer to as behavioral marital therapy (BMT).

BMT has had a significant impact on the field of marital therapy over the past decade, and has produced an impressive body of controlled research documenting its efficacy. In fact, it is really the only model of marital therapy that can claim a body of supportive research at this time.

Along with this supportive outcome research, there have been other concomitant research findings which are more sober in their appraisals of the effectiveness of BMT. Success rates, while substantial, are considerably less than 100%. Virtually all studies have found a residual minority of couples not responding positively to BMT. Moreover, there are also couples who improve significantly on our outcome measures but continue to experience varying degrees of marital distress. Therefore, along with the achievements of BMT, there is a growing recognition that there are more than a few couples who are not extensively aided by our technology.

As scientists and clinicians attempting to respond to both the achievements and the limitations of BMT, we could follow numerous possible directions. We could, for example, use clinical intuition to modify the treatment technology so that it is more widely applicable. Or, outcome data could be subjected to retrospective empirical analyses, to identify the factors that distinguish between successfully treated and failure cases. We have chosen still another path as the rationale for this article. Consistent with the behavior therapy tradition of applying principles from general psychology to clinical problems, we attempt to broaden the conceptual model of BMT by incorporating principles from social psychology, and then deriving clinical implications from this revised conceptual model.

For reasons that become apparent below, we have become convinced that cognitive interventions will strengthen the applicability and effectiveness of BMT. Thus, the primary purpose of this article is to develop a broader social learning model of marital distress based on cognitive constructs, and to apply this conceptual framework to the treatment technology commonly known as BMT. For reasons that also become apparent below, we have decided to focus on attribution theory as our base in general psychology. In Section II, we introduce BMT and provide a brief assessment of its historical development. Section III provides a brief overview of the attribution theory literature, and Section IV focuses on themes that are most relevant to attributional processes in intimate relationships. Section V provides a discussion of attributional processes in intimate relationships, along with a review of research that is directly relevant to understanding these processes. Finally, in Section VI, we discuss treatment innovations in the practice of marital therapy which follow from these concepts.

II. BEHAVIORAL MARITAL THERAPY AND COGNITIVE–BEHAVIORAL MARITAL THERAPY

In its earliest formulations, the application of behavior modification techniques to marital distress was little more than an adaptation of a monadic model of change to a dyadic situation. As O'Leary and Turkewitz (1978) remarked, clinical applications of principles from experimental psychology tend to support a therapeutic approach focused on the individual (Greer & D'Zurilla, 1975). Thus, early versions of BMT treated only one of the partners or treated spouses concurrently in individual sessions (Goldiamond, 1965), and emphasized typical behavioral treatments such as desensitization and assertion training (Lazarus, 1968). Stuart (1969) is typically credited with first presenting a marital treatment model explicitly recognizing the dyadic processes of social exchange and reciprocal reinforcement. More recently, BMT has been elaborated by Weiss, Hops, and Patterson (1973), Stuart (1980), and Jacobson and Margolin (1979). These approaches to BMT strive to increase couples' exchange of positive behaviors, diminish the use of aversive behaviors to control the partner, enhance communication, and teach problem-solving and contracting skills (O'Leary & Turkewitz, 1978). In addition, behavioral approaches share a philosophical preference for careful assessment, problem-focused therapy, and empirical verifications of treatment efficacy (Jacobson & Margolin, 1979).

While clearly grounded in empirically based theories of learning and reinforcement, BMT has always employed theoretical concepts that acknowledge the role of internal processes in marital distress. Behavioral models of marital distress depict spouses as rational, information-processing organisms who make decisions on the basis of their perceptions. Jacobson and Margolin (1979), among others (cf. O'Leary & Turkewitz, 1978; Stuart, 1980; Weiss, 1978, 1980), have indicated the importance of cognitive and perceptual processes in mediating the reinforcing and punishing impact of marital interactional behavior.

> People talk to themselves, they appraise their environments, and they make attributions and interpretations of their world. These self-statements, appraisals, and attributions mediate and moderate the effects of environmental stimuli on behavior, and can serve either as eliciting or discriminative stimuli. Attributions on the part of one's spouse regarding the "intent" of the partner's behavior can moderate the reinforcing effect of that behavior. . . . Emotional reactions can be elicited by specific self-statements, which often serve as interpretations of an environmental event. . . . The inclusion of cognitions as possible mediators of behavior will have important implications for the analysis and treatment of distressed relationships. (Jacobson & Margolin, 1979, p. 12)

Thus, social learning and behavior exchange notions emphasize that "spouses are not simply passive receptors of environmental stimuli, but rather actively evaluate and interpret such stimuli based on their idiosyncratic cognitive sets and schemata" (Jacobson, 1983). Indeed, O'Leary and Turkewitz (1978) argue that "much of what occurs in good marital therapy of any variety involves discussion of the assumptions that each spouse has: (1) about what was expected of the marriage, and (2) about what the marriage is providing relative to these expectations" (p. 247). Thus, effective treatment depends on changes in cognitive and affective domains as well as in overt behavior. Behavior change is best thought of as a means to an end rather than an end in itself (Jacobson, 1983). The end is increased marital satisfaction.

Jacobson (1983) summarized three broad categories of dysfunctional cognitive processes that can subvert desired changes targeted by BMT.

First, dysfunctional cognitive and perceptual processes may remain intact despite successfully induced behavior change. Though couples may exhibit behavior changes corresponding to stated treatment goals, such changes may not be noticed, may be regarded as impermanent, or may be interpreted in such a way that their impact is negligible. As a result, marital satisfaction may not be substantially altered. A stereotypic example is the wife who complains that her husband's increased affection is meaningless because it came "only" as a result of the therapist's directives. Second, dysfunctional cognitions may become autonomous from any behavioral referent. In this case, the wife may comment that while she enjoys a changed pattern of behavior involving kissing, hugging, and other affectionate behaviors, she still does not believe that her husband cares about her. In such cases, the cognitive and perceptual processes constitute the problem, and a continued exclusive focus on behavior change would be fruitless and unproductive. Third, dysfunctional cognitive processes can interfere with the behavior change itself, such that spouses will avoid complying with therapeutic directives or in other ways refuse to enact positive behavior changes. Dysfunctional cognitions may be directed toward the partner, the therapeutic context, or the process of change. For example, mistrust of a partner may lead one spouse to withhold potentially reinforcing behaviors with the expressed desire that the partner change first. The context or technology of therapy may not match clients' expectations, leading to a disengaged wait and see attitude. Or, as is frequently the case, one partner may blame the other for their marital distress and thus believe that therapy and change should be unilaterally directed.

As noted above, marital therapy evolved in a context of individual treatment. While the inclusion of social learning and behavior exchange theory has enabled therapists to expand their understanding of stimulus–response chains in dyadic situations, the underlying theoretical formulations are derived from what Kelley (1972b) has described as the minimal social situation, that is, a context in which subjects have no knowledge of each other or of their interdependence. Thus, while social exchange principles expand on the behavioral model by accounting for the presence of more than one individual, they do not account for the most salient characteristic of a marital pair, the presence of a committed, significant, and intimate relationship.

It is clear, for example, that the stimulus value of behavior will vary as a function of the relational context in which it is emitted. The stimulus value of behavior changes along a number of important dimensions when emitted in the presence of an intimate partner rather than a stranger. In addition, Goffman (1961) observed that the rules of social exchange change as well. While observing interpersonal transactions in a mental institution, Goffman noted two classes of exchanges: economic, in which a benefit may be bargained for a like-valued debt, and social, in which the value is essentially symbolic and defined in the context of the relationship. In an economic exchange, an individual buying a piece of jewelry will offer something of equivalent value, such as money. In a social exchange between intimates, a spouse receiving that piece of jewelry from the partner may respond (i.e., offer in return) with tears, expressions of joy or appreciation, or other affectionate behavior. Following from Goffman, Clark (1981) distinguished between exchange interactions, in which benefits of equivalent economic value are exchanged, and communal transactions, in which benefits are offered in response to a perceived need for the benefit. We would expect intimates to be involved in both economic and communal transactions; economic exchanges should predominate for instrumental behavior such as sharing of domestic chores, and communal offerings should be dominant for affection and intimate behaviors.

There are two interesting implications of Goffman's observation. First, the individual making a communal offering incurs the risk of being misperceived. It is therefore safer to offer benefits that are ambiguous regarding their communal or economic intent, so that the other cannot offer the rejecting response of treating the communal benefit as if it were economic. Second, since benefits that are bargained for typically imply an economic or exchange transaction, negotiations dealing with typically intimate behaviors may by implication be converted into economic or instrumental responses. This may help to explain why, as Jacobson (1983) remarks, certain traditional contingency management procedures prove to be self-defeating. For example, contingency contracting for physical affection may convert what is normally a communal offering into an economic exchange, and thereby undermine the reinforcing impact of the affectionate behavior resulting from the negotiation.

Because married couples engage in communal as well as economic transactions, many important marital behaviors are rewarding because of what they mean to the receiver. Marital relationships revolve around transactions that lead to each spouse feeling loved, esteemed, and respected. The derivation of such meaning depends on cognitive appraisal systems. Attribution theory addresses itself to the analysis of social appraisals, and provides a conceptual framework that has the potential to enhance our ability to describe and understand these transactions. The theory addresses the question of how a lay individual, acting as a "naive psychologist" (Heider, 1958, p. 12), comes to some particular conclusion about the causes or reasons for another's observed behaviors. The attribution theory literature leads to hypotheses that may help us in our attempt to understand intimate relationships.

The remainder of this article delineates an attributional framework for studying cognitive processes in married couples. We first provide an overview of relevant literature, followed by a discussion of attributional processes as they relate specifically to intimate dyads, and then conclude with a discussion of the implications for the process of marital therapy.

III. ATTRIBUTION THEORY: A SCHEMATIC OVERVIEW

Since Heider's seminal monograph introduced attribution theory to social psychology, the study of causal attributions has become one of the most prolific research areas in the field. During the 1970s alone, Kelley and Michela (1980) noted over 900 references. The field is diffuse and wide ranging, and is characterized by an abundance of reviews, reformulations, and additions (Jones, Kanouse, Kelley, Nisbett, Valins, & Weiner, 1972; Harvey, Ickes, & Kidd, 1976, 1978, 1981; Jaspers, Fincham, & Hewstone, 1983). Our goal is to present themes from this voluminous literature that have direct applications for conceptualizing and treating marital distress.

A. Prediction, Control, and Coordination

A central theme of attribution theory defines the underlying objective of attributional processing as effective control over the events occurring in one's life (Heider, 1958; Kelley, 1967, 1972b). Research consistently supports the concept that attributional processing functions not only by "providing the individual with the veridical view of his world, but [also] as a means of encouraging and maintaining his effective exercise of control in that world. The purpose of causal analysis—the function that it serves—is effective control" (Kelley, 1972b, p. 220). Miller, Norman, and Wright (1978) conducted a study in which subjects watched a bargaining game between one observable and one unobservable player. Subjects who had been told that they would soon be interacting with the unseen player reported that they had more dispositional information about that individual than did subjects who simply watched passively, even when given their expectancy information *following* their observation of the bargaining game. Thus, subjects who expected to interact with the player felt that they knew more about the player's personality. This finding cannot be due simply to visual orientation or attentional differences occurring during the course of the observation. Rather, the authors argue, the group differences most likely stem from the enhanced desire of the "interaction" subjects to understand and predict the actual or potential bargaining behavior of the unseen partner. Additional findings (Pittman & Pittman, 1980; Yarkin, Harvey, & Bloxom, 1981) tend to support the concept that attributions are motivated by a desire to control one's environment. Control of one's personal and physical environment is served by a variety of mental processes, most importantly the perception of an organized and stable world in which coordinated action may have a predictable effect (Brunswick, 1956). The perception of stability—the extraction of underlying invariance—is achieved at some cost; the power gained through the perception of underlying invariance is often accompanied by a loss of discriminative sensitivity. And so Hastorf, Schneider, and Palefka (1970) call our attention to the fact that attributions tend not to reflect real complexities, ambiguities, and multivalued states. It appears the complex, accurate perceptions of the world as it is cannot be accommodated into a stable, causal, and thus predictable world. As Kurglanski and Ajzen (unpublished) put it, the goal of cognitive processing is to create invariance out of variance "to impose order out of experience" (p. 44).

Kelley (1972b) divides attributional processing into two distinct categories: an unbiased and reasonable mirroring of correctly perceived data in which accuracy is limited but the process is rational, and a group of biased and erroneous processes which remain after one has accounted for those that are rational. However, as Kruglanski and Ajzen (unpublished) remark, the idea of error implies a secure criterion for inferential validity. Attributional processing is based on psychological rather than formally logical principles. Different individuals (or the same individuals at different times) will be biased in that they emphasize different aspects of a total field (Locke & Pennington, 1982) that cannot, in fact, be totally accounted for.

Kruglanski and Ajzen suggest a taxonomy of attributional biases with important implications for the understanding of couple transactions. According to the authors, biases may be either motivational or cognitive. Motivational biases include *ego enhancement and defense* (such as self-serving and egocentric biases), *effective control, hedonic relevance* (a desire to obtain control over situations in which another person is experienced as having the power to deliver positive or negative outcomes), *the belief in a just world* (in which one can enhance control over outcomes by acting in a worthwhile manner deserving of reward), and *the avoidability of physical harm*. Cognitive biases are grouped into two subheadings, those based on the salience or availability of data and those based on preconceptions. Salience and availability biases include *sampling bias* (in which the information available is not representative of the population as a whole), *selective attention* (though relevant information may be accessable to observers, they may focus selectively on those features of a situation that are, for one reason or another, perceptually salient), and *selective recall* (information retrieved from memory may itself be subject to a sampling bias). The subcategories of preconceptions include *presumed covariation* (the assumption that events or characteristics tend to covary or in some way be coordinated), *representativeness* (the placing of object A in class B according to the extent to which A is perceived to be representative of B), and finally, *causal theories* (a priori beliefs which represent peoples' understanding of the factors that *should* have an effect).

To summarize, people use causal attributions to create a more predictable world. In their quest for predictability and control over their environment, the world is inevitably simplified as attributional biases are created.

B. Attributional Schemes

In the attribution literature, a scheme has been variously described as a processing heuristic which represents content and structure of prior information (Kruglanski & Ajzen, unpublished); as a stored representation including a label, content information, and any elaborate thoughts or associations that may be used to facilitate the differentiation of later information (Upmeyer, 1981); and as organized elements of the qualities of some stimulus domain which control the tension and offer rules of inference (Tesser, 1978). A somewhat different view is offered by Kelley (1972a) based on his interest in how people process covariance information. For Kelley, causal schemes represent a person's conception "about how certain kinds of causes interact to produce a specific kind of effect. Each schema can be described in terms of a hypothetical matrix of data that summarizes the attributor's beliefs and assumptions about the distribution of the effect over various combinations of the causal factors. . . . Specifically, a causal schema is *an assumed pattern of data in a complete analysis of variance framework*" (pp. 151–152).

Attributional schemes allow people to process information very quickly in familiar situations. A number of authors have commented on the apparent ubiquity of scripted (Ableson, 1976) or mindless (Gibbs,

1979) behavior. For Langer (1978), scripted or unthinking behavior is defined by the relative absence of ongoing information processing. Bargh (1982) presents data supporting the notion that frequent and consistent experience with a particular constellation of percepts, thoughts, and feelings leads to a long-term chronic set of expectancies. Langer (1978) suggests that the result of such "overlearning" is that less information is processed on each repetition, so that eventually the behavior is based on minimal data. Taylor and Fiske (1978) suggest that the individual involved in automatic processing of information is generally responding to perceptual salience cues (intensity, duration, frequency, etc.), rather than cognitive cues such as novelty and significance (cf. Berlyne, 1960, 1974). Doherty (1981) presents the interesting notion that people who expect an aversive situation and enter an automatic mode of processing may experience depression from learned helplessness. Rather than learning any new information regarding the situation, the individual acts as if "he has heard it all before," and responds in an ineffectual and stereotypic fashion. The converse of automatic or mindless information processing has been described by Bargh (1982) as an active set involving conscious awareness of expectations, and by Taylor and Fiske (1978) as a controlled, active process elicited in situations perceived as difficult, novel, or uncertain.

It appears, then, that repeated presentations of an apparently similar situation result in expectations regarding the situation, and enhance the likelihood of mindless or automatic processing upon subsequent presentations. Research by Pyszczynski and Greenberg (1981) has shown that when an actor's behavior conforms to expectations, observers are less likely to seek out further information useful for inferring the causes of the actor's behavior. The implication is that people engage in less thorough attributional processing after observing an expected event. Rosenfield and Stephan (1977) found that the amount of responsibility attributed to any causal factor failed to change in light of additional plausible causes, if the behavior was expected. Newtson (1973) demonstrated that the "graininess" of distinctions made by an observer varied as a function of how expected an observed event was. Expected events were experienced in terms of large units of perceptions offering less information and permitting fewer distinctions, while unexpected events yielded finer units of perception and more available information. To summarize, familiar situations call for automatic and intuitive mental processes which generate expectancies based on the perception of cues thought to be causally related to an event. Fine-grain processing of perceptual information is minimal, and the apparent confirmation of an expected event reaffirms and reinforces the entire circular sequence.

If rapid, automatic processing is intimately connected with the establishment and realization of expectations, it is logical to suggest that unexpected events generate a more controlled and cognitively mediated sequence of search and process. Our interest is drawn to the latter situation because of its relevance to the issue of attributional change, since such change is unlikely in the context of mindless automaticity. Research has suggested a number of other events likely to initiate controlled processing and mindful attributional search.

C. Salience and the Self as a Stimulus

Given that we cannot attend simultaneously to all aspects of the perceptual field, the processes of selective attention and perceptual salience represent the by-products of attributional schemes. As Berlyne (1974) puts it, "many stimulus elements, present simultaneously, generally compete . . . for occupation of the nervous system's limited information-transmitting capacity. Events inside the organism may grant predominant influence to one property of a stimulus object, causing other properties of the same object to be ignored" (p. 124). Considering, then, potentially salient events as either inside the organism or a property of the stimulus object, we may examine attentional effects likely to predominate under situations of mindless vs mindful processing. In familiar, overlearned situations, we would expect salience to be a function of the intensity, duration, frequency, or motion of the stimulus object. Taylor and Fiske (1978) offer convincing evidence that this type of perceptual set predominates in most everyday situations. Perceivers tend to engage in minimal information processing, and make attributions "off the top of the head." In situations involving mindful processing, we would expect a lowered threshold for the standard categories of salient stimulus properties (a smaller "just noticeable difference"). Salience and attention are also partly a function of internal judgments that the stimulus or situation is novel, personally relevant, threatening, or ambiguous. The view that attributional processing may be either mindful or mindless suggests that there may be no conflict between Kelley's proposal that a perceiver makes attributions after logically weighing covariance information, and research supporting the concept that perceivers simply attribute causality to the most salient plausible cause. In most cases in which processing is automatic and mindless, salient causes may refer to a factor that is literally in the perceptual field (Taylor & Fiske, 1978; Tversky & Kahneman, 1974), or that is easily retrievable from memory (Pryor & Kriss, 1977).

There is a considerable body of research supporting the hypothesis that salience mediates causal attributions. Heider's (1958) assertion that, for an observer, "behavior . . . has such salient properties it tends to engulf the total field" has led researchers to argue that observers focus on the individual and his behavior, thereby overestimating the importance of dispositional factors in causing behavior (Jones, 1979; Synder & Frankel, 1976). It might also be noted that there is an important motivational bias that may account for this fundamental attribution error (Ross, 1977). As framed by Pittman and Pittman (1980), "the belief that the behavior of others is governed by stable internal characteristics makes the future more predictable and therefore controllable, whereas the lack of such determinants of one's own behavior allows for the flexibility required to meet the demands of a changing environment" (p. 378).

It is relatively easy to alter experimental subjects' attributions of causality by changing the salience or motivational aspects of the experimental context. McArthur and Post (1977) found that increasing the visual salience of an actor by manipulating the brightness of the image or the actor's physical movement led observers to attribute causality to the actor's dispositions. Conversely, Arkin and Duvall (1975) demonstrated that when the situation is dynamic, both actors and observers tended to make situational attributions. When the situation is stable (stationary), actors continue to make situational attributions while observers return to their focus on the actor's dispositional qualities. There is by now considerable support for the concept that observers will move from dispositional or internal attributions to situationally based or external attributions if aspects of the environment can be made more salient (Galper, 1976; Reagan & Totten, 1975; Storms, 1973).

D. Attributional Categories Utilized by Actors and Observers

Much of the early research on attribution theory investigated attributional categories employed by subjects for behavior originating in a stranger. The result has been an interesting array of attributional dimensions which may be used by individuals in explaining the causes of their own and others' behavior. Kelley (1967) has asserted that causality is typically assigned either to factors within the actor, in the person who is the object of the actor's behavior, or in the circumstances in which the action occurs. The distinction between causes attributable to something within the actor on the one hand and to aspects of the external environment on the other hand was initially popularized by

Jones and Davis (1965). Weiner's research (Weiner, Frieze, Kulka, Reed, Rest, & Rosenbaum, 1972) on causal attributions for success and failure also presents evidence for an internal/external, as well as a stable/unstable dimension. While there has been considerable argument regarding the logic, semantics, and naivete of an internal vs external dimension (Hamilton, 1980; Kruglanski, 1975; Locke & Pennington, 1982; Ross, 1977), the dimension has a powerful intuitive appeal. Moreover, there is considerable evidence that people are generally biased toward internal attributions as causal explanations for behavior.

Jones and Nisbett (1972) hypothesized that people tend to attribute their own behavior to external or situational factors, whereas they tend to attribute the behavior of others to dispositional or internal factors. This divergent perspectives hypothesis has received a great deal of attention, and has been subjected to a number of empirical tests. In a recent review of this literature, Watson (1982) concluded that actors and observers do indeed differ in the types of causal attributions they prefer. However, both actors and observers tend to favor dispositional causal attributions. They differ only in the relative causal importance typically ascribed to situations, with actors being more inclined toward situational attributions than observers.

E. Summary

The underlying objective of attributional processing is perceived control over the events occurring in one's life. The desire to create a predictable, stable environment often leads to attributional biases. Attributional schemes allow people to process information very quickly in familiar situations. However, unexpected, novel, or ambiguous events, when recognized, generate a more controlled and cognitively mediated sequence of attributional search and information processing. Perceptual salience cues serve as important mediators of causal attributions. In many situations, people are biased toward dispositional causal attributions in explaining both their own and others' behavior. However, there is some evidence that attributional categories differ depending upon whether one is attempting to explain one's own behavior or the behavior of another.

IV. CAUSAL ATTRIBUTIONS IN INTIMATE DYADS

As we now move to examine the nature and consequences of attributional schemes in intimate dyads, we apply the above themes extrapolated from basic research on attribution theory. It should be noted that relatively little research on attributional processes relates explicitly to intimate relationships. In particular, unique characteristics of intimate relationships influence attributional processes as a function of the following factors: the particular positive outcomes potentially available in the situation; the reciprocal control that each spouse exerts over those outcomes; the increased personal relevance or imagined relevance of a wide range of behaviors; the goals, purposes, and beliefs pertaining to a committed, ongoing relationship; the feelings and moods that an intimate relationship elicits; the lengthening history and increasing information regarding one's partner that accrues over the course of the relationship; and the particular individual and/or cultural beliefs that one brings to the relationship.

A. Reciprocal Determinism and Self-Confirmation

The research described in Section III is only indirectly applicable to attributional processes in ongoing dyadic interaction, because in no instance was the observer part of the actor's environmental field. In an intimate relationship, the observer who is making attributions about an event is also a participant in the event or at least has a stake in the outcome. In attempting to understand attributional processes in ongoing intimate relationships, it is important to ask the following questions: To what extent is each spouse aware of the contribution of his/her own behavior to salient relationship events? To what degree does each spouse recognize the reciprocal causality that governs dyadic behavior? Communication theorists have used the term *punctuation* to describe the arbitrary division of sequential dyadic interaction into hypothesized units of cause and effect (Watzlawick, Beavin, & Jackson, 1967). They observed that each spouse tends to view himself/herself as the victim or the recipient of the partner's behavior in conflict situations. That is, each partner views the other's behavior as the causal stimulus, and his/her own as the passive reaction. Each is insensitive to the reciprocal causality inherent in ongoing interactions between intimates.

In addition to punctuation errors, other consequences follow from each spouse's insensitivity to reciprocal causality. Each spouse may fail to recognize how his/her own behavior may place constraints on the behavior of the partner (Gibbs, 1979; Jones & Nisbett, 1972). Instead of viewing the partner's behavior as resulting from his/her own initiations, the observing spouse may misattribute that behavior to the partner/actor's dispositional qualities (Kelley & Stahelski, 1970). Moreover, the spouse may derive unwarranted interpersonal meaning (e.g., motivation) from the partner's behavior, and thereby create a biased attributional scheme which takes on a life of its own. Data that contradict this attributional scheme can be rejected as the exceptions that prove the rule, or reinterpreted as consistent with expectations. The result is a process which is analogous to the self-fulfilling prophesy (Merton, 1957). When people test interpersonal hypotheses, they tend to use confirmatory strategies which are likely to constrain others' behavior in ways that support the initial hypotheses (Kelly, 1955; Snyder & Gangestad, 1981). Moreover, early information regarding another will play a significant role in the developing sequence of transactions because subsequent processing activities may be conducted in such a way as to reinforce or bolster initial attributions (Berscheid & Graziano, 1979; Snyder, 1983).

B. Exchanges in Intimate Dyads

Returning to the initial premise that causal attributions enhance one's ability to predict or control the social environment, two concepts help to discriminate between intimate and stranger transactions: the translation of the control paradigm into one of reciprocal control, and the emergence of a subset of positive outcomes particularly, if not exclusively, available in the context of an intimate relationship. We have briefly discussed Goffman's (1961) distinction between economic and social exchanges, and Clark's (1981) differentiation between exchange relationships, in which the giving of a benefit is in response to the receipt of a benefit, and communal relationships, in which the giving of a benefit is in response to the perceived need for that benefit. While the research suffers from methodological difficulties, the results consistently support the utility of these distinctions. For example, Clark and Mills (1979) found that the request for a benefit after an offer of aid led to the expectation of an exchange relationship, and lowered interpersonal attraction if the subject had previously expected a communal relationship. These formulations have important implications for attributional processes in married couples. If we assume that the most important reinforcers in a marital relationship are those that convey liking, acceptance, and respect (cf. Foa, 1971; Hatfield, Utne, & Traupmann, 1979; Foa & Foa, 1974; Jones & Thibaut, 1958; Turner, Foa, & Foa, 1971), it becomes clear that the meaning attributed to spouse-delivered behaviors by the receiver plays an important role in determing their reinforcing impact. In other words, the value of many important relationship events cannot be determined by any extrinsic or exchange criteria, but rather are subject to the interpretations imposed on those events by each spouse. Such interpretations constitute the essence of what is meant by a communal exchange. Many events that would otherwise be reinforcing may be neutralized if they are attributed to motivations that fall within the framework of an economic relationship. For example, if the wife hugs the husband, he may attribute her affectionate behavior to her caring about him, her acceptance of him, etc; the affection feels good, i.e., is reinforcing. On the other hand, if he interprets it as a manipulative attempt to get something from him in return (as in an economic relationship), the reinforcing impact may very well be negated. Thus, causal attributions in communal relationships such as marriage may be critical determinants of the impact of important relationship behaviors. This is because the value of many relationship behaviors has no objective currency, as is the case in economic relationships.

C. Outcome Dependency

In applying the concept of reciprocal control to intimate relationships, the obtaining of significant rewards requires a spouse/partner who has some control over the availability of these desired outcomes. A situation in which one individual has the power to offer or withold desired outcomes has been variously described as hedonic relevance (Jones & Davis, 1965), fate control (Jones & deCharms, 1957), outcome dependency (Thibaut & Kelley, 1959; Berscheid, Graziano, Monson, & Durmer, 1976), and interdependence (Jones & Davis, 1965). Choices made by one partner have significant consequences for the other, and may promote or undermine the other's values, purposes, or outcomes.

What are the implications of the concept that intimate relationships are characterized by hedonic relevance or outcome dependency and depend on communal as well as social exchanges? If prediction and control of one's social environment are primary means for maximizing desirable outcomes, what does it mean to enter into a relationship in which control over interpersonal outcomes is relinquished, and in which the other has the power to dispense an important class of highly desirable behaviors? In an informal interview, Harold Kelley (quoted in Harvey et al., 1976) observed that

> a lot of attributional explanations given by couples revolve around concerns for the relationship. . . . In such [close] relationships, it's important to learn to analyze why you have done something, why your partner has done something, figuring out the partner's commitment to the relationship, portraying your own commitment, etc. There may [also] be some other motivation involved in the attributon process

than just being able to understand or control—such as intense interest in keeping the relationship smoothed over and going. (p. 383)

Concern for the relationship and an interest in maintaining it are reflections of the uniqueness and importance of relationship-relevant outcomes. In addition, economic and communal outcomes are of a different order of significance, and it is crucial to "figuring out the partner's commitment" that one accurately distinguish between the two. A need for accuracy is predicated on the desire to maximize positive outcomes as well as on the high cost of making a mistake (Kruglanski & Ajzen, unpublished). It thus behooves partners who are involved in a mindful, deliberate assessment of the current transaction to consider the potential meaningfulness of a large part of their partner's behavior. As Newman and Langer (1983) remark, the major point of relational attributions is the search for the meaning of behavior for them—"what the partner is like *in regard to them.*" The authors note that the context of interpersonal dependence or "embeddedness" is likely to lead partners to (1) perceive the other's behavior as a movement toward or away from the self rather than as an event, and (2) interpret the other's emotional and behavioral attribution as a function of self. They suggest that the fundamental attribution error in significant relationships may be a tendency to perceive a partner's behavior as interactive rather than as an expression of dispositional influences, and to exaggerate the communicative significance of noncommunicative behaviors. While communication theorists would take issue with the viewpoint that individuals can emit noncommunicative behavior, it is likely that the partners would be particularly vigilant regarding the emission and intent of a spouse's behavior, particularly when that behavior has a powerful emotional impact (cf. Harvey, Wells, & Alvarez, 1978).

The need to assess the meaning of a partner's behavior results in motivation to acquire a stable understanding of the environment. Since causal attributions are one important way that individuals uncover stability (through the analysis of covariance information) or create it (through the operation of attributional biases), we would expect to find that mindful attributional processing as well as motivated psychological biases would result. The greater the actor's power to control rewards or punishments, the more important it is for an observer to understand that behavior, and thus the greater the motivation for a causal analysis (Pittman & Pittman, 1980; Berscheid & Graziano, 1979; Newman & Langer, 1983). For example, Harvey, Yarkin, Lightner, and Towne (1980) found that as a person becomes more involved in a social situation and attempts to understand the dynamics of the observed event, "more elaborate interpretive and memorial processes will be engaged" (p. 552).

Spouses are likely to be involved, mindful, and deliberate in their efforts to understand the causes of a spouse's behavior; they are also likely to be biased toward attributions that provide the illusions of stability and/or predictability (Chaiken & Cooper, 1973). Jones and Davis (1965) remark that observers are more likely to make internal or dispositional attributions when an actor's behavior is rewarding or costly, arguing that the positive and negative experience of the observer is perceived as intended by the actor. Below, we present evidence that observers tend toward dispositional attributions regarding their intimate partners' negative behavior. Arias (1982) interprets this type of data in light of evidence that the ability to predict aversive events reduces stress (cf. Miller, 1981). The suggestion is that spouses create explanations for their partners' behavior which maximize its predictability. Finally, Snyder and Uranowitz (1978) demonstrated that memories as well as percepts are organized toward the construction of stable, predictable, and manageable images of other people. They conclude that by attributing stable traits to others, we may better understand and predict their actions and use these beliefs to guide our transactions with them.

It should be noted that the impetus toward mindful processing and dispositional attributions is not monolithic. First, as interpersonal attributions or relationship premises (Newman & Langer, 1983) evolve out of the ongoing stream of transactions, the need for thoughtful cognitive activity would decrease as it is replaced by more efficient, automatic modes of processing. Newman (1981) suggests that the extent of mindful cognitive activity is a function of the developmental phase of the relationship, the particular content of immediate transactions, and the availability of preestablished rules or stylized sequences of interaction. That is, it is not necessary for intimates to be chronically mindful about each other's behavior; clearly, the goal of cognitive efficiency is best served by expectations or relational premises that permit more automatic responses. Second, the tendency toward dispositional attributions should vary depending on the impact of the partner's behavior on the receiver. The relationship between behavioral impact and tendency toward dispositional attributions is expected to be complex, and to be mediated by the overall level of marital distress. Distressed couples should be particularly prone toward dispositional attributions when the impact of the partner's behavior is negative, whereas nondistressed couples should be inclined toward dispositional attributions when their partners' behavior is positive. Some support for these hypotheses is provided by research reviewed in the following section. The rationale for these predictions is relatively straightforward. Spouses are expected to produce causal attributions that are consistent with their predominant affect toward the partner. More specifically we expect them to produce dispositional attributions for actions that appear consistent with their affect toward the partner, and situational attributions for behaviors that are inconsistent with the predominant affect. In this way, positive behaviors are discounted by distressed spouses, thereby perpetuating their current level of distress, while negative behaviors are discounted by nondistressed couples, thereby maintaining their overall marital satisfaction.

D. Outcome Dependency and Reciprocal Control

In considering control-enhancing strategies such as the attribution of behavior to stable dispositions in a dyadic context, clearly control-enhancing attributions on the part of one partner have control-reducing implications for the other (Jones & Nisbett, 1972). As A gains predictive power by making trait attributions for B's behavior, B experiences a simultaneous loss of outcome control as the meaning of his/her behavior is constricted and reduced. The attribution of positive behavior to environmental causes or of negative behavior to stable dispositions effectively neutralizes the ability of one partner to perform certain classes of behavior in a limited number of categories. To take a common clinical example, the wife who attributes her husband's increased affectionate behavior to the therapist's influence effectively prevents her husband from enacting affectionate behaviors through her "refusal" to respond in a congruent manner. If dispositions have control-reducing implications for the actor, a reverse strategy might be what Snyder and Wicklund (1981) described as the pursuit of ambiguity: if a mutual motive of social interaction is prediction and control (including manipulation) of the interpersonal environment, one may attempt either to increase one's own comprehension of the underlying stability of a situation or to reduce the opportunity of others to perceive oneself as predictable and stable.

Snyder and Wicklund (1981) propose an additional motivation to maintain ambiguity in intimate relationships. If their own positive traits are perceived by a partner as the basis for their attractiveness to the other, they may gain control over aspects of themselves that their partners find rewarding and thus enhance the relationship. But to think and behave in this way is to perceive oneself as a means rather than an end and thus threatens the relationship's intrinsic quality. For example, a woman who is liked for her sexual responsiveness becomes an instrument to satisfy her partner's passion. Having become merely a means to an end, it is all too clear that someone else might be equally or more adept at serving the needs in question, thus threatening the *personal* nature of the relationship. In addition, this view of the relationship is no longer communal but has become defined by economic or value-for-value exchange, and calculating costs and benefits may be antagonistic to an intimate relationship. The authors conclude that such a relationship

> is practically defined in terms of its ambiguity of cause, and this is the magic that appeals to its participants. As soon as that other serves only as the end result of one's need for dominance, submissiveness, guilt reduction, or intellectual exchange, the raw specificity of such motivations breaks the magic. The relationship then turns into an extrinsically motivated one. (p. 218)

The increased motivation for stable perceptions in intimate relationship leads to circular and self-confirming attributional schemes. As Newman and Langer (1983) remark, "once individuals have formulated a stable repertoire of relationship premises and attributions, they may fail to consciously consider alternative explanations for partner's behaviors . . . and fail to establish a wide range of evaluative categories which more realistically reflect the information available to them" (p. 9). This hypothesized process provides a further rationale for the prediction that spouses interpret their partners' behavior in ways likely to maintain their current level of distress. As Knudson, Sommers, and Golding (1980) put it, an individual may tend to "minimize the communication of messages that reject or disconfirm the other person's definition of self and of the relationship" (p. 753).

E. Theoretical Statements on Attributional Categories Employed by Married Couples

It seems worthwhile to categorize attributional processes as they pertain to intimate relationships. Doherty (1981a) suggests five attributional dimensions that pertain to conflict in intimate relationships: (1) *source* (self, other family member, the relationship, the external environment, theological causes, luck, or fate), (2) *intent*, which refers to an attribution ranging from positive or helpful to negative or destructive, (3) *stability*, which ranges from permanent to transitory and unstable, (4) *voluntariness*, which refers to the quality of deliberateness or purposefulness and ranges from voluntary to involuntary, and (5) *specificity*, which "denotes the extent to which causal characteristics of an attributed source are viewed as a separate, narrow aspect of the source as opposed to representing a more global characteristic of the source" (p. 6).

Newman (1981) suggested an important difference between attributions offered by intimate vs stranger dyads: intimates are more likely to offer interpersonal attributions for emotional responses. In a more recent paper, Newman and Langer (1983) explain that the formation of a set of relational premises is based on a wide range of attributions regarding "what their partners are like" and "what they can expect from their relationships" (p. 5). Examples of cognitions such as "my partner respects my judgment" or "my partner knows what I'm feeling when I'm upset" indicate that the category does not consist exclusively of we attributions but refers generally to aspects of the state of being in a relationship.

F. Summary and Conclusions

We have suggested factors that are likely to influence attributional processes in significant relationships. First, with intimate relationships the quest toward predicting and controlling one's social environment in order to maximize positive outcomes is heightened. We expect this tendency to be particularly strong in the early phases of a relationship, when relationship rules have not been established, or following behavior whose impact is particularly negative.

Second, the potential for intimate as well as economic exchanges is likely to heighten the salience of a partner's behavior. Again, we expect this effect to be magnified when the relationship rules are not yet fully defined, or when they are being violated. Since communal or intimate exchanges may involve abstract, symbolic components, assessing the meaning of any partner-initiated exchange is a complex process, especially in the absence of a relationship rule or when the behavior is unusual. One consequence of this ambiguity is the threatening of one's perception of stability. We thus expect the motivation for stable attributions to be highest for partner-initiated behaviors that induce strong affect in the recipient. The perception of stability may be extracted from the available information or imposed upon it.

Based on these hypotheses regarding the heightened salience of a partner's behavior in marital relationships, we predict the following. First, in intimate relationships we expect couples to engage in attributional processes that are designed to define the meaning of the partner's behavior in terms of the relationship. In other words, attributions are designed to answer questions such as "What does this behavior say

about my partner's commitment to me?" Second, we expect attributional processes to work in the service of prediction and control, so that
each partner can maximize his/her own positive outcomes in the relationship. Perceiving the partner's behavior as stable and reflective of
internal dispositions is one example of an attribution that provides
stability and control. Third, we expect attributional schemes in intimate relationships to express themselves through beliefs and expectations which in turn guide behavior in ways likely to reinforce initial
presumptions.

Empirical research on attributional processes in intimate relationships is still in its infancy, with many of the hypotheses presented in
this section requiring empirical evaluation. However, there are studies
that are relevant to the issues raised, and they are reviewed in the next
section.

V. RESEARCH ON ATTRIBUTIONAL PROCESSES IN
NONSTRANGER DYADS

A. Categories of Dyadic Attributions

Orvis, Kelley, and Butler (1976) invited couples to list instances of
their own or their partners' behavior. The targets were behaviors for
which each spouse had a different causal explanation. The 41 couples
in the sample provided nearly 700 statements consisting of a behavior,
their own explanation, and their perception of the partner's explanation. The two major findings of the research were, first, that attributional differences tend to focus on unpleasant relationship events. Second, the general pattern of actor–partner differences suggested by Jones
and Nisbett (1972) was confirmed; actors tended to attribute their actions to situational contingencies while observers tended to attribute
the same actions to stable dispositions. Actors tended to use positive
dispositional explanations in accounting for their own behavior, although they were not nearly so benevolent in attempting to explain
their partners' behavior. The sample was composed of a mixture of
married, unmarried cohabitating, and dating couples. Unfortunately,
no information is provided regarding the effects of general relationship
satisfaction on attributional processes.

In an effort to empirically determine the underlying dimensions of
attributions offered by subjects in the study of Orvis et al., Passer,
Kelley, and Michela (1978) asked a sample of 114 college students to
respond to a questionnaire while imagining a scene in which members
of a couple were involved in a conflict. The questionnaire required

them to match 13 attributional categories with scenes worded to reflect either the perspective of the actor (self) or the target of the actor's behavior. The authors then applied a multidimensional scaling procedure to identify the most important attributional categories from both actor and observer perspectives. A dimension common to both conditions was labeled *positive vs negative attitude toward partner*, including items such as "actor doesn't care for partner," and "actor thought in partner's best interest." A second dimension in the actor condition was labeled *intentional vs unintentional*. In contrast, the second dimension in the partner/observer condition corresponded to an *actor's traits vs circumstances or states* distinction. Thus, subjects perceived actors as concerned with justification and rationalization of negative behavior, while perceiving observers as concerned with how characterological a behavior was.

Similarly, Kelley (1979) described a study in which married college students were asked to name things that they would most like their partners to start doing and stop doing. Despite the efforts to elicit mention of specific behaviors, subjects offered predominantly personality trait changes.

Thompson and Kelley (1981) requested 157 subjects to indicate their contribution to a list of relationship activities. All subjects were currently involved in an intimate relationship. Later, subjects were asked for the information upon which they had based their responses. Dispositional information was reported as forming the basis for the judgment in over 90% of the cases.

Thus, in all of these studies conducted by Kelley and associates, partners in intimate relationships exhibited tendencies toward dispositional attributions. Moreover pejorative trait attributions were most often evoked by observers to explain their partner's negative behavior.

However, none of the above studies looked directly at the valence of behavior (e.g., rewarding vs punishing) as a determinant of the type of causal attribution. Nor did these studies evaluate how causal attributions changed as a function of how well acquainted the observer was with the actor, since all subjects were either involved in intimate relationships or were asked to refer to hypothetical conflicts in intimate relationships.

B. Studies Exploring the Effects of Behavioral Impact and Marital Satisfaction

Taylor and Koivumaki (1976) asked married students to respond to a questionnaire listing a series of behaviors committed by either an acquaintance, a friend, one's spouse, or oneself. Each of the four stimulus persons was paired with three positive and three negative behaviors. For each statement the subject was asked the extent to which the stimulus person's behavior was caused by dispositions vs situations on an 11-point Likert scale. Subjects were more inclined to perceive persons as the cause of positive actions, while negative behaviors were attributed to situational factors. In addition, the tendency toward person attributions for positive behavior was strongest when the stimulus person was a spouse or a friend.

Two recent studies have explored differences between distressed and nondistressed married couples in their attributional tendencies. Fincham and O'Leary (1983) presented 16 distressed and 16 nondistressed married couples with an attribution questionnaire consisting of 12 hypothetical situations, 6 describing positive actions and 6 describing negative actions. For each situation, subjects were asked to name the major cause for the behavior and then rate the importance of a series of causal dimensions, using Likert scales. The first dimension contrasted causes having to do with a partner with those having to do with external circumstances. The next two dimensions were derived from the categories of Abramson, Seligman, and Teasdale (1978) of *stable–unstable* (referring to the extent to which the cause is likely to be manifested on future occasions) and *global–specific* (reflecting the extent to which the cause is viewed as specific to the behavior as opposed to global). The final dimension was that of *controllable–uncontrollable*, derived from the work of Weiner (1979) on achievement motivation. Subjects were also asked to rate their global affective response to each event on a 7-point scale ranging from *extremely negative* to *extremely positive*. For positive acts, distressed and nondistressed couples differed significantly on the dimensions of globality and controllability. That is, nondistressed spouses saw the causes of positive acts as being more global and more controllable than their distressed counterparts. For negative behaviors, distressed and nondistressed spouses differed only on the dimension of perceived globality, with distressed couples considering the cause to be more global than nondistressed couples. There was also a tendency for distressed couples to rate the cause of negative behavior as more controllable. There was no other main effects or interactions for either positive or negative behavior. The authors conclude that the study offers only partial support for the prediction that distressed and nondistressed spouses make different attributions for their partners' behavior, since consistent differences were found only on the perceived globality dimension. Unfortunately, this study is limited by a number of methodological problems. For example, the events serving as the basis for causal attributions were hypothetical rather than actual behaviors that occurred in the subjects' relationships. Therefore, we have no way of knowing whether or not these attributional tendencies would generalize to actual events in their relationship. Moreover, the validity of spouses' attributional ratings may be limited by their less than complete understanding of the terms used to define the various dimensions.

In the second study, Jacobson, McDonald, Follette, and Berley (1984b) assessed one spouse's attributions regarding the partner's behavior in a laboratory interaction. Unknown to one spouse, the partner was given instructions to act positively or negatively during a subsequent conflict resolution interaction. Following the task, the uninstructed spouse was given the opportunity to explain his/her partner's behavior by completing a questionnaire consisting of a series of internal and external causal attributions. They were asked to rate the importance of each of the causal explanations for their partner's behavior during the laboratory interaction. Subjects were also asked for their assessment of the overall impact of the partner's behavior. Analyses revealed an overall tendency for spouses to report internal causal attributions. As predicted, distressed spouses were particularly likely to offer internal attributions for their partners' negative behavior, while nondistressed couples were particularly likely to attribute positive behavior to internal factors.

These results support one of the hypotheses raised in the previous section. They suggest an expectancy or consistency effect; distressed couples, having established negative transactional patterns, attribute expected negative behaviors to stable partner characteristics, and unexpected positive behavior to environmental influences. As Heider's (1958) balance theory suggests, we expect good people to perform good actions and bad people to perform bad actions; when liked actors do good things or disliked actors do bad things, we can readily understand the action as caused by the characteristics of the actor. Spouses in distressed relationships are likely to feel helpless and ineffectual in generating behavior changes in their partners. Negative dispositional attributions can be used to justify the typical pattern in distressed relationships of escalating coercive exchanges. Consequently, by attributing their partners' negative behavior to internal, enduring characteristics, they justify their feelings of helplessness and enhance their own self-esteem.

Some additional support for these interpretations of the above findings is offered by Knight and Vallacher (1981), who asked subjects to observe a person via videotape under one of three randomly determined conditions. In one condition, subjects simply observed the videotape with no anticipated interaction with the actor on the tape. In a second condition, subjects were led to believe that they would be interacting with the actor on the tape subsequent to the experimental task. A third group of subjects was led to believe that they were currently interacting with the actor via a video hook-up. For half of the subjects, the actor conveyed positive messages regarding the subjects, while negative messages were conveyed for the other half. Following the interview, subjects completed a questionnaire evaluating the actor on the tape, and then indicated on a 9-point scale whether they thought the interviewee's behavior was a reflection of the situation or his personality. The attribution ratings supported the hypothesis that in the anticipated interaction condition subjects would demonstrate "hopefulness" by attributing the positive actor's behavior dispositionally and the negative behavior situationally. That is, subjects in this condition not only hoped for a positive response, but also attributed negative responses to factors that would be controllable during the interaction period. In the condition in which subjects believed they were actually interacting with the actor, the causal pattern was reversed. Observers attributed positive behavior to the situation and negative behavior to the actor's disposition. The authors interpret the data as representing an attempt to protect or enhance subjects' self-esteem. Having found the actor's behavior to be out of their control, the subjects took credit for whatever positive responses ensued and disowned the actor's negative behavior.

The Taylor and Koivumaki (1976) study cited earlier offers additional evidence for this hopefulness interpretation. The positivity effect (people seen as causing positive behaviors and situational factors regarded as causing negative behaviors) was found to operate more strongly for perceptions of intimate others such as spouses or friends and less strongly for strangers and acquaintances.

Finally, Reagan, Strauss, and Fazio (1974) provided a test of the effects of behavioral impact on the attribution process. They ran two experiments involving liked and disliked strangers (manipulated by the experimenter), and liked and disliked actual acquaintances. Subjects were led to believe that acquaintances were contacted and a sample of their behavior in a help-giving situation was assessed. Subjects were then asked to indicate the primary motive behind the target's behavior, and were given four response alternatives codable as either internal or external attributions. Results were consistent with the balance theory interpretation applied above to the Jacobson et al. (1984b) findings. Actions consistent with the subjects' attitudes toward the actor were attributed internally, and to characteristics of the actor, while actions inconsistent with affect for the actor were attributed externally to situational factors.

C. Egocentric and Self-Serving Biases

While the assessment of causality has been a classic domain of attribution research, some have suggested that dimensions other than causality may be more important in intimate relationships.

> Expectations . . . infuse the causal perceptions with their meaning and evaluative content. The expectation component has been implicitly assumed in previous writings and may explain why causal attributions are often equated with perceived blame. . . . From this analysis it is apparent that research on responsibility attribution is more relevant to relationship dysfunction than the study of perceived causality as traditionally conceived in the attribution literature. (Fincham, 1983, p. 11)

Thus, while the context of an intimate relationship heightens the need for prediction and planned coordination, empirical categories of attributions employed *in vivo* by partners may be causal in more of a legal (Fincham & Jaspers, 1980; Hamilton, 1980) than a logical sense. As Orvis *et al.* (1976) remark regarding their data on attributional conflict,

> Our actors and partners are clearly much more than simply "actors" and "observers," and differ in more dramatic ways than merely the information they possess. Our actor is a person who, in a close relationship with another person, has (in most cases reported . . .) behaved in an unfavorable or at least questionable manner. The relationship requires that he/she be concerned about justification and exoneration. Similarly, the partner is no mere observer. Having been affected negatively by the behavior, the partner is concerned about its meaning, about redress or retribution, and about preventing its recurrence. (p. 364)

In a study by Ross and Sicoly (1979), married couples were asked to estimate the extent of their responsibility for each of 20 relationship activities by marking a line with end points labeled *primarily wife* and *primarily husband*. The items included making breakfast, cleaning dishes, caring for children, planning leisure activities, making important decision, causing arguments, making the house messy, and irritating the spouse. Analyses revealed a significant bias; that is, spouses tended to consistently overestimate their own responsibility for relationship events. The authors suggest that the egocentric bias is mediated by selective recall for one's own behavior, since the tendency to recall self-relevant behaviors was highly correlated with overestimation of one's responsibility.

These findings were replicated by Thompson and Kelley (1981). In addition, there was a small but significant negative correlation between overall evaluation of the relationship and responsibility for positive events. That is, partners in more satisfactory relationships tended to give more credit to their partners for positive events. Because the number of self-instances recalled correlated significantly with a judgment of self-responsibility, the authors argue that the data support an availability or retrieval bias. Additional data supporting an egocentric bias were obtained by Christensen, Sullaway, and King (1983), who were interested in investigating the frequency of partner agreement on a behavioral checklist of couples' behavior. An egocentric bias based on the hypothesis that partners' disagreements, defined as a greater endorsement of I items than spouse or partner items, was found in both a sample of 50 married and a sample of 50 dating couples. Moreover, subjects showed an increased tendency to attribute responsibility for negative items to the partner as the length of the relationship increased.

In an analog study that has implications for intimate relationships, Sillars (1981) found that college student actors tended to overattribute responsibility for negative behaviors to their roommates and to underestimate the contribution of their own behavior to a conflict escalation. This was more true of dissatisfied roommate pairs, while more satisfied pairs tended to internalize conflict responsibility. In addition, other-directed blame and perceived stability of conflict were highest when satisfaction with the roommate was lowest.

Sillars discusses his research from a conceptual framework quite similar to our own. He argued that

> actor-partner attributional differences are likely to be more common and pronounced in interpersonal conflict than in most social conflicts, because ego-defenses and perceptual salience biases are likely to be greater, because it is especially difficult to make accurate dispositional attributions in an interactive setting, and because high drive levels and information overload may reduce the complexity of causal analysis. Actors appear to be relatively insensitive perceivers of mutually causal relationships that occur in conflict. Consequently, they tend to underestimate the extent to which their own behavior causes the style of the partner. (pp. 284–285)

Distressed couples are thus likely to experience great difficulty in decentering (Feffer & Suchotliff, 1966) and in objectively assessing the stimulus quality of their own behavior (cf. Berley, 1983).

The attribution of blame and responsibility in an intimate relationship has important implications for the perception of outcome control. Others can only be blamed for events over which they have control. In an investigation of blame, control, and marital satisfaction, Madden and Janoff-Bulman (1981) interviewed married women regarding two standard conflict situations and two conflicts from their own relationship. Results suggested that marital satisfaction was negatively associated with blaming one's husband for relationship difficulties and positively associated with perceived personal control over conflicts. Generally, the wife perceived her husband "as the one who determines how negative problems are in the marriage, and she perceives herself as the major force behind more positive aspects of the relationship, resolving or entirely avoiding conflicts" (p. 670). Ten of the 15 women who blamed their husbands most were among the least satisfied in the sample: "Of these ten women, nine specifically mentioned negative personality characteristics of their husbands as a source of their own marital conflicts" (p. 671). Thus, while husbands were perceived as controlling the recurrence and negativity of relationship problems, these wives' tendencies toward characterological blame implied that conflicts would be relatively permanent and unchanging.

In an effort to assess the relationship between a global attributional style and behavior in a laboratory interaction, Doherty (1982) presented couples with vignettes describing hypothetical conflicts of fictional couples. They were asked to generate causal attributions for the behavior of spouses in the vignettes. Wives who attributed marital problems to negative attitudes or personality traits in husbands were also more likely to verbally criticize their own partners during a subsequent problem-solving task. Doherty notes that the correlational nature of the study leaves open the direction of causality between attributions and negative behavior, and that the sample consisted only of newlywed couples and therefore cannot be generalized to other populations.

To summarize, there is some evidence that people in intimate relationships are biased in the way they apportion responsibility and blame. People tend to take credit for positive relationship events, a phenomenon that may have something to do with selective recall. However, a number of studies also indicate that people are likely to blame their partners for negative events. This latter tendency is particularly pronounced in couples who are generally dissatisfied with their relationships.

D. Effects of Communal and Economic Exchanges

Little research has been done on the differences between communal and economic exchanges. However, a study by Seligman, Fazio, and Zanna (1980) supports the intuitive notion that extrinsic (economic) rewards would tend to make the economic quality of a relationship more salient and thus decrease the intensity of the partners' emotional bond. Nineteen dating couples were randomly assigned to three conditions and given behavioral recording and attributional assessment questionnaires which were biased to produce a particular cognitive or attributional set. The results indicated that subjects who were made aware of possible extrinsic reasons for maintaining the relationship reported less love for their partner than subjects made aware of possible intrinsic reasons. This research provides further support for the concept that causal attributions can mediate the behavioral impact of another person's behavior. Research in other areas of social and clinical psychology also supports this. For example, Abramson et al. (1978), in their attributional reformulation of learned helplessness theory, suggest a treatment based on correcting self-esteem deficits and/or the acquisition of self-management skills. The vehicle proposed to foster these ends in a clinical setting involves techniques designed to foster self-attribution of behavior change. As another example, Kopel and Arkowitz (1975) review data supporting the conclusion that attribution of behavior change to oneself increases the likelihood of the maintenance of that change (cf. Fincham, 1983).

E. Summary and Conclusions

Most of the research that has been conducted thus far seems to support our speculations in the previous section. However, it also seems clear that much work remains to be done in uncovering attributional processes in intimate relationships. It appears that causal attributions for couples involve the assessment of attitude, intentionality, and source. There is some evidence that spouse/actors are more inclined toward situational, external, and variable attributions, whereas spouse/observers are inclined towards internal, dispositional, stable, or traitlike attributions. However, these effects are qualified by the overall level of distress in the relationship, as well as by the valence of the behavior's impact. The results suggest a kind of expectancy, balance, or discounting effect in which distressed couples attribute expected negative behavior to partners' dispositions, while positive behavior is discounted and attributed to external or situational causes. Conversely, happy couples attribute positive behavior to stable, repeatable characteristics of the spouse while minimizing the impact of negative behavior by attributing it to situational factors. Evidence also demonstrates an egocentric bias based on availability and selective retrieval in memory; self-serving biases show a valence effect such that partners are blamed for negative behavior while the self is credited for contributions to positive relationship events. These self-serving attributions appear to be more pervasive as couples experience increased levels of distress. Finally, as extrinsic rewards for behavior in an intimate dyad are made more salient, members report a diminution of love for their partners. The attribution of behavior change to oneself appears likely to enhance one's sense of personal outcome control, and thus increase the likelihood that behavior will be maintained.

The results of these studies must be considered tentative and preliminary. Research on attributional processes in intimate dyads has not succeeded in demonstrating that these sets of variables *cause* important marital phenomena. Moreover, these studies can be criticized for failing to tease apart attributional processes from instructional sets inherent in attribution questionnaires. It remains unclear whether or not spouses would exhibit or report these same attributional tendencies in the absence of requests from the experimenter to report attributions.

VI. ATTRIBUTION AND THE TREATMENT OF DISTRESSED RELATIONSHIPS

If we have learned anything by observing the evolution of BMT since Stuart (1969) first introduced behavior exchange treatment, it is that successful therapy must begin from a conceptual framework that does justice to the complexity of clients' presenting problems. While the bulk of controlled research efforts in the investigation of BMT support claims for its effectiveness (Jacobson, 1979), recent research as well as clinical material (Jacobson, Berley, Melman, Elwood, & Phelps, 1984a) have encouraged workers in the field to undertake a "mature reassessment" (Jacobson, 1983) of both the conceptual model and the treatment technology of BMT. Limitations to the skill deficit model endorsed by earlier versions of BMT have been highlighted. For example, Vincent and associates showed that distressed couples can communicate skillfully with strangers despite their failure to manifest these skills while talking to their partners (Vincent, Weiss, & Birchler, 1975). Moreover, when instructed to communicate well, distressed spouses can improve their communication to the point where they are indistinguishable from nondistressed couples, at least insofar as verbal behavior is concerned (Vincent, Friedman, Nugent, & Messerly, 1979). Thus, while at least some distressed spouses have the skills in their repertoire, each represents a S^Δ for the actual use of these skills. In order for treatment to be successful in maintaining desirable behavior changes in the natu-

ral environment, the therapist must change the couple's pattern of interaction such that each no longer serves as a discriminitive stimulus
for the other to emit aversive behavior. In the absence of such changes,
it appears possible for couples to learn complex sets of interactive skills
such as those taught in communication training without enhancing
marital satisfaction (Harrell & Guerney, 1976). While there have been
no direct tests of this hypothesis, an analog study by Margolin and
Weiss (1978) showed that a behavioral communication training program that included cognitive restructuring was more effective than the
behavioral training alone.

An important issue for the clinician relates to the role of cognitive
interventions in producing behavior change. There is no direct evidence that the modification of attributional processes leads to behavior
change. Research seems to indicate, however, that changing attributions does support the maintenance of behavior change, whether or not
the modification of attributions can directly result in such changes.
When a straightforward behavioral technology is found to be ineffective in producing desired changes, we have often found that dysfunctional attributional processes are interfering with the establishment
and the maintenance of desirable behavior. In other cases, dysfunctional cognitions have become autonomous from a specific behavioral
referent and therefore do not change in the expected manner even
when behavior changes do occur. In either case, some kind of cognitive
or attributional intervention is clearly required to establish or vivify
relationship-enhancing behavior.

As attributional models and research findings have become more
compelling, marital therapists have been increasingly inclined to incorporate cognitive interventions into their clinical work. There has recently been a proliferation of valuable and provocative contributions to
the field of cognitive–behavioral marital therapy (CBMT) (Arias, 1982;
Baucom, 1981; Birchler & Spinks, 1980; Doherty, 1981a,b; Epstein,
1982, Fincham, 1983; Jacobson, 1983; Jacobson & Margolin, 1979;
Schindler & Vollmer, 1983; Strayhorn, 1978; Stuart, 1980; Weiss, 1980).
While a number of authors have attempted to present a thematic basis
for treatment strategies, the field of CBMT is in relative disarray, and
lacks a systematic model for organizing a complex assembly of
therapeutic techniques (Schindler & Vollmer, 1983). CBMT is still in
the stage of compiling a range of interventions, and has yet to reach the
"tactile" (Weiss, 1980) phase of establishing sequence and/or selection
strategies. We hope to emphasize the possibilities as well as the uncertainties, limitations, and risks of an approach to CBMT derived from
attribution theory.

Our model of CBMT, founded in attribution theory, has three components. First, we apply six themes from the attribution theory literature. Second, we define CBMT as a training model, focusing on three basic types of cognitive change skills. These skills involve (1) learning to explain behavior using appropriate attributional strategies, (2) evaluating the resources and competencies available to each spouse, so that they can engage whatever skills they do have to improve the relationship, and (3) acquiring the behaviors necessary to utilize the other two sets of skills effectively. Third, a range of specific clinical strategies, based on our understanding of the attributional change process, are applied to modify dysfunctional attributions, appraise one's capacity for solving relationship problems, and implement the requisite behaviors.

A. Attributional Themes

When designing interventions to alter spouses' causal explanations, it is crucial for therapists to attend to their own theory regarding the role of cognitions in interpersonal interactions. Therefore, the themes from attribution theory we wish to highlight are summarized as follows:

1. Causal appraisals are utilized to facilitate the task of predicting one's social environment and coordinating interpersonal behavior.
2. Prediction and coordination are important because they appear to enhance the probability of positive outcomes, including instrumental gains, affectional rewards, and the maintenance of self-esteem.
3. Familiar situations may elicit or cue automatic causal schemes that support one's experience of stability.
4. Attributions may also be biased in ways that impose stability or that are egocentric or self-serving.
5. Automatic or biased attributions may be refractory to disconfirmation due to the complexities and nuances of behavior reciprocity. Partners tend to expect behavior consistent with causal attributions and consonant with their emotional response to the person or the situation. Biased cognitions process data in ways that bolster those expectations, and discount or tend not to accomodate to alternative explanations.
6. An intimate relationship involves a complex web of economic and communal transactions. While equity and justice are important concerns, the significant aspects of intimate relationships are delineated by the noneconomic transactions, generally consisting of symbolic statements of caring and regard. Much of the cognitive focus in intimate

relationships pertains to assessing the relational meaning of a partner's behavior.

Spouses' attributions constitute an account of the past, present, and future course of the dyad. Causal attributions for past behavior form the basis for efficacy and outcome expectations for the future (Weiss, 1980). When distressed couples who are still highly committed to one another seek therapy, it is crucial to help them modify their account of the relationship to mitigate the impact of negative behaviors. Over time, as negative behavior becomes automatic and expected, couples tend to remain distressed but become disengaged and distant. For these couples, the account serves merely to justify their lack of intimacy and chronic hostility. These dyads engage in self-fulfilling patterns of negative tracking and chronic blame. Keeping in mind the attributional themes noted above, the therapist must help these couples modify their account to increase their willingness to be involved with one another and thereby reverse their disengaged drift.

B. Cognitive Skills

Skills that may be taught to clients as part of CBMT fall into three categories. The first is learning explicitly about the attributional process, and how attributions are based on the covariation of distinctiveness, consensus, and consistency information (e.g., Baucom, 1981). Second, as a result of attributions regarding "why," clients have efficacy expectations regarding whether or not they "can" change behavior so as to improve the relationship (Doherty, 1981a,b; Epstein, 1982; Weiss, 1980). A skilled cognitive therapist can alter the conclusion from "we can't" to "we don't know how," as well as pinpointing the specific competencies partners need in order to fulfill and reinforce their potential. Third, following attributions regarding "why" and "can," spouses must learn to engage the skills in the appropriate context, the "when and how" of in vivo behavior change. This has been described as discriminative stimulus training (Schindler & Vollmer, 1983), training in self-control (Jacobson, 1983), and moving from stimulus to response control (Weiss, 1980). Causal attributions play a role in determining whether we do (or do not) emit well-learned behaviors in the appropriate context, as do attributions regarding the entire process of self-control.

For example:

Therapist: Now when you became mad at what you thought was Jack's hounding you, what did you do?

Wife: Well I know we agreed I would put on my Easter bonnet so he would know how upset I really was, since I wouldn't be willing to look that foolish unless it were really important to me . . . but I was just so mad at him and I didn't want to make a joke out of it.

Therapist: Well, you're not doing it to be funny, but to let him know that you're really upset.

Wife: I know. Now I am discouraged. . . . I wonder if we'll ever be able to do anything about this, since I don't know what to do when I get that way. I just want to kill!

Therapist: I can tell you have a real problem knowing what to do, and also, I would imagine, in doing it *even though* you are having a strong emotional response.

Thus, in the above example, the tendency of the wife to view herself as out of control leads to her failing to emit the relationship-enhancing behaviors.

C. Specific Interventions

The skill acquisition model of marital therapy fosters relationship-relevant competencies that are lasting and independent of direct influence by the therapist. By considering cognitions and attributions as learnable skills, the therapist projects the belief that the couple will be able to maintain treatment gains on the basis of their ongoing efforts.

CBMT expands the armamentarium of the therapist, thereby enhancing the effects of treatment. In general, the goals of these techniques are to eliminate dysfunctional, automatic attributions and replace them with more adaptive and functional causal assessments. These goals may be supported either by direct, overt techniques, or by those that are relatively indirect or covert. Both types are described in this section.

1. Challenging Myths, Expectations, and Beliefs

Spouses do not surrender their dysfunctional cognitions without a struggle. The modification of these processes provides the supreme test of clinical skill. Initiatives from therapists that are either too heavy-handed or too persistent can backfire; the cost may be therapist credibility. Logical appeals to mutual responsibility are often relatively weak ammunition against self-serving attributional biases. Such challenges may be accepted constructively only following a successful regimen of more indirect, subtle interventions.

One example of a subtler challenge is the provision of feedback, which permits a spouse to reconsider the data in a more deliberate fashion. This "challenge by data" may be directed at any relevant attributional dimension.

Husband: You never show any interest in my work. It's gotten to the point where I don't even bother to talk to you about it anymore. [One choice here might be to pursue what the husband means by "show interest" and model the skill of behavioral pinpointing. Let us focus, however, on an attributional approach.]

Therapist: What do you believe "not showing interest" tells you? [More information is needed before a challenge; note use of the word *believe.*]

Husband: I work hard all day and she doesn't appreciate it. I think she cares about getting what she wants but doesn't care about me as a person. I'm a meal ticket and a security blanket, and that's as far as her interest goes.

Therapist: Let me see if I have this straight. You're claiming that Karen never shows any interest in your work, and believe that means you are just a meal ticket for her, that she doesn't care about you as a person. [Attributional feedback presented as factual often leads people to soften their positions.]

Husband: You've got it!

Therapist: [Doubtful] She *never* showed any interest? [Change of tense questions historic as well as immediate consistency.]

Husband: Well, she used to question me all the time when we first got married.

Therapist: So something seems to have changed since then. How about now? Is it really never?

Husband: Well, sometimes over the weekend she'll ask about a project. But by then I'm angry and disgusted and don't care any more.

Therapist: That's interesting, Kenny! You say "never," but then you also say that when Karen does show interest in your work you find a way to discount it so that it's a negative experience rather than what you want. ["Why" training, calling attention to discounting and negative tracking, additional consistency information.]

Husband: Well, maybe. But it still feels like she doesn't care very much about me.

Therapist: Well, if you believed that was why she was doing it, I would understand why you might feel that way. But are you telling me that she never does anything that shows she cares? [Placing the attribution in a disconfirmable form] I'm wondering if what you see as her "not showing interest" is really aimed at you. [Decreasing personalism]

Husband: I guess I don't know. Karen, what's going on with you when I come home?

Through successive challenges and the modeling of attributional exploration, the therapist has created a context in which Kenny finally turns directly to Karen to get the information he needs. Equally important, he is in a receptive frame of mind and likely to carefully consider what Karen is about to say.

2. Relabeling

Along with challenging, relabeling is among the most common techniques suggested in the CBMT literature. Like challenging, relabeling may be directed at modifying a spouse's perception of intent, stability, voluntariness, globality, or source. Often relabeling and challenging may be alternated to create a smoother and more powerful sequence. The ambiguity of the relabeled attribution can be varied, depending on whether the therapist wants to heighten or diminish a mindful attributional search. As with attributional challenges, the clinician is using the power of his expertise and credibility to induce the adoption of causal schemes that promote therapeutic goals. Thus, it is crucial that the alternative attribution be psychologically plausible lest the therapist risk threatening the therapeutic relationship. It may be necessary to use additional techniques such as direct challenge and affect modification (see below) prior to presentation. If carefully done, however, relabeling can be a powerful intervention because the therapist has a virtually limitless range of benign and/or enhancing attributions to choose from. Appropriately used, relabeling is an important tool in enhancing self-esteem and attributing positive changes to stable aspects of self and other. Well-chosen alternative attributions can enhance positive expectancies. When distressing behavior is attributed to a skill deficit rather than a negative trait in the partner, feelings of control are enhanced. Let's do some relabeling with Karen and Kenny.

Husband: You never show any interest in my work. It's gotten to the point where I don't bother to talk to you about it anymore.
Therapist: Do you think she's trying to tell you something?
Husband: Well, I think I'm just a meal ticket to her. She doesn't care about me as a person, she cares about getting what she wants and needs from me.
Therapist: Give me an example of what you mean. [A plausible reframe requires additional data.]
Husband: Well, when I come home she's always distracted. If I try to

talk to her, she just keeps puttering around the kitchen. And if the kids do the slightest thing, she's on them immediately. She never really pays attention to me.

Therapist: It sounds like her attention is being split between a lot of different things. [Increasing ambiguity in attributional search; focusing attention on dimensions of voluntariness and source] If you were in her shoes what would you be trying to accomplish? [Increasing attributional search; decentering]

Husband: Well, I suppose a lot of things need to get done. But I still feel ignored.

Therapist: Maybe she simply doesn't know how to give you what you want and keep the kids happy and get dinner ready all at the same time. [Increasing attributional search regarding intent; suggesting attribution to skill deficit]

Husband: Yeah, well it is kind of crazy. I mean, I certainly wouldn't want to do it all. I just want to stop and sit down and have a drink.

Therapist: It does sound like she's trying really hard to do lots of things. [Positive tracking; reducing attributional search regarding intent]

Husband: Okay but when I come home, I still feel ignored.

As noted in the transcript, offering the plausible reframe requires a more complete understanding of the content and sequence of events than does a simple challenge. Note too that reattributions may be designed to foster or inhibit further mindful consideration of the possible causes for behavior. Similarly, the intimate or economic aspects of a transaction may be emphasized through alternative explanations. In this case, therapeutic goals were enhanced by reducing personalism and emphasizing the economic or task-relevant aspects of the transaction. As a fuller representation, Kenny might be reminded of how meaningful the relationship in the family must be to Karen for her to expend so much energy, and pointing out to Karen how important something as simple as her attention and interest is to her husband.

3. Behavioral Enactment

This rich and complex cluster of techniques includes behavioral experiments and diagnostic interactions, role playing, and behavioral rehearsal; the category might even be stretched to include homework assignments performed outside the therapy setting. The skill training techniques, such as problem solving, communication training, and behavior exchange, as well as discriminative stimulus and self-control training depend heavily on in-session behavioral diagnosis and re-hearsal. Including action in the treatment sessions adds immeasurably to the potency of challenges and reframes. While the tenets of BMT demand that the partners not argue during the sessions, the judicious use of controlled role-play can be extremely beneficial. In particular, the therapist can slow the entire process down by allowing each part-ner not only to recreate actions, gestures, and words, but also to express fully all of the thoughts and feelings that constituted the internal expe-rience of the argument. Spouses may be encouraged to explore their own and even their partner's attributions through decentering strat-egies. For example, by "stopping the action" and "walking out of the play" to ask participants some questions, exchanging seats, or using videotape feedback (Wright & Fichten, 1976), partners may be con-fronted with the impact their behavior has on the spouse. The strategic move of redefining the couple's fight as play offers a number of interest-ing possibilities: the notion that the entire process is carefully con-trolled and can be stopped at any moment, the analogy of scripted or automatic behavior, and so forth. Behavioral experiments provide a different source of data than do verbal challenges or reattributions. In-session behaviors may be pointed out to partners as a way of offering additional information for attributional processing.

Wife: He never really listens to what I have to say!
Therapist: Do you really mean that he has *never* heard what you've said?
Wife: Well, I suppose "never" is an exaggeration.
Therapist: So though he might sometimes not hear you, it's not true that he "never" does. How about right now, John? You look like you have been listening intently to what Nancy was saying. Can you tell us what that is?
Husband: Sure. She said I never listen to her, and then changed the "never" to "sometimes."
Therapist: Okay. So John, it's clear that you do hear what Nancy is saying at least sometimes. So what do you think, Nancy?
Wife: Well, I guess he does listen to what I am saying. But sometimes I just don't feel heard.
Therapist: What is John doing at those times?

In this case, Nancy accepted the therapist's challenge and revised her global estimate of the frequency of an aversive behavior on the basis of both data available from memory as well as information pointed out by the therapist regarding John's in-session behavior. If, however, Nancy's feeling of not being heard was part of an automatic or scripted (Able-son, 1976) cognitive process, Nancy might have been much less able to see the salience of potentially disconfirming behavior. It might also have been the case that her attributions regarding his perceived listening behavior served the purpose of stabilizing an aspect of her interpersonal environment and thus rendering it more predictable even if aversive. If this were the case, we might expect to see resistance on Nancy's part to accepting the therapist's intervention, and it would be necessary to consider the prediction and control implications of accepting John's behavior as situational. For example, Nancy might stabilize her perception of the interaction by attributing John's behavior to a negative trait of John's. Under these conditions, it would be important to challenge her perceptions in such a way as to encourage the perception of situational factors involved in John's behavior, even though the increased perception of responsibility may result in an initial response of blame and negative emotions. Until Nancy shifts to a more reciprocal understanding of John's behavior, she will not be motivated to make any attempt to alter it. In this case, Nancy's last comment might have been,

Wife: Well, he may hear me in here, but that's a front. He really isn't interested in me. We've lived together for 14 years, and I've had to learn that he's only interested in his work. . . . He's a workaholic and doesn't care very much about anyone else.

Therapist: You sound discouraged.

Wife: Well, there isn't much I can do about that.

Therapist: So if you believe that his lack of interest in you is based on a character trait, you feel you can't do much to change it. [Use of propositional form of belief] I suppose that's possible, but I wonder about the situations in which you see John "faking it," or listening and responding to you more attentively. Do you know *anyone* he responds attentively to?

Wife: Well, he can be a charmer at parties, sometimes. And he's kind to his mother.

Therapist: How about with you?

Wife: Well, maybe on special occasions, like my birthday.

Therapist: Okay. So we have some information that John's behavior isn't always the same. Partly, that seems to be due to what's going on inside him, and partly it's a result of what people around him are doing. For example, he was listening to you here a moment ago possibly because of my presence and the fact that this is therapy. So what I'm wondering is, since you can't control what goes on inside him, we look at whatever is going on outside him and consider what he might be responding to.

Wife: That's just it! He acts as if I was boring or not a part of his life. It makes me so mad!!

Therapist: Well, you sound both mad and maybe hurt and a little rejected.

Wife: That's how I feel.

Therapist: Let's try something. If you were to act in ways that you knew would make John even *less* interested and attentive, what might you do?

While the attempt to shift attributions from negative traits in the partner to mutual responsibility and reciprocal control must be done delicately, it offers an opportunity to mobilize change efforts in areas partners have stabilized and thus given up on.

Behavioral experiments may also be used in the context of learning exercises. For example, the skill of pinpointing and the use of sensory-based information can be highlighted by a behavioral experiment in which one partner is told to simply describe information about the other that he/she can *see*. As noted elsewhere (Jacobson, 1983), spouses are often not aware of the fact that they make inferences even when asked simply to observe behavior; they often have trouble distinguishing between observation and interpretation. When the situation is reduced to an absolute minimum, the difficulty partners have in limiting themselves to observable data becomes obvious. When the therapist asks "can you *see* his disinterest?" the case for the difference between behavior and interpretation is powerfully presented. A next step might be to allow the spouse to make a statement about what he/she sees and then describe what his/her interpretation or imagination adds to the behavioral data. The behavioral experiment as a microlearning tool is an exciting frontier in CBMT and awaits further creative exploration and elaboration (cf. Stevens, 1971, for a discussion of awareness exercises).

When role-play is used to generate alternative attributions, the therapist–director can change the script into a future-oriented behavioral rehearsal. Attributions are much easier to change in the controlled environment of a therapist's office than in the natural environment where any number of stimuli may function as a S^Δ for putting learned skills into effect. By manipulating props, time, and mental imagery or fantasy, the therapist can provide more and more realistic situations for couples to rehearse. Through continuous practice to the point of overlearning, new behavioral and cognitive responses become more automatic, and therefore more generalizable. Assuming that negative behaviors and potential provocations are inevitable in intimate relationships, we believe that it is important to focus discriminative stimulus and self-control training on the spouse who must respond to an aversive initiation from their partner. We know that marital distress is associated with heightened reactivity to negative behavior (Jacobson, Follette, & McDonald, 1982; Jacobson, Waldron, & Moore, 1980) and a tendency, not found in happy couples, to reciprocate negative behavior (Billings, 1979; Gottman, 1979; Margolin & Wampold, 1981). Research on happy couples suggests that someone, most typically the wife (Gottman, 1979), performs an editing function by exerting cognitive control over their reaction to negative behavior and thereby decreasing the tendency to reciprocate and escalate. While rehearsal may involve aspects of play, stimulus control techniques will not transfer to the home environment unless the in-session rehearsals are both realistic and emotionally powerful. For example, after a positive communication and problem solving session, Karen and Kenny have worked out an agreement as to how they will greet each other when Kenny comes home from work.

> *Therapist:* So let me summarize. What we've agreed to is that when Kenny comes home from work, Karen will stop what she is doing to give him a hug and say "hope you had a good day. I've got to finish some things and then I'll be able to talk with you." Is that right?
>
> *Wife:* That's it! I know I can do that much.
>
> *Husband:* And then I will get out of her way. Maybe take one of the kids and play somewhere else, or just read the mail, or just have a drink.
>
> *Therapist:* That sounds fine. Now I want you to imagine, Ken, that you've just come home after a satisfying but very difficult day. You are looking forward to being home with Karen as you come up the stairs and open the door. You walk over to her anticipating a warm welcome. She looks up, glares at you, and launches into an angry speech about something you'd promised you'd do last week and didn't get a chance to do and she had to do it today and the car broke down and why the hell can't you ever do what you said you would? And the least you could do is lend a hand now! What are you going to feel, Ken? And how are you going to deal with it?
>
> *Husband:* Well, I'll feel lousy. Guilty because I didn't do it, and angry because that's more important to her right now than I am. But I'm also going to tell myself that I can't always get what I want exactly when I want it, and that we'll be able to talk later when things have quieted down. So the best thing I can do right now is to try to help out.
>
> *Therapist:* Do you think you'll really be able to remember that?

Husband: Well yes, I'll remember it. The hard part will be doing it without acting resentful. But I can if I remind myself that that's the best way to get us back feeling close again.

Therapist: What other cues could you use to help remind you how you are going to deal with this situation?

Husband: Well, I don't know. Well, we have this pie-bird my grandmother gave me years ago. It whistles when a pie is cooked. I always notice it in the kitchen, and it could remind me to just keep whistling.

Therapist: Can you see that pie-bird right now?

Husband: Sure! It's on the second shelf over near the counter.

Therapist: And what does it remind you of?

Husband: Just whistling . . . staying cool and just whistling.

4. Mood and Affect Modification

There has been considerable recent interest in the role of affect in cognitive and behavioral responses (Zajonc, 1981), the interpretation of affective states and causal assessments (Smith & Kluegel, 1982; Weiner, Russell, & Lerman, 1978), and the effect of mood on memory (Snyder & White, 1982). As behavior therapists have explored the clinical implications of emotional states on behavior change, the suggestion that "we should aim to expand behavior modification to include affect modification" (Rachman, 1980, p. 289) has led behavior therapists (Wilson, 1982) and particularly behavioral marital therapists (Fincham & O'Leary, 1982) to suggest that affect is the new direction behavior therapy will take in the 1980s. Attributions are often difficult to alter in a clinical setting, perhaps due to the primacy of negative emotional states which continue to cue distressing attributional schemes. It is hypothesized, then, that an important component of effective CBMT will be the integration of affect-altering procedures at appropriate points in the ongoing stream of treatment.

To the extent that attributions and emotions are reciprocally related to one another in marital relationships, CBMT must effectively elicit and alter affect, just as it has begun to address issues regarding the elicitation and modification of cognitions. Certainly the evocation of positive affect has long been accepted as a therapeutic principle, for example, in generating positive expectations regarding treatment outcomes (Jacobson & Margolin, 1979). Heretofore, however, the range of techniques has been limited to a verbal request, e.g., "tell me about what it was like when you were happy together." As we noted earlier, not having any strategies to deal with an expression of negative feelings and not wanting treatment to become a discriminative stimulus for escalating arguments, BMT has typically eschewed soliciting feelings of anger, hurt, or sadness. While it is true that in some dyads the expression or even perception of a negative emotion will be immediately punished with an ever escalating stream of aversive behaviors, much of the necessary skill training involves the gradually increasing tolerance on the part of both partners for emotionally painful stimuli. It is also the case that challenging, relabeling, and behavioral tasks become more effective as alternative attributions are matched with appropriate affect. At a microlearning level, the behavioral experiment of "I see . . . and I imagine" can be expanded by adding "and I feel. . . ." The resulting sequence ("I see you looking at your feet, and I imagine you're not interested in me, and I feel sad and rejected") helps couples understand that their feelings cannot be totally accounted for by what is actually happening, but rather are embellished by what they imagine those events mean for them personally. The pernicious effects of beliefs, myths, and expectations are often transmitted through the negative feelings they engender. For example, a husband whose father would get periodically drunk and abuse the family stated, "When I come in the door after work I see you with a beer in your hand and I imagine you have been drinking all day, and I feel angry and scared and helpless because I believe that you can't control your drinking," clarifying the basis for his feelings as coming from his own personal history.

Because of the reciprocal relationship between mood and attribution, the therapist must be able to access current feelings in order to make an accurate assessment, and use fantasy techniques to establish more therapeutic moods which then may be associated with desired attributions. The most recent example of Karen and Kenny's dilemma might include the following interchange:

Therapist: So as you come up the stairs and put the key in the door; how are you feeling?

Husband: Tired and excited I guess. I'm really looking forward to sitting down and telling Karen about my day.

Therapist: Tell me about that feeling. What kinds of images or sounds or sensations do you associate with it?

Husband: Well [laughs] definitely to a wine glass! And to sitting on the couch and taking my shoes off.

Therapist: Okay, I want you to get that firmly in mind . . . the feeling of sitting on the couch and taking your shoes off and the wine glass. How about Karen? Is there anything you imagine about the way she might look?

Husband: Um hm. She is relaxed and smiling. She is walking toward the couch looking pleased to see me.

Therapist: Great! Add that to your picture. Do you have it all?

Husband: Yes! It feels great. [Laughs]

Therapist: Okay. Now you come in the door and she gives you this look of pure anger and just doesn't want to talk to you. How are you feeling now?

Husband: Terrible! Just like before, guilty and angry. And she doesn't care about me, she just wants me for the things I can do for her.

Therapist: Okay, can you feel that now?

Husband: Yes, I can feel my hands clenching.

Therapist: Okay, now what are you going to tell yourself?

Husband: That I'm glad she feels she can rely on me, so it makes sense she'd be left stranded if I didn't do what I said I would. And she's been hassled all day, and just because she's angry doesn't mean she doesn't care. In fact, she wouldn't be so upset unless she did care.

Therapist: Good, and what are you going to do?

Husband: Ask if I can lend a hand somehow.

Therapist: Good. Now how are you feeling?

Husband: Well, less guilty because I know that there is something I can do about the situation, but I still feel less important than all the things that need to get done.

Therapist: What else were you going to use as a cue?

Husband: The pie-bird. I remember it means I'm supposed to keep cool and whistling.

Therapist: Can you see the bird in your mind's eye.

Husband: Yes, I see it right over there.

Therapist: Good. Now, as you look at the bird, I want you to reexperience the feelings you had on the couch . . . of the glass of wine in your hand and taking off your shoes and Kathy coming towards you smiling and relaxed. Can you do that?

Husband: Yes. So the bird is not just whistling and being cool, it's also having a good time.

Therapist: Exactly. [Pause] Keep seeing the bird and seeing what it's like to sit on the couch and Kathy is smiling and relaxed and you are taking off your shoes and there is a glass of wine in your hand. And you can remember that all this will happen later on. [Pause] Now come back here to us.

Husband: Okay. That felt nice.

Therapist: Let's check things out. Ken, I want you to imagine that you've just come home. And Karen, I want you to imagine that you've had a terrible day, and Ken has failed to run an errand he promised and its caused you a lot of inconvenience. You've kept to the contract for the past couple of days, but this time you forgot because you're so hassled. Can you get that feeling of being so hassled?

Wife: Easily! [Laughs]

Therapist: Okay, now Ken, let the first feeling of being guilty and angry come up and use that as a signal to change your thoughts and feelings. Okay, Karen, begin now.

5. Strategic Interventions

Many of the methods for modifying dysfunctional attributions discussed thus far are best described as *direct* interventions. The acts of challenging dysfunctional cognitions, relabeling interventions, and behavioral enactments are all designed to affect and modify cognitive processes. In most cases, the rationale for these interventions is obvious to clients. Despite the potential utility of such techniques, they are limited in and of themselves. For one thing, they are of limited potency for some couples. For example, simply challenging an irrational cognition, however compelling that challenge might be, does not necessarily result in the modification of that cognition. Moreover, direct interventions often suffer from the disadvantage of a context effect. That is, the client is aware of the intervention being presented by a therapist in the clinical context, and this awareness may result in attributions that are not supportive of positive relationship changes. For example, when the therapist offers a more benign interpretation of a particular spouse behavior, the partner may be inclined to disregard it or minimize its importance because it came from the therapist rather than from the spouse. In many instances, attributional change is more likely when the therapist can either manipulate the context so that the spouse arrives at the new attribution on his/her own, or when the more benign interpretation comes from the partner rather than from the therapist.

By strategic interventions, we refer to attempts on the part of the therapist to induce behavior changes that will indirectly promote desirable changes in attributions as well. These interventions typically involve an attempt to design an environment that shapes and constrains cognitions and behaviors in therapeutic ways. Certain types of behavioral directives are more inclined than others to foster desirable cognitive and attributional changes.

One type of a strategic intervention attempts to shift client perceptions so that behavior change is accompanied by therapeutic causal attributions. Often, these interventions depart substantially from standard behavioral techniques. For example, contingency contracting was an important component of BMT historically. In the quid pro quo contract, each spouse agrees to a behavior change desired by the partner, and these changes are cross-linked such that each change is made contingent upon the other. In recent years there has been a growing tendency to be critical of contingency management procedures in general, and contingency contracting approaches in particular. The explicit specification of contingencies may be both fruitless and self-defeating: fruitless because the real reinforcers in most intimate relationships are very difficult to specify discreetly and provide on demand, and self-defeating because the act of contingency specification may serve to neutralize the reinforcing properties of both targeted behaviors and alleged reinforcers. Evidence is accumulating that immediate contingency control as a behavior change device is uniquely characteristic of distressed couples (Gottman, 1979; Jacobson et al., 1980, 1982). In satisfying relationships, immediate contingency control appears to be a less viable explanation for why positive behaviors occur at a high rate. Rather, happy couples seem to exchange high rates of noncontingent positive behaviors. The abundance of gratifying transactions appears to be under the control of a long history of stable and frequently provided rewards. Thus, a point-for-point exchange model based on the simplistic application of operant conditioning principles does not seem relevant to most satisfying marital relationships.

To the extent that distressed couples are taught in therapy to use contingency management procedures, we may be simply teaching them more of the same. The task of the therapist is to promote high rates of positive exchanges that are not linked by an immediate contingency. By using strategic interventions, marital therapy is structured in such a way that rewarding behaviors are perceived by their spouses as internally motivated. The types of directives issued by a behavioral marital therapist have changed in recent years to accommodate this reconceptualization of the change process.

First, contingency contracting is seldom used in our clinical research program. When written change agreements are used, the therapist specifically avoids the use of explicit reinforcers and punishers. This does not mean, of course, that contingencies are absent. But the emphasis in therapy is on directives that instigate simultaneous, parallel changes.

Second, directives are issued that maximize the number of options that clients have in fulfilling a particular homework assignment. For example, during the first few treatment sessions, homework assignments are stated rather generally, and we avoid prescribing specific behavior changes. The therapist might direct each spouse to "devote the next week to increasing your partner's overall satisfaction with the relationship," while leaving the specific mode of implementation to each spouse. Usually, such a directive follows training in pinpointing important reinforcers in the marriage. As task directives become less specific and client options become broader, the likelihood that subsequent changes will be well received is maximized. Consider a wife who chooses to fulfill the assignment by delivering more affectionate behaviors. Her husband has left the previous session not knowing what to expect from her during the coming week. She has not been given the assignment of increasing affectionate behavior, nor has she committed herself to providing more affection. Rather, both from the perspective of the husband and in reality, she is *choosing* to be affectionate. An external attribution that would neutralize the reinforcing impact of her behavior is unlikely. Despite the directive to make behavior changes, the particular changes that are made are less likely to be attributed to the homework assignment per se, and more likely to be perceived as internally motivated.

Third, in our behavior change directives, we typically avoid situations in which one spouse is requesting changes from the other, particularly during the early treatment sessions. Instead, we leave the initiative in the hands of the spouse whose behavior is changing. For example, we might begin by teaching each spouse to pinpoint important reinforcers in his/her repertoire. In other words, each spouse is taught to examine empirically the relationship between his/her own behavior and the partner's relationship satisfaction, and to generate hypotheses regarding what behaviors on their part, if delivered more often, would produce a happier spouse. This is then followed by a change directive such as the one mentioned above. With this type of assignment we circumvent the need for direct requests from the potential recipient. When the provider of rewards is in charge of determining what reward to deliver, rather than responding to a request from the receiver, the behavior changes are more likely to occur, and more likely to be reinforcing when they do occur. When the provider decides what to provide, he/she perceives himself/herself as being in control of the change process, and will therefore be less likely to feel coerced and constrained. Moreover, the changes that are forthcoming are more likely to be highly valued by the receiver because they occur at the provider's initiative.

While we have been discussing strategic interventions that attempt to shift client perceptions of control to themselves, at times it is more therapeutic for the therapist to be perceived as in control. For example, when a couple is experiencing unsatisfactory sexual relations, the therapist can forbid sexual activity for a limited period of time. This places an aversive situation under the therapist's control, and permits the couple to deny personal responsibility for an unsatisfactory state of affairs. Another example involves the therapist predicting that the couple will have a relapse. As long as this prediction is made in advance, and as long as the therapist normalizes this experience, the attributions for any relapses that do occur will be more benign than they would if they were unanticipated.

In considering when and how often to utilize strategic interventions, it is important to remember that behavior change is more likely to be maintained if couples take credit for the changes. Taking credit usually involves stable, esteem-enhancing causal attributions for success. While strategic interventions allow the therapist great flexibility in moving in and out of the change process, they do not, as Weiss (1980) notes, teach requisite skills. They must thus be considered only a limited part of an overall treatment plan.

6. Telling Stories

The telling of stories that embody therapy-enhancing themes is definitely the least discussed and most speculative cluster of therapeutic techniques we have to offer. Like strategic interventions, story telling has the advantage of not calling attention to the therapeutic context itself, and thus inhibiting attributions which credit change to an external source. Because of their variety and infinite flexibility, stories can involve all the components of challenging, relabeling, behavioral tasks, and mood effects, should the teller be skilled enough to invoke them. Stories can also weave in therapy-enhancing information regarding the attributional themes of control and prediction, positive outcomes, stability and automaticity, and so forth. For example, Ken and Karen might enjoy hearing the following story:

> Well, I can see that this is a long-standing and difficult problem. And that you both have tried at least a couple of things to help change the situation, but without much success. It's interesting, I remember a couple I saw some time ago, we can call them Nick and Jill. They were wrestling with something kind of similar, though certainly not as important. But it was important to them, and I'll bet that as soon as you hear it you'll be surprised at how much thought they gave this. As I remember it, one of the things they worked on was the fact that Nick sometimes felt used. Nick worked in one of these pet shops where they shampoo dogs like poodles, you know? And I guess he was good at it and he certainly liked what he did. But it seemed to him that Jill simply expected him to do the family dog. Now remember, you guys have never had to deal with a situation like this, so it may seem strange or confusing. But

somehow it became an issue for them, and that's why they ended up putting so much time and energy into it. So anyway, Nick felt that Jill ought to sit with him and keep him company while he was doing this. Otherwise, he felt like the family dog washer and not much more. While it may seem to you he was exaggerating his case, it probably was true that Jill was pretty insensitive to how unimportant he felt. Well, I don't know what you would do if you were trying to help them. Because while there might be lots of different ways of talking about what's going on or thinking about ways to resolve it, you have to at least begin with how the couple sees things. Anyway, this one was easy for me because I didn't have to do anything. Somewhere along the line they thought about what was going on and what might be useful to change, and one day they just surprised me with a copy of the agreement they had worked out. I guess by listening and talking to me and to each other they saw that there were lots of ways of considering the issue, and that they had simply gotten stuck with one that wasn't working for them. I didn't care, of course, what the details of the agreement were. That was a whole lot less important than the simple fact that they sat down together and discussed the situation with a clear objective of finding a mutually agreeable way of dealing with this. And found ways of seeing this through each other's eyes. Oh, I remember now, one thing they did was to make a mental list of all the situations in which he felt important and valued. So that he could remind himself whenever he needed to that washing the dog wasn't the sum total of his relationship. It's interesting that people often lose sight of that.

Story telling can also be useful in responding to questions to which a direct answer might limit the therapist's effectiveness. For example couples often inquire how common their particular problems are given the therapist's range of experience. Since responding that the couples' problems are uncommon may engender blame while suggesting that they are common to all distressed couples can lead to despair or hope-lessness, there may be no direct answer that supports the therapeutic goal of mobilizing energy for change by enhancing positive expectations. On the other hand, a story about a successfully treated couple implies both that they are not alone and that their problems are solvable.

Another nice example of story telling is offered by Weiss (1980) in the presentation of a universal truth. A universal truth is a statement backed up by the therapist's perceived expertise that presents a premise that is true of "all" couples, and particularly relevant though obscurely stated to the couple in treatment. By taking a positive statement describing what the couple is avoiding or unsuccessful at doing and placing it in the context of a universal truth, the therapist forces the couple to attend to how they will achieve particular relationship goals, and turn away from unproductive arguments regarding who is to blame for the fact that they are not engaging in the desired behavior. Partners who are extremely hesitant in expressing disagreement, or who withdraw because the perceived risk of conflict is too high, might be told that "a universal truth about relationships is that partners need to be clear and assertive in expressing their own needs and wants." This sets the stage for a discussion of how this might be better accomplished in their relationship. In couples for whom assertiveness and self-expression are complementary such that one partner dominates the other, the universal truth would be that "couples must be able to help each other be assertive in expressing their needs and wants." The implications of a reciprocal version press couples to examine how the dominant partner might support increased assertion on the part of the less dominant partner; this may help the latter examine how he/she may in fact encourage and reinforce the former's domination.

As a learning device, story telling represents a strategic method for integrating a rich variety of techniques such as challenging, relabeling, and affect manipulation in the service of increasing cognitive and behavior change skills. The explicit decentering of a therapeutic story allows a couple the necessary emotional and cognitive distance, and permits them to perceive therapeutic suggestions from a framework of choice, thus enhancing self-attributions for success.

D. Eroticizing CBMT

For many couples, issues of prediction, control, and negative attitude find their way into the bedroom. Satisfying sexual interaction requires a sensitive, moment-by-moment responsiveness which can be planned only in a vauge, general way. It is not surprising, then, that the need for control of potentially negative interactions leads most couples to experience difficulties in relationship behaviors such as affection and sex in which enjoyment is so predicated on spontaneous responsiveness. In addition, for many couples sexual involvement is an important source of symbolically intimate exchanges in addition to being a physical release. As an important intimate behavior, sexual activity produces a high degree of vulnerability and therefore the possibility of being injured. Intimate knowledge of oneself, as represented by sexual preferences, presents to one's partner knowledge that might be used to hurt as well as to please. While effective behavioral treatments exist for standard sexual dysfunctions, the behavioral marital therapist has little in the way of techniques designed to eroticize a relationship in which sexual excitement has been drained through conflicts in other areas. Since attributions and emotions regarding sexual behavior may easily

have become autonomous from other instigating problems in the relationship, it may not be the case that successful treatment of more instrumental or "rule-controlled" (Weiss, 1980) issues in the relationship
will have a salutary effect on sexual functioning.

The inclusion of indirect strategies in CBMT offers the therapist the
potential for eroticizing an otherwise flat sexual relationship by aiding
partners in "spontaneously" increasing their sexual feelings for each
other. For example, just as we develop positive expectations for the
course of treatment by having couples recall earlier and presumably
enjoyable times, the therapist can also cue feelings of sexuality and
sexual responsiveness which can be used as the basis for a cognitive
elaboration of renewed sexual desire. Partners might be asked to recall
their sexual feelings for each other when they first met, or the intensity
of their first awareness of sexual awakening. Assuring them that the
content of their fantasies will remain private, the therapist can slowly
encourage a heightening of imagery and intensifying of feeling. With
the client's cooperation, those feelings can be associated with currently
available objects, situations, or behaviors. In this way, erotic feelings
come spontaneously under discriminative and response control. While
clearly only a beginning, cognitive–affective skills such as discrimination training and response control portend an important expansion in
the range of problems responsive to indirect or direct therapeutic
intervention.

E. Considerations and Risks in CBMT

The extent to which a therapist relies on cognitive techniques in the
treatment of marital distress varies as a function of an assessment process that evolves out of the ongoing treatment. Given the clarity and
specificity of the standard behavioral technology, the clinician should
be thoroughly convinced of its inadequacies for a particular couple
before considering elaborate plans to include complex cognitive schemata in the change process. BMT may lead to therapeutic changes in
attributional processes without explicit cognitive interventions. Gra-
tuitous use of cognitive interventions can actually interfere with the
acquisition of behavioral competencies. CBMT is not a shotgun approach and should be used only when indicated.

A second consideration in the use of CBMT is the issue of whether
couples should be seen concurrently or conjointly. This is a complex
question for which no totally satisfying resolution exists. A number of
authors (Jacobson, 1983; Weiss, 1980) have suggested the use of indi-

vidual sessions when the mere presence of one spouse is a discriminative stimulus for coercive behavior. While the availability of both partners provides a richer context for the generation of healthier and more adaptive patterns, it may be important to remove such a stimulus from the immediate environment in order to develop positive expectations and emotions. It may also be useful to have a session or part of a session with the individual partners in order to prevent the other partner from engaging in potentially dysfunctional attributional processes. Training in response control, for example, may involve suggesting that one partner adopt attributions regarding the negative interaction that might be misinterpreted and/or objected to by the spouse. In our earlier transcript, Karen might have felt ignored by Ken's efforts to remain "cool" in the face of her agitation and distress. The therapist must, in any case, consider the cognitive effects of techniques presented in concurrent vs conjoint sessions, recognizing that clients will think about both the process and the context of treatment. Given the explicit role of dyadic, reciprocal transactions in the creation and resolution of marital distress, the choice of seeing partners separately should be exercised equitably and judiciously.

Beyond the risk of calling attention to cognitive processes in situations in which such mindful awareness is likely to reduce rather than increase relationship satisfaction, the major hazard of including attributions as part of the therapeutic methodology is that it may distract from the ultimate goal of enhancing the client's relationship. When used as a means of establishing or maintaining necessary behavior change, couples must be prevented from distracting themselves from useless verbiage. For some couples, the analysis of whys and wherefores in the relationship becomes an end in itself such that issues of behavior change are never adequately confronted. A second danger, particularly among hostile couples intent on attributing blame, is that attributional information will be used to support control and self-esteem needs. Couples who have been insufficiently imbued with a therapeutic understanding of the reciprocal and dyadic nature of their relationship will continue to use information learned from their partner and therapist regarding cognitions as justification for continued cross-complaining. This is likely to have an extremely negative effect on treatment since partners are unlikely to continue self-disclosure when they have been effectively punished for earlier efforts. It may also seriously impair the therapeutic relationship, since the therapist is no longer perceived as trustworthy or in control of the session. Clearly, for some couples a great deal of behavioral groundwork must be laid before dysfunctional cognitions can be safely approached.

VII. COGNITIVE–BEHAVIORAL MARITAL THERAPY:
SUMMARY AND PROSPECT

We began with two assumptions: that people do in fact seek causal explanations for interpersonal behavior as a means of stabilizing and coordinating goal-directed responses, and that an intimate relationship provides a unique context for the exchange of instrumental and affective rewards and tokens. An understanding of the ways in which information is organized to produce causal appraisals and attributional schemes is particularly valuable in helping behavior therapists personalize treatment strategies for dysfunctional couples who fail to respond to existent behavioral interventions.

While a number of intriguing implications have been drawn from the literature and used as the basis of a model for cognitive interventions, it is clear that both the hypotheses and particularly the therapeutic model are speculative and go beyond currently available clinical data. In the absence of literally any evidence regarding the efficacy of CBMT, the ubiquitous call for additional research is in this case particularly poignant.

REFERENCES

Ableson, R. P. Script processing in attitude formation and decision making. In J. S. Carrol & J. W. Payne (Eds.), *Cognition and social behavior*. Hillsdale, NJ: Erlbaum, 1976.

Abramson, L. Y., Seligman, M. E. P., & Teasdale, J. D. Learned helplessness in humans: Critique and reformulation. *Journal of Abnormal Psychology*, 1978, **87**, 49–74.

Arias, I. *Cognitive processes influencing marital functioning*. Paper presented at the annual convention of the American Psychological Association, Washington, DC, August 1982.

Arkin, R., & Duvall, S. Focus of attention and causal attribution of actors and observers. *Journal of Experimental Social Psychology*, 1975, **11**, 427–438.

Bargh, J. A. Attention and automaticity in the processing of self-relevant information. *Journal of Personality and Social Psychology*, 1982, **43**, 425–436.

Baucom, D. H. *Cognitive behavioral strategies in the treatment of marital discord*. Paper presented at the fifteenth annual convention of the Association for Advancement of Behavior Therapy, Toronto, 1981.

Berley, R. The effects of intimacy on causal attributions. Ann Arbor: University Microfilms, 1983.

Berlyne, D. *Conflict, arousal and curiosity*. New York: McGraw-Hill, 1960.

Berlyne, D. Attention. In E. Carterette & M. Freidman (Eds.), *Handbook of perception* (Vol. 1). New York: Academic Press, 1974.

Berscheid, E., & Graziano, W. The initiation of social relationships and interpersonal attraction. In R. L. Burgess & T. L. Huston (Eds.), *Social exchange in developing relationships*. New York: Academic Press, 1979.

Berscheid, E., Graziano, W., Monson, T., & Durmer, M. Outcome dependency: Attention, attribution, and attraction. *Journal of Personality and Social Psychology*, 1976, **34**, 978–989.

Billings, A. Conflict resolution in distressed and nondistressed married couples. *Journal of Consulting and Clinical Psychology*, 1979, **47**, 368–376.

Birchler, G. R., & Spinks, S. H. Behavioral-systems marital and family therapy: Integration and clinical application. *American Journal of Family Therapy*, 1980, **8**, 6–28.

Brunswick, I. *Perception and the representative design of psychological experiments.* Berkeley: Univ. of California Press, 1956.

Chaikin, A. L., & Cooper, J. Evaluation as a function of correspondence and hedonic relevance. *Journal of Experimental Social Psychology*, 1973, **9**, 257–264.

Christensen, A., Sullaway, M., & King, C. Systematic error in behavioral reports of dyadic interaction: Egocentric bias and content effects. *Behavioral Assessment*, 1983, in press.

Clark, M. S. *Distinguishing "communal" from "exchange" relationships: Implications for understanding friendships.* Paper presented at the annual meeting of the American Psychological Association, Los Angeles, 1981.

Clark, M. S., & Mills, J. Interpersonal attraction and exchange in communal relationships. *Journal of Personality and Social Psychology*, 1979, **37**, 12–24.

Doherty, W. J. Cognitive processes in intimate conflicts: I. Extending attribution theory. *American Journal of Family Therapy*, 1981, **9**, 1–13. (a)

Doherty, W. J. Cognitive processes in intimate conflicts: II. Efficacy and learned helplessness. *American Journal of Family Therapy*, 1981, **9**, 35–44. (b)

Doherty, W. J. Attributional style and negative problem solving in marriage. *Family Relations*, 1982, **31**, 202–205.

Epstein, N. Cognitive therapy with couples. *American Journal of Family Therapy*, 1982, **10**, 5–16.

Feffer, M., & Suchotliff, L. Decentering implications of social interactions. *Journal of Personality and Social Psychology*, 1966, **4**, 415–422.

Fincham, F. D. Clinical applications of attribution theory: Problems and prospects. In M. Hewstone (Ed.), *Attribution theory: Extensions and applications.* Oxford: Blackwell, 1983, in press.

Fincham, F. D., & Jaspars, J. M. Attribution of responsibility: From man as scientist to man as lawyer. In L. Berkowitz (Ed.), *Advances in experimental social psychology* (Vol. 13). New York: Academic Press, 1980.

Fincham, F. D., & O'Leary, K. D. *Affect in the 80's: A new direction in behavioral marital therapy?* Paper presented at the 90th annual convention of the American Psychological Association, Washington, DC, August 1982.

Fincham, F. D., & O'Leary, K. D. Causal inferences for spouse behavior in maritally distressed and nondistressed couples. *Journal of Social and Clinical Psychology*, 1983, **1**, 42–57.

Foa, U. G. Interpersonal and economic resources. *Science*, 1971, **171**, 345–351.

Foa, U. G., & Foa, E. B. *Societal structures of the mind.* Springfield, IL: Thomas, 1974.

Galper, R. E. Turning observers into actors: Differential causal attributions as a function of "empathy." *Journal of Research in Personality*, 1976, **10**, 328–335.

Gibbs, J. C. The meaning of ecologically oriented inquiry in contemporary psychology. *American Psychologist*, 1979, **34**, 127–140.

Goffman, I. *Asylums.* Garden City, NY: Doubleday, 1961.

Goldiamond, I. Self-control procedures in personal behavior problems. *Psychological Reports*, 1965, **17**, 851–868.

Gottman, J. M. *Marital interaction: Experimental Investigations.* New York: Academic Press, 1979.

Greer, S. E., & D'Zurilla, T. J. Behavioral approaches to marital discord and conflict. *Journal of Marriage and Family Counseling*, 1975, **1**, 299–315.

Hamilton, V. L. Intuitive psychologist or intuitive lawyer? Alternative models of attribution process. *Journal of Personality and Social Psychology*, 1980, **39**, 767–772.

Harrell, J., & Guerney, B. Training marital couples in conflict negotiation skills. In D. H. L. Olson (Ed.), *Treating relationships*. Lake Mills, IA: Graphic Publ., 1976.

Harvey, J. H., Ickes, W. J., & Kidd, R. F. (Eds.). *New directions in attribution research* (Vol. 1). Hillsdale, NJ: Erlbaum, 1976.

Harvey, J. H., Ickes, W. J., & Kidd, R. F. (Eds.). *New directions in attribution research* (Vol. 2). Hillsdale, NJ: Erlbaum, 1978.

Harvey, J. H., Ickes, W. J., & Kidd, R. F. (Eds.). *New directions in attribution research* (Vol. 3). Hillsdale, NJ: Erlbaum, 1981.

Harvey, J. H., Wells, G. L., & Alvarez, M. D. Attribution in the context of conflict and separation in close relationships. In J. H. Harvey, W. J. Ickes, & R. F. Kidd (Eds.), *New directions in attribution research* (Vol. 2). Hillsdale, NJ: Erlbaum, 1978.

Harvey, J. H., Yarkin, K. L., Lightner, J. M., & Towne, J. P. Unsolicited interpretation and recall of interpersonal events. *Journal of Personality and Social Psychology*, 1980, **38**, 551–568.

Hastorf, A. H., Schneider, D. J., & Polefka, J. *Person perception*. Redding, MA: Addison-Wesley, 1970.

Hatfield, E., Utne, M. K., & Traupmann, J. Equity theory of intimate relationships. In R. L. Burgess & T. L. Houston (Eds.), *Social exchange in developing relationships*. New York: Academic Press, 1979.

Heider, F. *The psychology of interpersonal relations*. New York: Wiley, 1958.

Hewstone, M. *Attribution theory: Extensions and applications*. Oxford: Blackwell, 1983, in press.

Jacobson, N. S. Behavioral treatments for marital discord: A critical appraisal. In M. Hersen, R. M. Eisler, & P. M. Miller (Eds.), *Progress in behavior modification* (Vol. 7). New York: Academic Press, 1979.

Jacobson, N. S. The modification of cognitive processes in behavioral marital therapy: Integrating cognitive and behavioral intervention strategies. In K. Hahlweg & N. S. Jacobson (Eds.), *Marital interaction: Analysis and modification*. New York: Guilford, 1983, in press.

Jacobson, N. S., Berley, R. A., Melman, K., Elwood, R., & Phelps, C. Failure in behavioral marital therapy. In S. Coleman (Ed.), *Failure in family therapy*. New York: Guilford, 1984, in press. (a)

Jacobson, N. S., Follette, W. C., & McDonald, D. W. Reactivity to positive and negative behavior in distressed and nondistressed married couples. *Journal of Consulting and Clinical Psychology*, 1982, **50**, 706–714.

Jacobson, N. S., & Margolin, G. *Marital therapy: Strategies based on social learning and behavior exchange principles*. New York: Brunner/Mazel, 1979.

Jacobson, N. S., McDonald, D. W., Follette, W. C., & Berley, R. A. Attributional processes in distressed and nondistressed married couples. *Cognitive Therapy and Research*, 1984, in press. (b)

Jacobson, N. S., Waldron, H., & Moore, D. Toward a behavioral profile of marital distress. *Journal of Consulting and Clinical Psychology*, 1980, **48**, 696–703.

Jaspers, J. M. F., Fincham, F. D., & Hewstone, M. *Attribution theory and research: Conceptual developmental and social dimensions*. New York: Academic Press, 1983, in press.

Jones, E. E. The rocky road from acts to dispositions. *American Psychologist*, 1979, **34**, 107–117.

Jones, E. E., & Davis, K. From acts to dispositions: The attribution process in person perception. In L. Berkowitz (Ed.), Advances in experimental social psychology (Vol. 2). New York: Academic Press, 1965.

Jones, E. E. & deCharms, R. Changes in social perception as a function of the personal relevance of behavior. Sociometry, 1957, 20, 75–85.

Jones, E. E., Kanouse, D. E., Kelley, H. H., Nisbett, R. E., Valins, S., & Weiner, B. Attribution: Perceiving the causes of behavior. Morristown, NJ: General Learning Press, 1972.

Jones, E. E., & Nisbett, R. E. The actor and the observer: Divergent perceptions of the causes of behavior. In E. E. Jones, D. E. Kanouse, H. H. Kelley, R. E. Nisbett, S. Valins, & B. Weiner (Eds.), Attribution: Perceiving the causes of behavior. Morristown, NJ: General Learning Press, 1972.

Jones, E. E., & Thibaut, J. W. Interaction goals as bases of inference in interpersonal perception. In Tagiurui & L. Petrullo (Eds.), Person perception and interpersonal behavior. Stanford, CA: Stanford Univ. Press, 1958.

Kelley, H. H. Attribution theory in social psychology. In D. Levine (Ed.), Nebraska Symposium on Motivation (Vol. 15). Lincoln: Univ. of Nebraska Press, 1967.

Kelley, H. H. Causal schemata and the attribution process. In E. E. Jones, D. E. Kanuse, H. H. Kelley, R. E. Nesbit, S. Valens, & B. Weiner (Eds.), Attribution: Perceiving the causes of behavior. Morristown, NJ: General Learning Press, 1972. (a)

Kelley, H. H. Attribution and social interaction. In E. E. Jones, D. E. Kanuse, H. H. Kelley, R. E. Nisbett, S. Valins, & B. Weiner (Eds.), Attribution: Perceiving the causes of behavior. Morristown, NJ: General Learning Press, 1972. (b)

Kelley, H. H. Personal relationships: Their structures and processes. Hillsdale, NJ: Erlbaum, 1979.

Kelley, H. H., & Michela, J. L. Attribution theory and research. In M. Rosenzweig & L. Porter (Eds.), Annual review of psychology (Vol. 13). Palo Alto, CA: Annual Reviews, 1980.

Kelley, H. H., & Stahelski, A. J. The social interaction basis of cooperators' and competitors' beliefs about others. Journal of Personality and Social Psychology, 1970, 16, 66–91.

Kelly, G. The psychology of personal constructs (Vols. 1 & 2). New York: Norton, 1955.

Knight, J. A., & Vallacher, R. R. Interpersonal engagement in social perception: The consequences of getting into the action. Journal of Personality and Social Psychology, 1981, 40, 990–999.

Knudson, R. M., Sommers, A. A., & Golding, S. L. Interpersonal perception and mode of resolution of marital conflict. Journal of Personality and Social Psychology, 1980, 38, 751–763.

Kopel, S., & Arkowitz, H. The role of attribution and self-perception in behavior change: Implications for behavior therapy. General Psychological Monographs, 1975, 92, 175–212.

Kruglanski, A. W. The endogenous-exogenous partition in attribution theory. Psychological Review, 1975, 82, 387–406.

Kruglanski, A., & Ajzen, I. Bias and error in human judgement. Unpublished manuscript.

Langer, E. J. Rethinking the role of thought in social interaction. In J. H. Harvey, W. J. Ickes, & R. F. Kidd (Eds.), New directions in attribution research (Vol. 2). Hillsdale, NJ: Erlbaum, 1978.

Lazarus, R. Behavior therapy and marriage counseling. Journal of American Society of Psychosomatic Dentistry and Medicine, 1968, 15, 49–56.

Locke, D., & Pennington, D. Reasons and other causes: Their role in the attribution process. Journal of Personality and Social Psychology, 1982, 42, 212–223.

Madden, M. E., & Janoff-Bullman, R. Blame, control, and marital satisfaction: Wives' attributions for conflict in marriage. *Journal of Marriage and the Family*, 1981, **43**, 663–674.

Margolin, G., & Wampold, B. E. Sequential analysis of conflict and accord in distressed and nondistressed marital partners. *Journal of Consulting and Clinical Psychology*, 1981, **49**, 554–567.

Margolin, G., & Weiss, R. L. A comparative evaluation of therapeutic components associated with behavioral marital treatment. *Journal of Consulting and Clinical Psychology*, 1978, **46**, 1476–1486.

McArthur, L., & Post, D. Figural emphasis and person perception. *Journal of Experimental Social Psychology*, 1977, **13**, 520–535.

Merton, R. *Social theory and social structure*. New York: Free Press, 1957.

Miller, D. T., Norman, S. A., & Wright, E. Distortion in person perception as a consequence of the need for effective control. *Journal of Personality and Social Psychology*, 1978, **36**, 598–607.

Miller, S. M. Predictability in human stress: Toward a clarification of evidence and theory. In L. Berkowitz (Ed.), *Advances in experimental social psychology* (Vol. 14). New York: Academic Press, 1981.

Newman, H. Communication within ongoing intimate relationships: An attributional perspective. *Personality and Social Psychology Bulletin*, 1981, **7**, 59–70.

Newman, H. M., & Langer, E. J. Investigating the development and courses of intimate relationships: A cognitive model. In L. Y. Abramson (Ed.), *Social-personal inference in clinical psychology*. New York: Guilford, 1983.

Newtson, D. Attribution and the unit of perception of ongoing behavior. *Journal of Personality and Social Psychology*, 1973, **28**, 28–38.

O'Leary, K. D., & Turkewitz, H. Marital therapy from a behavioral perspective. In T. J. Paolino Jr. & B. S. McCrady (Eds.), *Marriage and marital therapy: Psychoanalytic, behavioral, and systems theory perspectives*. New York: Brunner/Mazel, 1978.

Orvis, B., Kelley, H., & Butler, D. Attributional conflict in young couples. In J. H. Harvey, W. J. Ickes, & R. F. Kidd (Eds.), *New directions in attribution research* (Vol. 1). Hillsdale, NJ: Erlbaum, 1976.

Passer, M., Kelley, H., & Michela, J. Multidimensional scaling of the causes for negative interpersonal behavior. *Journal of Personality and Social Psychology*, 1978, **36**, 51–62.

Pittman, T. S., & Pittman, N. L. Deprivation of control and the attribution process. *Journal of Personality and Social Psychology*, 1980, **39**, 377–389.

Pryor, J. B., & Kriss, M. The cognitive dynamics of salience in the attribution process. *Journal of Personality and Social Psychology*, 1977, **35**, 49–55.

Pyszczynski, T. A., & Greenberg, J. The role of disconfirmed expectancies in the instigation of attributional processing. *Journal of Personality and Social Psychology*, 1981, **40**, 31–38.

Rachman, S. The primacy of affect: Some theoretical implications. *Behaviour Research and Therapy*, 1980, **18**, 51–60.

Reagan, D. Strauss, E., & Fazio, R. Liking and the attribution process. *Journal of Experimental Social Psychology*, 1974, **10**, 385–397.

Reagan, D., & Totten, J. Empathy and attribution: Turning observers into actors. *Journal of Personality and Social Psychology*, 1975, **32**, 850–856.

Ross, L. The intuitive psychologist and his shortcomings. In L. Berkowitz (Ed.), *Advances in experimental social psychology* (Vol. 10). New York: Academic Press, 1977.

Ross, M., & Sicoly, F. Egocentric biases in availability and attribution. *Journal of Personality and Social Psychology*, 1979, **37**, 322–336.

Rosenfield, D., & Stephan, W. G. When discounting fails: An unexpected finding. *Memory and Cognition*, 1977, **5**, 97–102.

Schindler, L., & Vollmer, M. Cognitive perspectives in behavioral marital therapy: Some proposals for bridging theory, research, and practice. In K. Hahlweg & N. S. Jacobson (Eds.), *Marital interaction: Analysis and modification*. New York: Guilford, 1984, in press.

Seligman, C., Fazio, R. H., & Zanna, M. P. Effects of salience of extrinsic rewards on liking and loving. *Journal of Personality and Social Psychology*, 1980, **38**, 453–460.

Sillars, A. L. Attributions and interpersonal conflict resolution. In J. H. Harvey, W. J. Ickes, & R. F. Kidd (Eds.), *New directions in attribution research* (Vol. 3). Hillsdale, NJ: Erlbaum, 1981.

Smith, E. R., & Kluegel, J. R. Cognitive and social bases of emotional experience: Outcome, attribution, and affect. *Journal of Personality and Social Psychology*, 1982, **43**, 1129–1141.

Snyder, M. On the self-perpetuating nature of social stereotypes. In D. L. Hamilton (Ed.), *Cognitive processes in stereotyping and intergroup behavior*. Hillsdale, NJ: Erlbaum, 1983.

Snyder, M. L., & Frankel, A. Observer bias: A stringent test of behavior engulfing the field. *Journal of Personality and Social Psychology*, 1976, **34**, 857–864.

Snyder, M., & Gangestad, S. Hypothesis-testing processes. In J. H. Harvey, W. Ickes, & R. F. Kidd (Eds.), *New directions in attribution research* (Vol. 3). Hillsdale, NJ: Erlbaum, 1981.

Snyder, M., & Uranowitz, S. W. Reconstructing the past: Some cognitive consequences of person perception. *Journal of Personality and Social Psychology*, 1978, **36**, 941–950.

Snyder, M., & White, P. Moods and memories: Elation, depression, and the remembering of events. *Journal of Personality*, 1982, **50**.

Snyder, M. L., & Wicklund, R. A. Attribute ambiguity. In J. H. Harvey, W. Ickes, & R. F. Kidd (Eds.), *New directions in attribution research* (Vol. 3). Hillsdale, NJ: Erlbaum, 1981.

Steven, J. O. *Awareness: Exploring, experimenting, experiencing*. Moab, UT: Real People Press, 1971.

Storms, M. D. Videotape and the attribution process: Reversing actors-observers-point of view. *Journal of Personality and Social Psychology*, 1973, **25**, 165–175.

Strayhorn, J. Social exchange theory: Cognitive restructuring in marital therapy. *Family Process*, 1978, **17**, 437–438.

Stuart, R. B. Operant-interpersonal treatment for marital discord. *Journal of Consulting and Clinical Psychology*, 1969, **33**, 675–682.

Stuart, R. B. *Helping couples change*. New York: Guilford, 1980.

Taylor, S. C., & Fiske, S. T. Salience, attention, and attribution: Top of the head phenomena. In L Berkowitz (Ed.), *Advances in experimental social psychology* (Vol. 11). New York: Academic Press, 1978.

Taylor, S. E., & Koivumaki, J. H. Perception of self and others: Acquaintanceship, affect, and actor-observer differences. *Journal of Personality and Social Psychology*, 1976, **33**, 403–408.

Tesser, A. Self-generated attitude change. In L. Berkowitz (Ed.), *Advances in experimental social psychology* (Vol. 11). New York: Academic Press, 1978.

Thibaut, J., & Kelley, H. *The social psychology of groups*. New York: Wiley, 1959.

Thompson, S. C., & Kelley, H. H. Judgements of responsibility for activities in close relationships. *Journal of Personality and Social Psychology*, 1981, **41**, 469–477.

Turner, J. L., Foa, E. B., & Foa, U. G. Interpersonal reinforcers: Classification in a relationship and some differential properties. *Journal of Personality and Social Psychology*, 1971, **19**, 168–180.

Tversky, A., & Kahneman, D. Judgement under uncertainty: Heuristics and biases. *Science*, 1974, **185**, 1124–1131.

Upmeyer, A. Perceptual and judgmental processes in social contexts. In L. Berkowitz (Ed.), *Advances in experimental social psychology* (Vol. 14). New York: Academic Press, 1981.

Vincent, J. P., Friedman, L. G., Nugent, J., & Messerly, L. Demand characteristics in observations of marital interaction. *Journal of Consulting and Clinical Psychology*, 1979, **47**, 557–566.

Vincent, J. P., Weiss, R. L., & Birchler, G. R. A behavioral analysis of problem solving in distressed and nondistressed married and stranger dyads. *Behavior Therapy*, 1975, **6**, 475–487.

Watson, D. The actor and the observer: How are their perceptions of causality different? *Psychological Bulletin*, 1982, **92**, 682–700.

Watzlawick, P., Beavin, J. H., & Jackson, D. D. *Pragmatics of human communication.* New York: Norton, 1967.

Weiner, B. A theory of motivation for some classroom experiences. *Journal of Educational Psychology*, 1979, **71**, 3–25.

Weiner, B., Frieze, I., Kukla, A., Reed, L., Rest, S., & Rosenbaum, R. M. Perceiving the causes of success and failure. In E. E. Jones, D. E. Kanuse, H. H. Kelley, R. E. Nisbett, S. Valins, & B. Weiner (Eds.), *Attribution: Perceiving the causes of behavior.* Morristown, NJ: General Learning Press, 1972.

Weiner, B., Russell, D., & Lerman, D. Affective consequences of causal ascriptions. In J. H. Harvey, W. Ickes, & R. F. Kidd (Eds.), *New directions in attribution research* (Vol. 2). Hillsdale, NJ: Erlbaum, 1978.

Weiss, R. L. The conceptualization of marriage from a behavioral perspective. In T. J. Paolino & B. S. McCrady (Eds.), *Marriage and marital therapy: Psychoanalytic, behavioral, and systems theory perspectives.* New York: Brunner/Mazel, 1978.

Weiss, R. L. Strategic behavioral marital therapy: Toward a model for assessment and intervention. In J. P. Vincent (Ed.), *Advances in family intervention, assessment, and theory* (Vol. 1). Greenwich, CT: JAI Press, 1980.

Weiss, R. L., Hops, H., & Patterson, G. R. A framework for conceptualizing marital conflict, a technology for altering it, some data for evaluating it. In L. A. Hamerlynck, L. C. Handy, & E. J. Mish (Eds.), *Behavior change: Methodology, concepts, and practice.* Champaign, IL: Research Press, 1973.

Wilson, G. T. Psychotherapy process and procedure: A behavioral mandate. *Behavior Therapy*, 1982, **13**, 291–312.

Wright, J., & Fichten, C. Denial of responsibility, videotape feedback and attribution theory: Relevance for behavioral marital therapy. *Canadian Psychological Review*, 1976, **17**, 219–229.

Yarkin, K. L., Harvey, J. H., & Bloxom, B. M. Cognitive sets, attribution, and social interaction. *Journal of Personality and Social Psychology*, 1981, **41**, 243–252.

Zajonc, R. Feeling and thinking: Preferences need no inferences. *American Psychologist*, 1981, **35**, 151–175.

Recovering Social-Cognitive Schemata: Descriptions and Applications of Multidimensional Scaling for Clinical Research

THOMAS E. RUDY[1] AND THOMAS V. MERLUZZI

Department of Psychology
University of Notre Dame
Notre Dame, Indiana

I. GENERAL THEORETICAL FRAMEWORK

"Although research on social cognition has discovered much about the consequences of categorization (as in 'stereotyping'), much less is

[1]Present address: Psychology Service, West Haven Veterans Administration Medical Center, West Haven, Connecticut.

ADVANCES IN COGNITIVE–BEHAVIORAL RESEARCH
AND THERAPY, VOLUME 3

known about the structure and growth of people's natural categories about the social world" (Mischel, 1981, p. 487).

There has been in recent years a growing interest on the part of clinical and social researchers in schemata or "schemas." Several articles in this series (Turk & Speers, 1983; Goldfried & Robins, 1983) and in other volumes (Hastie, 1981; Landau & Goldfried, 1981; Kuiper & Derry, 1981) attest to the utility of the schema concept, in spite of the variety of usages and definitions ascribed to the term *schema*.

In general terms a schema might be considered "an abstract, general structure that established relations between specific events or entities; and, that any specific event or entity can be evaluated as congruent, or irrelevant with reference to the schema" (Hastie, 1981, p. 41). It is assumed that this structure (or these structures in the case of social interaction) mediates our interpersonal behaviors. The basic premise that interpersonal processes are mediated by cognitive representations of self, others, and the situation in which behavior occurs can be found in several general theories of interpersonal behavior (e.g., Sullivan, 1953; Kelly, 1955) and in interactionist theory (e.g., Magnusson & Endler, 1977). A central assumption in these theories is that social reality for an individual is a product of that individual's experiences with other individuals, groups, and organizations. These experiences of self, others, and interaction episodes are symbolized and represented in organized cognitive structures, which in turn regulate future interactions. In other words, "on the person side of the interaction, cognitive and motivational factors are essential determinants of behavior and on the situation side, the psychological meaning of situations for the individual is the important determining factor" (Magnusson & Endler, 1977, p. 4).

From this perspective a basic process of social cognition is assumed to involve the classification of perceived events into an organized set of categories according to their meaning for an individual. One quickly recognizes that this line of thought is highly consistent with social learning theory (Mischel, 1981). Further, Mischel (1980) has acknowledged that this aspect of his thinking has been greatly influenced by George Kelly (1955). In Kellian terms, the discriminating or construing process provides a means of representing the way in which, for example, social situations are alike in certain respects and simultaneously different from other situations (Neimeyer & Neimeyer, 1981). The assumption in this process is that the social environment acquires meaning and enables the perceiver to understand the present and anticipate the future. Thus, social constructs can be viewed as "significant guideposts for the business of living" (Neimeyer & Neimeyer, 1981, p. 191). A major implication of this position and of Hastie's definition of schema which was presented above is that an individual's structured construct system may not only facilitate but also restrict his or her interpersonal behavior. That is, a schema can account for distortions of reality by affecting information during the encoding stages (i.e., in perception, classification, storage) and by selective or inaccurate retrieval of previously processed information. Thus, psychopathology can be thought of as the adoption of a schema (or schemata) that may contribute to systematic distortions that, in turn, maintain dysfunctional behaviors. The clinical importance of this process has been well presented by other contributors to this series (Turk & Speers, 1983; Goldfried & Robins, 1983) as well as by other researchers in this area (Kuiper & Derry, 1981). The reader is encouraged to consult those sources.

Another major position in personal construct theory that is relevant to the research model to be presented in this article is that all constructs are bipolar; that is, they imply some type of contrast. Furthermore, the nature of these contrasts may be more or less idiosyncratic to the individual. However, as Kelly's Communality Corollary states, one person may employ a construction of experience that is similar to that empoyed by another; that is, individuals may employ psychological processes that are similar to each other. Yet Kelly's theory is based on the premise that the individual's construct system is a unique representation of the individual's constructions. Thus, communality should be viewed in relative terms. For example, two people may employ a similar construct but weigh that construct's importance differently and, therefore, employ it differently. Thus, the distortion in one's schematic representation of information may not be that one uses dimensions totally aberrant, rather that one over- or underemphasizes dimensions that a group of people may share relative to a specific set of stimuli. In sum, there may be common variance (communality) in the utilization of certain psychological dimensions (constructs), yet group or individual differences in the salience of those dimensions.

Recent advances in psychometric methods suggest that some of Kelly's theoretical formulations may be quantitatively verifiable. In the class of statistical models described in this article, similar and/or different constructs and their bipolar arrangement can be thought of as regions in an n-dimensional space. Within this space, social situations involving different behaviors, persons, and environments can be represented as points. Specifically, the methods of multidimensional scaling that will be discussed offer the necessary flexibility to assess both differences and similarities in terms of individuals' interpretation of social situations. In keeping with Kellian theory, the psychometric models illustrated in this article allow the researcher to maintain a clear and important distinction between objective social fields (for example, the factorial arrangement of the social stimuli employed) and perceived social fields, that is, the actual cognitive constructs and dimensions individuals use to process social situations and to render meaning and organization to them. In essence, the challenge posed by Mischel in the quotation that opened this article may be able to be approached through the methods reviewed here.

II. A RESEARCH MODEL TO ASSESS SOCIAL-COGNITIVE SCHEMATA: MERGING PSYCHOLOGICAL THEORY AND PSYCHOMETRIC METHODS

A. Overview

The research model that we are proposing here and have employed in an ongoing research program, along with the methods and analytic procedures that it incorporates, is compatible with the general theories of interpersonal perception and behavior mentioned in Section I. This model, which is quite versatile, unified, and psychometrically sound, permits precise definition and measurement of the major constructs of these theories. Additionally, it permits several levels and units of analysis, and includes some that are not possible with more commonly employed research models.

A basic assumption that we are making by using the present research model is that individual differences in personality and interpersonal perception are central to understanding social experience and behavior. The statistical methods employed are multivariate by virtue of the fact that both social stimuli and the process by which we organize and interpret our experiences are multidimensional. It should be emphasized from the outset that the theoretical framework presented earlier and the research model outlined below are not intended to be complete. Rather, they simply represent what we consider to be a powerful framework for asking questions and testing hypotheses about the cognitive processes that may be involved in social skills. In addition, it allows assessment of the possible effects of demand on these cognitive processes, it is a coherent method by which to organize the resulting data, and it is a way of providing precise descriptions of the cognitive structures presumed to mediate social behavior.

B. Measurement Issues

The present research model departs rather markedly from traditional research methods that have been used to analyze and represent the major structural components involved in social situations. It is our belief that methods that only rely on the rating of prespecified attribute scales, trait terms, or situational labels can only lead to very limited understanding of the social perception processes that are involved in interpersonal behavior. The fact that an individual can make judgments on a variety of rating scales tells us nothing about whether or not he or she routinely uses these dimensions. Factor analytic studies of the covariation among attribute scale ratings believed to be related to social skills rely on strong yet often unacknowledged assumptions. The scales used typically come from the investigator's theories, hunches, or naturalistic data. These sources may miss important attributes and, at best, result in a set of attributes that are only relevant to the group being studied. There is no reason to believe that the set of attributes derived is relevant to any particular individual.

The basic unit of analysis employed in the present assessment approach is at the individual level as well as at the more traditional group level. The underlying assumption is that an individual may employ different schemata or dimensions in his or her perception of the structure involved in social situations. It is quite possible, of course, that he or she may use some of the same dimensions others use in their interpretational processes; however, the relative saliences of these dimensions may be uniquely different for him or her. Multidimensional scaling methodology, by using direct similarity judgments between several situations involving social interaction, provides the necessary flexibility to answer the question of how individuals are similar as well as different in their processing of social situations. Furthermore, the measurement of similarity judgments is less subject to experimenter contamination and is more likely to contain the relevant cognitive structure individuals use in social situations. Thus, the primary strength of using similarity judgments is that this approach does not require a priori assumptions about the dimensions relevant to social situations. In other words, the present approach gives individuals more freedom to let the researcher know what the important dimensions are in their construct processes. The dimensional space resulting from this approach may be seen as superior to a space based on adjective or attribute ratings because the adjective space runs the risk of being a biased arrangement of the social stimuli (Schiffman, Reynolds, & Young, 1981). In order to create a multidimensional space based on adjective ratings, the number and types of scales that are assumed to be relevant to the social stimuli under question must be chosen in advance, and thus, important attributes may be missed.

C. An Introduction to Multidimensional Scaling

Multidimensional scaling (MDS), like factor analysis (FA), refers to a collection of mathematical techniques that enable a researcher to uncover hidden structure in a data base. These techniques usually use proximities among objects as input. A proximity refers to a number that indicates how similar or how different two objects are or are perceived to be. The chief output is a spatial representation consisting of a geometric configuration of points. In the spatial representation of a set of proximities, the larger the dissimilarity between two stimuli (as indicated by their proximity value), the further apart they should be in the resulting spatial map. In other words, computer-based MDS procedures attempt to find positions in space, or coordinates, for each of the stimuli such that the distances between them will correspond as closely as possible to the proximity values. Thus, after subjects' similarity ratings are empirically obtained, MDS can then be used to represent "psychological distance" as some type of geometric distance. The axes or other transformations of the geometric space are assumed to represent the psychological bases or attributes along which individuals compare stimuli. In sum, the scaling of subjects' judged similarities of stimuli can be used to develop a perceptual space in terms of those attributes that are jointly evoked by the subjects, the stimulus set, and the task (Green & Wind, 1973).

Most frequently the data used as input into a two-way MDS program is a simple symmetric matrix of proximities, usually stimulus by stimulus. More useful to the clinical and social researcher, however, is the three-way MDS approach. Three-way MDS uses as input two or more matrices of proximities, all of which pertain to the same set of stimuli. Each matrix typically contains one subject's proximities data, although it could also be based instead on data from another type of data source, such as one of several experimental conditions, occasions, or instructional tasks.

In our research program we have chosen to use a three-way technique called Individual Differences Multidimensional Scaling (INDSCAL) developed by Carroll and Chang (1970). First, INDSCAL allows one to scale proximities data by means that retain individual or experimental group differences while computing a common group stimulus space. Although INDSCAL is similar to FA in that both identify the number of dimensions underlying a set of data, the output from INDSCAL includes a set of dimension weights for each person or experimental group indicating how salient or important each dimension is to them in making their similarity judgments. When the dimensions of the group stimulus space are appropriately normalized[2] the square of a subject's weight on a particular dimension indicates the proportion of variance in his or her proximities data that can be accounted for by that dimension[3] (Wish, Deutsch, & Beiner, 1972).

Another important aspect of INDSCAL that sets it apart from FA concerns dimensional uniqueness. By using the variation among the individual input matrices, INDSCAL is able to orient the underlying dimensions uniquely, and thus avoids the difficulty of rotation for interpretability.[4] Basically, the coordinate axes derived from an INDSCAL analysis correspond to the fundamental psychological dimensions underlying the group stimulus space, assuming, of course, a sufficient amount of variance has been accounted for. Additionally, the solutions resulting from INDSCAL (as well as from other MDS approaches) are often more readily interpretable and of lower dimensionality than those resulting from FA (Schiffman et al., 1981). Several important differences between MDS and FA appear to contribute to this observation. First, the FA model is based on the angles between vectors, whereas the MDS model is based on distances between points. Schiffman et al. (1981) conclude that it is often easier to interpret distances between points than angles between vectors. Second, the MDS approach is not based on the assumption of linear relationships between variables (as is the case for most FA approaches), and therefore MDS solutions often result in lower dimensionality.

Before providing a basic conceptual understanding of the INDSCAL model, we discuss some of the methods used to collect proximities data appropriate for MDS.

1. Data Collection Methods and Issues

A variety of procedures for obtaining proximities data appropriate for multidimensional scaling have been developed. The more commonly

---

[2]The dimensions are normalized so that the sum of squared coordinates on each stimulus dimension equals 1.

[3]If the stimulus dimensions are correlated, the squared weight for a dimension underestimates the proportion of variance accounted for.

[4]Wish and Carroll (1974) note that the property of uniqueness of orientation of INDSCAL does not apply if all of the subjects have the same pattern (proportional profiles) of dimension weights, or in other words, if there is little or no variability between subjects' judgments.

used data collection methods are discussed briefly in this section. The creation or selection of a stimulus set, especially the types and number of stimuli appropriate for MDS, is discussed in Section II,D,1.

The classic MDS procedure for obtaining proximities data is to ask subjects to make similarity judgments between pairs of stimuli. More specifically, all possible pairs of stimuli are presented and after each pair, subjects are asked to rate "how similar or different are these two stimuli." Traditionally, these direct similarity judgments have been used as the primary data for recovering the underlying structure of the relationships among a group of stimuli. For some applications, comparisons based on relatedness, dependence, complementarity, and so forth may be more useful than similarity or dissimilarity judgments (Kruskal & Wish, 1978). Additionally, it may be appropriate to ask for specific kinds of similarity; for example, in our research we have found it more useful to ask subjects to rate social situations in terms of the similarity in difficulty for them to respond to the social situations as opposed to simply asking for the similarity between the social situations. Thus, although the researcher may choose to place some restriction on similarity ratings, the specific attributes on which the stimuli are to be judged should not be specified. This is done in order to discover rather than impose the dimensions or constructs that subjects use to process a set of stimuli.

The actual method used to record pairwise similiarity judgments is open to some debate. In an experiment of the differences in perceived similarity of nations, Wish et al. (1972) collected similarity ratings on a 9-point scale, ranging from 1, extremely dissimilar, to 5, moderately similar, to 9, extremely similar. Schiffman et al. (1981), however, recommend the use of a 5-inch undifferentiated line scale with descriptors such as *very similar* versus *very different* at either end. Subjects record their similarity judgments by making a mark through this line. Judgments are then recorded in millimeters (the scale becomes 0–127). We tend to favor the latter approach, not only because Schiffman et al. have made a systematic study of different response scales, but also because response scales with only a few discrete categories result in numerous ties in the data—a situation that can lead to "noisier" MDS solutions. After all pairwise similarity judgments have been recorded, a square matrix, stimulus × stimulus, of ratings is then created for each subject. Because this square matrix is symmetric, that is, the order of presentation of the two stimuli in a pair is irrelevant, many MDS computer programs will also accept a lower triangular matrix. To illustrate this type of data matrix, consider having collected pairwise similarity ratings for four different General Motors cars on a 5-inch scale ranging from very similar to very different. Table I (pairwise ratings method) displays how a subject's proximities data (as recorded in millimeters) would be prepared for a MDS analysis. Each entry represents a subject's or a group of subject's rating of the similarity of two GM cars. For example, a Fleetwood and Impala were seen as more similar (i.e., a similarity rating of 23) to one another than were the Chevette and Fleetwood (i.e., a similarity rating of 92).

An alternate method of collecting a complete set of similarity ratings for each subject is the conditional rank ordering approach. For this method of data collection, each stimulus in turn is used as a standard, and the subject is asked to rank the remaining stimuli in order of their

TABLE I
Examples of Different Types of Proximity Data Matrices

	Fleetwood	Impala	Chevette	Corvette
Pairwise ratings method				
Fleetwood				
Impala	23			
Chevette	92	45		
Corvette	57	96	61	
Conditional rank ordering method				
Fleetwood	0	1	3	2
Impala	2	0	1	3
Chevette	3	2	0	1
Corvette	1	3	2	0
Similarity sorting method				
Fleetwood				
Impala	4			
Chevette	8	5		
Corvette	4	7	3	
Preference ranking method—raw data				
Subject				
1	1	2	4	3
2	3	4	2	1
3	3	1	2	4
4	1	3	4	2
5	2	4	3	1
Preference ranking method—profile proximities				
Fleetwood	.0	3.7	4.6	3.3
Impala	3.7	.0	3.3	5.4
Chevette	4.6	3.3	.0	3.7
Corvette	3.3	5.4	3.7	.0

similarity to the standard. For most subjects, this is a relatively easy task to perform, can be used effectively with children (see, for example, Young, 1975), and from our experience is a somewhat more ego-involving task than the pairwise rating approach. Additionally, when a large number of stimuli are involved, the experimenter may wish to simplify this task by having subjects rank only some of the stimuli against each standard (Schiffman et al., 1981). For example, subjects might be requested to rank the five stimuli most like each standard and the five stimuli least like each standard. Another possible variation that can be used to reduce the time needed to collect these data would be to exclude from the stimulus set each standard after it has been used. Returning to our hypothetical GM experiment, if we had chosen to use the conditional rank ordering approach, we would organize a subject's data as displayed in Table I (conditional rank ordering method). For example, when the Fleetwood was presented as the standard, this particular subject chose the Impala as most similar, next the Corvette, and finally, the Chevette as least similar. Note that we assume that the subject would have picked the standard stimulus as being most similar to itself if that had been possible, and therefore a 0 is entered for those comparisons. Also, note that although this data matrix is square, these data are asymmetric (i.e., the rank position of stimulus i with respect to standard j is not necessarily the same as the rank position of stimulus j with respect to standard i). In sum, conditional rank ordering data must be analyzed with computer programs that (1) support a row-conditional option since the meaning of a particular datum depends entirely on the row in which it appears and (2) allow data to be treated as ordinal.

Although the above methods of data collection offer the advantages of being able to assess individual differences and allowing for certain internal consistency checks, as pointed out by Wish, Deutsch, and Biener (1970) the INDSCAL model "would be limited in its applicability if it were dependent upon such tedious data collection procedures as paired-comparison ratings of similarity" (p. 371). Not only are such tasks repetitive and tedious for subjects, but as the number of stimuli or their complexity increases, the time required of subjects often exceeds that available to the researcher. For example, if 20 stimuli are employed in an experiment, in order to collect paired-comparison ratings subjects would be required to make 190 separate judgments (i.e., $N(N - 1)/2$). We have found in our research program, using 18 brief social vignettes, that a paired-comparison or complete conditional rank ordering approach to data collection required approximately 1.5 hours for subjects to complete. Fortunately, there are several other methods of collecting proximities data appropriate for MDS that require only a minimal amount of time and, thus, are more useful in field research.

Several investigators (Rosenberg & Kim, 1975; Benton, 1975; Drasgow & Jones, 1979) have explored the use of sorting procedures as an alternative to the paired-comparison approach. In a typical application of the sorting method, subjects are presented with the total stimulus set and asked to sort stimuli into an arbitrary number of unlabeled groups, with similar stimuli sorted into the same group and dissimilar stimuli sorted into different groups. As previously stated, the experimenter may choose to qualify the type of similarity judgments to be used or may use alternate terms, for example, relatedness or co-occurrences. When the sorting is completed, the researcher simply records which stimuli were placed in the same group. A square matrix is then constructed for each subject and the entries in the matrix are binary coded, using 0 if a stimulus pair was placed in the same group and 1 if placed in a different group. The matrices are then summed over subjects (or experimental groups) to yield dissimilarity judgments. These dissimilarity measures reflect the degree to which a sample of subjects did not sort any two stimuli into the same group and, thus, provide measures of the psychological distance between the two stimuli. For example, if in our hypothetical GM experiment we asked 10 subjects to sort the four different car models into categories of similarity (naturally, in a real experiment we would use a larger number of model types), we would prepare their data for an MDS analysis as displayed in Table I (similarity sorting method). If 7 of the 10 subjects placed the Corvette and the Chevette in the same group, a 3 would be entered into the matrix because most scaling programs call for dissimilarities. Thus, while 7 of 10 subjects saw the Chevette and Corvette as similar, dissimilarity would be the difference (10 minus 7). In sum, one of the main advantages of sorting as a data gathering method is its economy, particularly in dealing with large numbers of stimuli. On the other hand, one of the chief disadvantages of this method of data collection is that the MDS solutions are based on group data rather than individual data.

A second less cumbersome, frequently used approach to obtain proximities from data that are not proximities in their original form (thus inappropriate for MDS) is to compute some measure of profile similarity or dissimilarity from single rank ordering or rating methods of data collection. To illustrate this type of data collection and preparation for an MDS analysis, we return to the GM experiment. Perhaps in addition to understanding the major dimensions consumers use in comparing and contrasting model types, GM is also interested in what types of constructs individuals use to determine their preferences for different models. To answer this question, we might ask five subjects (for the sake of this example) to rank the four car models from 1, most preferred, through 4, the least preferred model. We would then prepare these preference rankings for an MDS analysis in the following ways. First of all, a rectangular response matrix, subjects (5) × stimuli (4), would be constructed, as displayed in Table I (preference rank- ings–raw data). Next, following a procedure outlined by Kruskal and Wish (1978) and often referred to as the computation of profile prox- imities, dissimilarity or distance measures between stimuli (car mod- els) would be computed using the following Euclidean distance formula:

$$d_{ij} = \sqrt{\sum_{s=1}^{n} (X_{is} - X_{js})^2}$$

In words, this translates as the square root of the sum of squared dif- ferences between pairs of stimuli (the columns of the raw data matrix). Continuing with our GM example this produces a 4 × 4 symmetric matrix of distances or profile proximities between stimuli (see Table I, preference ranking—profile proximities). In other words, this matrix reflects the mean differences that this group of consumers perceived between pairs of GM models. The matrix of Euclidean distances is appropriate to use in an MDS analysis, which is somewhat equivalent to performing a principal components analysis (Rodgers & Young, 1981). Naturally, given that these data are ordinally based, we would use a nonmetric approach to MDS.

A number of variations can also be used with the profile proximities approach. For example, if more than one experimental group is used, Euclidean distance matrices can be computed separately for each group and then all of these matrices can be submitted to an INDSCAL analy- sis. Additionally, preferences can be collected using an undifferenti- ated 5-inch line (described earlier) instead of employing a rank order- ing approach. Also, the instructions given to subjects need not be in terms of preference. For example, in our research we have found it more useful to have subjects produce a single rank ordering in terms of the difficulty for them to respond to various social situations or the likelihood that they would initiate a refusal in social situations involv- ing unreasonable requests. In sum, although this method of data collec- tion is relatively simple and straightforward, numerous researchers (e.g., Rodgers & Young, 1981; Wish & Carroll, 1974; Wish, Deutsch, & Kaplan, 1976; Schiffman, Musante, & Conger, 1978) have found the profile proximities approach to MDS to be quite useful.

With some basic understanding of several of the methods of data collection used in MDS, we now return to describing more fully the INDSCAL approach to multidimensional scaling and the major methods used to interpret stimulus and subject spaces. After that discussion we demonstrate how the INDSCAL model and one method of data collection discussed in this section can be applied to recover social-cognitive schemata.

2. The INDSCAL Model

Based on a three-way Eckart–Young (1936) decomposition of N sets of proximities, the INDSCAL model solves for a unique (nonrotatable) object space that all individuals are assumed to share and a set of weights for each individual that are applied to the dimensions of the common space. This corresponds to the observable phenomenon of individual variation in the importance assigned to the various attributes of the objects being judged. The model, therefore, provides an estimate of each individual's stimulus configuration, which is obtained by stretching or shrinking the group object space according to the weights the individual applies to each dimension. Although two-way MDS, like FA, employs the use of the Young–Householder theorems (1938), MacCallum (1974) has shown that these two psychometric approaches are quite different in their objectives and their representation of data and solutions.

Tucker (1972), however, has shown that the INDSCAL model is in reality a special case of three-mode FA. In more statistical terminology, the algorithm developed by Carroll and Chang (1970), i.e., the INDSCAL model, adapts the nonlinear iterative least-squares method to the canonical decomposition of the three-way $N \times N \times M$ matrix of stimuli by stimuli by individuals to obtain the following: (1) a metric configuration of the N stimuli in an orthogonal coordinate space and (2) the weights of the orthogonal dimensions of this space for each of the M individual subjects or experimental conditions (Shepard, 1980). An important consequence of this approach is that this larger three-way matrix of data can support the extraction of a larger number of dimensions than is usually possible in the analysis of two-way matrices (Carroll, 1972). Thus, large individual differences can be accommodated in a single MDS solution.

To summarize, the aim of the INDSCAL approach to MDS is to determine (by means of an iterative least-squares procedure) the stimulus coordinates (plotted in a group stimulus space) and the subject weights (which can be plotted in a subject space) that account for as much total variance as possible in all subjects' data. In the process, the INDSCAL algorithm finds the orientation of axes that maximize several goodness-of-fit measures. While this approach assumes that the subjects use a common set of dimensions, some of the dimensions may have little or no importance to some subjects. Thus, subjects may have high weightings on some dimensions and simultaneously zero or near-zero weightings on others.

A very simple hypothetical illustration of the type of output provided by INDSCAL may help to clarify the above description. Assume that we were employed by General Motors to determine what are the major schemata or constructs used by consumers to compare different models of cars produced by GM. In order to answer this question five subjects were asked to rate the similarity between four different models produced by General Motors (naturally in an actual experiment more car models and subjects would be used). A matrix of pairwise similarity ratings for each subject was used as input into the INDSCAL computer program. Again for illustrative purposes only, assume that the results of the INDSCAL analysis indicated that a two-dimensional solution was most appropriate for these data.

Figure 1 displays the typical output produced by MDS computer programs that analyze data according to the INDSCAL model. Two basic rectangular matrices (and a corresponding plot if requested) are printed. The first matrix contains the coordinate values for the stimuli and is called the group stimulus space. The dimensionality of this matrix is always the number of stimuli by the number of dimensions. In the present example, this corresponds to a 4 (model types) × 2 (dimensions) matrix. The second matrix given is a set of points, one point for each subject, in another space called the subject (or weight) space. The dimensionality of this matrix is the number of subjects (or in some applications of INDSCAL, experimental conditions) × the number of dimensions. In Fig. 1, the subject weight matrix is 5 (subjects) × 2 (dimensions). In Sections II,C,3 and 4, the major differences between stimulus and subjects spaces are highlighted. For our present purposes, however, subject weights basically can be viewed as measures that tell us the relative saliences of each dimension of the stimulus space for each subject (as indicated by the projections of their points on the axes of the subject space).

If these were real experimental results to be interpreted, we first would determine if the group stimulus space is interpretable. Examination of the group stimulus plot contained in Fig. 1 suggests that dimension 1 appears to be discriminating GM models according to cost and that dimension 2 seems to be related to a size factor. Inspection of the subject weights indicates that only the first dimension is primarily relevant to subject 5, only the second dimension is of primary impor-

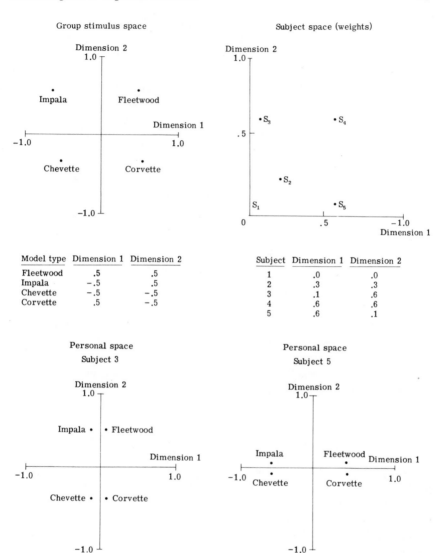

Fig. 1. An example illustrating the INDSCAL model using hypothetical data.

tance to subject 3, and both dimensions are relevant to subjects 2 and 4. Additionally, it should be noted that the distance of a subject from the origin (the length of that subject's weight vector) indicates, approximately, the amount of variance in that subject's data accounted for by the INDSCAL solution. Thus, as displayed in Fig. 1, because subjects 3 through 5 are further from the origin, we conclude that this solution provided a better accounting of their data than the data of subjects 1 and 2. In fact, none of the data of subject 1 could be accounted for by these dimensions because that subject's vector length is 0 (i.e., at the origin). This may suggest two possibilities, either that person used completely idiosyncratic dimensions (perhaps "marching to the beat of a different drummer") that were not uncovered in this two-dimensional solution or that responses to stimuli were completely random. The lower diagrams in Fig. 1 illustrate how personal spaces can be created. Geometrically, the subject weights stretch and shrink the dimensions of the group stimulus space to yield each subject's personal space. In other words, the stretching and shrinking are done separately for each subject according to that subject's own idiosyncratic weighting scheme. As displayed in Fig. 1, because subject 3 placed almost exclusive emphasis on dimension 2, the size dimension is stretched and the cost dimension is shrunk. These judgment criteria were reversed for subject 5 whose personal space is also plotted in Fig. 1.

One additional observation should be made in relation to the interpretation of this hypothetical example. Because the weight vectors for subjects 2 and 4 are in the same direction, we would conclude that these two subjects used approximately the same constructs or judgment processes but that this solution provided a better fit for the data of subject 4 than of subject 2. This latter observation is especially important to keep in mind, and we return to this issue.

3. Interpreting Stimulus Spaces

Frequently, the resulting stimulus configuration produced by INDSCAL is not self-explanatory, especially when complex stimuli are used. Although it is always important to assess which stimuli loaded highest on the ends of each dimension (the dimensions resulting in an MDS analysis are bipolar) and attempt to determine intuitively why they clustered in that particular way, several more objective methods have been proposed. For the most commonly used interpretational aids, it is necessary to have information about the stimuli in addition to the similarity information used in the INDSCAL analysis. Thus, to do what has been termed property fitting, it is necessary to have some type of information about the basic properties of each stimulus, for example, psychological attribute ratings. In this section, the use of multiple regression and canonical correlation to do property fitting is discussed.

The approach most commonly used to help interpret stimulus spaces is based on a multiple regression or vector model (Kruskal & Wish, 1978). Ratings on bipolar or attribute scales believed to be theoretically relevant to the stimuli in question are collected for all stimuli after similarity judgments have been completed. The mean ratings for each of the stimuli on these bipolar scales are then computed. After appropriate normalization, these bipolar vectors can be fit into the stimulus space by using linear multiple regression. Chang and Carroll (1968) have written a computer program called PROFIT specifically tailored for this purpose and have included an option to conduct nonmetric multiple regression if desired. Basically, this multiple regression analysis uses coordinate values of the stimuli on the dimensions derived from INDSCAL (or any MDS solution) as predictor variables, and mean values on the bipolar scales as the criterion variable. The regression weights resulting from this analysis are direction cosines of the vector through the MDS space that best represents that bipolar construct. The multiple correlation (R) measures the goodness-of-fit of the vector in the selected multidimensional space. Kruskal and Wish (1978) suggest that in order for a rating scale to provide satisfactory interpretation of a dimension two conditions are necessary: (1) the multiple correlation for the scale must be high (indicating that the scale can be well fitted by the coordinates of the MDS configuration) and (2) the scale must have a high regression weight on one dimension (indicating that the angle between that dimension and the direction of the associated scale is small).

Similar in spirit to the multiple regression approach outlined above, Schiffman et al. (1981) have recently proposed that canonical correlation can be used to aid in the interpretation of stimulus spaces. Whereas the multiple regression approach relates ratings to the stimulus space one at a time, canonical correlation can simultaneously relate an entire set of bipolar ratings to an MDS stimulus space. In the terminology of canonical correlation, the stimuli become the observations or cases, the MDS dimension coordinates become one of the sets of variables, and the mean ratings on the bipolar scales become the variables in the other set. Similar to the regression weights resulting from the multiple regression approach, canonical correlation analysis produces canonical variable loadings for each of the bipolar ratings (these loadings, of course, are also given for each of the MDS dimensions). These loadings can then be used to aid in the interpretation of the MDS space. More importantly, these canonical loadings along with the canonical correlation coefficients can be used to calculate measures of redundancy (Stewart & Love, 1968). These redundancies allow us to calculate how much of the data in the first set of variables are explained by the data in the second set of variables. Thus, for example, we can determine how much of the variance in an MDS stimulus space is accounted for by a set of bipolar rating scales. Therefore, canonical correlation offers an important aspect not contained in the far more frequently used multiple regression approach. An example of both of these approaches to stimulus space interpretation are contained in Section III,B.

The analysis of variance (ANOVA) can also be used as an ancillary method to interpret stimulus spaces when the stimuli employed are based on a factorial arrangement. For example, in the research study reviewed in Section III, the social situations that were used were a factorial arrangement of types of behavior, target persons, and environmental contexts. Thus, a main effects ANOVA can be performed on the stimulus coordinates for each dimension resulting from the group INDSCAL solution in order to determine if one or more of these three factors were significant on a particular dimension. If so, post hoc comparisons can be used to assess the specific levels in a factor that contributed to the significant F ratio.

4. Interpreting Subject Spaces

In order to use statistical procedures to aid in the interpretation of the subject space resulting from an INDSCAL analysis, relevant information about the subjects used in the experiment must also be obtained. This information may range from demographic information about each subject to experimental conditions in which subjects were assigned.

Unlike the methods for interpreting stimulus spaces, the methods used to interpret subject spaces are not based on more common statistical methods such as multiple regression. The reason is that matrix conditionality becomes an important consideration when weighted Euclidean models (e.g., INDSCAL) are employed to analyze individual or experimental group differences. While the mathematical derivation of this problem is well beyond the scope of this article, the issue needs to be discussed briefly because, according to MacCallum (1977), numerous researchers have misinterpreted their results. Briefly, the type of matrix conditionality employed in an MDS analysis determines the nature of the normalization applied to the data prior to analysis. If the data are conditional, which means large individual (or experimental group) differences are allowed between subjects' proximity matrices (the INDSCAL model), then normalization of the data is done separately for each subject. The most important consequence of this type of normalization is that it is not permissible to compare directly raw subject weights for different subjects on a given dimension because the normalization process is unique to a specific subject. The outcome of this process, as has already been discussed, is that the variance accounted for by an INDSCAL solution can vary widely between subjects. In sum, there is a crucial difference in the fundamental nature of the two MDS spaces resulting from an INDSCAL analysis: (1) the stimulus space contains points, one point for each stimulus, and (2) the subject space contains vectors, one vector for each subject. Thus, as Schiffman *et al.* (1981) demonstrate, the important aspect of stimulus points is their linear separation (the distance between them), whereas the corresponding aspect of subject vectors is their angular separation (the angle between them).

Perhaps one way to make the above discussion more salient to the reader is to refer back to Fig. 1. In interpreting that hypothetical example, the statement was made that it appeared as though subjects 2 and 4 were using approximately the same judgment processes. The points plotted in the subject space are not really coordinate points but rather represent the position of subject vectors. Thus, because subjects 2 and 4 have the same vector direction in relation to dimensions 1 and 2, we can conclude they used similar constructs (although, of course, we would still conclude that the data of subject 4 fit this INDSCAL solution better than that of subject 2).

Several methods have been proposed to interpret subject spaces that at the same time take into account the matrix conditionality issue. Two of these methods are reviewed briefly here, and another is illustrated in Sections II,A and B. MacCallum (1977) has noted that if weight ratios between dimensions are computed for each subject, these ratios can then be meaningfully compared across subjects and experimental groups. For example, the subject weights (vector locations) for subjects 2 and 4 in Fig. 1 were .3, .3 and .6, .6, respectively. The ratio of dimension 1 to dimension 2 for both subjects is 1. Thus, if we were to employ weight ratios in analyzing these data we would correctly conclude that these two subjects used similar schemata in their judgment of these stimuli. On the other hand, if we only observed the raw weights for subjects provided by INDSCAL and concluded, for example, that dimension 1 was twice as important for subject 4 as it was for subject 2, we would be in error. Because these weight ratios are calculated for each subject, we then can use these ratios and apply standard statistical methods to test for differences between experimental groups. For example, Nygren and Jones (1977) in a study of individual differences in perceptions for political candidates used these weight ratios in discriminant analysis to test for differences between groups of subjects based on their political affiliation.

Schiffman *et al.* (1981) have proposed a second solution to interpreting subject spaces. Their method is part of a new branch of statistics called directional statistics, based largely on the work of Mardia (1972). While the mathematics behind their method become rather involved, the statistical logic is rather straightforward. Subjects' weight vectors are first normalized to unit length. The primary concern in subject space has to do with the angular separation between subjects; thus, Schiffman *et al.* developed a procedure called the analysis of angular variation (ANAVA), which is based on the same logic as the analysis of variance (ANOVA). That is, mean angular directions and standard deviations of these angular directions can be computed for each experimental group. As in ANOVA, ANAVA separates the total sums of squares into within-group and between-group classes, computes mean squares, and forms an *F* ratio. ANAVA is now available in a FORTRAN program called SUBJSTAT, written by Forrest Young (see Schiffman *et al.*, 1981, p. 314f, for a source listing of this program).

Although we have found in our research program both of these methods to be useful interpretational aids, we have come to prefer the ANAVA approach. Unfortunately, at the present time there is no ANAVA analog of multiple-way ANOVA. Additionally, the use of the ANAVA approach becomes questionable if experimental groups display large differences in the variance accounted for by the INDSCAL solution. More specifically, because the ANAVA approach normalizes all subject vectors to a length of 1, differences in variance accounted for between subjects are removed. In fact, this normalization process is a necessary prerequisite to the calculation of angular differences, the heart of the ANAVA approach. If, for example, the average variance accounted for in one experimental group is only half of that accounted for in the other groups, it does not seem legitimate that all groups receive equal weighting in the ANAVA analysis. From another perspective, however, the problem may indeed not be with the ANAVA approach but rather with the INDSCAL solution itself. In other words, if such an imbalanced situation in the variance accounted for arises from an INDSCAL analysis, the researcher must seriously question whether or not all the experimental groups can be compared meaningfully in a single INDSCAL solution. For more details regarding the development of the ANAVA approach, the reader is directed to Chapter 13 of the Schiffman *et al.* (1981) text.

5. Nonmetric Multidimensional Scaling

Nonmetric MDS models recently have been developed, primarily due to the difficulty in justifying the strong assumption of the metric model; that is, the raw proximities are a linear transformation of the true underlying interpoint distances. MacCallum (1974) states that the metric model must be viewed as hazardous because stable configurations are very rare in practice, due to the presence of nonlinear distance functions. The newer approach in MDS requires only that these distance functions be monotonic; that is, the scale of measurement underlying the raw data is assumed to be an ordinal rather than an interval scale. The goal of the nonmetric MDS model is to seek a configuration of n points in minimum dimensionality such that the interpoint distances are monotonically related to the observed proximities. The basic computational procedure is based on Shepard's (1962) proposal that if nonmetric constraints are imposed in sufficient number, they begin to act as metric constraints. By employing relations among interpoint distances as specified by inequalities only, the nonmetric MDS model has proven to be very powerful and apparently has definite advantages over metric MDS (Kruskal & Wish, 1978). It is generally accepted that the nonmetric model results in solutions of lower dimensionality than does the metric version, simply because the latter requires more dimensions to account for nonlinearities in the distance functions. In effect, the nonmetric MDS model effectively converts an ordinal scale of proximities to a ratio scale of interpoint distances (Carroll & Arabie, 1980). Recently, Takane, Young, and deLeeuw (1977) have incorporated a nonmetric version of the INDSCAL model into a comprehensive computer program called ALSCAL. Since gross violations of the weak assumptions involved in nonmetric MDS seem to be much less likely than gross violations of the strong assumptions of the fully metric model, the study reported in Section III utilized the nonmetric approach to MDS.

D. Planning an MDS Experiment:
Major Considerations

Using multidimensional scaling procedures to assess social-cognitive schemata generally requires the experimenter, first of all, to consider carefully each of the following major issues: (1) the selection of a stimulus set, (2) the type(s) of data collection method(s) to employ, (3) whether or not to collect ratings of stimuli on descriptors (such as bipolar adjective scales) in addition to similarity judgments, (4) how much time and how many sessions will be needed to complete the experiment, (5) how the stimuli and the instructions to the different judgment tasks should be presented, and (6) how subjects will be selected and what, if any, experimental manipulations should be used.

Obviously, some of these issues need to be considered in any experimental endeavor and are undoubtedly familiar to the reader. Due to space limitations we only highlight two key issues that we have found deserve special consideration in planning an MDS experiment. Time constraints and data collection issues have already been discussed in Section II,C,1. Stimulus presentation and instructional issues are addressed in the context of an actual MDS experiment, presented later in Section III,A,3.

1. Selecting a Stimulus Set

Numerous applications over the past 10 years illustrate the wide range of stimuli as well as experimental methods that can be studied by INDSCAL and other MDS techniques. The stimuli that have been employed in MDS experiments have ranged from very concrete and physically well-defined stimuli such as colors (Wish & Carroll, 1974), musk odors (Schiffman & Dackis, 1976), and food flavors (Schiffman & Pasternak, 1978), to very general and abstract stimuli such as assertion vignettes (Rudy, Merluzzi, & Henahan, 1982), a wide variety of interpersonal situations (Wish et al., 1976), phobic objects (Landau, 1980), and prose passages (LaPorte & Voss, 1979). It is generally desirable to include as many stimuli as practically possible in an experiment. This is because the number of dimensions that can be explored increases with the number of stimuli. More specifically, from a statistical point of view Kruskal and Wish (1978) recommend that at least 9 stimuli are needed to support a two-dimensional MDS solution, at least 13 stimuli are needed for three dimensions, and at least 17 stimuli are needed for four dimensions.

Naturally, as the complexity of the stimuli increases, the amount of time required for subjects to process the stimuli and make judgments about them similarly increases. Thus, in some instances the researcher may be forced to use a somewhat smaller stimulus set. It should be recognized, however, that a smaller stimulus set may result in a loss of the more subtle discriminations being made by subjects which can be observed only at higher dimensionalities.

In addition to selecting a reasonably large number of stimuli, the quality and diversity of the stimuli are equally important considerations. For example, if the stimuli all represent extreme examples of the hypothesized underlying attributes, the resulting MDS solution is a rather meaningless collection of clusters. On the other hand, if the stimuli are all very similar, it is difficult to determine whether or not the resulting MDS dimensions represent psychologically meaningful and reliable judgments. It is, therefore, vital to select stimuli that have sufficient variation on potential dimensions for them to have a chance to appear.

After 4 years of using MDS to assess the social-cognitive schemata that may be related to social skill differences, we have concluded that the systematic construction of a stimulus set is probably the most important component in planning an MDS experiment. Rather than simply selecting intuitively a number of specific social situations and using these as stimuli, we first systemtically studied subjects' perceptions of some of the major components believed to be involved in social situations. That is, using MDS and clustering methods, we assessed subjects' judgments of different types of interpersonal behaviors, target persons, and environmental contexts, and then factorially combined the results of these separate solutions into complete, specific, complex social vignettes (for more details see Rudy et al., 1982). In sum, this approach yielded a meaningfully diverse set of social stimuli. Moreover, this set of stimuli has proven to be more useful in subsequent MDS experiments than social stimuli derived in less systematic ways.

2. Collecting Bipolar Attribute Ratings

As discussed in the section on interpreting stimulus spaces (Section II,C,3), when stimuli as complex as social situations are used in an MDS experiment, the resulting MDS stimulus configuration is often not self-explanatory. As a result of laboring long hours over numerous MDS solutions involving complex stimuli, we have concluded that collecting ratings on bipolar scales believed to be relevant to the stimulus set in question is an essential component of an MDS experiment. Not only does the use of bipolar scales effectively aid the interpretation of stimulus spaces, especially when the dimensionality of the solution is greater than two and spatial visualization becomes quite difficult, but these scales also help to guard against the human tendency to find patterns or constructs whether or not they exist.

In light of this position, the construction of a set of relevant attribute rating scales can be as important as the selection of a stimulus set. As with the selection of a stimulus set, the set of attribute rating scales selected should reflect a diversity of concepts. Due to time constraints, it is often not feasible to have subjects rate the stimuli on a large number of bipolar scales after they have made their similarity judgments. Thus, after selecting or creating a stimulus set, the experimenter may want to create a relatively large number of bipolar scales believed to be theoretically relevant to the stimulus set in question. These scales along with the stimulus set than can be used in a pilot study with a small group of subjects. If the stimulus set and/or the number of bipolar scales are large, it may be more efficient to divide, randomly, the stimulus set in half and ask half of the pilot group to rate one-half of the stimuli on all the bipolars and the rest of the subjects to rate the other half of the stimulus set. Factor analytic procedures then can be used to reduce the number of bipolar scales. That is, highly correlated bipolars can either be merged into a higher order construct or some of them can be eliminated. Additionally, those scales that appear to be "noisy" or do not load particularly well on any factor can be eliminated. In sum, although a carefully tailored set of bipolar attributes will never recover completely all of the variance in MDS stimulus spaces, systematically tailoring a set of attributes to a specific stimulus set in order to maintain a diversity of concepts will nonetheless make the bipolar scales more useful interpretational aids.

III. AN ILLUSTRATION OF USING MDS TO ASSESS SOCIAL-COGNITIVE SCHEMATA

At this point, a concrete example of an application of multidimensional scaling methods to assess social-cognitive schemata should help clarify some of the issues presented. As is typical of examples presented to clarify methodological issues, only a limited range of issues can be illustrated by describing a particular application. In spite of this limitation, we present in some detail part of a recent experiment we have conducted in hopes of more clearly demonstrating some of the MDS techniques available to the clinical researcher, rather than creating possible confusion by briefly, and most likely incompletely, reviewing a number of clinical applications of MDS.

The study reviewed here for illustrative purposes was one in a series of studies (Rudy, 1982) we have conducted recently to assess the utility of MDS methods of data collection and analysis to measure cognitive schemata or constructs that may be important in asssertiveness. Another purpose of the study was to assess the effects of demand on MDS methods of cognitive assessment. If this exploratory endeavor did, in fact, suggest that some MDS methods were resistant to demand, it seemed to us that the MDS methodology may be useful in developing cognitive assessment instruments that can be used as both initial screening instruments as well as providing cognitively oriented treatment outcome measures. After an abbreviated yet hopefully informative method section, we highlight some of the ways in which MDS data can be analyzed and how the results can be displayed and interpreted.

A. Method

1. Subjects

Sixty undergraduate males were recruited from introductory psychology courses and received experimental credit for their participation. All subjects were tested for level of assertiveness with the Conflict Resolution Inventory (CRI) developed by McFall and Lillesand (1971). Following a procedure outlined by Schwartz and Gottman (1976), assertiveness classification was done with a bivariate criterion using both assertion and nonassertion scores on the CRI. Based on their CRI scores 12 low-assertive, 6 moderate-assertive, and 6 high-assertive subjects were selected to complete the rest of the experiment.

2. Experimental Conditions

Low-assertive subjects were matched on their nonassertion scores on the CRI and were assigned to one of two experimental conditions. Half of these subjects along with the six moderate- and six high-assertive subjects completed three rank ordering tasks and a bipolar rating task under a standard instructional set (only one of the rank ordering tasks and the bipolar rating tasks are discussed in this example; see Rudy, 1982, and Rudy & Merluzzi, 1982, for more details). The other half of the low-assertive subjects completed these four tasks under high-demand instructional sets asking them to make all of their responses from the perspective of themselves as highly socially skilled individuals who are capable of refusing unreasonable requests in most situations.

3. Materials

The primary stimuli used in this experiment were 18 assertion vignettes developed from a previous study (Rudy et al., 1982) which utilized mutlidimensional scaling and hierarchial clustering procedures to develop systematically complex assertion vignettes that were a factorial arrangement of three major components: types of assertion, target persons, and environmental contexts. More specifically, the present study used the factorial arrangement of 3 types of assertion (someone asking to borrow $25, someone asking you to change tables, and someone cutting in front of you while you are waiting in line) × 3 target persons (intimates, friends and acquaintances, and status/authority people) × 2 environmental contexts (formal and informal). In sum, each of the stimuli involved some type of an unreasonable request that occurred in differing environments and with different types of people.

In addition to the 18 assertion vignettes, 12 bipolar scales were also used to aid in the interpretation of the INDSCAL group space. Originally, the majority of these bipolar scales were those that had proven useful in studying other types of social situations (e.g., Wish et al., 1976). These scales were later refined in a study on assertion (Rudy et al., 1982). As described in the section on interpreting stimulus spaces, by using multiple regression and canonical correlation these 12 bipolar rating scales had been tailored specifically to rating assertion vignettes and had displayed a good ability to recover MDS stimulus spaces.

The data relevant to our present example were collected in the following manner. Subjects first were asked to create a single, absolute rank ordering of the 18 assertion situations in terms of how difficult it would be for them to respond to each of the social situations. A three-page booklet was presented to each subject. The first page contained a set of instructions that informed the subject of the nature of the tasks and provided him with a description of how to record his responses, the second page contained a brief questionnaire designed to serve the dual purpose of a manipulation check as well as assessing whether or not subjects correctly understood the instructions, and the third page contained a list of all 18 of the assertion vignettes. Two computer randomized forms were used. The standard instructional set used for this single rank ordering difficulty of responding task was as follows:

In this part of the experiment, your task will be to read 18 social situations and then rank order them in terms of how difficult it would be for you to respond to the request being made in each of these situations. In making these rankings, please observe the following procedure:.

1. First of all, carefully read all 18 situations before you start making your rankings. As you read each social situation briefly imagine yourself actually in that particular social situation, paying attention to what thought, feelings, and behaviors you might have in that particular situation.

2. Next, decide on which one of the 18 social situations would be the easiest situation for you to respond to the request being made and place a number "1" on the line below that situation. Then place an "X" over that situation so that you no longer consider it in subsequent judgments.

3. Proceed to choose the second easiest situation for you to respond

to, place a number "2" under that situation and then cross out that situation.

4. Proceed in this way until you have rank ordered all 18 situations in terms of the difficulty for you to respond to the request being made in each situation. Thus, when you are finished with your rank ordering each situation should have been assigned a "difficulty number" ranging from "1"—the situation that you see as the easiest for you to respond to through "18"—the situation that you feel would be the most difficult for you to respond to.

5. Throughout this difficulty rank ordering process, carefully consider all aspects of a particular situation and make as finely tuned difficulty discriminations as possible. Please assign each situation a unique difficulty number, that is, do not use any ties in your rank ordering.

6. Please note that this is not a timed experiment and that there are no right or wrong answers. Simply read each situation carefully and give your honest first impressions regarding the difficulty for you to respond to each of the 18 social situations.

After subjects completed their difficulty of responding rankings, they then were asked to rate each of the 18 assertion vignettes on 12 bipolar scales. This order of presentation of the tasks was deemed necessary because in MDS, similarity of ranking judgments are the primary means for recovering the underlying structure of relationships among a group of stimuli. Bipolar rating tasks rely more on subjective and often conceptually incomplete lists of verbal descriptors, and may contaminate similarity or ranking judgments if they precede the collection of these judgments.

Each page of the bipolar scales rating booklet contained six vignettes on the left of the page with a 9-point rating scale on the right of each vignette. At the top of each page was listed the bipolar scale to be rated, which changed every fourth page. Two computerized forms of this booklet were created. The computer program not only randomized the order of the bipolar scales, but also randomized the order in which each of the vignettes occurred under each of the bipolar scales. Additionally, a brief instructional reminder occurred every seventh page and was worded differently for the standard and demand condition. This task was completed by most subjects in 1 hour, however, due to the large amount of judgments required of subjects (216) and the possible effects of fatigue, which often leads to random responding, two sessions were used to collect these data. An example from the booklet is presented below.

While you are waiting in a long line in your hall's food
sales, a guy who lives across the hall from you asks to   Easy   Difficult
cut in front of you because he's in a hurry.   1 2 3 4 5 6 7 8 9

B. Results

The subjects' single rank ordering of the assertion situations was
prepared for an INDSCAL analysis in the following way. Rectangular
response matrices, subjects (6) by stimuli (18), were constructed for
each of the four experimental groups. Next, following a procedure outlined in Section II,C,1, dissimilarity or distance measures between
stimuli (i.e., assertion vignettes) were computed using the Euclidean
distance formula. This produced an 18 × 18 symmetric matrix of distances or profile proximities between stimuli for each of the four
groups. Thus, these matrices reflected the mean differences each experimental group perceived between pairs of vignettes.

The four 18 × 18 symmetric proximity matrices created by the procedure outlined above were then submitted to the ALSCAL computer
program (Takane et al., 1977), and a nonmetric (ordinal level) INDS-
CAL analysis was conducted. A three-dimensional solution appeared
to be adequate for these data and accounted for 69.4% of the variance.
Adding a fourth dimension only accounted for 2.5% more variance,
and only using two dimensions decreased the variance accounted for
by 10%. Table II displays the variance accounted for in each of the four
matrices. More specifically, the squared correlations (RSQ) show the
proportion of variance accounted for by the INDSCAL model for each
group. Schiffman et al. (1981) suggest that RSQ is probably the best
indication of the appropriate dimensionality. Stress, another goodness-
of-fit measure, as well as interpretability, ease of use, and stability are
also important considerations (see Kruskal & Wish, 1978 for a clear and
concise treatment of these issues).

Table II also contains the raw and normalized subject weights. In our
hypothetical GM experiment, these dimensions weights corresponded
to individual subject matrices. Here, however, the dimension weightings apply to an experimental group instead of to an individual subject.
This method of using averaged proximity matrices for each experimental group is not a new approach to the INDSCAL model; in fact, in their
introduction of the INDSCAL model, Carroll and Chang (1970) noted
that this approach may also prove to be useful, in addition to using
INDSCAL to assess individual differences. Numerous research efforts
(e.g., Wish & Carroll, 1974; Wish et al., 1976; Rudy et al., 1982) have
verified this prediction.

Before addressing the question of dimensional weight differences

TABLE II

INDSCAL Dimension Weights and Variance Accounted for from the Single Rank
Order Difficulty of Responding Task for Each Experimental Group[a]

	Dimension			
Group	1	2	3	RSQ
Low	.639	.136	.501	.675
	(.775)	(.165)**	(.610)***	
Moderate	.552	.461	.285	.599
	(.713)	(.596)	(.368)	
High	.889	.159	.077	.822
	(.981)**	(.175)***	(.085)***	
Demand	.549	.549	.275	.679
	(.666)	(.666)*	(.333)	
		Average RSQ across matrices		.694
Random sampling				
Mean	.790	.476	.368	
Standard deviation	.072	.087	.049	

[a]Numbers in parentheses are normalized dimension weights so that their sum of
squares equals 1. The mean and standard deviation for the random sampling procedure
are based on normalized weights. RSQ, Squared correlations or variance accounted for.
  *$p < .05$.
  **$p < .01$.
  ***$p < .001$.

between experimental groups, the INDSCAL stimulus space is interpreted. As described in Section II,C,3, multiple regression (PROFIT,
Chang & Carroll, 1968) and canonical correlation (BMDP6M, Dixon &
Brown, 1979) procedures were used to interpret the three-dimensional
group stimulus space that resulted from the INDSCAL analysis. Table
III contains the basic results of these analyses. Examination of the total
redundancies contained in Table III indicates that the canonical correlation analysis between the three INDSCAL dimension coordinates
and the 12 bipolar scales demonstrated that 94.1% of the variance in
the INDSCAL group space could be accounted for by the bipolar scales.
Thus, as was hypothesized, it seemed statistically legitimate to use
these bipolar scales to interpret this particular INDSCAL group space.
Additionally, given the large percentage of highly significant multiple
R values on the bipolar scales, the INDSCAL dimensions were apparently psychologically meaningful and unique and could generally be
recovered in an objective manner.

Consideration of the high regression weights on Dimension 1 (Table

TABLE III

Multiple Regression and Canonical Correlation of Bipolar Ratings on INDSCAL
Dimensions from the Single Rank Order Difficulty of Responding Solution

| Bipolar scales | INDSCAL dimensions regression weights (direction cosines) | | | |
	1	2	3	R
Socially appropriate vs socially inappropriate	.772	.194	.606	.815***
Informal vs formal	−.505	−.208	.838	.629
Irritating vs nonirritating	−.748	−.461	−.478	.868***
Threatening vs nonthreatening	−.426	−.349	−.835	.881***
Tense vs relaxed	−.204	−.275	−.940	.699*
Exactly equal power vs very unequal power	−.554	−.071	.829	.742**
Cooperative vs competitive				
Fair vs unfair	.688	.521	.506	.875***
Easy vs difficult	.675	.381	.631	.804***
Similar roles and behavior vs different roles and behavior	−.186	.338	.923	.616
	.211	.150	.966	.703*
Unfamiliar vs familiar	−.202	.640	−.741	.748**
Friendly vs hostile	.303	.770	.561	.894***

| Canonical variate | Canonical correlation | Redundancies | | Total redundancies | |
		INDSCAL set	Bipolar set	INDSCAL set	Bipolar set
First	.999***	.326	.171	—	—
Second	.970**	.300	.299	.626	.470
Third	.943*	.315	.135	.941	.605

*p < .05.
**p < .01.
***p < .001.

III) suggested that this dimension primarily concerned the level of social appropriateness or propriety that subjects perceived in these assertion situations. That is, at one end of this dimension were situations
that appeared to subjects as socially appropriate and nonirritating;
those at the opposite end were rated as irritating and socially inappropriate. Table IV contains the order of the stimuli on this dimension
coded in terms of their three-way factorial construction. Using the dimension coordinates as the dependent variable, ANOVA main effects
were calculated for this dimension in order to aid interpretation. The
ANOVA main effects results indicated that both the type of assertion

factor and the target person factor were significant, $F(2, 12) = 4.87$, p $<.02$ and $F(2, 12) = 10.21$, p $<.002$, respectively. The type $\times$ person interaction was also significant, $F(4, 8) = 5.14$, p $<.02$, although this test can only be considered to be suggestive because in order to form this interaction only two stimuli existed per cell. Post hoc Duncan tests were also calculated for both significant main effects, and the results are contained in Table IV. In summary the PROFIT results (Table III) and the Duncan results (Table IV) suggest that, apparently, subjects felt that it was inappropriate and irritating for acquaintances to ask them to change tables, but that it was okay for intimates and status persons to ask to borrow \$25 or to cut in front of them in line.

Dimension 2 was only recovered well by the friendly vs hostile bipolar scale (Table III). There was, however, a significant main effect for the type of assertion factor, $F(2, 12) = 30.05$, p $<.0001$. As indicated in Table IV, subjects apparently perceived being asked to change tables or someone cutting in line as a hostile request, whereas someone asking to borrow \$25 was rated as a more friendly type of request.

Dimension 3 appeared to be related primarily to the target person, $F(2, 12) = 1098$, p $<.002$. The results of the Duncan test contained in Table IV revealed that this dimension separated intimates from acquaintances and status persons. The bipolar regression weights displayed in Table III not only supported the hypothesis that this was primarily a target person dimension, but also helped to finely tune its interpretation. That is, assertion situations that involve intimates were viewed by subjects as relaxed and nonthreatening, and situations involving status persons were seen as tense and threatening. In some ways, this dimension can be interpreted as an emotional arousal dimension.

In sum, the interpretation of the dimensions resulting from the INDSCAL analysis of the single rank ordering in terms of the difficulty to respond to the assertion situations were as follows: (1) Dimension 1 primarily dealt with the level of perceived social appropriateness, (2) Dimension 2 seemed to address the level of hostility in the situation, and (3) Dimension 3 was interpreted as an emotional arousal dimension which related to the status of the target person.

Because the matrices used in this INDSCAL analysis were group rather than subject matrices, the ANAVA approach could not be used.[5]

[5]The basic logic and normalization approach contained in the SUBJSTAT computer program were used to slightly modify the statistical approach outlined below. Normalization of dimension weights to unity vectors was considered to be important so that differences in variance accounted for and in the effect that these differences have on dimension weights would not have an impact on the statistical procedures that follow.

TABLE IV

Coordinate Values and Stimulus Arrangement of the Group Space Resulting from the INDSCAL Analysis of the Single Rank Order Difficulty of Responding Task

Dimension 1	Dimension 2	Dimension 3
.399 CHA–ACQ–FORMAL	.308 CHA–STATUS–FORMAL	.388 LINE–STATUS–INFORM
.370 $25–ACQ–INFORM	.307 LINE–STATUS–FORMAL	.330 CHA–STATUS–INFORM
.322 CHA–ACQ–INFORM	.279 CHA–INT–INFORM	.299 LINE–ACQ–FORMAL
.276 CHA–INT–INFORM	.223 LINE–INT–INFORM	.263 $25–ACQ–INFORM
.192 $25–ACQ–FORMAL	.222 LINE–ACQ–INFORM	.171 CHA–STATUS–FORMAL
.168 LINE–ACQ–FORMAL	.162 LINE–ACQ–FORMAL	.150 LINE–STATUS–FORMAL
.162 CHA–INT–FORMAL	.152 LINE–INT–FORMAL	.103 $25–STATUS–FORMAL
-.009 LINE–INT–INFORM	.068 LINE–STATUS–INFORM	.041 LINE–ACQ–INFORM
-.086 CHA–STATUS–FORMAL	.052 CHA–STATUS–INFORM	.027 $25–ACQ–FORMAL
-.102 LINE–ACQ–INFORM	.041 CHA–ACQ–INFORM	.023 CHA–ACQ–FORMAL
-.106 $25–STATUS–FORMAL	-.005 CHA–ACQ–FORMAL	-.065 $25–STATUS–INFORM
-.118 CHA–STATUS–INFORM	-.021 CHA–INT–FORMAL	-.138 $25–INT–INFORM
-.153 LINE–INT–FORMAL	-.189 $25–INT–FORMAL	-.142 $25–INT–FORMAL

-.182 $25–STATUS–INFORM   -.196 $25–INT–INFORM   -.172 CHA–ACQ–INFORM
-.218 LINE–STATUS–FORMAL   -.281 $25–ACQ–INFORM   -.242 LINE–INT–INFORM
-.259 LINE–STATUS–INFORM   -.346 $25–ACQ–FORMAL   -.262 CHA–INT–INFORM
-.280 $25–INT–FORMAL   -.367 $25–STATUS–FORMAL   -.294 CHA–INT–FORMAL
-.375 $25–INT–INFORM   -.410 $25–STATUS–INFORM   -.480 LINE–INT–FORMAL

Coordinate means and Duncan test results for significant main effects

A	.159	CHA	A	.189	LINE	A	.179	STATUS
B	-.063	$25	A	.109	CHA	A	.080	ACQ
B	-.095	LINE	B	-.298	$25	B	-.259	INT
A	.224	ACQ						
B	-.063	INT						
B	-.161	STATUS						

[a]The INDSCAL dimension coordinates have been normalized to a mean of 0 and the sum of squares equal to 1. For the Duncan tests, means with the same letter are not significantly different, and α was set at .05. The coding for the stimuli is as follows: the first factor relates to the type of assertion, the second to the target person, and the third to the environmental context. For each factor the following abbreviations represent the levels of the factors. CHA, Changing tables; LINE, line cutting; $25, borrowing $25. INT, Intimates; ACQ, acquaintances; STATUS, status persons. FORMAL, Formal environments; INFORM, informal environments.

Determination of statistically significant differences between experimental groups involved a type of Monte Carlo procedure that was first proposed by Wish *et al.* (1976). Using the actual rank ordering data from subjects, 10 mean distance profile proximity matrices—each computed from 6 randomly selected individuals (with replacements) from the entire population of 24 subjects—were formed. Using an option provided in the ALSCAL computer program to keep the stimulus space fixed and to solve for the weights by a least-squares procedure, dimension weights were then determined for each of the random samples. These dimension weights were normalized to unity and used to create sampling distributions and derive confidence intervals. The dimension weights for each experimental group were also normalized to unity vectors. The normalized group weights were compared to the confidence regions that resulted from the Monte Carlo procedure. The results of these comparisons are contained in Table II. As displayed in Table II, although all groups used Dimension 1, this dimension was found to be significantly more important to the high-assertive group. In fact, it appeared as though these subjects created their rank orderings based on an almost exclusive use of some type of social appropriateness criterion. It should be noted that Dimension 1 was not significantly less important for any group. Dimension 2, related to the degree of perceived hostility, was used primarily by the moderate-assertive, high-demand groups and was found to be significantly less important for both the low- and high-assertive groups. The third dimension, the arousal/status dimension, was significantly more important to low assertives and significantly less important to the high-assertive group. In sum, these results suggested that the low-, moderate-, and high-assertive groups differed from each other regarding the importance that they placed on the three INDSCAL dimensions. Additionally, and perhaps of most importance, it appeared that low assertives under high-demand instructions performed more like moderate assertives than like low assertives under a standard instructional set. Thus, this method was not impervious to demand.

C. Discussion

The schema differences found in this assessment task for the low-, moderate-, and high-assertive groups under standard instructions raise some interesting speculations concerning the attitudinal differences that may have been involved in the subjects' difficulty of responding judgments. Since all 18 assertion vignettes implied varying degrees of unreasonable requests or impositions, perhaps these subjects were using somewhat different criteria to assess the level or degree of imposition. Low assertives, who weighted the status level dimension as significantly more important, may have felt that it was acceptable for a higher status person to impose upon them, but perhaps reacted differently to the imposition if the request was made by an individual of lower status.

The difficulty of responding judgments made by the moderate- and high-assertive groups did not appear to be as status oriented. Rather, these subjects appeared to make more finely tuned evaluative judgments. The moderate assertives seemed to be linking imposition with negative arousal or anger. Perhaps as the level of perceived imposition increased, so did their feelings of resentment and irritation. On the other hand, the high assertives seemed to use a less emotional construct to represent the degree of imposition. Specifically, it appeared as though they used some type of criterion based on an inverse relationship between social propriety and the level of imposition. That is, perhaps they felt requests that were more imposing were also less socially appropriate. Additionally, it is important to note that the dimension of primary importance to the high-assertive group (Dimension 1) appeared to represent an interaction between the type of request and the target person. For example, this group believed that it would be socially inappropriate for an acquaintance to ask them to change tables, but socially appropriate for an intimate to ask to borrow $25. Neither the perceived level of hostility dimension (weighted as more important by the moderate- and the high-demand groups) nor the status level dimension (weighted as more important by the low-assertive group) appeared to represent as complex a relationship.

It should be noted that although the importance placed on the social propriety dimension varied between experimental groups, none of the groups weighted this dimension as significantly less important. This finding suggested all groups were apparently in agreement that some type of social propriety schema was useful in making judgments about the difficulty involved in responding to the assertion situations. Of most interest, however, was the finding that instead of weighting another dimension as being of relatively equal importance to the social propriety dimension (as was the case for the moderate- and low-assertive groups), the high-assertive group appeared to be almost unidimensional in their judgments. Specifically, the INDSCAL dimension weights for the high-assertive group indicated that the social propriety dimension received a very high loading and the perceived hostility and status dimension had low weights. Although these results may indicate high-assertive individuals have a more finely tuned sense of social propriety, an equally plausible interpretation would be that high-assertive individuals may be somewhat rigid in their assessment of assertion situations. In other words, by focusing primarily on the "social rightness" or "social wrongness" of a request, other important emotional and interpersonal components may be ignored.

Finally, it appears that the instructional set for low assertives to complete the tasks as if they were highly socially skilled did have a modest effect. The low assertives under demand had dimension weights similar to moderate-assertive subjects. Thus, the single rank order method was not impervious to instructional demand. At the same time the low-assertives under demand did not look similar to high-assertive individuals. Other methods of data collection should be tested for sensitivity to demand, and the findings presented here should be replicated.

IV. CONCLUSION: SPECULATIONS ON THE UTILITY OF MULTIDIMENSIONAL SCALING IN ADVANCING THEORY AND CLINICAL ASSESSMENT

The methods, examples, and theoretical underpinnings of MDS as we have used it have been presented in the hope that these methods will be used to advance theory and research in psychopathology.[6] With respect to theory, MDS may be useful in uncovering basic cognitive structures that may help elucidate certain theories of psychopathology. For example, while the self-schemata of depressives and nondepressives have been described by Beck's theory and studied, although using a different methodology, by Kuiper and Derry (1981), MDS may offer information that elaborates on the dimensions or constructs that constitute those self-schemata (or schemata about situations) and on the importance of those dimensions. We might speculate, for example, that depressives and nondepressives both might use a valence dimension (or evaluative dimension) in constructing social situations. However, we might also speculate that depressives would have higher weights on that dimension. Thus, these methods might be helpful in discovering what clinical and nonclinical populations have in common (i.e., the group space) and what might be unique about the groups or individuals (i.e., the personal space).

In some instances we might conclude that a common group space is

---

[6]Portions of this section were presented in Merluzzi and Rudy (1982).

not warranted. For example, the variance-accounted-for for a group (or individuals) may be very low compared to other groups (or individuals), whereas when scaled separately, an acceptable solution is obtained for that group. In that case, a common group space cannot be achieved and we might conclude that the dimensions extracted for that group are uncorrelated with those extracted for other groups. We might even check this assumption by looking at the simple correlations (or perform canonical correlations) between the dimension coordinates derived from the aberrant group (individual) and those obtained from the other groups (individuals). In that way, we can test whether there is any common variance between the MDS solutions. Perhaps there is one common dimension, and the remaining dimensions are uncorrelated.

While this discussion is speculative, it is nonetheless provocative in that theoretical assumptions may be made more testable using MDS. Also, MDS may provide a method of converging operations when used in conjunction with other methods of assessing schemata.

Another area in which MDS may advance research and theory is in cognitive assessment. Recently, a number of researchers (Arnkoff & Glass, 1982; Glass & Merluzzi, 1981; Goldfried & Robins, 1983; Kendall, 1983; Mischel, 1981) have commented on the status of cognitive assessment models and offered either suggestions or new directions in both method and theory. A common problem inherent in much of the work in cognitive assessment is that little attention has been paid to the conceptual aspects of the various methods. Mischel (1981) and Arnkoff and Glass (1982) draw out attention to this problem and have suggested areas in which we might begin to examine the concepts and constructs that guide the development of cognitive assessment methods. A compelling paper by Diane Arnkoff (1980) and, later, a chapter by Arnkoff and Glass (1982) have presented an overarching construct, level of inference, that may be a useful construct in conceptualizing cognitive assessment methods. Arnkoff (1980) proposed a cognitive framework from which to view clinical events and the process of psychotherapy. This perspective is based on the assumption that each individual creates a model of the structure of the world. This model or framework guides an individual's behavior and provides structure for inferring the meaning of events.

An individual's model, to a large extent, is not part of conscious awareness (Arnkoff, 1980); that is, much of an individual's knowledge of the world may be tacit. This concept of tacit knowledge is related to Chomsky's linguistic theory involving the distinction between deep structure and surface structure. The tacit deep structure rules determine the meaning of surface structure or observable behavior; that is, meaning relates to deep structure and there is only surface evidence of it.

For change in psychotherapy to be maintained and generalized, the deep structure must be altered. Changing deep structure means shifting the pattern of relations seen in the world and involves moving from one way of understanding the world to another. Temporary shifts in surface structure can be easily achieved, as evidence by the initial success of many therapies. Change in deep structure or cognitive–perceptual schemata is much more difficult (Arnkoff, 1980).

This conceptualization of change is very consistent with that of George Kelly (1955). The deep structure may be the complex template of constructs that one erects and uses to understand the world. One's overt behaviors and thought reflect that underlying system of constructs.

The level of inference construct was related by Arnkoff and Glass to Arnkoff's surface–deep structure analysis of psychotherapy. Further, the authors mentioned that the surface to deep structure connection may not be easily observed because there are unique, individualized relationships between overt events and the meaning structure. Again, Kelly's theory is very consistent with this line of thought.

The concepts of surface and deep structure may also be applied to cognitive assessment as suggested by Glass and Merluzzi (1981) and Arnkoff and Glass (1982). Therefore, it becomes necessary to look at cognitive assessment methods from the perspective of the surface-to-deep structure or level of inference construct. Self-statements and overt behaviors appear to be surface representations of a deeper cognitive schema. Accordingly, self-statement measures, such as the Social Interaction Self-Statement Test (Glass, Merluzzi, Biever, & Larsen, 1982) and thought listing (Cacioppo & Petty, 1981), assess surface structure, whereas assessment of the underlying meaning of the self-statements involves deep structure assessment. We propose that MDS may be a method of assessing deep structure. However, Mischel warns us, "If one wants to go beyond the information given, beyond what is reported or observed directly in its own right, one must justify the resulting inferences and generalizations" (Mischel, 1981, pp. 499–500). It is interesting to note that a basic assumption of MDS is that the geometric representation of data must be reasonably close to the original similarity (or dissimilarity) judgments made by subjects. If this correspondence is not attained, the obtained solution is not valid. Thus, while the inferences are deep, they are based very closely on the actual data reported or observed.

There appears to be several challenges that we must confront if we are to postulate that MDS data may represent a deeper level of inference than self-statement or behavioral data. First, we must test its imperviousness to demand and transient fluctuations. Second, we must show that there is change in the deep structure as a function of therapy and that this change is stable once achieved. Third, we must show a correspondence between surface structure (i.e., overt behaviors) and deep structure (i.e., dimension weights). As is evident from the substance of this article, our research program is beginning to focus on these issues. We feel that MDS is flexible and robust enough to confront these challenges. Finally, because in many uses of MDS there is an emphasis on the individual, we feel that the uniqueness of the individual may be preserved. And we believe that is the way George Kelly would have wanted it.

REFERENCES

Arnkoff, D. B. Psychotherapy from the perspective of cognitive theory. In M. J. Mahoney (Ed.), *Psychotherapy process: Current issues and future directions.* New York: Plenum, 1980.

Arnkoff, D. B., & Glass, C. R. Clinical cognitive constructs: Examination, evaluation and elaboration. In P. C. Kendall (Ed.), *Advances in cognitive-behavioral research and therapy* (Vol. 1). New York: Academic Press, 1982.

Benton, M. L. Dissimilarity measures for unconstrained sorting data. *Multivariate Behavioral Research,* 1975, **10**, 409–423.

Cacioppo, J. T., & Petty, R. E. Social psychological procedures for cognitive response assessment: The thought listing technique. In T. V. Merluzzi, C. R. Glass, & M. Genest (Eds.), *Cognitive Assessment.* New York: Guilford, 1981.

Carroll, J. D. Individual differences and multidimensional scaling. In A. K. Romney, R. N. Shepard, & S. B. Nerlove (Eds.), *Multidimensional scaling: Theory and applications in the behavioral science* (Vol. 1). New York: Seminar Press, 1972.

Carroll, J. D., & Arabie, P. Multidimensional scaling. *Annual Review of Psychology,* 1980, **31**, 607–649.

Carroll, J. D., & Chang, J. J. Analysis of individual differences in multidimensional scaling via an N-way generalization of "Eckart-Young" decomposition. *Psychometrika,* 1970, **35**, 283–319.

Chang, J. J., & Carroll, J. C. *How to use PROFIT, a computer program for property fitting by optimizing nonlinear or linear correlation.* Unpublished manuscript, Bell Laboratories, 1968.

Dixon, W. J., & Brown, M. B. (Eds.). *BMDP-79: Biomedical computer programs.* Berkeley: Univ. of California Press, 1979.

Drasgow, F., & Jones, L. E. Multi-dimensional scaling of derived dissimilarities. *Multivariate Behavioral Research,* 1979, **14**, 227–244.

Eckart, C., & Young, G. The approximation of one matrix by another of lower rank. *Psychometrika,* 1936, **1**, 211–218.

Glass, C. R. & Merluzzi, T. V. Cognitive assessment of social evaluative anxiety. In T. V.

Merluzzi, C. R. Glass, & M. Genest (Eds.), *Cognitive Assessment*. New York: Guilford, 1981.

Glass, C. R., Merluzzi, T. V., Biever, J. L., & Larsen, K. H. Cognitive assessment of social anxiety: Development and validation of a self-statement questionnaire. *Cognitive Therapy and Research*, 1982, **6**, 37–55.

Goldfried, M. R., & Robins, C. Self-schemas, cognitive bias, and the processing of therapeutic experiences. In P. C. Kendall (Ed.), *Advances in cognitive-behavioral research and therapy* (Vol. 2). New York: Academic Press, 1983.

Green, P. E., & Wind, Y. *Multiattribute decisions in marketing: A measurement approach*. Hinsdale, IL: Dryden Press, 1973.

Hastie, R. Schematic principles in human memory. In E. T. Higgins, C. P. Herman, & M. P. Zanna (Eds.). *Social Cognition: The Ontario Symposium*. Hillsdale, NJ: Erlbaum, 1981.

Kelly, G. H. *The psychology of personal constructs*. New York: Norton, 1955.

Kendall, P. C. Methodology and cognitive-behavioral assessment. *Behavioral Psychotherapy*, 1983, in press.

Kruskal, J. B., & Wish, M. *Multidimensional scaling* (Sage University Paper Series on Quantitative Applications in the Social Sciences, No. 07-011). Beverly Hills, CA: Sage Publications, 1978.

Kuiper, N. A., & Derry, P. A. The self as a cognitive prototype: An application to person perception and depression. In N. Cantor & J. F. Kihlstrom (Eds.), *Personality, cognition and social interaction*. Hillsdale, NJ: Erlbaum, 1981.

Landau, R. J. The role of semantic schemata in phobic word interpretation. *Cognitive Therapy and Research*, 1980, **4**, 427–434.

Landau, R. J., & Goldfried, M. R. The assessment of schematic structure: A unifying focus in cognitive, traditional, and behavioral assessment. In P. C. Kendall & S. P. Hollon (Eds.), *Assessment strategies for cognitive behavioral interventions*. New York: Academic Press, 1981.

LaPorte, R. E., & Voss, J. F. Prose representation: A multidimensional scaling approach. *Multivariate Behavioral Research*, 1979, **14**, 39–56.

MacCallum, R. C. Relations between factor analysis and multidimensional scaling. *Psychological Bulletin*, 1974, **81**, 505–516.

MacCallum, R. C. Effects of conditionality on INDSCAL and ALSCAL weights. *Psychometrika*, 1977, **42**, 297–305.

Magnusson, D., & Endler, N. S. Interactional psychology: Present status and future prospects. In D. Magnusson & N. S. Endler (Eds.), *Personality at the crossroads: Current issues in interactional psychology*. Hillsdale, NJ: Erlbaum, 1977.

Mardia, K. V. *Statistics of directional data*. New York: Academic Press, 1972.

McFall, R. M., & Lillesand, D. B. Behavioral rehearsal with modeling and coaching in assertion training. *Journal of Abnormal Psychology*, 1971, **77**, 313–323.

Merluzzi, T. V., & Rudy, T. E. Cognitive assessment of social anxiety: A "surface" and "deep" structure analysis. In M. R. Leary (Chair), *Recent research in social anxiety: Social, personality, and clinical perspectives*. Symposium presented at the meeting of the American Psychological Association, Washington, DC, August 1982.

Mischel, W. George Kelly's anticipation of psychology: A personal tribute. In M. J. Mahoney (Ed.), *Psychotherapy process: Current issues and future directions*. New York: Plenum, 1980.

Mischel, W. A cognitive-social learning approach to assessment. In T. V. Merluzzi, C. R. Glass, & M. Genest (Eds.), *Cognitive assessment*. New York: Guilford, 1981.

Neimeyer, G. J., & Neimeyer, R. A. Personal construct perspectives on cognitive assessment. In T. V. Merluzzi, C. B. Glass, & M. Genest (Eds.), *Cognitive assessment*. New York: Guilford, 1981.

Nygren, T. E., & Jones, L. E. Individual differences in perceptions and preferences for political candidates. *Journal of Experimental Social Psychology*, 1977, **13**, 182–197.

Rodgers, J. L., & Young, F. W. Successive unfolding of family preferences. *Applied Psychological Measurement*, 1981, **5**, 51–62.

Rosenberg, S., & Kim, M. P. The method of sorting as a data gathering procedure in multivariate research. *Multivariate Behavioral Research*, 1975, **10**, 489–502.

Rudy, T. E. *The effects of demand on the cognitive assessment of assertion: A measurement approach.* Unpublished doctoral dissertation, University of Notre Dame, 1982.

Rudy, T. E., & Merluzzi, T. V. *The effects of demand on the cognitive assessment of assertiveness.* Paper presented at the meeting of the American Psychological Association, Washington, DC, August 1982.

Rudy, T. E., Merluzzi, T. V., & Henahan, P. T. Construal of complex assertion situations: A multidimensional analysis. *Journal of Consulting and Clinical Psychology*, 1982, **50**, 125–137.

Schiffman, S. S., & Dackis, C. Multidimensional scaling of musks. *Physiology and Behavior*, 1976, **17**, 823–829.

Schiffman, S. S., Munsante, G., & Conger, J. Application of multidimensional scaling to rating of foods for obese and normal weight individuals. *Physiology and Behavior*, 1978, 21, 417–422.

Schiffman, S. S., & Pasternak, M. Decreased discrimination of food odors in the elderly. *Journal of Gerontology*, 1978, **34**, 73–79.

Schiffman, S. S., Reynolds, M. L., & Young, F. W. *Introduction to multidimensional scaling: Theory, methods, and application.* New York: Academic Press, 1981.

Schwartz, R. M., & Gottman, J. M. Toward a task analysis of assertion behavior. *Journal of Consulting and Clinical Psychology*, 1976, **44**, 910–920.

Shepard, R. N. The analysis of proximities: Multidimensional scaling with an unknown distance function. *Psychometrika*, 1962, **27**, 125–140.

Shepard, R. N. Multidimensional scaling, tree-fitting, and clustering. *Science*, 1980, **210**, 390–398.

Stewart, D., & Love, W. A general canonical correlation index. *Psychological Bulletin*, 1968, **70**, 160–163.

Sullivan, H. S. *The interpersonal theory of psychiatry.* New York: Norton, 1953.

Takane, Y., Young, F. W., & deLeeuw, J. Nonmetric individual differences multidimensional scaling: An alternative least squares method with optimal scaling features. *Psychometrika*, 1977, **42**, 7–67.

Turk, D. C., & Speers, M. A. Cognitive schemata and cognitive processes in cognitive-behavioral interventions: Going beyond the information given. In P. C. Kendall (Ed.), *Advances in cognitive-behavioral research and therapy* (Vol. 2). New York: Academic Press, 1983.

Tucker, L. R. Relations between multidimensional scaling and three-mode factor analysis. *Psychometrika*, 1972, **37**, 3–27.

Wish, M., & Carroll, J. D. Applications of individual differences scaling to studies of human perception and judgment. In E. C. Carterette & M. P. Friedman (Eds.), *Handbook of perception: Vol. 2. Psychophysical judgment and measurement.* New York: Academic Press, 1974.

Wish, M., Deutsch, M., & Biener, L. Differences in conceptual structures of nations: An exploratory study. *Journal of Personality and Social Psychology*, 1970, **16**, 361–373.

Wish, M., Deutsch, M., & Biener, L. Differences in perceived similarity of nations. In A. K. Romney, R. N. Shepard, & S. B. Nerlove (Eds.), *Multidimensional scaling: Theory and applications in the behavioral sciences* (Vol. 2). New York: Seminar Press, 1972.

Wish, M., Deutsch, M., & Kaplan, S. J. Perceived dimensions of interpersonal relations. *Journal of Personality and Social Psychology*, 1976, **33**, 409–420.

Young, F. W. Scaling replicated conditional rank order data. In D. R. Heise (Ed.), *Sociological Methodology*. San Francisco: Jossey-Bass, 1975.

Young, G., & Householder, A. S. Discussion of a set of points in terms of their mutual distances. *Psychometrika*, 1938, **3**, 19–22.

Covert Modeling

ALAN E. KAZDIN

Department of Psychiatry
Western Psychiatric Institute and Clinic
University of Pittsburgh School of Medicine
Pittsburgh, Pennsylvania

I. INTRODUCTION

In behavior therapy, several techniques based on the use of imagery have emerged over the last decade. The development of imagery-based techniques in behavior therapy is significant for several reasons. First, the use of imagery for treatment purposes directly acknowledges the potentially crucial role of private events, in this case imaginal processes, in controlling behavior. This is significant because behaviorism as a larger movement has often held private events in varying degrees of disrepute (Koch, 1964). Second, there are many practical advantages in using imagery in clinical work. Imagery allows the client to rehearse

103

ADVANCES IN COGNITIVE–BEHAVIORAL RESEARCH
AND THERAPY, VOLUME 3

covertly many different responses under a wide array of situations. The flexibility and ease of administration often make covert rehearsal preferred over overt rehearsal or in vivo practice. Third, the use of imagery may help to create conceptual and procedural bridges between behavioral and more traditional therapies. Imagery is used extensively in various forms of psychotherapy, particularly in Europe (see Singer, 1974; Singer & Pope, 1978). The use of imagery in behavior therapy has developed independently of these other techniques. Yet, the common use of imaginal processes may provide the opportunity for rapprochement among different conceptual schools.

In behavior therapy, imagery-based techniques require the client to imagine a series of carefully planned scenes that are directed toward behavior change. The most familiar technique that meets this general description is systematic desensitization in which the clients usually imagine themselves engaging in various behaviors to overcome anxiety (Wolpe, 1958). Indeed, other imagery-based techniques emerged in part because of the initial applications of desensitization (Cautela, 1966, 1967). Several techniques, referred to as covert conditioning, have been developed over the last 15 years by Cautela (1971a, 1972, 1977).

Covert conditioning techniques were derived from extrapolations of specific learning principles developed in laboratory research. The techniques include covert sensitization, covert positive reinforcement, covert negative reinforcement, covert extinction, covert punishment, and covert modeling (see Kazdin & Smith, 1979; Upper & Cautela, 1979). Techniques such as covert reinforcement, punishment, and extinction are considered to be direct applications of operant conditioning principles. Covert sensitization relies on operant principles such as punishment and negative reinforcement as well as on classical conditioning and aversion relief. Covert modeling is derived from observational or vicarious learning.

The covert conditioning techniques are based on the assumption that imagined events influence behavior in a fashion similar to actual events. For example, in covert reinforcement, the clients imagine themselves performing a behavior they wish to develop. After the behavior is performed in imagination, the client is immediately instructed to imagine some reinforcing (favorable) consequence. It is assumed that this sequence in imagination (i.e., imagined behavior followed by imagined consequences) exerts similar control over overt behavior as the direct operation of reinforcing consequences (i.e., overt behavior followed by the actual delivery of reinforcing consequences). The general assumption about the influence of imagined events has been very useful in generating specific treatment techniques. The viability of these techniques is attested to by the successful application they have enjoyed across a wide range of disorders. Covert conditioning techniques have been used to treat behaviors related to social inadequacy, fears, sexual deviance and dysfunctions, obsessions and compulsions, obesity, drug addiction, alcoholism, and other problems (Cautela, 1971a, 1972; Kazdin & Smith, 1979).

One of the more recently developed covert conditioning techniques is covert modeling. The purpose of the present article is to describe the practice of covert modeling and to evaluate the outcome literature pertaining to its efficacy and range of applicability. In addition, parameters of imagery that appear to influence the efficacy of treatment are reviewed. Finally, salient issues in covert modeling treatment are discussed.

II. CHARACTERISTICS OF COVERT MODELING

A. Background and Underlying Rationale

Covert modeling, first presented in 1971, is derived from the modeling or vicarious learning literature (Cautela, 1976).[1] Modeling refers to learning based primarily upon merely observing someone else (a model) perform a response. To acquire a response, an observer need not perform the response but only observe the response performance of a model. The effects of modeling have been well established both in laboratory research and clinical applications (see Perry & Furukawa, 1980; Rachman, 1976; Rosenthal & Bandura, 1978).

In general, several different interpretations of modeling effects are available. The most widely discussed interpretation has been proposed by Bandura (1970), who has accounted for observational learning on the basis of covert coding processes on the part of the observer. Bandura has suggested that observing a live or film model conveys cues to the observer. These cues are symbolically coded through representational processes based on imagery or verbalizations. Bandura (1970) has noted that observational learning refers primarily to the representational processes by which the modeled responses are coded rather than by the form in which these events are conveyed to the observer.

Emphasizing the cognitive processes that account for performance of the observer suggests that viewing or observing a model is not an essen-

---

[1]This published report of covert modeling was first presented as a paper delivered to the Association for Advancement of Behavior Therapy, Washington, DC, September 1971.

tial ingredient for behavior change. Rather, altering the representational processes that guide behavior is responsible for behavior change. Covert modeling provides an alternative means of altering representational processes assumed to be important in live modeling. Rather than observing behavior, a client may imagine a model performing a behavior that the client wishes to develop. Thus, the modeling goes on covertly or in the imagination.

As usually conducted, covert modeling requires that a client imagine several situations in which someone other than himself or herself performs behaviors that the client wishes to develop (see Cautela, 1971b). Scenes or situations are constructed in which the client can picture the behavior that is to be changed (e.g., approach toward some feared object, appropriate social interaction). For example, a client who is severely withdrawn would be asked to imagine a number of scenes in which a model engages in social interaction. Initially, the model would be described in scenes in which he or she performs relatively minimal social behaviors (e.g., perhaps merely greeting someone). Over the course of treatment, the scenes might illustrate behaviors that reflect more demanding interactions (e.g., maintaining a conversation, initiating an interaction at a party). The scenes are constructed in consultation with the client and focus upon the range of situations in which the behavior needs to be changed or developed.

B. Illustration of the Procedures: Assertion Training

Much of our own work has focused on the use of covert modeling in developing social skills, particularly assertive behavior for persons who claim they have difficulty communicating their feelings to others or in standing up for their rights.[2] Participants of our programs have received covert modeling, or some variation, to develop their social skills across a wide range of situations. Treatment is administered by a therapist in individual sessions and usually is conducted over a period of 2–5 weeks.

At the beginning of treatment, clients receive a rationale that describes the basis of modeling and covert conditioning in general. Prior

[2]Assertion training encompasses teaching individuals to express themselves more effectively and may include both the expression of positive and negative feelings such as affection or anger. In our own work, the majority of client goals pertain to refusing to comply with unreasonable demands, making requests of others, and in general sticking up for one's rights. Hence, this relatively narrow focus has served as the primary focus of treatment.

to actual treatment, clients receive practice in imagining various scenes and are instructed to focus on detail of the scenes. Also, clients practice imagining a model (someone other than themselves) who will be used in the treatment scenes. In light of research, reviewed later, clients usually are instructed to imagine a model similar to themselves (e.g., in age and same sex). After practice in imagery, clients are given several scenes in which the model performs assertively.

Scenes are described by a therapist. For purposes of standardization, they often are tape-recorded and presented by audiotapes controlled by the therapist during the sessions. The client tries to imagine the material presented. When the image is clear, the client signals by raising a finger and maintaining his or her eyes closed. The client then is told to hold the image as best as possible until a predetermined time period has elapsed (e.g., 30 seconds). After the interval, the client is told to stop imagining the scene. The same scene is repeated or a new scene is presented. Treatment consists of traversing several scenes that elaborate diverse aspects of the behaviors the client wishes to develop. Three of the scenes that are used in the treatment of assertive behavior illustrate the general task provided for the client.

1. Imagine the person (model) in his (her) apartment around dinnertime. The person has an important appointment later in the evening, but friends drop in for a visit. The friends have spent time there. They have finished their coffee but look like they are going to stay for some time. The person is getting somewhat bothered about the appointment and has to leave in a few minutes. While the friends are sitting there and everyone is chatting, the person breaks into the conversation and says, "Say, I'm really glad you dropped in but I have a meeting and have to leave. Perhaps we can get together sometime when we are both free."

2. Picture yourself at a concert with a friend. A few people in the row behind you are making a lot of noise and disturbing everyone. It seems they have a comment to make every few minutes that everyone can hear. A person sitting next to you (the model) turns around and says, "Will you people please be quiet?"

3. Imagine that the person (the model) is staying in a hotel. After one night there, he (she) notices that the bedsprings must be broken. The bed sags miserably and was very uncomfortable during the night. In the morning, the person goes to the clerk at the desk and says, "The bed in my room is quite uncomfortable. I believe it is broken. I wish you would replace the bed or change my room."

The above scenes and the manner of their presentation mentioned earlier should be taken only as illustrations for implementing covert modeling. Each scene has two basic or core components, namely, the context which makes an assertive response appropriate and the assertive response on the part of the model. Several other features can be added to the basic scenes to enhance treatment effects, as reviewed later.

III. OUTCOME EVIDENCE

The outcome evidence has addressed different questions about covert modeling including efficacy of the basic procedure, parameters that contribute to behavior change, and adjunctive procedures that can be added to the basic covert modeling treatment. The research has provided a few empirically based guidelines for how covert modeling should be implemented.

A. Efficacy of the Basic Procedure

The initial question for evaluating covert modeling is whether the treatment as proposed can effect therapeutic change. Initial applications of covert modeling consisted exclusively of case studies that served primarily to illustrate the procedure (Cautela, 1971b). Covert modeling was applied to individual therapy cases covering various maladaptive approach and avoidance responses and behavioral deficits such as fear of blushing, social criticism, entering a homosexual bar, excessively consuming food, and responding assertively to others. In other case reports, covert modeling administered alone or in conjunction with other procedures has been shown to reduce agoraphobia, addiction to drugs, and excessive consumption of alcohol (e.g., Flannery, 1972a,b; Hay, Hay, & Nelson, 1977). In some of the case applications, single-case experimental designs have been reported. In two such demonstrations using multiple-baseline designs, covert modeling was shown to alter obsessive–compulsive behaviors (Hay et al., 1977, Case 2) and cross-gender behaviors (Hay, Barlow, & Hay, 1981). In general, the cases suggest the applicability of covert modeling across diverse problems but do not establish that covert modeling specifically was responsible for change.

A number of outcome studies have evaluated covert modeling. The majority of these have been with relatively mild behavior problems of college students rather than with clinically debilitating disorders of patients. The mild problems have included subphobic levels of fear of rats or harmless snakes. In one of the first studies completed, Cautela, Flannery, and Hanley (1974) demonstrated that covert modeling was as effective as overt (film) modeling in reducing fear of rats in college students on behavioral and subjective measures of fear. Both overt and covert modeling groups were superior to a control group that merely discussed the nature of the fear that was treated. Subsequent studies also have demonstrated the efficacy of covert modeling in reducing subphobic levels of fear in college students (Harris & Johnson, 1983; Kazdin, 1973, 1974a,b,c; Tearnan, Lahey, Thompson, & Hammer, 1982; Thase & Moss, 1976).

Aside from the analog fear studies, covert modeling has been investigated with a target problem and treatment population that more closely resembles clinical applications than do college students with small animal fears. In separate projects, individuals recruited from a community for problems in asserting themselves have been solicited and screened on several criteria for severity of their problem to serve in an assertion training clinic (Kazdin, 1974d, 1975, 1976a). Clients who received covert modeling imagined a model engaging in assertive interactions in a variety of different scenes over four treatment sessions. These clients showed markedly greater improvement on behavioral and self-report measures of assertion skills immediately after treatment and at several months follow-up relative to subjects who imagined similar scenes without the modeling component or who received no treatment.

Demonstration that covert modeling leads to greater changes than no treatment is an important, even if quite rudimentary, step in attesting to the efficacy of the treatment. Of greater interest is the finding that the effects of covert modeling surpass the changes achieved among clients who imagine training scenes that exclude a model who behaves assertively. The findings suggest the importance of the model in the scenes and also make less plausible the view that nonspecific effects (e.g., merely attending treatment, engaging in problem-related activities, focusing on the target problem) account for covert modeling effects. Other studies have shown that covert modeling is effective in altering social behavior (e.g., Nietzel, Martorano, & Melnick, 1977; Rosenthal & Reese, 1976).

Covert modeling has not been effective in all experimental tests. For example, in an application to children's dental fears, Chertock and Bornstein (1979) found variations of covert modeling to be no more effective than a no-model control condition (see Tearnan & Graziano, 1980). Of course, few covert conditioning studies have emerged with children, so the results are difficult to evaluate. In general, the number of demonstrations with adults that have failed to show significant changes with covert modeling is not readily available since they are likely to be infrequently published. At this point, the evidence suggests that covert modeling can produce behavior change with adults in the areas of anxiety and social skills. Findings in these areas have been replicated.

B. Important Parameters of Treatment

The basic covert modeling procedure requires that a client imagine a model performing the behavior he or she wishes to develop. An important question is whether imagery might be varied in such a way as to enhance the effects of the basic covert modeling procedure. The question can be answered tentatively by drawing on the findings from investigations on live and film modeling in the context of laboratory and therapy research (e.g., Perry & Furukawa, 1980; Rosenthal & Bandura, 1978). Several dimensions can be varied to enhance the efficacy of covert modeling. Many of these have been explored in analog therapy research with fearful college students and remain to be explored in the context of clinical research.

1. Model–Client Similarity

The basic covert modeling paradigm requires that a client imagine a model but does not specify who the model is or the kind of model used. Research on live and film modeling suggests that the more similar the model and observer, the greater the effect of modeling on observer behavior (Bandura, 1971). This relationship has been found in several laboratory investigations which demonstrate that individuals informed that they share qualities in common with an unfamiliar model are more likely to imitate the model's responses than individuals who initially share no common qualities (e.g., Burstein, Stotland, & Zander, 1961; Stotland, Zander, & Natsoulas, 1961). Also, similarity of the model across age, sex, and socioeconomic and racial status has facilitated performance on the part of the observer (Bandura, 1971).

Similarity of the model and subject has been examined in the context of covert modeling in an analog treatment study. In one project, subjects who feared harmless snakes participated in a covert modeling treatment study in which similarity of the model and subject were manipulated along the dimensions of sex and age (Kazdin, 1974b). Subjects who imagined a model similar in age and of the same sex showed a greater reduction in avoidance behavior and self-report anxiety than did subjects who imagined an older and opposite-sexed model. Although this study suggests that similarity of the model and client is important in covert modeling, it did not indicate the specific dimension along which this similarity is important (e.g., sex or age alone or their combination). Research in film modeling has not always shown that model–observer similarity along the dimension of age consistently relates to behavior change (e.g., Bandura & Barab, 1973; Kornhaber & Schroeder, 1975).

Model similarity has been shown to be important along dimensions other than sex and age. In film modeling, research has shown that adult subjects who are anxious and avoidant in the presence of a particular stimulus are more likely to imitate models who initially display some anxiety and eventually overcome their anxiety than those who do not display any anxiety (Meichenbaum, 1971). Similarly, in the area of covert modeling, fearful subjects who imagine models who initially are fearful (similar to themselves) but eventually overcome their anxiety perform more approach responses at the end of treatment than those who imagine nonanxious models (Kazdin, 1973, 1974b). The effects attributed here to model–client similarity might be due to the effect of viewing models who engage in coping behavior. In another study for the treatment of anxiety, covert modeling in which the model engaged in coping self-instructions was more effective than covert modeling alone (Tearnan et al., 1982). The influence of the model's similarity to the client and the influence of coping behavior are difficult to separate clearly, since a model who shows some initial anxiety either through verbal or nonverbal behavior is likely to be more similar to the client than one who does not.

At present, it appears that covert modeling is enhanced by increasing the similarity between the model and the client. Indeed, if the model and client are very dissimilar (e.g., differ in sex and approximate age), covert modeling may produce little change in the client (Kazdin, 1974b). The more dimensions along which the model and client are similar, the greater the behavior change (Kazdin, 1974b). Several questions about the influence of model–client similarity remain to be explored. The most salient question is determining the range of dimensions along which similarity may be important.

2. Model Identity

Another dimension that might be important in modeling is who the model is. The identity of the model may be confounded with similarity but presumably can be separated conceptually and empirically. One question that arises is whether the covert model should be the client himself or herself or someone else. When covert modeling was initially posed as a treatment technique, it was defined as a procedure in which the client imagined someone other than himself (Cautela, 1971b). Conceptually, there is no clear reason to maintain this distinction. Indeed, imagery-based procedures that rely upon imagining oneself rather than another individual have proven to be effective. The best example of this is systematic desensitization in which clients imagine themselves performing gradations of various behaviors they would like to develop in themselves. Because desensitization typically requires clients to imagine themselves performing responses, it might be viewed as a version of covert modeling, i.e., covert self-modeling.

In two covert modeling investigations of fear reduction, imagining oneself as the model versus imagining someone else were compared (Kazdin, 1974c; Thase & Moss, 1976). Subjects who imagined either themselves or someone else improved equally well in performing responses in a fear situation. Apparently, whether one imagines oneself or someone else does not bear on the efficacy of covert modeling. As Cautela (1971b) suggested when initially describing the covert modeling procedure, the selection of the model might be determined by convenience. Some clients might find it easier to imagine either themselves or someone else performing the target behavior. In such cases, pragmatic considerations might dictate selection of the model.

3. Multiple Models

In covert modeling, only one model is required for the scenes over the course of treatment. The client needs to imagine a given person engaging in the response that is to be developed. Yet, research on overt modeling suggests that observing several models is more effective in altering an observer's behavior than is observing only one model (e.g., Bandura & Menlove, 1968; Marburg, Houston, & Holmes, 1976).

The relationship of the number of models and behavior change has been examined in covert modeling studies. In the treatment of fear and unassertive behavior, studies have shown that clients who imagine several different models across treatment sessions show greater behavior change than those who imagine a single model across the sessions (Kazdin, 1974a, 1976b). Thus, over the course of treatment or from session to session the individual who is imagined should be varied in covert modeling.

It is unclear whether imagining several models is part of a larger dimension, namely, the extent to which the scenes that the client imagines vary. Possibly, the greater the variation of the scenes across several dimensions, the greater the behavior change. Imagining several different models may merely increase the diversity of cues across which the new responses are learned. If this is accurate, varying the types of scenes that are imagined also might enhance treatment.

4. Model Consequences

Modeling research has shown that observing behavior of a model is sufficient to learn a response. Yet, the learned response may not be performed until appropriate incentive conditions are available in the environment (Bandura, 1970, 1971). The incentive conditions refer either to the consequences that follow the model's performance or response or to the observer's subsequent performance of the response after observing the model. As might be expected, individuals who observe a model receiving favorable or reinforcing consequences for performing a behavior tend to engage in the response more than individuals who observe the model receive aversive consequences or no consequences at all (Bandura, 1965).

Several studies outside of the context of covert modeling have explored the effects of imagined consequences on behavior. In laboratory and therapy studies, imagining positive or negative consequences following overt behavior increases or decreases subsequent performance of the behavior, respectively (e.g., Bellack, Glanz, & Simon, 1976; Weiner, 1965). These studies suggest that imagined consequences may influence overt behavior in the same way as do overt consequences.

A few covert modeling studies have examined the influence of imagining positive consequences on behavior. Specifically, assertion training studies have compared the effects of imagining scenes with and without positive consequences following the model's assertive response (Kazdin, 1974d, 1975). In these studies some clients received covert modeling in which they imagined a model engage in assertive behavior across several situations. Other clients received covert modeling plus reinforcement in which they imagined situations with the addition of positive model consequences following behavior.

For example, covert modeling clients might imagine a situation in which a model returns food that has been incorrectly prepared in a restaurant. Covert modeling plus reinforcement clients would imagine the same situation with an added consequence such as the final receipt of the correctly prepared food and an apology from the waiter. Throughout treatment the only differences were the imagination of consequences as part of the scenes. The results have shown that clients who imagine positive consequences perform more assertively at the end of treatment on self-report and behavioral measures than do clients who imagine the scenes without the consequences. These results suggest the advisability of incorporating positive consequences into covert modeling scenes that are used to develop behaviors.

5. Scene Elaboration

In the usual practice of covert modeling, the therapist describes the scene and allows the client a brief period to develop the image. Generally, it is assumed that the client's imagery adheres closely to the scene that the therapist describes. Yet, clients frequently have claimed that their imagery deviated from the scenes described by the therapist (e.g., Davison & Wilson, 1973; Weinberg & Zaslove, 1963; Weitzman, 1967). The scene presented by the therapist occasionally is reported to initiate an ongoing movielike series of images that is not confined to the material presented.

Examination of the imagery process requires assessment procedures that can compare the scenes presented by the therapist with those actually imagined by the client. In our work, we have assessed imagery content by asking clients to narrate aloud the scenes that they are imagining during the treatment sessions (Kazdin, 1975, 1976a). After the scene is presented, the clients are allowed time to develop the imagery. When the scene is clear and while the image is still held, the client narrates the scene. These narrations are tape-recorded and subsequently evaluated to determine their similarity to the scenes presented.

Interestingly, assessing imagery has revealed that clients introduce features into their scenes that have not been presented. For example, clients in a model-only condition in one study occasionally introduced favorable model consequences even though these ingredients had not been presented in the scenes (Kazdin, 1975). Essentially, these subjects had been assigned to the model-only group but had imagined an assertive model plus reinforcing consequence. Perhaps of even greater interest were the scene-control subjects who received scenes in which an assertive response was appropriate with no model performance. Some of these subjects imagined an assertive model as well as reinforcing consequences following the model's assertive behavior, even though neither of these latter components had been presented in their scenes. Overall, covert modeling subjects occasionally deviate from the scenes presented to them. Moreover, the deviations are systematic in that certain ingredients that are relevant to the efficacy of treatment (e.g., model consequences) are introduced.

The finding that spontaneous emergence of elaborated scenes was related to outcome does not establish a causal role of this variable. Possibly, clients who elaborated the scenes and showed greater therapeutic change did so as a result of a correlated variable (e.g., cognitive skills, intelligence) related to both elaboration and outcome. However, the above results were replicated in an experiment in which some clients were instructed and trained to elaborate their imagined scenes and others were not (Kazdin, 1979b). These results suggest that clients who participate in covert modeling should be encouraged to elaborate their scenes rather than to adhere strictly to the scenes as presented. However, complete elaboration appears to be limited by findings that certain ingredients remain critical to the procedure. For example, scene elaboration by itself is not helpful, unless the model who engages in the desired behavior is still included in the scenes (Kazdin, 1979b).

C. Additional Variations and Procedures to Enhance Outcome

The above studies refer to variations of features that are inherent to the covert modeling procedure but that remain largely unspecified. Additional procedures have been evaluated as well that are adjuncts to the treatment rather than variations of parameters within the basic procedure.

1. Modality of Rehearsal

Covert modeling can be viewed as a treatment in which a client imagines someone else rehearsing or performing the behaviors he or she wishes to develop. Imagining someone else rehearsing behaviors offers several practical advantages because of the flexibility that imagery affords in arranging situational and stimulus cues required for treatment. However, in many situations, procedures based on imagery or actual performance of the target behavior are equally applicable. Rather than imagining a model performing the behaviors, the clients might actually perform the behaviors. An obvious question is the relative effectiveness of procedures based on imagery or overt performance.

Few studies are available that contrast covert and overt rehearsal. Related research in the areas of systematic desensitization and flooding suggests that actual exposure to the anxiety-provoking stimuli leads to greater anxiety reduction than does exposure to imagined representations of these stimuli (see Kazdin & Smith, 1979). Modeling research suggests that imagining a model apparently is less effective than observing the modeling sequence and then overtly performing the model behaviors, i.e., participant modeling (Rosenthal & Bandura, 1978).

The literature might lead to the general view that exposure to the actual stimuli rather than to imagined representations of these stimuli and overt rather than covert rehearsal of behavior maximize therapeutic change. However, little research has addressed directly whether covert and overt rehearsal differ in their effectiveness.

In one investigation that addressed the effects of covert and overt rehearsal, clients were presented with identical training situations over the course of treatment (Kazdin, 1980). The treatments differed primarily in whether the situations were rehearsed in imagination or overtly within the sessions. Overt practice consisted of rehearsal (role playing) with the therapist, in which the client enacted the behavior to be developed. The results indicated that at posttreatment and at a 6-month follow-up covert modeling and overt rehearsal were equally effective in altering assertive behavior. In a subsequent study, this relationship was replicated (Kazdin, 1982).

Additional research evaluated the combination of covert and overt rehearsal. In this variation of training, a client is first presented with the situation in imagination. Then, the situation is enacted overtly. Treatment proceeds by rehearsing each situation first in imagination and then in direct role-play. Separate studies demonstrated that the combination of covert and overt rehearsal is superior to either constituent modality used alone (Kazdin, 1982; Kazdin & Mascitelli, 1982b).

2. Homework Practice

Previous investigations mentioned above have suggested that overt rehearsal within the treatment sessions can enhance the effects of covert modeling. A logical extension of this work is to encourage clients to rehearse the desired behaviors outside of the treatment sessions where opportunities to practice and develop the desired behaviors are prominent. The use of extratreatment practice or "homework" is relatively pervasive in therapy in general. Indeed, approximately 60% of all outpatient behavior therapy studies have incorporated extratherapy practice (Shelton & Levy, 1981). The impact of therapeutically relevant activities that clients perform outside of treatment has been evaluated in the context of covert modeling.

As part of covert modeling treatment, clients and therapists identified situations the clients felt they could perform. Between treatment sessions, clients engaged in practice in the situations they identified during treatment. Adherence to the practice was monitored by interviews and questionnaires in the treatment sessions. The results of separate investigations indicated that homework practice greatly enhanced treatment outcome (Kazdin & Mascitelli, 1982a,b).

Interestingly, in these studies, the additive effects of overt rehearsal within the treatment sessions (role playing) and outside of treatment (homework practice) were evaluated. The results indicated that both procedures enhance the effects of covert modeling. Thus, enacting by separate methods overt behaviors that are to be developed or perhaps enactment in different situations contributes to outcome. Research is needed to evaluate what aspects of homework practice account for its effects.

3. Other Procedures Briefly Noted

The above procedures do not exhaust the techniques that enhance overt and covert rehearsal. For example, in the context of covert modeling, one study has examined the impact of engaging in coding strategies of the training stimuli (Kazdin, 1979a). Among clients who engaged in the standard covert modeling treatment, some clients also were trained to develop verbal summary codes of the modeled material. The utility of developing coding strategies was suggested from laboratory investigations showing that coding strategies enhance retention of modeled responses (e.g., Bandura, Jeffery, & Bachicha, 1974; Jeffery, 1976). In covert modeling, both the acquisition and maintenance of modeled behaviors in treatment appear to be enhanced by engaging in coding strategies.

Not all of the variations of covert modeling and adjunctive treatments have enhanced outcome. For example, the impact of self-instruction training has been evaluated as part of the assertion training studies of covert and overt rehearsal (Kazdin & Mascitelli, 1982a). In this study, training persons to make comments to themselves prior to enacting their assertive response enhanced treatment effects at posttreatment. However, by a 6-month follow-up assessment, self-instruction training was no longer a significant factor in treatment outcome. In the context of treating test anxiety, Harris and Johnson (1983) examined the impact of relaxation training as an adjunctive procedure with covert modeling. Relaxation did not enhance the effectiveness of treatment.

D. General Comments

In general, the outcome research for covert modeling has utilized different treatment evaluation strategies. Several studies have suggested that the basic treatment package leads to behavior change. Most demonstrations have focused on analog fear or social skills of college students or volunteer clients rather than focusing on persons who have sought treatment at a clinic. Other studies have examined the parameters of treatment that can be varied to enhance treatment. Many of the parameters selected for investigation such as the number of models, the consequences following model performance, and use of coding strategies were derived from direct extrapolations of findings from the live and film modeling literature. Additional studies of adjunctive procedures have identified further ways of enhancing treatment. Overt rehearsal and extratreatment practice appear to be particularly robust additions to the basic covert modeling treatment.

IV. ISSUES IN CONTEMPORARY RESEARCH

Although several studies of covert modeling have been completed, very basic questions about the procedure and its effects remain unanswered. The most salient questions pertain to the clinical effectiveness of the procedure, the reasons why covert modeling produces behavior change, characteristics of imagery that are related to change, and whether imaginal rather than overt rehearsal offers special advantages in terms of treatment outcome.

A. Clinical Efficacy

The single most salient issue for covert modeling pertains to its effectiveness with clinical populations and disorders. In many ways, the research has progressed as if basic questions about the efficacy of the procedure were resolved. To be sure, studies with college students and volunteer clients have frequently shown that covert modeling produces change and that these changes are often maintained. However, covert modeling research has focused almost exclusively on nonpatient samples. The risk of such a focus, heavily discussed in clinical research circles, is that the findings may not generalize to clinical populations.

A close examination of the covert modeling studies indicates that the participants in many investigations extend beyond the familiar and overly utilized college student whose dysfunction and adjustment may not warrant intervention. For example, in the assertion investigations reviewed earlier, clients who participated showed clear deficits in their social behavior prior to treatment, when compared to persons who considered themselves to be functioning adequately in interpersonal situations (see Kazdin, 1979b, 1980, 1982). Thus, the persons who have been treated have evinced deficits in the area of treatment. In research with adolescents, aggressive or unassertive students were identified by teachers and treated with covert modeling (Pentz & Kazdin, 1982). Even though the above samples are not formally identified patient populations, their deficiencies in the area of treatment have been identified by different criteria. Occasionally, patient samples have been treated with covert modeling. For example, in one study, covert modeling was shown to increase the assertive behavior of psychiatric patients (psychotic, neurotic, and character disorder) (Hersen, Kazdin, Bellack, & Turner, 1979).

The above studies suggest that covert modeling can be implemented with different populations, particularly for the treatment of social behavior. However, the studies do not provide convincing evidence that the technique can be applied to a particular clinical problem, can improve the presenting complaints and adjustment, and can sustain treatment gains over time. The bulk of the above studies which might be used to support the clinical effectiveness of treatment have evaluated changes in social behavior as assessed by behavioral role-playing tests. The generality of results from role-play performance to everyday situations has been seriously questioned in light of the multiple problems with that measure (see Bellack, 1979; McNamara & Blumer, 1982). Although social behavior might be a useful initial focus for further tests of covert modeling, given the amount of literature in this area, measures of community adjustment would need to be included to provide convincing evidence of treatment effects.

It might be tempting to speculate about the types of populations and problems for whom covert modeling might be particularly appropriate. However, considerable reserve is called for given the current status of the evidence. There has been a propensity to suggest from case studies that covert conditioning techniques can be used effectively to treat the full gamut of problems seen in outpatient treatment with both children and adults. Yet, the field awaits direct tests of covert modeling with clearly identified clinical populations and disorders. Until such work emerges, the clinical use of covert modeling remains a matter of surmise.

B. Conceptual Bases

Relatively little attention has been devoted to the conceptual bases of covert conditioning techniques in general. As noted earlier, most techniques have been explicitly formulated in terms of operant conditioning principles (Cautela, 1977). Although extrapolation from the principles of operant conditioning to imagery processes may have heuristic value, there are important limitations to be recognized as well. First, the principles prove to be violated in covert conditioning techniques when one examines how the procedures in fact are implemented. For example, reinforcement and punishment paradigms in laboratory research utilize consequences that are defined on the basis of their impact on behavior. In covert analogs of reinforcement and punishment, clients merely report on the subjective appeal of alternative events which are then used as imagined consequences to increase or decrease the frequency of behavior (Cautela & Kastenbaum, 1967; Wolpe & Lang, 1964). The use of terms such as reinforcement and punishment really does not parallel their use in laboratory work on operant conditioning. Also, reinforcing and punishing consequences in laboratory applications increase or decrease the behaviors they follow. When imagined consequences are applied to imagined behaviors, they might be expected to alter the frequency of imagined behaviors. The impact of imagined consequences on overt behavior when overt behavior is not included in the contingency would not be predicted from operant conditioning. Overall, operant conditioning principles and laboratory paradigms bear faint resemblance to the operations of covert conditioning.

Second, direct tests of operant principles made with covert conditioning techniques have not always supported the putative basis of the procedures. For example, imagining reinforcing or aversive consequences may be effective in changing behavior even when the usual contingent response–reinforcer relationship is violated, as when the consequence is imagined before the behavior or is not contingent on the behavior (e.g., Blanchard & Draper, 1973; Hurley, 1976; Ladouceur, 1974; Marshall, Boutilier, & Minnes, 1974). Thus, a strict application of operant principles does not easily account for major findings in the covert conditioning literature.

To determine the applicability of particular concepts to explain covert conditioning techniques, the techniques need to be examined individually (see Kazdin & Smith, 1979). As for covert modeling, there is no clear theoretical explanation that accounts for the findings obtained to date. The parallel is often drawn between overt and covert modeling, with the implication that the latter produces changes for the same reasons as the former. This is of little assistance in explaining the basis for covert modeling effects. Modeling itself is not an explanation of the mechanism of change but rather merely describes the relationship between particular events (e.g., observing or imagining a model) and the effects (e.g., increases in the propensity to behave in a particular way).

One possible explanation that might be advanced to explain covert modeling effects is the self-efficacy theory (Bandura, 1977). The theory, beyond the scope of the present article, attributes therapeutic change from diverse techniques on the basis of altering clients' expectations for success in performing the behaviors in the area of the target problem. Although several studies have shown that changes in anxiety in volunteer clients are associated with changes in self-efficacy, there is by no means universal agreement that self-efficacy explains the changes (see Rachman, 1978). Also, assessment of self-efficacy in the context of covert modeling treatment has produced mixed results (Bandura, Adams, Hardy, & Howells, 1980; Kazdin, 1979b, 1980). Changes in self-efficacy do not correlate highly with success in treatment of social behavior using behavioral role-play and self-report measures. Self-efficacy needs to be tested further before it can be evaluated more definitively.

Overall, there is a void in the conceptualization of covert modeling and other covert conditioning techniques. No unified theory can be offered with any genuine support. Typically, to fill such a void, concepts are borrowed from other areas of research (e.g., learning theories) or laboratory paradigms (Wilkins, 1974). Alternatively, general concepts are advanced such as "nonspecific treatment factors" that are designed to account for the impact of diverse treatments.

Meichenbaum (1978) advanced the view that imagery-based treatments produce change because they induce self-awareness, they generate new thoughts and behavior, and they foster *in vivo* uses of mental rehearsal. Imagery-based treatments are considered to operate by conveying a sense of control over one's imagery and behavior and changing for the client the meaning of his or her maladjusted behavior. This view raises important points that can apply generally to diverse treatments. They need to be followed up with empirical tests in the context of research on imagery to provide a viable conceptual view. As yet, specific tests of the theoretical mechanisms underlying covert modeling, covert conditioning, or imagery-based treatments more generally have not emerged to elucidate the bases for treatment effects.

C. Assessment of Imagery

Assessment of imagery raises a large number of issues that have not begun to be addressed adequately in the context of treatment. An obvious initial question is what to assess. Different facets of imagery can be assessed such as the properties or characteristics of imagery, the content of imagery, the relationship between imagery and perception, and the contexts in which imagery is evoked (Horowitz, 1970). What should be assessed in imagery-based treatment presumably depends on the processes that are considered to be responsible for or to contribute to therapeutic change.

Assessment of imagery in covert modeling and in other covert conditioning treatments has suffered from the lack of clear conceptions of those features of imagery that lead to therapeutic change. Consequently, assessment has focused on some of the more obvious and generic features such as self-reported clarity and vividness. One might expect that individuals whose imagery is particularly clear, vivid, and detailed would profit more from covert modeling than those persons whose images are less adequate. Many investigations have examined the relationship between these and other characteristics of imagery and treatment outcome. Results have frequently failed to identify a relationship between such characteristics as vividness, clarity, anxiety experienced during imagery, controllability of imagery, and amount of material imagined in relation to what was presented, and therapeutic improvements (e.g., Davis, McLemore, & London, 1970; Kazdin, 1973, 1974d; McLemore, 1972).

As noted earlier, a few studies have examined the content of imagery in covert modeling by asking clients to narrate aloud what they were imagining (Kazdin, 1975, 1976a). After a scene is presented, clients develop the images described by the therapist. When the scene is clear and while the clients continue to imagine the scene, they narrate what is imagined. These narrations are tape-recorded and subsequently evaluated to determine the correspondence of the scenes imagined to those presented. The results, highlighted earlier, have yielded interesting information about the systematic departures that clients introduce into their imagery. Even so, the assessment has been exploratory and designed primarily to check on the manipulation of gross features of imagery. Much more sophisticated work is needed to understand the mechanisms of imagery that produce therapeutic change.

The assessment of imagery raises obvious problems because of the nature of private events. Also, measures have been based primarily on self-report and have been criticized because of their susceptibility to response sets and styles and limited evidence concerning their psychometric characteristics (e.g., Danaher & Thoresen, 1972; Hiscock, 1978; White, Sheehan, & Ashton, 1977). Yet, considerable advances have been made in recent years in the assessment of imagery using a variety of questionnaires, perceptual and visual tasks, projective tests, and psychophysiological measures (see Tower, 1981; Tower & Singer, 1981). These measures have emerged primarily from experimental research rather than from treatment studies. Also, diverse facets of imagery can be assessed such as the ease of generating imagery, the spontaneous use of imagery, active and passive participation of the subject in the imagined scenes, and others. Although many of the measures that might be incorporated into treatment seem relevant on prima facie grounds (Tower & Singer, 1981), additional guidelines need to be developed about the relevant dimensions that underlie intervention effects.

The facets of imagery that are assessed need to be based on theories about the nature of imagery as a mechanism of change or on views about how particular treatment techniques operate (see Strosahl & Ascough, 1981). A promising line of work that illustrates this approach has been provided by Anderson (1981), who has designed assessment based on interpretations of how imagery operates. Specifically, he drew on propositional and perceptual process interpretations of imagery (see Lang, 1977; Neisser, 1976) and speculated that the kind and amount of imagery provided are relevant to behavior change. Preliminary research was conducted to show that type of imagery relates to changes on physiological and subjective measures of fear (Anderson & Borkovec, 1980). Thus, drawing on interpretations of imagery processes, procedures to assess the content of imagery were developed and tested. Further work that draws on theories of imagery processes needs to be completed.

D. Imagery-Based and Overt Rehearsal

Research reviewed earlier addressed the relative efficacy of covert rehearsal (covert modeling) and overt rehearsal (role playing). The results consistently indicated that these variations were equally effective. At first glance, the results would suggest that whether the desired behaviors are enacted or imagined should be decided on criteria other than effectiveness. The practical advantages and flexibility might favor imagery, because the presentation of actual events and situations in everyday life can be cumbersome, if not prohibitive, for many clinical problems.

The relative effectiveness of covert and overt rehearsal cannot be resolved definitively, given the evidence currently available. What has emerged from studies reviewed earlier is that overt rehearsal in the form of role playing in the treatment sessions or therapeutically planned activities outside of treatment (i.e., homework) can add greatly to treatment outcome. Further work is needed to determine whether covert modeling and an in vivo practice rehearsal procedure differ in efficacy. A direct comparison is warranted because of the repeated demonstrations in related areas showing that direct practice and in vivo experiences contribute greatly to behavior change (e.g., Crowe, Marks, Agras, & Leitenberg, 1972; Röper, Rachman, & Marks, 1975; Thase & Moss, 1976). Research on the relative effectiveness of a covert procedure and overt practice procedures on target responses and nontarget responses at posttreatment and at follow-up would address a critical issue. Although covert modeling may remain an interesting area of research, it would be useful to assess its clinical efficacy by direct comparison with overt and *in vivo* practice.

V. CONCLUSIONS

Covert modeling research has demonstrated that the basic procedure produces behavior change and that parameters of the technique can be varied to enhance these changes. Additional research is needed to determine the overall efficacy of the techniques and the problems to which the technique is well suited, the conceptual basis of the technique, the imaginal processes that influence outcome, and the efficacy of imagery-based and *in vivo* rehearsal techniques.

Because covert modeling has been proposed as a therapy technique, there is a special need to evaluate the effectiveness of the procedure with clinical populations or problems. Case applications of covert modeling suggest that the procedure can be applied clinically. Yet, instances in which covert modeling has been applied to clinical problems generally represent those areas in which inferences about the procedure cannot be drawn. Given the evidence to date, it would be difficult to argue that covert modeling is a treatment of choice or an effective treatment for a particular clinical problem. The appropriate outcome studies simply have not been conducted.

The bulk of research has been conducted with volunteer clients or college students. Such research may continue to be very important to address other outstanding issues in covert modeling. To begin with, the conceptual basis of the technique and the nature of client imagery in treatment require programs of research in their own right. Clinical trials of covert modeling may not be the best place to address questions about the underpinnings of the treatment. At this point, a conceptual interpretation of covert modeling would need to incorporate data on parameters that have been shown to influence the effects of the procedure. No single interpretation has been advanced toward this end.

Cognitive psychology may provide especially useful leads for examining the imagery processes. The impact of imagery on overt behavior and the assessment of imagery have been more well developed in experimental research than in the treatment literature (see Klinger, 1981). Research on covert modeling has yet to draw from the rich laboratory literature on imagery.

Finally, the relative effectiveness of imagery and overt rehearsal raises many questions, only a few of which have begun to be addressed. It is interesting to note from studies reviewed earlier that covert and overt rehearsal appear to be equally effective but less effective than their combination. Apparently covert and overt rehearsal make separate but additive contributions to behavior change. The separate contributions of covert and overt rehearsal are conceptually intriguing. However, clinically, it is not yet clear that covert modeling and *in vivo* practice are equally effective. Of course, overt rehearsal may not be feasible for some of the problems that are treated in therapy. Yet, whether covert modeling should serve as a prime treatment modality when *in vivo* rehearsal is feasible remains to be determined.

ACKNOWLEDGMENTS

Completion of this article was supported by a Research Scientist Development Award (MH00353) and by a grant (MH37801) from the National Institute of Mental Health. The research upon which the article is based was supported by an earlier grant (MH31047) for which the author is grateful.

REFERENCES

Anderson, M. P. Imagery assessment through content analysis. In E. Klinger (Ed.), *Imagery: Vol. 2. Concepts, results, and applications*. New York: Plenum, 1981.

Anderson, M. P., & Borkovec, T. Imagery processing and fear reduction during repeated exposure to two types of phobic imagery. *Behaviour Research and Therapy*, 1980, **18**, 537–540.

Bandura, A. Influence of model's reinforcement contingencies on the acquisition of imitative responses. *Journal of Personality and Social Psychology,* 1965, **1**, 589–595.

Bandura, A. Modeling theory. In W. S. Sahakian (Ed.), *Psychology of learning: Systems, models, and theories*. Chicago: Markham, 1970.

Bandura, A. Psychotherapy based upon modeling principles. In A. E. Bergin & S. L. Garfield (Eds.), *Handbook of psychotherapy and behavior change*. New York: Wiley, 1971.

Bandura, A. Self-efficacy: Toward a unifying theory of behavioral change. *Psychological Review*, 1977, **84**, 191–215.

Bandura, A., Adams, N. E., Hardy, A. B., & Howells, G. N. Tests of the generality of self-efficacy theory. *Cognitive Therapy and Research*, 1980, **4**, 39–66.

Bandura, A., & Barab, P. G. Processes governing disinhibitory effects through symbolic modeling. *Journal of Abnormal Psychology*, 1973, **82**, 1–9.

Bandura, A., Jeffery, R., & Bachicha, D. L. Analysis of memory codes and cumulative rehearsal in observational learning. *Journal of Research in Personality*, 1974, **7**, 295–305.

Bandura, A., & Menlove, F. L. Factors determining vicarious extinction of avoidance behavior through symbolic modeling. *Journal of Personality and Social Psychology*, 1968, **8**, 99–108.

Bellack, A. S. A critical appraisal of strategies for assessing social skill. *Behavioral Assessment*, 1979, **1**, 157–176.

Bellack, A. S., Glanz, L. M., & Simon, R. Self-reinforcement style and covert imagery in the treatment of obesity. *Journal of Consulting and Clinical Psychology*, 1976, **44**, 490–491.

Blanchard, E. B., & Draper, D. O. Treatment of a rodent phobia by covert reinforcement: A single subject experiment. *Behavior Therapy*, 1973, **4**, 559–564.

Burstein, E., Stotland, E., & Zander, A. Similarity to a model and self-evaluation. *Journal of Abnormal and Social Psychology*, 1961, **62**, 257–264.

Cautela, J. R. A behavior therapy treatment of pervasive anxiety. *Behaviour Research and Therapy*, 1966, **4**, 99–109.

Cautela, J. R. Covert sensitization. *Psychological Record*, 1967, **20**, 459–468.

Cautela, J. R. Covert conditioning. In A. Jacobs & L. B. Sachs (Eds.), *The psychology of private events: Perspectives on covert response systems*. New York: Academic Press, 1971. (a)

Cautela, J. R. *Covert modeling*. Paper presented at the fifth annual meeting of the Association for Advancement of Behavior Therapy, Washington, DC, September 1971. (b)

Cautela, J. R. Rationale and procedures for covert conditioning. In R. D. Rubin, H. Fensterheim, J. D. Henderson, & L. P. Ullmann (Eds.), *Advances in behavior therapy*. New York: Academic Press, 1972.

Cautela, J. R. The present status of covert modeling. *Journal of Behavior Therapy and Experimental Psychiatry*, 1976, **7**, 323–326.

Cautela, J. R. Covert conditioning: Assumptions and procedures. *Journal of Mental Imagery*, 1977, **1**, 53–64.

Cautela, J. R., Flannery, R., & Hanley, E. Covert modeling: An experimental test. *Behavior Therapy*, 1974, **5**, 494–502.

Cautela, J. R., & Kastenbaum, R. A reinforcement survey schedule for use in therapy, training, and research. *Psychological Reports*, 1967, **20**, 1115–1130.

Chertock, S. L., & Bornstein, P. H. Covert modeling treatment of children's dental fears. *Child Behavior Therapy*, 1979, **1**, 249–255.

Crowe, M. J., Marks, I. M., Agras, W. S., & Leitenberg, H. Time-limited desensitization, implosion and shaping for phobic patients: A crossover study. *Behaviour Research and Therapy*, 1972, **10**, 319–328.

Danaher, B. G., & Thoresen, C. E. Imagery assessment by self-report and behavioral measures. *Behaviour Research and Therapy*, 1972, **10**, 131–138.

Davis, D., McLemore, C. W., & London, P. The role of visual imagery in desensitization. *Behaviour Research and Therapy*, 1970, **8**, 11–13.

Davison, G. C., & Wilson, G. T. Processes of fear-reduction in systematic desensitization: Cognitive and social reinforcement factors in humans. *Behavior Therapy*, 1973, **4**, 1–21.

Flannery, R. B. Covert conditioning in the behavioral treatment of an agoraphobic. *Psychotherapy: Theory, Research and Practice*, 1972, **9**, 217–220. (a)

Flannery, R. B. Use of covert conditioning in the behavioral treatment of a drug-dependent college dropout. *Journal of Counseling Psychology*, 1972, **19**, 547–550. (b)

Harris, G. M., & Johnson, S. B. Coping imagery and relaxation instructions in a covert modeling treatment for test anxiety. *Behavior Therapy*, 1983, **14**, 144–157.

Hay, W. M., Barlow, D. H., & Hay, L. R. Treatment of stereotypic cross-gender motor behavior using covert modeling in a boy with gender identity confusion. *Journal of Consulting and Clinical Psychology*, 1981, **49**, 388–394.

Hay, W. M., Hay, L. R., & Nelson, R. O. The adaptation of covert modeling procedures to the treatment of chronic alcoholism and obsessive-compulsive behavior: Two case reports. *Behavior Therapy*, 1977, **8**, 70–76.

Hersen, M., Kazdin, A. E., Bellack, A. S., & Turner, S. M. Effects of live modeling, covert modeling and rehearsal on assertiveness in psychiatric patients. *Behaviour Research and Therapy*, 1979, **17**, 369–377.

Hiscock, M. Imagery assessment through self-report: What do imagery questionnaires measure? *Journal of Consulting and Clinical Psychology*, 1978, **46**, 223–230.

Horowitz, M. J. *Image formation and cognition*. New York: Appleton, 1970.

Hurley, A. D. Covert reinforcement: The contribution of the reinforcing stimulus to treatment outcome. *Behavior Therapy*, 1976, **7**, 347–378.

Jeffery, R. W. The influence of symbolic and motor rehearsal in observational learning. *Journal of Research in Personality*, 1976, **10**, 116–127.

Kazdin, A. E. Covert modeling and the reduction of avoidance behavior. *Journal of Abnormal Psychology*, 1973, **81**, 87–95.

Kazdin, A. E. Comparative effects of some variations of covert modeling. *Journal of Behavior Therapy and Experimental Psychiatry*, 1974, **5**, 225–231. (a)

Kazdin, A. E. Covert modeling, model similarity, and reduction of avoidance behavior. *Behavior Therapy*, 1974, **5**, 325–340. (b)

Kazdin, A. E. The effect of model identity and fear-relevant similarity on covert modeling. *Behavior Therapy*, 1974, **5**, 624–635. (c)

Kazdin, A. E. Effects of covert modeling and model reinforcement on assertive behavior. *Journal of Abnormal Psychology*, 1974, **83**, 240–252. (d)

Kazdin, A. E. Covert modeling, imagery assessment, and assertive behavior. *Journal of Consulting and Clinical Psychology*, 1975, **43**, 716–724.

Kazdin, A. E. Assessment of imagery during covert modeling treatment of assertive behavior. *Journal of Behavior Therapy and Experimental Psychiatry*, 1976, **7**, 213–219. (a)

Kazdin, A. E. Effects of covert modeling, multiple models, and model reinforcement on assertive behavior. *Behavior Therapy*, 1976, **7**, 211–222. (b)

Kazdin, A. E. Effects of covert modeling and coding of modeled stimuli on assertive behavior. *Behaviour Research and Therapy*, 1979, **17**, 53–61. (a)

Kazdin, A. E. Imagery elaboration and self-efficacy in the covert modeling treatment of unassertive behavior. *Journal of Consulting and Clinical Psychology*, 1979, **47**, 725–733. (b)

Kazdin, A. E. Covert and overt rehearsal and elaboration during treatment in the development of assertive behavior. *Behaviour Research and Therapy*, 1980, **18**, 191–201.

Kazdin, A. E. The separate and combined effects of covert and overt rehearsal in developing assertive behavior. *Behaviour Research and Therapy*, 1982, **20**, 17–25.

Kazdin, A. E., & Mascitelli, S. Behavioral rehearsal, self-instructions, and homework practice in developing assertiveness. *Behavior Therapy*, 1982, **13**, 346–360. (a)

Kazdin, A. E., & Mascitelli, S. Covert and overt rehearsal and homework practice in developing assertiveness. *Journal of Consulting and Clinical Psychology*, 1982, **50**, 250–258. (b)

Kazdin, A. E., & Smith, G. M. Covert conditioning: A review and evaluation. *Advances in Behaviour Research and Therapy*, 1979, **2**, 57–98.

Klinger, E. (Ed.). *Imagery: Concepts, results, and applications* (Vol. 2). New York: Plenum, 1981.

Koch, S. Psychology and emerging conceptions of knowledge as unitary. In T. Wann (Ed.), *Behaviorism and phenomenology*. Chicago: Univ. of Chicago Press, 1964.

Kornhaber, R. C., & Schroeder, H. E. Importance of model similarity on extinction of avoidance behavior in children. *Journal of Consulting and Clinical Psychology*, 1975, **43**, 601–607.

Ladouceur, R. An experimental test of the learning paradigm of covert positive reinforcement in deconditioning anxiety. *Journal of Behavior Therapy and Experimental Psychiatry*, 1974, **5**, 3–6.

Lang, P. J. Imagery in therapy: An information processing analysis of fear. *Behavior Therapy*, 1977, **8**, 862–886.

Marburg, C. D., Houston, B. K., & Holmes, D. S. Influence of multiple models on the behavior of institutionalized retarded children: Increased generalization to other models and behaviors. *Journal of Consulting and Clinical Psychology*, 1976, **44**, 514–519.

Marshall, W. L., Boutilier, J., & Minnes, P. The modification of phobic behavior by covert reinforcement. *Behavior Therapy*, 1974, **5**, 469–480.

McLemore, C. W. Imagery in desensitization. *Behaviour Research and Therapy*, 1972, **10**, 51–57.

McNamara, J. R., & Blumer, C. A. Role playing to assess social competence: Ecological validity considerations. *Behavior Modification*, 1982, **6**. 519–549.

Meichenbaum, D. H. Examination of model characteristics in reducing avoidance behavior. *Journal of Personality and Social Psychology*, 1971, **17**, 298–307.

Meichenbaum, D. Why does using imagery in psychotherapy lead to change? In J. L. Singer & K. S. Pope (Eds.), *The power of human imagination: New methods in psychotherapy*. New York: Plenum, 1978.

Neisser, U. *Cognition and reality: Principles and implications of cognitive psychology*. San Francisco: Freeman, 1976.

Nietzel, M. T., Martorano, R. D., & Melnick, J. The effects of covert modeling with and without reply training on the development and generalization of assertive responses. *Behavior Therapy*, 1977, **8**, 183–192.

Pentz, M. A., & Kazdin, A. E. Assertion modeling and stimuli effects on assertive behavior and self-efficacy in adolescents. *Behaviour Research and Therapy*, 1982, **20**, 365–371.

Perry, M. A., & Furukawa, M. J. Modeling methods. In F. H. Kanfer & A. P. Goldstein (Eds.), *Helping people change: A textbook of methods* (2nd ed.). Oxford: Pergamon, 1980.

Rachman, S. J. Observational learning and therapeutic modelling. In M. P. Feldman & A. Broadhurst (Eds.), *Theoretical and empirical bases of the behaviour therapies*. New York: Wiley, 1976.

Rachman, S. J. (Ed.). Perceived self-efficacy: Analysis of Bandura's theory of behavioural change. *Advances in Behaviour Research and Therapy*, 1978, **1**, 137–-269.

Röper, G., Rachman, S., & Marks, I. Passive and participant modelling in exposure treatment of obsessive-compulsive neurotics. *Behaviour Research and Therapy*, 1975, **13**, 271–279.

Rosenthal, T. L., & Bandura, A. Psychological modeling: Theory and practice. In S. L. Garfield & A. E. Bergin (Eds.), *Handbook of psychotherapy and behavior change* (2nd ed.). New York: Wiley, 1978.

Rosenthal, T. L., & Reese, S. L. The effects of covert and overt modeling on assertive behavior. *Behaviour Research and Therapy*, 1976, **14**, 463–469.

Shelton, J. L., & Levy, R. L. A survey of the reported use of assigned homework activities in contemporary behavior therapy literature. *The Behavior Therapist*, 1981, **4**, 13–14.

Singer, J. L. *Imagery and daydream methods in psychotherapy and behavior modification*. New York: Academic Press, 1974.

Singer, J. L., & Pope, K. S. (Eds.). *The power of human imagination: New methods in psychotherapy.* New York: Plenum, 1978.

Stotland, E., Zander, A., & Natsoulas, T. The generalization of interpersonal similarity. *Journal of Abnormal and Social Psychology,* 1961, **62**, 250–256.

Strosahl, K. D., & Ascough, J. C. Clinical uses of mental imagery: Experimental foundations, theoretical misconceptions, and research issues. *Psychological Bulletin,* 1981, **89**, 422–438.

Tearnan, B. H., & Graziano, W. G. Covert modeling and children's fears: A methodological critique of Chertock and Bornstein. *Child Behavior Therapy,* 1980, **2**, 73–77.

Tearnan, B. H., Lahey, B. B., Thompson, J. K., & Hammer, D. The role of coping self-instructions combined with covert modeling in specific fear reduction. *Cognitive Therapy and Research,* 1982, **6**, 185–190.

Thase, M. E., & Moss, M. K. The relative efficacy of covert modeling procedures and guided participant modeling on the reduction of avoidance behavior. *Journal of Behavior Therapy and Experimental Psychiatry,* 1976, **7**, 7–12.

Tower, R. B. Imagery measurement in clinical settings: Matching the method to the question. In E. Klinger (Eds.), *Imagery: Vol. 2. Concepts, results, and applications.* New York: Plenum, 1981.

Tower, R. B., & Singer, J. L. The measurement of imagery: How can it be clinically useful? In P. C. Kendall & S. D. Hollon (Eds.), *Assessment strategies for cognitive-behavioral interventions.* New York: Academic Press, 1981.

Upper, D., & Cautela, J. R. (Eds.). *Covert conditioning.* Oxford: Pergamon, 1979.

Weinberg, N. H., & Zaslove, M. "Resistance" to systematic desensitization of phobias. *Journal of Clinical Psychology,* 1963, **19**, 179–181.

Weiner, H. Real and imagined cost effects upon human fixed-interval responding. *Psychological Reports,* 1965, **17**, 659–662.

Weitzman, B. Behavior therapy and psychotherapy. *Psychological Review,* 1967, **74**, 300–317.

White, K. D., Sheehan, P. W., & Ashton, R. Imagery assessment: A survey of self-report measures. *Journal of Mental Imagery,* 1977, **1**, 145–170.

Wilkins, W. Parameters of therapeutic imagery: Directions from case studies. *Psychotherapy: Theory, Research and Practice,* 1974, **11**, 163–171.

Wolpe, J. *Psychotherapy by reciprocal inhibition.* Stanford, CA: Stanford University Press, 1958.

Wolpe, J., & Lang, P. A fear survey schedule for use in behavior therapy. *Behaviour Research and Therapy,* 1964, **2**, 27–30.

Cognitive–Behavioral Interventions in Educational Settings

ANDREW W. MEYERS AND ROBERT COHEN

Department of Psychology
Memphis State University
Memphis, Tennessee

I. INTRODUCTION

As this review series indicates, attention to cognitive factors has spread throughout the psychological study of human behavior. This cognitive revolution has had widespread effects in the experimental areas of learning, social, and developmental psychology, and given the historic ties between behavior therapy and experimental psychology, it was inevitable that cognitive influences would invade the behavioral domain (Wilson, 1982). Indeed these cognitive incursions have been apparent in theory (cf. Bandura, 1969) and practice (cf. Beck, 1967) for well over a decade.

131

ADVANCES IN COGNITIVE–BEHAVIORAL RESEARCH
AND THERAPY, VOLUME 3

In his 1981 presidential address to the Association for Advancement of Behavior Therapy, Wilson (1982) suggested that the increased attention to cognitive variables has produced three measurable changes in behavior therapy. The first development was a movement beyond conditioning-based interventions to the introduction of new therapeutic strategies such as Beck's (1976) cognitive therapy for depression and Meichenbaum's (1977) self-instruction training. Second, existing therapeutic interventions have received new theoretical interpretations [e.g., Bandura's (1977) self-efficacy theory] which have led to different therapeutic outcome predictions and novel therapeutic applications. Finally, this cognitive shift has given behavior therapists a framework for understanding those variables formerly considered to be nonspecific factors in therapy. Client expectancies, the therapeutic relationship, and resistance to treatment compliance have all become viable targets for the behavioral clinician.

The investigation of cognitive influences on human behavior and in therapeutic interventions on dysfunctional behavior has recently found favor in the educational setting. Both academic performance and social and behavioral problems in the classroom are receiving increasing attention from cognitive behavior therapists (Meyers & Cohen, 1982). The rationale for the emphasis on the school-based treatment of childhood dysfunction relies on evidence that childhood difficulties are predictive of more severe adolescent and adult maladjustment (Craighead, Wilcoxon-Craighead, & Meyers, 1978). The study of childhood disorders should give us an increased understanding of the development of later behavioral dysfunction; the treatment of childhood disorders may serve a preventive mental health function.

The significance of the school as a locus of intervention is illustrated by an Achenbach and Edelbrock (1981) study which indicated that the only reported behavior problems that discriminated large samples of clinic-referred from nonreferred children were depression and poor school performance. Other categories, such as childhood fears, did not differentiate the samples. This evidence suggests that the school will serve as a crucial point for the initial identification and subsequent professional assessment and treatment of problem children.

The cognitive–behavioral orientation in school interventions is based on increasing evidence of the significance of the individual's information-processing activities. Many psychologists across a variety of disciplines and theoretical perspectives have argued that the individual is actively selecting, elaborating, and transforming information in the process of interacting with the environment. Within this information-processing activity, Litrownik (1984) has identified four levels of cognitive functioning: at the sensory receptor level, in the initial selection and screening process, at higher levels of organization of information, and in the executive process of information retrieval response generation and selection. Kendall (1977) summarized evidence which suggests that impulsive children, aggressive boys, and "classroom problem" children all show verbal mediational deficits compared to nonlabeled children. These deficits may represent inappropriate or incomplete cognitive activity at any of Litrownik's (1984) four levels.

The growing adoption of a cognitive–behavioral perspective in work with children and the increasing recognition of the importance of the educational environment, both socially and academically, for child development have helped to shape this review. The school provides an attractive environment to evaluate the contributions of cognitive processing skills and deficits and of functional and dysfunctional cognitive styles to child social behavior and academic performance. In return, the development of a viable cognitive–behavioral assessment and treatment model should offer the school a set of strategies for remediating children's academic, social, and behavior problems as well as interventions designed to strengthen children to prevent the occurrence of those problem situations.

In this article, we briefly overview the history of psychological interventions in the schools, and then document and review the use of cognitive–behavioral procedures applied to academic and social problems within this environment. A critical appraisal of this literature reveals limitations of the generalizability of cognitive–behavioral training effects. This leads us to a discussion and critique of the concept of cognition in cognitive behavior therapy with children and the contribution that cognitive developmental psychology can make to an applied cognitive model. We conclude by illustrating this "developmental-clinical" model in a review of our research on the development of generalizable interventions with elementary school children and by discussing the implications of this new perspective for cognitive behavior therapy with children.

II. HISTORY OF SCHOOL INTERVENTIONS

As O'Leary and O'Leary (1977) pointed out, the contemporary view of child behavior dysfunction has been a relatively recent development. It is only in this century that these problems have been conceptualized within educational, physical illness, psychological illness, or social systems paradigms. This contemporary approach to the problems of children can be traced to the activities of Lightner Witmer and the founding of his Psychological Clinic at the University of Pennsylvania in 1896 (Meyers & Craighead, 1984). Witmer's work with children experiencing learning difficulties employed directive educational intervention strategies based on experimental principles from the study of perception and learning, and so may be thought of as an antecedent of modern behavior therapy with children.

Other early influences on the behavioral treatment of children were the work of Watson and colleagues (Watson & Rayner, 1920) on the development and elimination of children's fears, the Mowrer and Mowrer (1938) bell and pad procedure for the treatment of enuresis, and operant interventions with severely dysfunctional children in institutional and classroom environments in the late 1950s and early 1960s.

These initial behavioral efforts were forced to compete with the prevailing theoretical approach to clinical intervention with children, the Freudian or psychoanalytic position. This psychoanalytic perspective emphasized the child's unconscious processes and the therapist–patient relationship, but in the 1950s the therapeutic effectiveness of this model came under suspicion (Levitt, 1957). While some therapists and counselors turned to humanistic, specifically client-centered, approaches, many turned to the emerging area of behavior therapy.

The earliest behavioral interventions with children were with the severely dysfunctional children that more traditional therapies had largely ignored or with whom the traditional therapies had proven relatively ineffective (Meyers & Craighead, 1984). This groundbreaking behavioral work was marked by the applied research programs of Bijou and colleagues (Bijou, 1966) with children experiencing academic skill, social skill, and motor performance deficits, by Lovaas's work with autistic children (Lovaas, 1967), and by the classroom interventions of Becker, Baer, and others (for a history of behavior modification see Kazdin, 1978).

Behavior therapy with children through the early 1970s relied almost exclusively on operant conditioning procedures. However, the successful impact of behavioral procedures over the last decade has brought behavior therapy in contact with less severely disturbed child and adult clients in less restrictive noninstitutional settings. In addition, operant conditioning procedures have not consistently produced generalized behavior change across settings and tasks. These facts, and what Kazdin (1978) has identified as a conceptual stagnation in applied behavior analysis, have prompted behavior therapists to look beyond the conditioning literature to other areas in experimental psychology in order to develop more sophisticated, comprehensive, and potentially more effective therapeutic interventions.

The major expansion in behavior therapy has been the consideration of the client's cognitive activity as both a target and as a mechanism of therapeutic change. The influential factors in this shift to cognitive behavior therapy with children (which has in many ways paralleled a shift in behavioral approaches to adult dysfunction) have come from both laboratory and clinical research. These influences have included Bandura's (1969) information-processing explanation of modeling, Meichenbaum's (1977) cognitive–developmental view of children's self-instructional behavior, work in self-control and Bandura's (1977) concept of reciprocal determinism, problem-solving training (D'Zurilla & Goldfried, 1971), and Beck's (1967) cognitive therapy for depression. Specific evidence from research on semantic conditioning, symbolic self-stimulation, the role of awareness in human learning, and observational learning has also been instrumental in broadening behavioral perspectives.

Though Kazdin (1982) has stated recently that the development of cognitive behavior therapy has yet to be elaborated in a comprehensive historical account, cognitive–behavioral approaches have had great impact on the treatment of children. The next section briefly examines cognitive–behavioral interventions with children in the educational domain. This review is meant to be illustrative rather than exhaustive, and interventions conducted in noneducational settings with relevance to educational issues are included.

III. COGNITIVE–BEHAVIORAL INTERVENTIONS IN EDUCATION

Cognitive–behavioral interventions with children can be traced to the work of the Soviet scientists, Luria (1961) and Vygotsky (1962), and their pioneering research on the developmental interaction of verbal and nonverbal behavior. Their work had major impact on Meichenbaum's (1977) development of self-instructional interventions with children. However, contemporary cognitive–behavioral work with children has gone beyond self-instruction training and now includes direct verbal instruction, modeling, reinforcement strategies, role-play and behavioral rehearsal, self-reinforcement, and feedback, as well as a variety of self-instructional strategies (Urbain & Kendall, 1980). As Hobbs, Moguin, Tyroller, and Lahey (1980) pointed out, independent of the strategy used cognitive–behavioral interventions with children share at least one distinctive feature. Children attempt to learn and perform mediating responses or strategies for controlling their behavior under a variety of circumstances.

In our examination of cognitive–behavioral interventions in education, we identified four target areas that have received significant research attention. These areas are attentional problems, aggression, problem-solving and prevention, and academic performance.

A. Attentional Problems

Attentional problems affect a broad range of normally functioning and clinically identified children. Child behavior problems with hypothesized attentional deficit components include impulsivity, underachievement, learning disabilities and hyperactivity, and neurological impairment (Craighead et al., 1978). While this broad array of diagnostic categories encompasses other problem behaviors, attentional problems appear to be central in that they affect the child's ability to learn in both educational and clinical settings.

The label of impulsivity has been given traditionally in response to children's inability to maintain attention and to delay responding on visual discrimination and other problem-solving tasks (Hobbs et al., 1980). And, impulsivity has often been considered a correlate and a hypothesized cause of learning disabilities. Impulsivity is also a major cause of children's referral to psychological services and is related to problems of aggression, classroom conduct disorders, academic deficiencies, and dysfunctional problem solving (Schleser & Thackwray, 1982).

Whereas impulsivity has been identified by children's strategic performance on problem-solving tasks, attention has been measured in a wide variety of ways. Assessment targets have included overt behaviors, academic performance, and the recording of eye movements to identify scanning strategies (Craighead et al., 1978). However, although several operational definitions of attention have been employed, most research efforts have relied on conceptual tests to label impulsive responding. This focus on implusivity as a measure of dysfunctional attention has served to influence clinicians to adopt specific training programs designed to modify particular attentional deficits.

The earliest of these programs used instructional interventions to delay the impulsive child's responding. For example, Kagan, Pearson, and Welch (1966) gave impulsive children instructions to study and think about task stimuli until told to respond by the experimenter. This delay training resulted in significantly greater Matching Familiar Figures Test (MFFT) response latencies by the experimental group compared to a no-treatment control group. However, no differences were observed in MFFT error scores. Similar findings were obtained in a study by Denney (1973). These experiments demonstrated that instructions to delay responding can influence conceptual tempo but do not necessarily modify the child's use of cognitive strategies. Studies that reinforce the child for increased response latency (Messer, 1976) or employ a self-instructing, reflective model (Debus, 1970) also generally experience this limitation.

Several investigators have taught directly cognitive strategies to facilitate attention. Egeland (1974) trained impulsive second-grade children to use scanning strategies on the MFFT by presenting them with a self-instructing model and then teaching them to break the standard down to its component parts, compare each part across all alternatives, and refer back to the standard to eliminate incorrect choices. The group trained in scanning strategies was compared to a group simply instructed to delay responding and to a no-treatment control group. Both training groups significantly increased response latency and decreased errors on the MFFT at posttest and performed significantly better than the control group. However, at a 2-month follow-up only the scanning strategy group maintained performance improvements. Egeland (Egeland, Wozniak, Schrimpf, Hage, Johnson, & Lederberg, 1976) extended his work on the training of visual information-processing skills to learning-disabled second graders. After 8 weeks of training, these children showed significant improvements on reading and visual processing tasks compared to two control groups. While training effects generalized to MFFT latency scores, no improvement was observed on MFFT error rate; effects on academic performance were not evaluated.

More comprehensive cognitive treatment packages, typically labeled self-instruction training, have shown some promising results with attentional problems. These interventions generally include a cognitive model who verbalizes the appropriate cognitive strategies, and a gradual fading of the presented strategies from the model to the child. The self-instructions typically consist of statements identifying and describing task demands, plans for task performance, self-guiding statements to facilitate monitoring task performance and coping with errors, and self-reinforcement for successful performance.

Meichenbaum and Goodman (1971) conducted the earliest self-instruction work with impulsive second-grade children from a remedial class. In the first study, children received either a self-instruction intervention or an attentional control treatment and these two groups were compared to an assessment-only control group. The self-instruction group improved relative to the other two groups on MFFT latencies, Porteus Maze scores, and WISC Performance IQ; no generalization effects were found for MFFT errors, teacher ratings, or observation of classroom behaviors. A second study revealed that the self-instruction group improved significantly on a set of measures similar to those employed in the first study when compared to cognitive modeling and attention control conditions.

Robertson and Keeley (1974) applied the Meichenbaum program with five first- and second-grade impulsive children in the classroom using a multiple case study design. To improve the educational relevance of the treatment, the number of sessions was increased, self-instruction cue cards were used, and social and token reinforcement was administered for satisfactory performance. Robertson and Keeley reported that subjects showed improvement on MFFT error scores and academic achievement, but no change on MFFT latency scores or observation of classroom behavior.

In 1978, Kendall and Finch evaluated the effects of a combined self-instruction plus response cost intervention versus an attentional control condition on the behavior of impulsive children. The experimental group significantly outperformed the control group on MFFT latencies and errors and on teacher ratings of impulsive classroom behavior immediately after and 3 months after treatment. No differences were obtained on self-report measures or on teacher and staff ratings of locus of conflict.

One of the most comprehensive programs dealing with attentional problems was conducted by Douglas, Parry, Marton, and Garson (1976). These authors trained hyperactive boys (mean age approximately 8 years) over 24 sessions on cognitive, academic, and social tasks using specific attentional strategies, general problem-solving strategies, and social interaction strategies. Twelve sessions were conducted with the child's teacher and six sessions with the child's parents. These sessions were used to instruct care givers in the cognitive strategies and the application of contingency management techniques to encourage use of self-instructions and to control problem behaviors. Compared to a no-treatment control group, the intervention group improved on MFFT errors and latencies, realistic coping responses on a story completion test, time on the Bender-Gestalt test, and reading scores. However, no significant group differences were obtained on Bender-Gestalt errors, memory tests, mathematics measures, and the Connors Teacher-Rating Scale measure of hyperactivity.

Kendall and Braswell (1982) reported perhaps the most methodologically sophisticated study of children manifesting attentional and self-control problems. They assigned 27 teacher-referred non-self-controlled 8- to 12-year-old children to either cognitive–behavioral, behavioral, or attention placebo groups. All groups received training in a variety of academic and interpersonal tasks. The cognitive–behavioral group was given this training through self-instructional-based problem-solving strategies, social and token reinforcement, and response cost contingencies. The behavioral group received only the modeling and contingency arrangements, while the attention placebo group was reinforced for cooperation and effort on the training tasks. Kendall and Braswell (1982) employed an exceptionally broad set of dependent measures including parent, teacher, and student self-report, performance measures, and behavior classroom observation. Over most measures, groups receiving cognitive–behavioral and behavioral training were superior to the attention placebo group, and the cognitive–behavioral group consistently outperformed the behavioral group at posttest and a 10-week follow-up. Unfortunately most group differences were not apparent at a 1-year follow-up.

Cognitive–behavioral work with children's attentional problems has demonstrated a consistent ability to improve children's performance on a variety of tasks requiring sustained attention. Straight instructional interventions appear to influence positively children's conceptual tempo but not their problem-solving strategy use. Self-instruction and more comprehensive cognitive–behavioral interventions have demonstrated at least short-term maintenance but only limited generalization. Children's impulsive responses have been modified successfully only when the training tasks have been analogous to the dependent measures (Keogh & Hall, 1984). Generalization to classroom observational measures and teacher ratings of appropriate attentional behavior has been especially disappointing, and evidence of long-term maintenance of improvement in attentional problems has yet to be presented.

B. Aggression

Frequent aggressive behavior is one of the best predictors of referral of children for psychotherapy (Miller, Hampe, Barrett, & Noble, 1971). Excessive verbal and physical aggression disrupts the classroom and the learning process and provokes rejection from peers, punishment from adults, and psychological labels from professionals. Labeled aggressive children have also been found in both prospective longitudinal studies and retrospective analyses to be at risk for academic failure, delinquency, and adult psychopathology (Kennedy, 1982; Kirschenbaum & Ordman, 1983).

Although aggression may be related to attentional deficits and problems of impulsivity, aggressively responding children are not classified typically by performance on conceptual and other standardized tests such as the MFFT. The aggressive label is most often generated by parents, teachers, and other significant care givers based on observation of the child in the natural environment (Hobbs et al., 1980).

Cognitive–behavioral efforts to ameliorate aggressive behavior began with programs that either presented children with instructions or displayed strategies to enable children to inhibit their aggressive responses. MacPherson, Candee, and Hohman (1974) evaluated the effects of self-instruction-based mediation essays (which required children to identify disruptive behavior, desirable behavior, and operative contingencies so that a discrimination among alternatives was apparent) and a behavior modification program involving social and material reinforcers, withdrawal of reinforcement, and time-out on the disruptive lunchroom behavior of 6- to 13-year-old elementary school children. This program effectively reduced disruptive behavior and was more successful than a punishment essay (which required children to copy sentences containing corrective feedback, e.g., "I must not . . . .") plus the behavioral program or the behavioral program alone.

A different approach to the aggressive behavior question was taken by Goodwin and Mahoney (1975). Three uncontrolled case studies were conducted with boys ages 6–11 judged to be aggressive in the classroom and seen as outpatients at a mental health center. The boys participated in four taunting exercises in which they stood inside a circle of children who taunted them in order to prompt aggressive behavior. After the first exercise, the boys viewed a 3-minute videotape of a boy adaptively coping with similar taunts. The videotape was viewed again after the second exercise, and in addition the experimenter pointed out and discussed the coping responses. Coping responses by the target boys improved dramatically during the third and fourth taunting exercises. Classroom observation revealed pre- to posttreatment reductions in disruptive behavior though the case study design precluded any cause–effect conclusions.

Robin, Schneider, and Dolnick (1977) applied the "Turtle Technique" in a multiple baseline design with two classrooms of aggressive children. Classroom observation of aggressive behavior served as the dependent variable. The Turtle Technique is a strategy in which children are taught to control aggression by imitating a turtle and withdrawing inside their shells. This process is cued by the teacher or a peer using the word *turtle*. During the turtle response, the child is taught to relax and use problem-solving skills. A significant decrease in aggressive behavior was found during use of the program. However, in one of the classrooms this decrease began before the initiation of treatment thus confounding any conclusions about treatment effectiveness.

Several studies made more active attempts to train aggressive children to utilize nonaggressive problem-solving strategies. Snyder and White (1979) employed discussion, modeling, imaginal rehearsal, and role playing to enable five adolescent delinquents who had failed to respond to a token economy to reappraise aggression-producing situations and to use self-instructions to cope with failure. Six weeks after treatment, trained delinquents, relative to untrained controls, showed greater improvements in academic, self-care, and social behaviors, and greater reductions in disruptive and aggressive responses.

Chandler (1973) trained 10- to 13-year-old delinquent boys in role-taking skills. Paid delinquents working in small groups wrote and videotaped role-playing skits about social situations involving adolescents. The skits were performed enough times so that each individual played each part, and then everyone viewed all versions of the skit. Relative to no-treatment and attention control groups, those receiving role-taking training showed significant improvement on Chandler's measure of role-taking skill, and they experienced approximately 50% fewer delinquency contacts over an 18-month follow-up (Chandler, Greenspan, & Barenboim, 1974).

In an experiment with 8- to 11-year-old elementary school students referred for aggressive behavior, Forman (1980) used scripts of aggression-provoking situations, problems identification, rational reappraisal, role taking, and self-instructions to reduce aggressive responses. This intervention was significantly more effective than an attention placebo condition and as effective as a response cost condition, as assessed on teacher ratings, teacher records, and classroom observation of aggressive behavior.

Perhaps the most comprehensive intervention for children's aggressive behavior was documented by Camp and colleagues (Camp, Blom, Hebert, & van Doorninck, 1977). In an earlier study, Camp (1977) had found that aggressive first- and second-grade boys possessed adequate verbal mediation skills but failed to use those skills appropriately. From this she concluded that aggressive boys demonstrated a "control deficiency." Camp's "Think Aloud" program was designed to remedy this deficiency.

In the Think Aloud program, aggressive boys were trained in small groups by a regular classroom teacher. The 30 half-hour sessions included self-instruction training on cognitive, motor, and interpersonal problem-solving skills. A group of treated aggressive boys was compared with a group of untreated aggressive boys and a group of nonaggressive boys. On cognitive tasks such as the MFFT, treated aggressive boys improved significantly over untreated aggressive boys and matched the performance of normal boys. The treatment group also showed an increase in prosocial behavior; however, these boys did not show a significantly greater decrease in teacher-rated aggressive behavior than the control groups. No improvement was observed in problem-solving behavior, and solutions used by the treatment group were often aggressive.

The support for cognitive–behavioral treatment of aggressive behavior is less consistent than similar approaches to attentional deficits. When cognitive–behavioral interventions have been successful, the target populations has been older children and adolescents (Kennedy, 1982). There is little evidence of maintenance and generalization of treatment-initiated nonaggressive behavior. Kennedy (1982) has suggested that the limited impact of cognitively oriented interventions for aggression may be due to the narrow focus of these programs. Cognitive deficits are potential contributors to aggressive behavior, but social skill deficits and motivational problems must also be considered and may necessitate broader intervention strategies.

C. Problem Solving and Prevention

Kirschenbaum and Ordman (1984) argued that despite the growth of paraprofessional and community-based professional services, psychology has failed to meet the needs of individuals experiencing personal and social problems. These authors joined the long list of psychologists advocating the development of prevention-oriented services as a solution to this problem. One major approach to prevention in the mental health area is the development of general and interpersonal problem-solving skills (Craighead et al., 1978). Others have argued extensively that problem-solving skills can contribute significantly to positive mental health (cf. Jahoda, 1958), and that poor problem-solving skills are related to social disfunction (Spivack, Platt, & Shure, 1976). While problem-solving interventions have been discussed in the preceding sections, those programs covered here are directed specifically towards problem-solving skills building and prevention.

Much of the contemporary work on problem solving can be traced to D'Zurilla and Goldfried's (1971) problem-solving model. They suggested that problem solving be broken down into these steps: the development of a problem-solving set, identification of the problem, evaluation of solutions and selection of the most appropriate alternative, and implementation and evaluation of the selection.

The most extensive research on the development of problem-solving skills has been presented by Spivack and Shure (Spivack et al., 1976). These authors argued that problem-solving skills consist of the following component skills: an awareness of social problems and the potential for such problems, generation of alternative solutions to problems, means–end thinking (i.e., the specification of steps necessary to carry out problem solutions), consequential thinking (i.e., an understanding of the consequences of behavior on self and others), and cause–effect thinking (i.e., an understanding that social interaction is a reciprocal process affected by the feelings and acts of others).

In a large-scale evaluation of the Spivack and Shure (1974) program, 113 preschool children received from their teachers 12 weeks of daily problem-solving training and 106 preschool children served as control subjects. Both pre- and posttreatment, teachers rated students as impulsive, inhibited, or adjusted, and also rated them on scales of popularity, initiative, and independence. Students' problem-solving skills were assessed using the Preschool Interpersonal Problem Solving Test (Spivack & Shure, 1974).

Trained students demonstrated a significant improvement in number of alternative solutions suggested and the social appropriateness of those solutions. Improvement in consequential thinking and cause–effect thinking was also observed for the trained group. Children rates as impulsive or inhibited showed the greatest improvement on problem-solving measures. Children in the trained group were also more likely than control children to improve from being rated as impulsive or inhibited to being rated as adjusted, and trained children also received better teacher ratings of other classrooms and social behavior. Conclusions drawn in this study are weakened by the use of teachers as both trainers and raters and by the failure to include an attention control group.

The findings of Spivack and Shure and the results of similar programs (e.g. Stone, Hinds, & Schmidt, 1975) may indicate that problem-solving training can be effectively conducted in the educational setting and may serve preventive mental health functions. However, there is little evidence in these experiments to support assertions of adjustment and mental health benefits. Several large-scale investigations have attempted to examine the wide ranging effects of problem-solving training.

In a primary prevention project, Allen, Chinsky, Larcen, Lochman, and Selinger (1976) used components of both the D'Zurilla and Goldfried and the Spivack and Shure models to present 150 third and fourth graders with 24 half-hour problem-solving lessons conducted by classroom teachers. The teachers employed videotapes, classroom and small group activities, reinforcement, and role playing in the lesson sequence.

Problem-solving training was evaluated using a means–end problem-solving test, and a subset of students were given a test of ability to generate efficient alternative problem solutions. Teachers rated students' behavioral adjustment. Also, measures of locus of control, self-esteem, level of aspiration, and sociometric status were taken. Analyses of these measures indicated that trained children improved on both problem-solving measures compared to no-treatment control children. Treatment children showed a more internal locus of control than control students, though other self and peer ratings and teacher rating of students' behavioral adjustment revealed no group differences. Problem-solving improvements were not maintained at a 4-month follow-up.

A project conducted through the University of Rochester evaluated a 17-lesson teacher-administered problem-solving program for second- and third-grade children (Gesten, Flores-de-Apodaca, Rains, Weissberg, & Cowen, 1979). Like the Allen et al. (1976) effort, this problem-solving training borrowed from both the Spivack and Shure and the D'Zurilla and Goldfried models. Children receiving the complete program were compared to a brief five-lesson treatment group and a control group. The results were strikingly similar to the Allen et al. findings. Treatment children showed significantly better problem-solving skills than children in the brief treatment or control groups. However, these problem-solving gains did not affect adjustment as measured by sociometric measures and teacher ratings. More extensive interventions with this problem-solving training led to inconsistent adjustment improvements which did not appear to be related to problem-solving skill gains (Weissberg, Gesten, Rapkin, Cowen, Davidson, Flores-de-Apodaca, & McKim, 1981b; Weissberg, Gesten, Carnike, Toro, Rapkin, Davidson, & Cowen, 1981a). A large-scale application of the problem-solving skill training produced similar conclusions (Kirschenbaum & Ordman, 1984).

Whereas the Spivack and Shure (1974) problem-solving training program demonstrated improvements in children's problem-solving skills, improvements in rated adjustment, and a positive relationship between problem-solving skills and improvements in adjustment, other training programs have been unable to replicate these optimistic findings (Kirschenbaum & Ordman, 1984). Intervention gains have been limited typically to component problem-solving skills without any demonstration of generalized problem-solving abilities or improved adjustment (Weissberg & Gesten, 1982). Lahey and Strauss (1982) also argued that these programs require extensive teacher cooperation, possess questionable cost effectiveness, show little evidence of relative effectiveness compared to other treatments, and have not been evaluated with dysfunctional populations.

D. Academic Performance

As noted, unsatisfactory academic performance is one of the few childhood problems that discriminated clinic-referred from nonreferred children (Achenbach & Edelbrock, 1981). The significant role of academic and school performance in children's lives has led to initial attempts to apply cognitive–behavioral interventions to such performance.

In one of the earliest cognitive–behavioral applications to academic problem behaviors, Denney, Denney, and Ziobrowski (1973) trained 5- and 6-year-old elementary school children to ask constraint-seeking questions in a game of "Twenty Questions." Children in three groups observed cognitive models using constraint-seeking questions on the "Twenty Questions" task. Each group received a slightly different version of the model. When compared to a practice control group, all treatment groups asked a significantly greater percentage of constraint-seeking questions at two posttest evaluations.

Robin, Armel, and O'Leary (1975), working with kindergarten children, compared a self-instruction intervention with direct skill training in letter writing and a no-treatment control condition. Both treatments produced significantly better letter-writing performance than no treatment, and self-instructions were significantly more effective than skill training on trained letters. On a generalization test with untrained letters, no differences among groups were found. Additionally, Robin et al. reported no relationship between children's self-instruction behavior and letter-writing performance, and they found the self-instruction training difficult and time consuming.

A number of instructional studies have successfully developed children's reading recognition skills by increasing children's decoding accuracy and fluency. However, the area of reading comprehension is more complex, involving decoding skills and the additional areas of attentional skills and strategies for deriving information from the reading materials (Lloyd, Kosiewicz, & Hallahan, 1982). Interventions to improve children's attentional skills were discussed in Section III,A; and Hallahan, Marshall, and Lloyd (1983) demonstrated that a self-motivating procedure improved learning-disabled boys' attention to a reading comprehension task.

Strategies for deriving information from reading materials were evaluated by Bommarito and Meichenbaum (in Meichenbaum & Asarnow, 1979). Seventh- and eighth-grade children with reading comprehension deficits received a self-instructional intervention that led them to identify major themes, significant details, organization of events, and character motives in the readings. Other reading-deficient students participated in practice-only or no-treatment conditions. At both posttest and a 1-month follow-up, self-instruction subjects performed significantly better on two reading comprehension measures than control groups.

Mathematics is perhaps the most explored area in cognitive–behavioral interventions for academic performance (cf. Genshaft, 1982; Lloyd, Saltzman, & Kauffman, 1981). One of the first experiments in this area was conducted by Lovitt and Curtis (1968). In a single-subject case study, they directed an 11-year-old boy to read subtraction problems aloud before answering. This strategy increased the proportion of correct answers compared to baseline performance.

In a more comprehensive effort, Genshaft and Hirt (1980) selected 36 seventh-grade girls with math achievement scores below grade level and reading achievement scores above grade level. One-third of the subjects received 16 40-minute math tutoring sessions over an 8-week period. A second group received the math tutoring plus a self-instruction intervention with attentional self-reinforcement, arousal reduction, and self-efficacy building components. The third group attended regularly scheduled math classes with no additional tutoring. On the math applications section of the Stanford Diagnostic Mathematics Test (SDMT), all groups showed significant pre- to posttreatment improvement. However, on the computations section of the SDMT, only the self-instruction group demonstrated significant pre- to posttreatment improvement. The self-instruction group also developed a significantly favorable attitude toward mathematics while the other two groups showed no significant change.

Cognitive–behavioral interventions for academic performance have shown some promising signs, but these largely isolated experiments have yet to demonstrate long-term maintenance of educational tasks. These cognitive–behavioral interventions must also be compared for effectiveness and efficiency with alternative educational programs.

E. Critical Appraisal

As Kazdin (1982) noted, the effect of cognitive–behavioral work has expanded the content of behavioral research, broadened the attention of behavior modifiers to include information from cognitive and developmental psychology, and facilitated the development of interventions that integrated internal and external mediators of behavior. Our review of cognitive–behavioral interventions in educational settings reveals some optimistic feelings. Instructional interventions typically improve children's performance on trained tasks but rarely affect children's use of cognitive strategies. More comprehensive problem-solving and self-instruction interventions show short-term maintenance of behavior change and strategy change but only limited generalization and limited long-term maintenance. Research findings are most discouraging in the areas of aggressive behavior change and academic performance improvement.

As in all research areas, methodological and procedural problems abound in educationally based cognitive behavior therapy. The evaluation of cognitive–behavioral intervention strategies varies from laboratory to laboratory, and often experimenters rely on psychometric measures of response to intervention rather than developing a comprehensive assessment of cognitive and behavior change (Urbain & Kendall, 1980). Urbain and Kendall (1980) and Kazdin (1982) recommended including in assessment packages self-report measures, teacher, parent, and peer ratings, and more importantly, behavioral observation and measures of target task performance. A comprehensive set of cognitive dependent measures is also necessary if we are to identify children's cognitive–behavioral deficits and relationships between their behavioral performance and measures of cognitive capacities and skills. Other methodological recommendations include the use of credible attention placebo groups, comparisons with alternative treatment strategies (Urbain & Kendall, 1980), complete specification of the treatment program and the clinical population, and the use of appropriate statistical techniques (Lahey & Strauss, 1982).

The crucial problems with cognitive–behavioral interventions are the lack of evidence for maintenance of behavior change and the failure to show generalization of behavior change across tasks and settings. Lahey and Strauss (1982) found that few studies in this area present follow-up data, and that where such evaluation is available the time period is typically less than 2 months. The 1-year follow-up data presented by Kendall and Braswell (1982) failed to support treatment gains achieved earlier.

The failure to achieve generalization of behavior change is a more serious concern because only rarely is the intent of interventions to produce change on an isolated task or in a single setting. Urbain and Kendall (1980) recommended that more intensive, longer term training involving both cognitive and behavioral components may be necessary to consistently produce academic and social behavior change.

IV. AN ORGANISMIC PERSPECTIVE

The preceding section reveals both the strengths and weaknesses of the cognitive–behavioral approach to behavior change in general and to children in school settings in particular. As noted, the move to considering internal mental events has generated a wealth of potentially important assessment and intervention techniques as well as opened the door to perhaps a richer theoretical and conceptual base for clinical work.

An important goal for all practitioners is to promote an enduring change in behavior following intervention. It is hoped that the child will continue to use the skills and strategies learned, both on tasks used during training (a maintenance issue) and on tasks or in settings not explicitly used during training (a generalization issue). While some researchers report successful generalization following a cognitive–behavioral intervention, a general weakness of these approaches is the failure to consistently demonstrate significant generalization effects.

This weakness is important for two reasons. First, it is rarely the case that we wish our interventions to affect single target behaviors for single situations. Second, this weakness was one of the motivating forces in the movement away from conditioning-based interventions. The hope of cognitive behaviorists for an alleviation of the generalization problem rested on the assumption that giving the child an internal system for assessing and controlling his or her own behavior would prove to be a more powerful means of instigating and maintaining change.

In the preceding section, we have tried to document faithfully (if sketchily) the state of the art of clinical interventions in the school setting. Note that the language used to describe children not meeting some standards set by teachers, parents, or the general social system involved terms such as *deficiency* and *lack of* some presumably important aspect of behavioral and/or cognitive functioning. For us, this use of a terminology emphasizing what a child does *not* possess relative to some standard implicates a particular conceptualization of the child and of development—a conceptualization we feel hinders the search for interventions having a greater range of impact. In the remainder of this article, we develop the argument for a very different conceptualization of clinical interventions with children in the schools. We advocate a move to an organismic model for developmental and clinical change over the traditional use of a "deficit" model. Proponents of an organismic perspective emphasize different periods of development, a series of qualitative changes through these periods, an organism with an active role in confronting and interpreting experiences, and a structure/function analysis of change (see Reese & Overton, 1970, for a detailed discussion of this perspective). In short, reliance on an organismic perspective channels the focus of study away from a conceptualization of deficits toward a conceptualization of developmental differences.

As an introduction, and to provide a framework for the distinctions to be made, a brief consideration of the term *cognition* is in order. There seems to be general agreement that the term *cognition* refers both to the content (i.e., organization and knowledge base) and to the processing (i.e., acquisition,manipulation, and retrieval) of thought (e.g., see Bower, 1975; Meichenbaum, 1977; Neisser, 1976). Although this agreement exists, different theoretical perspectives within psychology seem to emphasize one or the other in their "cognitive" approach. For example, contemporary social learning theory (Bandura, 1977) certainly advocates the importance of the processes of attention, retention, etc., but the focus of the theory rests on the modeling of behavior and the conditions under which a child will assume those behaviors. This is a focus on the content of thought. To provide a counterpoint, Paigetian theory (Flavell, 1963), while making some statements about the content of thought at different developmental periods, nonetheless strongly emphasizes the processes of thought that characterize these stages.

Achenbach (1978) noted that the majority of clinical interventions with children is dominated by an adaptation of adult-oriented interventions. It is our contention that a focus on the content of thought in cognitive behavior therapy perpetuates this approach. A focus on content naturally leads to a conceptualization of child behavior as being deficient relative to older children, to "normal" children, or to adults.

We propose a conceptualization of child behavior that emphasizes the processes of thought. In Volume 1 of this series, Arnkoff and Glass (1982) argued for a process-oriented view of cognition. They stressed the role of the function of cognition for subsequent behavior and behavior change. While our position is essentially in agreement with these authors, we are extending and modifying the perspective for work with children. Our position draws heavily from the developmental work of Piaget and his emphasis on the processes of thought. As such, this leads us to an organismic model for the analysis of developmental and clinical change.

We present this position in three sections. In the first, we elaborate our view of the intervention setting per se, a view which places at its core the cognitive functioning of the child. Next we present our program of research based on this conceptualization of the intervention setting. Finally, we present a summary and conclusions of our thoughts, and provide some implications of adopting this perspective. We feel that this conceptualization can affect many aspects of the educational and clinical needs of children, but foremost we feel that we are offering an improved means by which to foster the generalization of training.

A. The Intervention Setting

All theories of cognition view the individual as an active problem solver. Experiences are not simply incorporated in a simple fashion; rather, experiences are encountered, assessed, and understood in relation to the cognitive and emotional state of the person. Thus, even though we primarily address issues of direct instruction or intervention, in a very real sense every setting every day for the child can be viewed as an instructional experience.

Our conceptualization of the intervention setting is adapted from Bransford (1979). Four components operate interdependently to determine the outcome of training: learning activities, nature of materials, criterial tasks, and cognitive status of the learner. Learning activities refer to the cognitive and behavioral exercises provided to the learner. These can be verbal rehearsal, role playing, participant modeling, etc. Nature of materials refers to the content of the materials used during learning, such as the use of props or aids, and the type of material provided as a training task. Criterial tasks are the assessment measures used to measure immediate learning, maintenance of learning, and generalization of learning. Finally, and to us, most importantly, the cognitive status of the learner must be considered. The exercises engaged in, the materials used, and the standards for assessment are all understood only in relation to the extant cognitive ability of the learner.

Thus far in our presentation of the intervention context, we doubt that there is little disagreement even from quite different cognitive "camps." Let us go an important step further. Given this conceptualization of the intervention setting, how do we characterize the conditions which promote change? Obviously, those conditions that optimally engage the cognitive activity of the learner will be the conditions that best facilitate change. It is here that we depart from traditional cognitive–behavioral approaches. Because we feel that children pass through different developmental periods (rather than overcoming deficits inherent to age), we feel that children of different developmental periods will optimally respond to different regimens of instruction—regimens that capitalize on those differences as opposed to eliminating presumed deficits. We suggest that those interested in provoking behavior change in children can do so best by assessing the developmental/cognitive status of the child and optimally engaging the processing of the child through a manipulation of the materials, activities, and criterial tasks. We present just such an endeavor in the next section.

B. Our Program of Research

Over the past 5 years, in conjunction with Robert Schleser and a number of others, we have explored the value of the above conceptualization. Our progress is documented here by a brief presentation of the results of six of our projects. Details of three of the studies may be found in Cohen and Meyers (1983). In four of the experiments reported below, we used samples of "normal" children; in the other two, we extended the findings to children having difficulties in school settings.

In our first project (Schleser, Meyers, & Cohen, 1981) we systematically varied three of the components of our intervention model. As learning activities, we presented children with a set of traditional self-guiding self-statements, fashioned after Meichenbaum and Goodman (1971), either through the typical five-step, overt-to-covert fading procedure, or through a didactic procedure in which the experimenter simply read the statements to the child. The nature of materials was manipulated by presenting half of the trained children a set of task specific self-instruction statements and presenting the remainder a set of general content statements. The specific statements were designed to aid performance on the task used during training, the MFFT. The general content statements were designed to be a broadly based set of strategies, applicable to a variety of problem-solving tasks. To exemplify this distinction, children in the specific content group would rehearse (or listen to) the statement, "I must match every part of these pictures to every part of this one," while those in the general content group would rehearse (or listen to) "I must think about all the answers before choosing the best one."

Cognitive status of the learner was assessed by identifying Piagetian-defined preoperational and concrete operational children among first and second grades. Age was kept equivalent across experimental conditions. Preoperational children live in a kind of here-and-now reality. They rely more heavily on their perceptions of a situation rather than on a conceptual understanding. Their thought has been characterized as egocentric in nature (inability to take another's perspectives), and they seem to have difficulty shifting their focus of attention among dimensions of a problem. Concrete operational children have much more stable thought processes than preoperational children. These children are very systematic in their reasoning abilities. Their thought processes have been characterized as having the ability to reverse certain logical operations, to take different perspectives, and to engage in systematic classification of stimuli, and in general, as possessing a quantitative, analytical approach to the world. A more detailed description of the characteristics of these children may be found in Flavell (1963, 1977). For our purposes here, the point to be made is that these groups of children possess qualitatively different processes of thinking. In a very real sense, they live in different realities.

Cognitive level of children was identified on the basis of performance on two Piagetian tasks (Flavell, 1963), conservation of number and conservation of continuous quantity. To be considered preoperational, the child had to answer incorrectly each part of both tasks. To be considered concrete operational, the child had to successfully conserve on both tasks and provide appropriate verbal explanations. Each child served in two sessions following screening for cognitive level. In the first session, the child was pretested on the MFFT and a perceptual perspective-taking task designed to resemble in format the MFFT. That is, the child was presented a standard display of geometrical objects and six choice displays. The task was to choose the alternative from the choice displays that matched what the experimenter viewed sitting 90° to the right of the standard. Thus, like the MFFT, the child was required to analyze a standard and find a match among six alternatives; for the MFFT, this match was a direct perceptual match, and for the perspective-taking task the match required an inference about the arrangement of parts.

Following testing on the two tasks the child served in one of five experimental groups. Four of these groups represented the factorial combination of content of instruction (specific versus general) with delivery procedure (fading versus didactic). A fifth group served as a no-instruction control. At the second session, the child received a second presentation of assigned instruction condition and was posttested on the MFFT and perspective taking tasks. The MFFT was used during the delivery of the various instruction packages and thus performance on this task served as a measure of the immediate gains of training. The perspective-taking task served as our generalization instrument.

On the MFFT training task, those children receiving the specific self-instructions delivered through the fading procedure witnessed the greatest pretest to posttest gains. Children in the fading/general content group showed modest, but nonsignificant improvement. On the generalization measure, only those children receiving the general content instructions delivered through fading showed significant gains. Concrete operational children outperformed preoperational children on both tasks, and both groups of children showed similar patterns of performance across instructional groups.

Similar to Kendall and Wilcox (1980), children given more conceptually oriented self-guiding statements were able to transfer the acquired strategy to another task better than those children given a concrete, task specific set of instructions. Rehearsing the strategy proved to facilitate both training task and generalization task performance relative to simply listening to the strategy statements. Interestingly, although concrete operational children outperformed the preoperational children in an absolute sense, the manipulation of the intervention setting through the means used here provoked change in both cognitive level groups in a similar fashion.

We replicated the effects of specific versus general content of instructions using a group of third- and fourth-grade children identified by teachers as performing poorly in math (Thackwray, Meyers, Schleser, & Cohen, 1982). Children were assigned to one of three groups, using addition math problems as a training task: a general content self-instruction group, a specific content self-instruction group, and a specific content, didactic control group. Children in the specific content group demonstrated significant gains on the math subtest of the Peabody Individual Achievement Test (PIAT). As in the study reported above, only those children in the general group displayed generalization effects from training, as witnessed by significant gains on the PIAT spelling and general information subtests.

The effect of specific versus general content of strategy statements is a nature of materials issue within our conceptualization of the intervention setting. We next turned to an analysis of learning activities. While fading or rehearsal proved to be more influential than simply listening to a strategy in the first study, it seemed to us that this was a weak manipulation of optimal involvement of the child. Certainly the child is more physically active, and perhaps attends more to the training when asked to rehearse as opposed to simply listening, yet perhaps other forms of instructional procedures can better capture the child's cognitive activity and involvement.

Thus in the third experiment (Cohen, Meyers, Schleser, & Rodick, 1980), we again used same-aged preoperational and concrete operational children and again used the MFFT and perspective-taking tasks. Also, we saw the children for two sessions following initial screening—pretesting and instructing in the first session, instructing then posttesting in the second session. What we varied in this study was the delivery procedures of the instructions, keeping content of instruction constant across experimental groups receiving instruction. Here we used specific content of instructions, a conservative choice of content given the lack of generalization which resulted from this content in the first two experiments.

In addition to a no-training control group, we assigned children to three types of instruction groups: a didactic group, a fading group, and a discovery group. The didactic and fading groups received the same instructional procedure as similar groups in the first experiment. The procedure followed for the discovery group was designed to maximize a priori the cognitive involvement of the child. These children received the same set of self-guiding statements presented to the didactic and fading groups, but these children were led to discover these statements through a programmed question-and-answer Socratic dialogue with the experimenter. For example, the following interchange would occur for getting the child to discover the first self-guiding statement. Experimenter: "What's the first thing you should ask yourself when given this task?" Child: "I guess I need to know what I'm supposed to do." Experimenter: "I see. So you need to ask yourself, 'What is it I need to do?'" The child was led to discover each of the self-guiding statements in this fashion with the experimenter prompting and shaping the responses. Each statement was repeated by the child and successive statements were cumulatively rehearsed, but no fading of instructions occurred.

On the MFFT training task, both the group receiving fading of instructions and the group receiving discovery instruction significantly improved their performance. Again, a main effect for cognitive level revealed that concrete operational children outperformed the preoperational children, but both groups, as in Experiment 1, responded to the different procedures in a similar way. Importantly, only the concrete operational children in the discovery group showed significant generalization of performance on the perspective-taking task.

Whereas both cognitive level groups responded to a manipulation of content in Experiment 1, only the concrete operational children were able to benefit, in terms of generalization of training, from the high level of cognitive involvement generated in the discovery condition. This effect due to learning activities is predictable from the characteristics of the learners. Concrete operational children, unlike peroperational children, are able to separate form from content in a situation. This implies that in Experiment 3 the concrete operational child was able to understand and benefit from a learning activity that systematically puts on display not only a set of self-guiding statements, but also a procedure for generating and adapting a strategy. Preoperational children were able to learn from the process of discovery. What they learned was the content of the instructions that they took with them for the training task. These children could not go beyond this content and glean the generation and application procedure inherent to the discovery learning activity.

An interesting question can be posed based on the two experiments varying cognitive level. Preoperational and concrete operational children both showed significant generalization when the content of the instructions was general in nature and was rehearsed through fading of instructions. Yet, with specific content of instructions delivered through discovery procedures, only concrete operational children showed significant generalization effects. The obvious question, then, is what happens when general content is delivered via discovery procedures?

Nichol, Cohen, Meyers, and Schleser (1982) performed this comparison using the same tasks and procedures as the previous studies. General content instructions were taken from the first experiment and the discovery procedures were adapted from the second experiment. Once again, only the concrete operational children in the general content/discovery condition demonstrated significant generalization.

Thus a manipulation of delivery procedures, in this experiment what we call a discovery procedure, led to differential generalization effects as a function of Piagetian stage. This occurred whether the nature of materials was specific or general content self-instructions. Our interpretation of this cognitive level × instruction group interaction rests on an analysis of these cognitive stages in terms of the ability to glean strategy generation and adaptation processes from the discovery procedure, an ability within the realm of the concrete operational child but not of the preoperational child, who focuses on only the content of instruction.

Perhaps it seems to the reader (as indeed it did to us) that an interpretation of the cognitive level × instruction group effects based on the presentation of strategy generation and adaptation effects is on tenuous grounds. As a more direct analysis of this interpretation, Good-night, Cohen, and Meyers (1983) tested preoperational and concrete operational children in three sessions. In the first session, one-third of the children at each cognitive level were assigned to a no-treatment group, and the remainder were given standard specific content, fading procedure self-instructions using the MFFT as the training task. In the second session, those children from the self-instruction group were divided in half. One of these groups received direct instruction on how to adapt the strategy they had learned for use on a new training task, the perspective-taking task. The other group was told to adapt the strategy and were given the opportunity to do so, but without the benefit of adaptation training. We call the first condition a passive adaptation group since the adaptation training was given to them, and we call the second adaptation group an active group since they had to work out the adaptation themselves. At the third session, all children were tested on the MFFT and perspective-taking tasks as well as a Tower of Hanoi task (Klahr, 1978) which served as the measure of generalization.

Both preoperational and concrete operational children, in either adaptation group, were able to improve their performances on both the MFFT and perspective-taking tasks relative to the no-training group. Once again, only the concrete operational children showed generalization on the Tower of Hanoi task. Interestingly, it did not matter if the adaptation training was active or passive for the concrete operational children to improve on the generalization task. Although not statistically significant, it is worthwhile to point out that while the preoperational children did not solve more problems following adaptation training, they did show signs of solving the problems more efficiently at posttest than they had at pretest.

We have performed one study testing the benefits of the discovery procedure on a clinically relevant population (Schleser, 1982). Teacher-referred non-self-controlled third- and fourth-graders were divided into four groups: specific content/didactic procedure, specific content/fading, general content/fading, and specific content/discovery. Children were seen in four sessions. Math problems served as the training materials. Thus the specific content instruction packages were designed to be helpful on similar types of math tests.

A variety of dependent measures were taken: a math quiz, the PIAT, prorated Wechsler IQ score, the MFFT, and the Nowicki–Strickland Locus of Control Scale. Children in the didactic condition showed no significant change on the measures at posttest. The specific content/fading group improved significantly on the math quiz and the math subtest of the PIAT. Children in the general content/fading group

experienced gains on the MFFT, and on the spelling, general information, and total test scores of the PIAT. Those children in the discovery
condition showed the same improvement on all these measures as the
other groups and in addition showed improvement in internal locus of
control, an increase in prorated IQ scores, and improved reading recognition PIAT subtest scores.

The pattern of results in this final study confirms our findings from
the previous experiments, using children with teacher-identified self-
control problems. Telling the child to listen to a strategy has little
value. If employing rehearsal, which is a relatively simple cognitive
activity, the range of generalization seems to be dictated by the degree
to which the content of the instructions map onto the critical tasks
including generalization tasks. That is, specific content instructions
lead to admirable performance gains on the task used during training;
broadly based general content instructions foster generalization of performance gains on untrained tasks. If delivery procedure is manipulated, in this case as a cognitively active discovery procedure, the range
of generalizability seems to be greatly expanded over the content of
instructions manipulation. How you train seems to be at least if not
more important than what is being trained. Finally, and a point that we
discuss shortly, all of these manipulations rely for their effectiveness
on the cognitive ability of the child to acquire, manipulate, and apply
the strategy being trained.

C. Summary of Research

The program of research affirms several assumptions typically held
by clinicians and educators. Children of the same chronological age can
possess different cognitive abilities. In addition, based on these cognitive differences, different training practices can be expected to meet
different degrees of success, both in direct benefits from training and in
the generalization of training effects. What we have done with our
research is to empirically assess a particular perspective on the intervention setting—a perspective that considers several components of
that setting and places a primary emphasis on important individual
differences of children.

When defining and executing the four components of our intervention model, perhaps the cognitive status of the learner component allows for the greatest range of potential theoretical candidates. We have
chosen a developmental perspective that proposes the existence of successive, qualitative stages of development. This Piagetian perspective
is an organismic model of development. More importantly, and derived

from this model, conditions of change are believed to be governed by the degree of cognitive activity generated in the intervention setting. Not all types of cognitive activity, however, are equally effective. Those conditions that are moderately discrepant from the cognitive structures of the child are those conditions that will promote the greatest cognitive change. In Piagetian terminology (Flavell, 1963), experiences that provoke states of moderate disequilibrium cause the greatest evocation of the processes of assimilation and accommodation to reduce the disequilibrium.

Based on our model, we suggest that moderate disequilibrium can be produced in intervention and educational settings by manipulating the remaining three components: nature of materials, learning activities, and critical tasks. The key of structuring training, then, is to assess the cognitive status of the child and manipulate the other components to provide an optimal mismatch. Our data suggest that this optimal mismatch for preoperational children can be achieved through a manipulation of the content of instructions (nature of materials) as long as the training procedures (learning activities) are kept relatively simple. These children can then demonstrate both training and generalization gains to the extent that the content of what is being taught maps onto the various criterial tasks. Concrete operational children, on the other hand, seem to be more sensitive to manipulations of learning activities. An activity that highlights a strategy generation and adaptation procedure helped these children regardless of the particular content of the instruction package.

V. CONCLUSIONS

Although the strengths of cognitive–behavioral approaches to childhood problems have been well documented, a critical examination of the data reveals particular weaknesses. Some of these weaknesses involve methodological and assessment issues, but the major issue that we have chosen to highlight is the problem of the generalization of behavior change. We chose this particular issue not only for its obvious relevance to practitioners, but also to use it as a vehicle for elaborating an alternative conceptualization for work with children.

A number of theorists have offered suggestions for fostering generalization. Bransford (1979) and Brown (1977) suggest that generalization can be enhanced by teaching concepts in multiple contexts and by teaching an awareness of future benefits (a metacognitive concern).

Kendall and Wilcox (1980) recommend the use of conceptual rather than concrete self-instruction packages. Kendall (1977) also suggested the use of contingent incentives along with self-instruction training. In addition, our work suggests that the goal of the practitioner must be to provide an optimal mismatch for the child, that is, provide a context for the child during instruction that will best provoke the activation of cognitive activity. As we noted, this provocation will take different forms for children of differing cognitive abilities. In a sense, these accounts are complementary. They all advocate the conscientious attempt first to help children acquire a strategy or set of strategies and then to encourage the child to adopt, adapt, and apply what was learned as situations warrant. In sum, all accounts posit the child in the role of an active participant in the intervention enterprise.

While our research presented in this article offers, we hope, some new ways to use some familiar tools, we also wish to offer a conceptualization divergent from much of the other work done with children in clinical and educational settings. We are advocating what has been called an organismic paradigm or world view as a set of assumptions about development and developmental change (Reese & Overton, 1970). For us, development is best conceptualized as children being qualitatively different organisms at different developmental stages. Much developmental change, then, is discontinuous in form, and the focus of analysis becomes that of structure change and function fitting. Operantly based interventions with children, in contrast, follow a set of what Reese and Overton (1970) call a mechanistic world view. Here children are seen as quantitatively less skilled than an older child or adult. Through a gradual process of accretion the child acquires more and more skills, behaviors, etc., and develops. Thus, notions of stages are rejected, developmental change is seen as entirely continuous in form, and the focus of analysis is strictly that of antecedent–consequent behavior change.

While the influx of cognitive concerns in the fields of clinical psychology and education has certainly broadened the scope of inquiry, we contend that, by and large, the paradigmatic assumptions underlying the work have remained largely mechanistic in nature. Much of the self-instruction work implicitly (or explicitly) rests on the assumption that any child can successfully mediate behavior if only an appropriate internal dialogue is adopted. The emphasis is on the materials and procedures of learning with only a passing interest in personal characteristics of the learner/child. This, of couse, brings us back to the distinction made earlier about deficit versus organismic models of development. We feel that much is to be gained by adopting an organismic position and by structuring interventions upon the strengths of the child rather than structuring them to alleviate proposed weaknesses.

Many researchers, obviously, are not as committed to this Piagetian perspective as we are. Alternative conceptualizations of cognition, such as information-processing approaches, metacognitive approaches, and social learning theory approaches, share with the Piagetian approach a view of the child as an active participant in all settings. For us, the strength of the Piagetian approach lies in its recognition of different cognitive abilities in different-aged children. We would urge researchers and practitioners from other theoretical orientations not necessarily to adopt a Piagetian perspective, but to strongly consider the issue of distinct differences in problem-solving abilities with development, a consideration of developmental differences rather than developmental deficits.

Mention must be made of the distinction between skills and strategies, a distinction related to the one posed earlier concerning the knowledge versus processes of cognition. Our research to date offers little information about the roles these play during interventions. Educators have been quite diligent at dissecting and ordering the various skills necessary for performance of academic tasks. Developmental and child clinical researchers mainly have focused on strategy acquisition, and useful work can be done relating the two. The concept of optimal discrepancy, which we introduced earlier, would lead us to believe that the success of strategy-based interventions may be dependent on the skill level of the child. It would be very interesting to match children on skill level and vary the types of strategies taught or vice versa. Furthermore, it would be important to note the generalization effects that occur as a function of these optimal mismatches.

Although we have focused primarily on academic and problem-solving tasks, the position we offer is readily adaptable to social and emotional issues as well. As an example, Dodge (1980) found that aggressive children did not process hostile, benign, and neutral social cues differently. They did differ on their attribution of intent, however, for the neutral cues situation. Normal children interpreted the neutral condition as benign, while the aggressive children interpreted it as an aggressive intent. From our perspective, then, the aggressive children were not cognitively deficient; rather their processes of attributing intent were different. Intervention then, for these particular children, should probably not focus on alleviation of social skill deficits; rather it should focus on prompting the child to reconsider and reevaluate social cues when in doubt as to intent.

The scope of our conceptualization merits further work. That is, much more developmental and child clinical research is needed in the area of emotional development and its relation to cognitive development. In addition, there is no one context for intervention, nor are typical contexts truly isolated. Much more information is needed about the influence of parents, siblings, and peers on the child's school performance. The interrelationships among family, neighborhood, and school influences are not well documented.

In conclusion, we have tried to provide to practitioners and researchers alike a new conceptualization of the intervention enterprise. We advocate an analysis of clinical/educational change within the context of developmental change, particularly within the context of cognitive–developmental change. Factors within the intervention setting (i.e., nature of materials, delivery procedures, and criterial tasks) must be designed in reference to the extant cognitive functioning of the individual child. We suggest that this design should attempt to provoke the child's cognitive involvement in the intervention by striving for an optimal mismatch between these factors and the child's cognitive functioning. We hope to see continued work on what we call developmental-clinical psychology as opposed to traditional child clinical psychology. We feel that a significant melding of developmental and clinical/educational interests will prove to be a fruitful union.

REFERENCES

Achenbach, T. M. Psychopathology of childhood: Research problems and issues. *Journal of Consulting and Clinical Psychology*, 1978, **46**, 759–776.

Achenback, T. M., & Edelbrock, C. S. Behavioral problems and competencies reported by parents of normal and disturbed children aged four through sixteen. *Monographs of the Society for Research in Child Development*, 1981, **46** (1, Serial No. 188).

Allen, G., Chinsky, J., Larcen, S., Lochman, J., & Selinger, H. *Community psychology and the schools: A behaviorally oriented multilevel parentive approach.* Hillsdale, NJ: Erlbaum, 1976.

Arnkoff, D. B., & Glass, C. R. Clinical cognitive construct: Examination, evaluation, and elaboration. In P. C. Kendall (Ed.), *Advances in cognitive-behavioral research* (Vol. 1). New York: Academic Press, 1982.

Bandura, A. *Principles of behavior modification.* New York: Holt, 1969.

Bandura, A. *Social learning theory.* New York: Prentice-Hall, 1977.

Beck, A. T. *Depression: Clinical experimental and theoretical aspects.* New York: Harper (Hoeber), 1967.

Beck, A. T. *Cognitive therapy and the emotional disorders.* New York: Int. Univ. Press, 1976.

Bijou, S. W. A functional analysis of retarded development. In N. R. Ellis (Ed.), *International review of research in mental retardation* (Vol. 1). New York: Academic Press, 1966.

Bower, G. H. Cognitive psychology: An introduction. In W. H. Estes (Ed.), *Handbook of learning and cognitive processes* (Vol. 1). Hillsdale, NJ: Erlbaum, 1975.

Bransford, J. D. *Human cognition: Learning, understanding, and remembering.* Belmont, CA: Wadsworth, 1979.

Brown, A. L. Development, schooling, and the acquisition of knowledge about knowledge. In R. C. Anderson, R. J. Spiro, & W. E. Montague (Eds.), *Schooling and the acquisition of knowledge.* Hillsdale, NJ: Erlbaum, 1977.

Brown, A. Knowing when, where, and how to remember: A problem of metacognition. In R. Glaser (Ed.), *Advances in instructional psychology.* Hillsdale, NJ: Erlbaum, 1981.

Camp, B. Verbal mediation in young aggressive boys. *Journal of Abnormal Psychology,* 1977, **86**, 145–153.

Camp, B., Blom, G., Hebert, F., & van Doorninck, W. "Think aloud": A program for developing self-control in young aggressive boys. *Journal of Abnormal Child Psychology,* 1977, **5**, 157–169.

Chandler, M. Egocentrism and antisocial behavior: The assessment and training of social perspective-taking skills. *Child Development,* 1973, **9**, 326–443.

Chandler, M., Greenspan, S., & Barenboim, C. Assessment and training of role-taking and referential communication skills in institutionalized emotionally disturbed children. *Developmental Psychology,* 1974, **10**, 546–553.

Cohen, R., & Meyers, A. W. The generalization of self-instructions. In B. Gholson & T. L. Rosenthal (Eds.), *Applications of cognitive-developmental theory.* New York: Academic Press, 1983, in press.

Cohen, R., Meyers, A. W., Schleser, R., & Rodick, J. D. *The generalization of self-instructions as a function of cognitive level and delivery procedures.* Paper presented at the biennial meeting of the Southeastern Conference on Human Development, Alexandria, VA, April 1980.

Craighead, W. E., Wilcoxon-Craighead, L., & Meyers, A. W. New directions in behavior modification with children. In M. Hersen, R. Eisler, & P. Miller (Eds.), *Progress in behavior modification* (Vol. 6). New York, Academic Press, 1978.

Debus, R. Effects of brief observation of model behavior on conceptual tempo of impulsive children. *Developmental Psychology,* 1970, **2**, 22–32.

Denney, D. Reflection and impulsivity as determinants of conceptual strategy. *Child Development,* 1973, **44**, 614–623.

Denney, D., Denney, N., & Ziobrowski, M. Alterations in the information processing strategies of young children following observation of adult models. *Developmental Psychology,* 1973, **8**, 202–208.

Dodge, K. A. Social cognition and children's aggressive behavior. *Child Development,* 1980, *51*, 162–170.

Douglas, V., Parry, P., Marton, P., & Garson, C. Assessment of a cognitive training program for hyperactive children. *Journal of Abnormal Child Psychology,* 1976, **4**, 389–410.

D'Zurilla, T., & Goldfried, M. Problem solving and behavior modification. *Journal of Abnormal Psychology,* 1971, **78**, 107–126.

Egeland, B. Training impulsive children in the use of more efficient scanning techniques. *Child Development,* 1974, **45**, 165–171.

Egeland, B., Wozniak, R., Schrimpf, V., Hage, J., Johnson, V., & Lederberg, A. *Visual information processing: Evaluation of a training program for children with learning disabilities.* Paper presented at the meeting of the American Educational Research Association, San Francisco, April 1976.

Flavell, J. H. *The developmental psychology of Jean Piaget.* Princeton, NJ: Van Nostrand-Reinhold, 1963.

Flavell, J. H. *Cognitive development.* New York: Prentice-Hall, 1977.

Forman, S. A comparison of cognitive training and response cost procedures in modifying aggressive behavior of elementary school children. *Behavior Therapy*, 1980, **11**, 594–600.

Genshaft, J. The use of cognitive behavior therapy for reducing math anxiety. *School Psychology Review*, 1982, **11**, 32–34.

Genshaft, J., & Hirt, M. The effectiveness of self-instructional training to enhance math achievement in women. *Cognitive Therapy and Research*, 1980, **4**, 91–97.

Gesten, E., Flores-de-Apodaca, R., Rains, M., Weissberg, R., & Cowen, E. Promoting peer related social competence in young children. In M. Kent & J. Rolf (Eds.), *The primary prevention of psychopathology: Social competence in children.* Hanover, NH: Univ. Press of New England, 1979.

Goodnight, J. A., Cohen, R., & Meyers, A. W. *Generalization of self-instructions: The effect of strategy adaptation training.* Paper presented at the biennial meeting of the Society for Research in Child Development, Detroit, April 1983.

Goodwin, S., & Mahoney, M. J. Modification of aggression through modeling: An experimental probe. *Journal of Behavior Therapy and Experimental Psychiatry*, 1975, **6**, 200–202.

Hallahan, D., Marshall, K., & Lloyd, J. Self-recording during group instruction: Effects on attention to task. *Learning Disabilities Quarterly*, 1983, in press.

Hobbs, S. A., Moguin, L. E., Tyroller, M., & Lahey, B. B. Cognitive behavior therapy with children: Has clinical utility been demonstrated? *Psychological Bulletin*, 1980, **87**, 147–165.

Jahoda, M. *Current concepts of positive mental health: A report to the staff director, Jack R. Ewalt, 1958.* New York: Basic Books, 1958.

Kagan, J., Pearson, L., & Welch, L. Modifiability of an impulsive tempo. *Journal of Educational Psychology*, 1966, **57**, 359–365.

Kazdin, A. *History of behavior modification: Experimental foundations of contemporary research.* Baltimore, MD: Univ. Park Press, 1978.

Kazdin, A. E. Current developments and research issues in cognitive-behavioral interventions: A commentary. *School Psychology Review*, 1982, **9**, 75–82.

Kendall, P. C. On the efficacious use of verbal self-instructional procedures with children. *Cognitive Therapy and Research*, 1977, **1**, 331–341.

Kendall, P. C., & Braswell, L. Cognitive-behavioral self-control therapy for children: A components analysis. *Journal of Consulting and Clinical Psychology*, 1982, **50**, 672–689.

Kendall, P. C., & Finch, A. J. A cognitive-behavioral treatment for impulsivity: A group comparison study. *Journal of Consulting and Clinical Psychology*, 1978, **46**, 110–118.

Kendall, P., & Wilcox, L. A cognitive-behavioral treatment for impulsivity: Concrete versus conceptual training. *Journal of Consulting and Clinical Psychology*, 1980, **48**, 80–91.

Kennedy, R. E. Cognitive-behavioral approaches to the modification of aggressive behavior in children. *School Psychology Review*, 1982, **11**, 47–55.

Keogh, B. K., & Hall, R. J. Cognitive training with learning disabled pupils. In A. W. Meyers & W. E. Craighead (Eds.), *Cognitive behavior therapy with children.* New York: Plenum, 1984.

164   Andrew W. Meyers and Robert Cohen

Kirschenbaum, D. S., & Ordman, A. M. Preventive interventions for children: Cognitive-behavioral perspectives. In A. W. Meyers & W. E. Craighead (Eds.), *Cognitive behavior therapy for children*. New York: Plenum, 1984.

Klahr, D. Goal formation, planning, and learning by pre-school problem solvers or: "My socks are in the dryer." In R. S. Seigler (Ed.), *Children's thinking: What develops?* Hillsdale, NJ: Erlbaum, 1978.

Lahey, B. B., & Strauss, C. C. Some considerations in evaluating the clinical utility of cognitive behavior therapy with children. *School Psychology Review*, 1982, **11**, 67–74.

Levitt, E. The results of psychotherapy with children: An evaluation. *Journal of Consulting Psychology*, 1957, **21**, 189–196.

Litrownik, A. J. Cognitive behavior modification with psychotic children: A beginning. In A. W. Meyers & W. E. Craighead (Eds.), *Cognitive behavior therapy with children*. New York: Plenum, 1984.

Lloyd, J., Kosiewicz, M., & Hallahan, D. Reading comprehension: Cognitive training contributions. *School Psychology Review*, 1982, **9**, 35–41.

Lloyd, J., Saltzman, N., & Kauffman, J. Predictable generalization in academic learning as a result of preskills and strategy training. *Learning Disability Quarterly*, 1981, **4**, 203–216.

Lovaas, O. A behavior therapy approach to the treatment of childhood schizophrenia. In J. P. Hill (Ed.), *Minnesota symposium on child psychology*. Minneapolis: Univ. of Minnesota Press, 1967.

Lovitt, T., & Curtis, K. Effects of manipulating an antecedent event on mathematics response rate. *Journal of Applied Behavior Analysis*, 1968, **1**, 329–333.

Luria, A. R. *The role of speech in the regulation of normal and abnormal behavior*. New York: Liveright, 1961.

MacPherson, E. M., Candee, B. L., & Hohman, R. J. A comparison of three methods for eliminating disruptive lunchroom behavior. *Journal of Applied Behavior Analysis*, 1974, **7**, 287–297.

Meichenbaum, D. *Cognitive behavior modification*. New York: Plenum, 1977.

Meichenbaum, D., & Asarnow, J. Cognitive-behavior modification and metacognitive development: Implications for the classroom. In P. C. Kendall & S. D. Hollon (Eds.), *Cognitive behavioral interventions: Theory, research, and procedures*. New York: Academic Press, 1979.

Meichenbaum, D., & Goodman, J. Training impulsive children to talk to themselves. *Journal of Abnormal Psychology*, 1971, **77**, 115–126.

Messer, S. Reflection-impulsivity: A review. *Psychological Bulletin*, 1976, **83**, 1026–1052.

Meyers, A. W., & Cohen, R. (Eds.). Cognitive-behavioral interventions for classroom and academic behaviors. *School Psychology Review*, 1982, **11**, 4–82.

Meyers, A. W., & Craighead, W. E. Cognitive behavior therapy with children: An historical, conceptual and organizational overview. In A. W. Meyers & W. E. Craighead (Eds.), *Cognitive behavior therapy with children*. New York: Plenum, 1984.

Miller, L., Hampe, E., Barrett, C., & Noble, H. Children's deviant behavior within the general population. *Journal of Consulting and Clinical Psychology*, 1971, **37**, 16–22.

Mowrer, O. H., & Mowrer, W. M. Enuresis—A method for its study and treatment. *American Journal of Orthopsychiatry*, 1938, **8**, 436–459.

Neisser, U. *Cognition and reality*. San Francisco: Freeman, 1976.

Nichol, G., Cohen, R., Meyers, A. W., & Schleser, R. Generalization of self-instruction training. *Journal of Applied Developmental Psychology*, 1982, **3**, 205–216.

O'Leary, K. D., & O'Leary, S. G. *Classroom management: The successful use of behavior management.* Oxford: Pergamon, 1977.

Reese, H. W., & Overton, W. F. Models of development and theories of development. In L. R. Goulet & P. B. Baltes (Eds.), *Life-span developmental psychology.* New York: Academic Press, 1970.

Robin, A., Armel, S., & O'Leary, K. D. The effects of self-instruction on writing deficiencies. *Behavior Therapy*, 1975, **6**, 178–187.

Robin, A., Schneider, M., & Dolnick, M. The turtle technique: An extended case study of self-control in the classroom. In K. D. O'Leary & S. G. O'Leary (Eds.), *Classroom management: The successful use of behavior modification* (2nd ed.). Oxford: Pergamon, 1977.

Robertson, D., & Keeley, S. *Evaluation of a mediational training program for impulsive children by a multiple case study design.* Paper presented at the meeting of the American Psychological Association, New Orleans, August 1974.

Schleser, R. *Individual differences in response to self-instructional training.* Paper presented at the annual meeting of the Association for Advancement of Behavior Therapy, Los Angeles, November 1982.

Schleser, R., Meyers, A. W., & Cohen, R. Generalization of self-instructions: Effects of general versus specific content, active rehearsal, and cognitive level. *Child Development*, 1981, **52**, 335–340.

Schleser, R., & Thackwray, D. Impulsivity: A clinical-developmental perspective. *School Psychology Review*, 1982, **11**, 42–46.

Snyder, J., & White, M. The use of cognitive self-instruction in the treatment of behaviorally disturbed adolescents. *Behavior Therapy*, 1979, **10**, 227–235.

Spivack, G., Platt, J., & Shure, M. *The problem-solving approach to adjustment.* San Francisco: Jossey-Bass, 1976.

Spivack, G., & Shure, M. *Social adjustment of young children.* San Francisco: Jossey-Bass, 1974.

Stone, G., Hinds, W., & Schmidt, G. Teaching mental health behaviors to elementary school children. *Professional Psychology*, 1975, **6**, 34–40.

Thackwray, D., Meyers, A. W., Schleser, R., & Cohen, R. *Achieving generalization with self-instructions: Effects on teacher-referred academically deficient children.* Paper presented at the annual meeting of the Association for Advancement of Behavior Therapy, Los Angeles, November 1982.

Urbain, E. S., & Kendall, P. C. Review of social-cognitive problem-solving interventions with children. *Psychological Bulletin*, 1980, **88**, 109–143.

Vygotsky, L. S. *Thought and language.* New York: Wiley, 1962.

Watson, J. B., & Raynor, R. Conditioned emotional reactions. *Journal of Experimental Psychology*, 1920, **3**, 1–14.

Weissberg, R. P., & Gesten, E. Considerations for developing effective school-based social problem-solving (SPS) training programs. *School Psychology Review*, 1982, **11**, 56–63.

Weissberg, R., Gesten, E., Carnrike, C., Toro, P., Rapkin, B., Davidson, E., & Cowen, E. Social problem-solving skills training: A competence-building intervention with second- to fourth-grade children. *American Journal of Community Psychology*, 1981, **9**, 411–423. (a)

Weissberg, R., Gesten, E., Rapkin, B., Cowen, E., Davidson, E., Flores-de-Apodaca, R., &

McKim, B. The evaluation of a social problem-solving training program for suburban and inner-city third-grade children. *Journal of Consulting and Clinical Psychology*, 1981, **49**, 251–261. (b)

Wilson, G. T. Psychotherapy process and procedure: The behavioral mandate. *Behavior Therapy*, 1982, **13**, 291–312.

Linking Social-Cognitive Processes with Effective Social Behavior: A Living Systems Approach

MARTIN E. FORD

School of Education
Stanford University
Stanford, California

ADVANCES IN COGNITIVE–BEHAVIORAL RESEARCH
AND THERAPY, VOLUME 3

I. INTRODUCTION

Therapy is an interpersonal process in which the primary objectives are to resolve intrapsychic conflict and to promote more effective behavior on the part of clients. In many cases, effective social behavior is of central concern, and cognitive interventions are important therapeutic tools. In such cases therapy can be appropriately construed as an effort to improve or enhance the social-cognitive processes of clients so that they may be more effective in their everyday social interactions and social relationships.

From this premise follows a crucial research question: Do social-cognitive skills contribute to effective social behavior? Surprisingly, relatively little effort has been invested in this problem either theoretically or empirically. Although a few prominent exceptions can be nominated from branches of psychology directly concerned with the promotion of behavioral competence (primarily clinical and industrial psychology), basic theory and research in cognitive social psychology and social-cognitive developmental psychology have clearly been focused primarily on the question of how people acquire, process, and represent social information rather than on the question of how people use this information to guide their social behavior. For example, Flavell and Ross (1981) have commented that the link between social cognition and social behavior "remains almost virgin terrain for the developmentalist" (p. 314). This impression is confirmed in Shantz' recent comprehensive review of the field of social-cognitive development, which devotes only a few of its many pages to the question of how social cognition impacts social behavior (Shantz, 1983). Similarly, Nisbett and Ross (1980) introduced their summary of the field of cognitive social psychology by noting that

> We . . . say little about precisely *how* people's judgments affect their behavior. This is neither an oversight nor a deliberate choice. We simply acknowledge that we share our field's inability to bridge the gap between cognition and behavior, a gap that in our opinion is the most serious failing of modern cognitive psychology. . . . There is surely no more important task for cognitive psychologists than to bring . . . noncognitive response classes under their theoretical umbrella. (p. 11–12)

There appear to be two major reasons for the historical and current emphasis on cognitive rather than behavioral outcomes of social-cognitive processing. First, methodologically it is usually easier to study cognitive dependent variables than social behavioral dependent variables. Cognitive dependent variables can often be assessed using verbal reports or simple nonsocial behavioral responses such as pushing a button on a response device or checking a line on a questionnaire.

Alternatively, even though these types of assessments are sometimes used in research on social competence, social behavioral dependent variables can usually only be validly assessed by observing interactions in settings that have some ecological validity or by asking people who have had the opportunity to make such observations (e.g., peers, parents, the subject) to provide knowledgeable ratings. Even these procedures may not be adequate, as validity is often significantly threatened by observer or rater biases (M. Ford, 1982). Consequently, measures of social-cognitive processes are relatively abundant compared to those pertaining directly to social behavioral effectiveness (Butler & Meichenbaum, 1981; Kendall, Pellegrini, & Urbain, 1981). Furthermore, measures of social competence that are available typically focus on younger age groups in which social behavior can be more readily observed for lengthier periods of time (e.g., young children are more likely to be in a single classroom throughout a school day and school year, and are less likely to be concerned about issues such as privacy and confidentiality). Thus, this measurement obstacle has been especially acute with regard to adolescent and adult populations.

The second plausible explanation for the lack of research dealing with the impact of social-cognitive processes on social behavior is that very few contemporary psychological theories speak directly to this question. Shantz (1983) also noted this problem in her review, concluding that "There is not specific and detailed theory guiding the research on social-cognitive/social-behavior relations" (p. 526). For example, causal attribution theories have very little to say about the behavioral consequences of attributions (Nisbett & Ross, 1980; Weiner, 1979). Information-processing theories also typically focus on the construction and maintenance of cognitive representations rather than the ways in which cognitive processes shape behavior (Flavell, 1974). Behavioral outcomes of social-cognitive processing are also of secondary concern for cognitive developmental theories such as Kohlberg's theory of moral development and Selman's theory of interpersonal awareness. Fortunately, cognitive theories that have developed within the clinical psychology literature have been somewhat more attentive to the cognition–behavior link. This is especially evident in the various manifestations of cognitive social learning theory (e.g., Bandura, 1977; Mischel, 1973; Thoresen & Mahoney, 1974). Nevertheless, even these theories do not provide a complete picture of the cognitive processes involved in social interactions. In each case the tendency has been either to focus on a relatively narrow subset of the relevant processes (e.g., Bandura, 1977; Beck, 1976), or to provide a somewhat more comprehensive list of relevant processes without clearly specifying the ways in which these processes are organized (e.g., Meichenbaum, 1977; Mischel, 1973).

II. AN ALTERNATIVE CONCEPTUAL FRAMEWORK: DONALD FORD'S LIVING SYSTEMS THEORY

A. Overview

Although these brief descriptions do not adequately characterize the significant contributions each of the cognitive theories mentioned above has made to our understanding of human functioning and development, there is nevertheless a clear need for an integrative conceptual framework that focuses on the ways in which the full range of social-cognitive processes are organized to direct, control, and regulate social behavior. The primary purpose of this article is to describe such a framework, or more specifically, to describe those parts of a more general framework relevant to the topic of this article. This framework is a recently developed version of living systems theory that seeks to integrate various streams of influence focusing on the need to adequately characterize the complexly organized nature of living systems such as humans (e.g., Allport, 1960; Baltes, 1979; Baltes, Reese, & Lipsitt, 1980; Bronfenbrenner 1977, 1979; Jantch, 1980; Koestler, 1967; Lerner, 1978; Maturana, 1975; Miller, 1978; Powers, 1978; Riegel, 1976; vonBertalanffy, 1968). Donald Ford, the theorist attempting this imposing integrative effort, is a clinical psychologist with a long-standing concern for the need to somehow combine the scientist's regard for empirical verification and methodological sophistication with the therapist's regard for the richness and subtlety of human experience (Ford & Urban, 1963; D. Ford, 1984). This is of course precisely the theme underlying the cognitive–behavioral approach to research and therapy (Kendall & Hollon, 1979).

Just as the cognitive–behavioral approach to psychotherapy has been described as "a joining of forces rather than a break for independence" (Kendall & Hollon, 1979, p. 6), living systems theory can perhaps be best construed as a heuristic tool for organizing the many useful ideas that have been offered in the various literatures dealing with social cognition and social behavior. Indeed, the integrative power of this approach has already been illustrated, both with regard to adolescent social competence (M. Ford, 1982) and children's communication development (McDevitt & Ford, 1983). Thus, although living systems theory is much more than a simple summation of previous theoretical parts, it would clearly be inappropriate to construe it as a new entry in some contrived theoretical competition. As an integrative conceptual framework, living systems theory is in many respects congruent with existing theories of cognitive functioning and development. In fact, some of these theories, namely those at lower levels of abstraction that deal with more detailed aspects of functioning in specific system components or in specific content domains, will no doubt be necessary to help explicate the general framework described here. Nevertheless, it is important that these "mini-theories" be developed in the context of a larger framework that adequately characterizes the organized complexity of human behavior and human development (D. Ford, 1984).

B. Basic Concepts

A system is essentially any set of units with relationships among them (Miller, 1978). At least some of these relationships must be nontrivial to make it useful to construe the units as components of a system. One type of system is an open system, which is characterized as such because it must exchange energy, materials, and/or information with its environment in order to continue functioning. A living system is a special kind of open system possessing autopoietic (self-constructing) properties (Maturana, 1975). That is, living systems are able to take energy, materials, and information and transform them in order to increase the size and complexity of their structure and functioning, as well as release energy, materials, and information into the environment in order to create consequences favorable to the system and to get rid of waste products that might produce consequences unfavorable to the system. This description implies that there is a strong interdependence between living systems such as humans and their contexts. That is, in order for people to function effectively in their environment there must be both a skillful person and a responsive environment (e.g., Bandura, 1982). Thus, efforts to promote social competence may need to include both "competence building" interventions, such as those that stimulate cognitive restructuring or train specific social skills, and "social reform" interventions, such as those that create social support networks or provide opportunities or incentives for effective social behavior (Albee, 1980).

The physical structure and organization of living systems makes possible four sets of functions which D. Ford (1984) has described as follows:

1. *Biological functions:* Growth, maintenance, operation, and repair of the biological structure; energy production.
2. *Transactional functions:* Exchange of materials essential for biological functioning; body movement and other energy exchange processes; information collection and transmission.

3. *Arousal functions:* Varying the amount, rate, or intensity of system activity to meet situational demands.

4. *Governing functions:* System organization and coordination—direction, control, and regulation of behavior; information processing; information storage.

A representation of the governing, transactional, arousal, and biological subsystems and some of the most important ways in which they interact is given in Fig. 1.

Social-cognitive processing generally refers to the functioning of the governing subsystems in contexts involving interpersonal transactions. Consequently, most of this article is devoted to an explication of the governing subsystems' contributions to effective social behavior.[1] However, one must recognize that all four subsystems are continuously interacting with each other and their environments in a dynamic stream, so that while it is possible and often useful to disentangle these interdependent components in order to conceptually understand and empirically identify their unique characteristics, one takes the risk of losing important information about the ways in which they are organized. Thus, although the strategy of this article is to conceptually disentangle different types of social-cognitive processes in order to consider their individual contributions to social competence, a serious effort is made to point out the limitations of this strategy and the importance of "trying to put Humpty Dumpty back together again" (D. Ford, 1984).

C. Overview of the Governing Subsystems: A Functional Taxonomy of Social-Cognitive Processes

1. Directive Process

This process defines desired (and undesired) consequences toward which the person's activity is to be directed and coordinated. A therapist interested in a client's directive cognitions might ask, "What can I help you accomplish?" "What do you want to happen (or to avoid)?" "What outcomes do you hope for (or fear)?" "What's important to you?" "What kind of a person do you want to be?" "Why do you do

---

[1]In this article the term *behavior* is used to refer to the transactional functions, as is the tradition in much of psychology, although in his presentation of the living systems framework D. Ford (1984) makes a cogent argument for using the term *behavior* to refer to all types of human functioning.

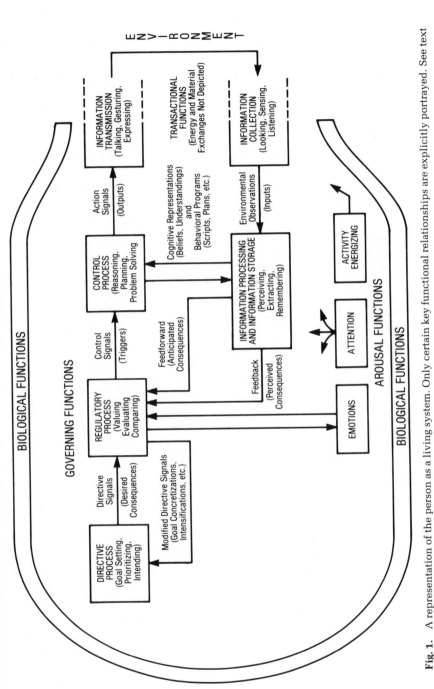

Fig. 1. A representation of the person as a living system. Only certain key functional relationships are explicitly portrayed. See text for further details. (Modified from D. Ford, 1984.)

what you do?" "What do you intend to do next?" "What are your goals? Your priorities?"

In an ongoing stream of activity, a cognition representing a desired consequence may be activated by a variety of mechanisms. For example, a prosocial goal may be activated by perceived or anticipated situational demands, remembered states or experiences that were pleasurable or rewarding in the past, learned emotional associations with real or imagined objects or events, biological impulses, and so forth. These mechanisms may or may not involve conscious or rational thought; consequently, it is sometimes difficult for people (especially children) to verbalize their goals or bring them into awareness. Indeed, this may be one of the therapist's most important tasks, since it is virtually impossible to effectively help people accomplish their goals if it is not clear what those goals are (cf. Locke, Shaw, Saari, & Latham, 1981). This does not mean that goals must be in awarenesss to efficiently direct behavior; much of cognitive functioning is not (and need not) be represented in consciousness (D. Ford, 1984). However, when people are having difficulty accomplishing their objectives, it may become important to try to represent those objectives in consciousness in order to help produce more efficiently organized behavior.

Living systems theory assumes that most behavior is goal directed. In some cases a person's goals might tend to be transient or unstable, but this does not mean that their behavior is not generally directed by goals. It simply means that their goals are more likely to be set and pursued reactively (i.e., by responding to situational opportunities or pressures) rather than actively (i.e., by shaping or creating situations that will provide desired consequences). In such cases one useful goal of therapy might be to increase a client's goal directedness.

For a systems theorist, accepting the validity of a directive process is crucial to understanding the overall functioning of a system. Without such a process, systems would be unable to "stay a steady course" in the face of varying environmental conditions. In some cases the goals may be built in when the system is created (as in the case of an infant with a caretaker-seeking goal); however, living systems, because they have autopoietic capabilities, may also create goals in the course of their transactions with the environment. In either case, the directive process is a necessary component of effective system functioning.

The omission of directive cognitions may be the most important limitation of therapies based on Skinnerian theory. Both living systems theory and operant conditioning theory emphasize the idea that people generally behave in order to obtain desired consequences. However, whereas the assumption of operant conditioning theory is that the consequences (i.e., the inputs) control behavior (i.e., the outputs), living systems theory assumes that we behave in order to control our consequences (i.e., outputs control inputs) (Powers, 1973). In other words, systems theorists operate on the premise that people both shape and are shaped by their contexts in mutual interaction (D. Ford, 1984). Thus, unless they permanently alter a person's natural environments (i.e., unless they create social reform), therapies based on operant conditioning principles—including those that allow for cognitive mediational processes—are likely to be effective in creating lasting changes in behavior only if they produce a lasting change in the person's ability to attain their "intrinsic" goals through competence-building techniques (e.g., by enhancing self-efficacy or teaching new methods for goal attainment).

2. Regulatory Process

This process evaluates the degree to which a person has achieved, is achieving, or is likely to achieve desired outcomes, as well as the degree to which various means that were used, are being used, or are being considered to attain these goals meet certain criteria such as social acceptability, situational appropriateness, and efficiency. A therapist interested in a client's regulatory cognitions might ask, "Where do you stand with respect to your goals?" "How does what you want to happen compare with what's currently happening?" "Do you think you can get what you want?" "How do you feel about yourself?" "How do you think you compare to other people?" "Are your methods of goal attainment efficient (e.g., are there some undesired side effects)?" "Are your methods of goal attainment situationally appropriate? Socially acceptable? Ethical?"

Evaluations of goal-directed behavioral progress or potential progress are conducted by comparing cognitions representing desired outcomes with those representing actual or anticipated outcomes. Evaluations of behavioral means are conducted by comparing cognitions representing desired characteristics of behaviors (e.g., effectiveness, situational appropriateness, social acceptability) with cognitions representing the characteristics of actual or anticipated means to goal attainment. The results of these evaluations are used to either (1) trigger cognitive and behavioral activity intended to improve one's goal-seeking and rule-following efforts, or (2) inhibit activity if the desired consequences are evaluated as unattainable due to constraints imposed by personal inefficacy, environmental unresponsiveness, regulatory rules, and so forth.

Two types of information may be used to make evaluations of one's goal-seeking and rule-following efforts, and of persons and situations in general: feedback, which is obtained from the environment, and feedforward, which is obtained from within the system. Examples of feedforward include self-efficacy expectations (Bandura, 1982) and stimulus-outcome and behavior-outcome expectancies (Mischel, 1973). Thus, feedforward is future oriented, representing anticipated outcomes rather than actual consequences. Because social life involves both consistency and unpredictability, the combined use of feedback and feedforward greatly enhances the efficiency and adaptiveness of living systems.

Since social behavior is often directed toward multiple goals, and is typically guided by a wide variety of personal and social rules, social competence is highly dependent on the effective functioning of the regulatory process. This is especially true when the various goals and rules are not all compatible (the usual case). In such instances the regulatory process becomes a kind of cost–benefit analyzer responsible for making decisions about what goals to pursue and what means to use to pursue them. For example, the pursuit of a social relationship goal may involve task goals, self-esteem goals, sex-role rules, ethical rules, rules concerning the appropriate use of language, rules for showing respect and deference, rules pertaining to one's personal appearance, and so forth.

This use of multiple goals and rules underlines the difficulty of assessing an individual's social competence. When there is more than one criterion that can be used to evaluate a given behavior pattern, it becomes possible for the observer and the subject (or the therapist and client) to disagree about the behavior's effectiveness. For example, individuals with a strong concern for interpersonal harmony may view assertive behavior less favorably than therapists who train such behavior (Wine, 1981). Conversely, highly ambitious or competitive individuals may often behave in ways that are personally satisfying but also hurtful, unfair, or selfish from an observer's perspective. Some impulsive people may also be quite satisfied with their behavior despite social disapproval. Thus, while behavior that appears to be ineffective may indicate a deficit in the person's ability to regulate his or her behavior along relevant dimensions, it may also simply indicate a lack of agreement about what dimensions are relevant.

Good decision making requires not only the effective use and weighting of multiple evaluative criteria, but also the availability of reliable information about the current and probable future status of the system with regard to each of these criteria. Many cognitive and cognitive–behavioral therapies have made this latter problem their primary focus of intervention. This is true, for example, of therapies designed to enhance self-efficacy expectations (Bandura, 1982), as well as those that focus on cognitive distortions that may yield inaccurate feedback or feedforward information (e.g., Beck, 1976). Such interventions are likely to be particularly effective in cases in which social incompetence results primarily from deficits in behavioral regulation skills rather than behavioral control skills (see below).

One other important feature of the regulatory process is that it is the primary antecedent of emotional arousal (see Fig. 1). In other words, living systems theory asserts that most emotional responses are triggered by evaluations of perceived, remembered, or imagined persons, objects, or events that are relevant to goal-seeking and rule-following efforts already in progress or activated by the situation. These emotions may then serve a regulatory function by helping to activate or inhibit cognitive and behavioral activity (D. Ford, 1984). For example, frustration or anger energizes behavior so that one can deal more effectively with obstacles to goal attainment. Helplessness or depression inhibits activity so that one will not continue to pursue goals that are unattainable. Guilt may serve a similar function for goals that are considered unacceptable. Positive emotions such as interest, satisfaction, and hope may also promote effective behavior by energizing new goal-seeking behavior or maintaining ongoing goal attainment efforts. Thus, emotions are generally adaptive. In fact, they appear to have an evolutionary basis, although in evolutionary terms they are probably a more primitive form of regulation than cognitive regulation (D. Ford, 1984). Of course, emotions that are overamplified or overgeneralized across situations or across time are likely to eventually produce negative behavioral consequences. Emotions may also be maladaptive if they are based on inaccurate evaluations. However, since humans are capable of cognitive as well as emotional regulation of behavior, emotional problems such as phobias or chronic depression may be highly responsive to therapies that promote accurate evaluations and/or evaluative cognitions incompatible with the problematic emotion (e.g., self-efficacious thoughts, relaxing thoughts, thoughts about attainable goals).

3. Control Process

This process is responsible for the construction and selection of cognitive representations and behavioral plans relevant to goals that have been activated by the directive process, within the constraints imposed by the regulatory process. A therapist interested in a client's control cognitions might ask, "What could you do to get what you want?" "What do you usually do?" "What else could you do?" "Are there better ways to get what you want?" "How do you go about solving this kind of problem?" "How do you find out what you need to know?" "What do you do when something goes wrong?" "How do you make yourself feel better?" "How can you get one thing without giving up the other?"

M. Ford (1982) has distinguished between two major types of control processes. *Representation construction* control processes must be used when producing desired consequences requires means for increasing one's understanding of a person or event. For example, role taking can be used to better understand another person's point of view, and causal attributions can be made to help explain why an event occurred. However, *behavioral planning* control processes must also be used when producing desired consequences requires means for successfully transacting with the environment. For example, getting someone to provide a desired service or resource requires a plan such as making a verbal request or suggesting a bargain. Of course, impoverished cognitive representations and inaccurate cognitive theories may lead to the selection or construction of ineffective or maladaptive behavioral plans. Nevertheless, control processes that provide enriched social-cognitive representations may sometimes be unnecessary for effective social behavior. One may often behave competently with only a simple or superficial understanding of a situation. Indeed, it would be difficult to cope with everyday social life if every situation required conscious, effortful social inferencing processes. Even in relatively complex social contexts one may often behave effectively by simply relying on previously learned scripts or plans activated by directly observable situational or social cues. Thus, sophisticated representation construction processes such as role taking and theory testing may be useful primarily in contexts involving unfamiliar people or uncertain or unexpected events (i.e., in contexts in which adequate representations do not already exist).

A related feature of representation construction control processes is that they will rarely be sufficient for social competence. No matter how profound or complete one's understanding of a person or social event, one cannot behave effectively if appropriate social scripts or plans are not available or cannot be invented. Moreover, the information needed to guide behavior is generally only a small subset of that which is available in one's social environment and which is likely to be cognitively represented. Nisbett and Ross (1980) have commented on this issue in their book on social judgment processes.

> It seems clear that many inferences have no behavioral consequences or result in only inconsequential behavior. In fact, it seems likely that this is true for the great majority of our beliefs and inferences, whether correct or incorrect. (p. 269)

A related point is made by Harrison (1975). He asserts that not only do people typically guide their behavior using minimal information, they also do not know how to efficiently use rich data even when they have them.

This characterization of what has become the central focus of basic theory and research in social cognition suggests that the study of representation construction processes may be a difficult area in which to find strong or consistent links between cognition and behavior. If such relationships do exist, they are likely to be found only when the belief or understanding helps one construct more effective behavioral plans, or when it helps regulate behavior by serving as feedback (i.e., by helping the individual gauge behavioral progress) or feedforward (i.e., by helping the individual decide whether to inhibit to activate behavior).

In contrast to representation construction control processing, in which influence on behavior is theoretically indirect and idiosyncratic, behavioral planning control processes are likely to make a stronger contribution to social competence than perhaps any other set of social-cognitive processes because they directly precede behavior and serve the function of enhancing the probability that one's behavior will produce desired outcomes. In some cases this function may be accomplished simply by selecting an appropriate plan of action that has already been developed and stored in memory. These kinds of plans, which are often automated and consequently may require little attention or awareness, may be stored in the form of specific event patterns (i.e., scripts; Abelson, 1976) or in the form of more general or less elaborate behavior-outcome expectancies (Mischel, 1973).

However, since most people experience extensive variability in their contexts, and since relatively few situations will be without some unique properties that must be considered in one's behavioral planning, it is usually unwise to rely completely on habituated plans (e.g., Langer, Blank, & Chanowitz, 1978). There is a constant need to develop new plans and update old ones. As noted above, the success of these plans may depend in some instances on sophisticated representation construction control processes; nevertheless, social insight is often unaccompanied by and unnecessary for effective social behavior. In contrast, social problem-solving activity is not only much more likely to be accompanied by behavior, it is also more likely to be a prerequisite for social competence since its function is to produce effective behavioral sequences. Thus, from a living systems theoretical perspective, the ability to resourcefully think of means for controlling environmental inputs to the system—whether they involve single motoric acts or complex behavioral patterns, or whether they are general strategies or specific step-by-step solutions—is likely to be strongly related to effective social behavior.

4. Information Processing and Information Storage

Information-processing and storage capabilities allow humans to go beyond their genetically preprogrammed instructions to develop new or improved ways of thinking, feeling, and behaving. These capabilities include the perceiving, filtering, extracting, integrating, storing, and recalling of information. These processes may also involve the control function, since it is responsible for allocating available information and information-processing resources. Together, then, these foundational processes provide humans with their unique capability for acquiring and elaborating goals, rules, understandings, emotional associations, and behavioral programs that were not initially built into the system (D. Ford, 1984).

Because all other social-cognitive processes rely on information-processing and storage capabilities, it is difficult to evaluate the unique contribution of this latter set of processes to effective social behavior. They are clearly important in a fundamental sense, since at least a minimal level of basic perceptual and/or memory skills are required to effectively engage the social environment. Nevertheless, living systems theory would predict that, in general, these processes would play a secondary, supportive role rather than a primary role in the production of socially competent behavior. That is, even though skills such as perceiving contextual details and remembering seldom encountered names and faces may be required for goal attainment in some social situations, information-processing and storage skills can by themselves really only help resolve the preliminary problem of supplying an adequate data base from which goals, rules, and expectations may be selectively activated and plans developed. Their central role is to enhance social learning rather than social competence. In this respect they are similar to the more inferential representation construction processes described under the control function rubric.

5. Summary

This effort to link social-cognitive processes with effective social behavior suggests that one must adopt a differentiated view of social cognition in order to meaningfully address this issue. Living systems theory appears to be a very useful conceptual framework in this regard, in that it provides a taxonomy of social-cognitive processes differentiated by their function. In general, the framework suggests that social-cognitive processes that are used to produce desired *cognitive* consequences (i.e., processes such as person perception, role taking, and causal attribution) will account for little of the variance in measures of social behavioral effectiveness because the influence of these processes on behavior is indirect and because they often are used simply to promote social understanding. Alternatively, social-cognitive processes that are used to produce desired *behavioral* consequences (i.e., processes such as social goal setting, social decision making, and social problem solving) should be strongly related to indices of social behavioral effectiveness because of their focus on action and accomplishment. This relationship should be particularly strong for behavioral planning control processes when the measure of social competence has a strong "skill" (i.e., problem-solving) component; alternatively, when the outcome measure is focused primarily on motivational factors such as behavioral inhibition, behavioral persistence, or conformity to social rules, the regulatory process should be of primary importance. Since the directive process theoretically has its influence on behavior through its impact on the regulatory and control processes, its relationship to social competence should be of intermediate magnitude.

These hypotheses are highly researchable, and the central objective of the next section is to explore selected research literatures that address these propositions. However, it is useful to keep in mind the principle that all of these social-cognitive processes are interrelated components of a larger system. Consequently, they typically are not functioning in a completely autonomous fashion. Thought often occurs in "packages" of goals, plans, expectancies, perceptions, memories, etc. This of course has significant consequences for research methodology and the interpretation of research results. Moreover, it also suggests the possibility that interventions to enhance social-cognitive skills may be designed to take advantage of the natural interrelationships among various social thought processes.

III. THE CONTRIBUTION OF DIFFERENT TYPES OF SOCIAL-COGNITIVE PROCESSES TO EFFECTIVE SOCIAL BEHAVIOR

A. Basic Premises and Limitations

Research on social cognition and social behavior is scattered throughout a variety of literatures and subdisciplines; moreover, there is a great diversity of labels and organizing rubrics used to characterize this research. Consequently, any review of these literatures must necessarily be selective, highlighting certain individuals and topics and neglecting others that are potentially relevant and deserving. The review that follows will be no exception. It should therefore be interpreted not as an attempt to exhaustively catalog all relevant studies, but rather as an effort to describe the general thrust of research findings in each category of the functional taxonomy outlined above by providing some particularly salient examples of these findings.

Of course, the validity of the conclusions that result from this strategy depends on the representativeness of the examples selected. The possibilities for theoretical bias are numerous and should be carefully considered in evaluating the conclusions described below. Exacerbating this potential problem is the lack of good data for some categories in the social-cognitive taxonomy as well as the almost total absence of data directly comparing the contributions of different types of social-cognitive processes to effective social behavior. Nevertheless, there is a growing body of evidence that can be brought to bear upon the social cognition–social behavior question, and this evidence limits to some extent the degree to which living systems theory might unintentionally serve as a biased conceptual filter rather than as a useful organizing heuristic.

As implied in the preceding paragraph, there has been more research done on some social-cognitive processes than others. Consequently, the hypotheses tested in the illustrative studies cited below are not necessarily at equivalent stages of development in terms of either conceptual sophistication or empirical support. Related to this point is the problem of trying to categorize studies that do not fit neatly into the living systems taxonomy. In some cases investigators have not differentiated social cognitions by their function (e.g., cognitive developmental theorists are often more interested in the overall organization of social-cognitive processes), and in other cases their concepts are simply fuzzy or ambiguous. Finally, like social cognition, social competence is neither a unidimensional nor a well-explicated concept. There are many different criteria one can use to define competence or effectiveness. Moreover, deciding what criteria to apply always involves value judgments. These judgments may be based on the welfare of the individual (i.e., internal system equilibration), the welfare of the individual's social context (i.e., equilibration between the system and its environment), or both (D. Ford, 1984). Therefore, the contribution of different types of social-cognitive processes to effective social behavior may depend to some extent on the criteria one uses to define effectiveness.

Two other qualifying factors should be kept firmly in mind when interpreting the results described below. First, although social-cognitive processes are theoretically of central importance for social competence, they are clearly not the whole story. For example, arousal processes (selective attention, emotional lability, etc.) and transactional processes (motor skills, speech skills, etc.) may also play a crucial role in a variety of social outcomes. Thus, one should not expect social-cognitive processes to account for all of the variance in social competence. Second, the contribution of different kinds of social-cognitive processes to effective social behavior may change with age and/or experience. For example, it seems likely that basic information-processing and storage skills might be of greater salience for children than for adolescents or adults, since early cognitive development seems to involve dramatic changes in memory capacity and in the efficiency of basic cognitive processing (e.g., Chapman, 1981; Ford & Keating, 1981) as well as more gradual changes in skills with an apparently more extended developmental course (e.g., M. Ford, 1982; Spivack, Platt, & Shure, 1976). Similarly, poor social performances in contexts where one has had little or no experience may be primarily attributable to simple knowledge deficits rather than to more generalized problems in the regulation or control of one's social behavior. Thus, the question of where and how to cognitively intervene in order to effectively promote competent social behavior is very much a developmental question. Early on it may be necessary to invest a sizable portion of one's efforts in helping a person acquire the basic building blocks of social interaction, namely, information regarding the fundamental rules, goals, meanings, and patterns of social life. However, living systems theory predicts that as social learning and cognitive development progress, and especially as a child's capabilities for self-direction, self-regulation, and self-control increase, it will become increasingly true that the more direct and more effective strategy for promoting social competence will be to teach social goal-setting, social decision-making, and social problem-solving skills.

B. The Directive Function and Effective Social Behavior

After a lengthy period characterized by a bias toward behavioristic conceptions and a concern about teleological implications, there is finally emerging a sizable and coherent literature on goal-related processes (e.g., Locke et al., 1981; Wadsworth & Ford, 1982). However, perhaps because there are almost no measures of social goals or social goal-setting processes, the number of studies focusing on social goal-related processes is startlingly low. Moreover, only a few of these studies have tried to relate directive social cognitions to indices of social competence. Therefore, the evidence described in this section should be considered preliminary and not really extensive enough to warrant confident conclusions. Two concepts related to the directive function are considered, goal setting and goal hierarchies.

1. Goal Setting

Locke et al. (1981) assert that "the beneficial effect of goal setting on task performance is one of the most robust and replicable findings in the psychological literature" (p. 145). They review evidence showing that challenging goals nearly always lead to more effective behavior than easy goals, as do specific goals in comparison with vague goals or no goals. Locke et al. attribute these impressive results to the pervasive effects of goal setting. They explain that goals affect performance by directing attention and action, by mobilizing energy expenditure and interest, by motivating strategy development, and by increasing behavioral persistence. Klinger (1975, 1977) adds to this list by noting that "goal commitment" also increases one's sensitivity to goal-related stimuli and makes goal-related thoughts more available. Thus, consistent with a living systems view, the activation of personally meaningful directive cognitions appears to enhance behavioral effectiveness by instigating and maintaining coordinated activity from all components of the system.

Unfortunately, it is not yet clear whether the well-documented association between goal setting and task performance is generalizable to social goals and accomplishments. M. Ford (1982) addressed this question using a 16-item scale assessing adolescents' tendency to set goals, to be aware of their goals, and to effortfully persist in attempting to reach their goals. He found that "goal directedness" accounted for a significant, although modest, portion of the variance in measures of adolescents' ability to behave effectively in challenging or stressful social situations (approximately 10% in the more heterogeneous sample used in this study). This positive result was obtained even though the measure of goal directedness did not specifically pertain to social goals. In order to test the possibility that the strength of the relationship between goal setting and social competence may have been underestimated in the M. Ford (1982) study as a result of this global measurement strategy, Ford, Burt, and Bergin (1984) constructed a new measure of social goal directedness and related it to eight different types of social competence: individuality, belongingness, self-determination, social responsibility, superiority, equity, acquiring resources, and providing resources. Overall, the results of this study suggest that goal-setting skills may be associated with many different types of social competence, although it does not appear that focusing the assessment of these skills specifically on social goals substantially increases the resulting correlations (i.e., these skills may be fairly traitlike).

2. Goal Hierarchies

This attribute of the directive function refers to the ways in which individuals prioritize multiple goals when they are in conflict or when an individual can choose to invest his or her limited time and energy resources in different types of activities and achievements. Goal hierarchy conceptualizations have been very useful to psychologists working in a variety of areas, including, for example, vocational interests (Holland, 1973; Strong, 1943), values (Rokeach, 1968), and human motivation (Maslow, 1943). However, despite the fact that many of these goal hierarchies include a social component (e.g., Holland's social personality type; Maslow's love and esteem needs), they have generally not been studied in terms of their possible impact on social behavioral effectiveness. This may be an important omission, since as Shantz (1983) has commented, "social information and understanding . . . can be used for social good or ill" (p. 526).

Several recent studies have tried to fill this empirical gap by more directly addressing the hypothesized relationship between social goal investment and social competence. Jennings (1975) assessed "people vs object orientation" in a sample of 38 nursery school children, and found that children high in object orientation scored higher on tests of physical knowledge, while children high in people orientation scored higher on measures of peer popularity, peer leadership, and getting along with others. However, not all of these latter correlations were significant, leading the author to comment that these children "might be described as more congenial although not necessarily more effective in their interactions with others" (p. 517). M. Ford (1982) also examined the relationship between interest in social goals and social competence in his two high-school-aged samples, as did Ford and Tisak (1982) in their study evaluating a social-cognitive skill training program for adolescents. In each case greater interest in social goals was associated with a greater ability to handle challenging social situations. These correlations, all of which were significant, ranged from .21 to .36.

Very few studies have tried to test the social goal investment hypothesis by contrasting different types of social goals, although this may be a stringent test of the hypothesis. In one potentially relevant study, Gerson and Damon (1978) found that inconsistencies between moral behavior and moral reasoning in a distributive justice situation could be accounted for in part by taking into account the child's goals. They observed that children at similar levels of reasoning behaved quite differently depending on whether they gave priority to self-assertive goals such as acquiring resources or to integrative goals such as equity or social responsibility (the latter group was much less likely to give themselves a disproportionately large share of the resource being distributed). Ford, Burt, and Bergin (1984) also tried to explore the effects that preferences for self-assertive or integrative goals might have on adolescents' social competence, with their overall results providing fairly consistent support for the hypothesis that individuals assigning high priority to a goal are likely to be more effective in accomplishing that goal.

Despite these encouraging results, the correlations between social goal importance and social success seem to be a bit lower than one might expect given the reliable and extensive effects of goal setting on performance described by Klinger (1975, 1977) and Locke et al. (1981). A recent study conducted by Wadsworth (1982) and D. Ford (personal communication, February 1982) may shed some light on this problem. They examined male college students' and middle-aged blue-collar workers' priorities for accomplishing self-defined goals in various life domains over both short and extended periods of time. Although the focus of this study was on comparing the goal hierarchies of the two groups to test certain developmental hypotheses, these researchers discovered in informal follow-up interviews that despite many consistencies between goals and behavior, stated priorities sometimes did not match up well with an individual's actual accomplishments. The results of these interviews suggest that goals promote behavioral effectiveness only to the extent that they are actually used to guide behavior. In some cases a personally important goal may lie dormant either because the individual has failed to think about it or because there are few opportunities to pursue it. The interviews also appeared to serve a useful counseling function in that they explicitly brought to the subjects' attention the discrepancies between their desired and actual behavioral consequences. This impression is consistent with research indicating that goal setting must be accompanied by feedback before it will have any beneficial effects on performance (Locke et al., 1981).

C. The Regulatory Function and Effective Social Behavior

According to living systems theory, three conditions must be met in order for the regulatory process to effectively guide social behavior: (1) socially appropriate goals and rules must be activated and used as criteria for evaluating or predicting behavioral accomplishments, (2) good information about current and future behavioral accomplishments must be available so that accurate evaluations and predictions can be made, and (3) evaluations of social ineffectiveness must trigger emotions that arouse the system to respond in ways that will help promote more effective social behavior. This section is organized around these three topics. A fairly respectable body of evidence has accumulated on the latter two of these three aspects of regulatory functioning; less is known about the behavioral consequences of failing to activate and use socially appropriate rules and goals.

1. Activation and Use of Relevant and Acceptable Social Rules and Goals

The study described earlier by Wadsworth (1982) and D. Ford (personal communication, February 1982) seems relevant to this issue. Although some subjects' goal attainment problems appeared to be attributable to a failure to attend to their goals (a directive process concern), other cases seemed to be better described in terms of self-regulatory deficits. That is, some subjects seemed to have given certain high-priority goals a great deal of thought and yet were not using them to guide their behavior. This pattern was associated with the habituated pursuit of short-term goals along with an increasing dissatisfaction regarding failures to attain long-term goals.

Also relevant to this issue is recent work on the kinds of goals and rules typically associated with common social situations (Argyle, Graham, Campbell, & White, 1979; Graham, Argyle, & Furnham, 1980). These researchers argue that socially inadequate people may simply be unaware of what goals or rules are appropriate in a given situation. However, it seems likely that this knowledge-deficit explanation may be valid only in a narrow range of circumstances. As Argyle et al. (1979) note, it is primarily socially inexperienced people who are ignorant or mistaken about the rules that apply in a given social situation. Also, the most important social rules (e.g., be friendly, be polite, don't hurt or embarrass people) tend to be fairly universal (Argyle et al., 1979) and learned at a very early age (Hogan, 1973). Situation-specific rules, although there are many (Argyle et al., 1979), are almost all of the less obligatory social convention type (Turiel, 1983). Thus, most serious failures to follow social rules are likely to be problems of self-regulation rather than information storage failures. A possible exception to this generalization is noted by Pressley (1979), who concluded that rule statement rationales are effective in promoting young children's social competence. This position is of course consistent with the developmental hypothesis stated earlier in the article.

Research on the impact of using or failing to use one important category of social rules—moral rules—to guide behavior has been plagued by an overreliance on a theoretical framework not really designed to answer this question, Kohlberg's cognitive developmental theory. As Colby (1978) has explained, "the relationship of the . . . structural aspects of moral judgment to moral conduct . . . is not completely clear. That is, the answers to the broader questions are not contained within the stage construct itself" (p. 103). As a result, research on the relationship between moral judgment processes and moral behavior is characterized by a great deal of inconsistency and controversy (Blasi, 1980). Nevertheless, there are indications that individuals' active use of moral rules may have considerable impact on the effectiveness of their social behavior. For example, in a study of first graders' social competence, Enright and Sutterfield (1980) obtained significant correlations between several measures of social success and Damon's moral judgment measure, which assigns high (levels one and two) and low (level zero) scores to individuals using and not using moral rules, respectively. O'Leary (1968) and Monahan and O'Leary (1971) found that increasing the salience of a rule prohibiting cheating through self-verbalization was effective in reducing the incidence of cheating behavior in this same age group. In a somewhat different kind of study, Klass (1980) found that sociopaths tended to view victimizing behaviors as causing less self-discrepancy than either normal subjects or nonsociopathic methadone outpatients, suggesting that the sociopaths were less likely to use moral rules to evaluate the adequacy of their behavior (since a comparison of a moral rule with an immoral action should produce conceptual discrepancy). Finally, Smetana (1981) found that one could accurately predict the abortion decisions of pregnant unmarried women by determining whether they used moral rules to evaluate the appropriateness of having an abortion. In this study 91% of those who continued their pregnancy viewed abortion as a moral issue, while only 19% of those who had an abortion did so. Of course, which of these behavioral choices is viewed as more "effective" depends on one's evaluative criteria. In any case, these results indicate that under some circumstances there may be a very strong connection between social rule usage and behavioral outcomes.

2. Adequacy of Feedback and Feedforward Information

A fundamental prerequisite for successful goal attainment, at least in situations involving active problem solving, is the ability to collect and effectively use relevant and accurate information regarding behavioral progress. This monitoring capability involves a composite of skills, including the efficient allocation of attentional resources, the accurate deployment of information collection and social perception skills, and the ability to use feedback to regulate goal-directed behavior. Although most of the work demonstrating the importance of monitoring skills has been done with regard to nonsocial tasks, Flavell and colleagues have convincingly shown that monitoring is an important factor in the development of at least one kind of social competence as well, namely, communicative competence (Flavell, Speer, Green, & August, 1981).

Another way in which feedback-related processes may help social competence is by correcting cognitive distortions and biases that lead to the maladaptive activation or inhibition of behavior. However, Nisbett and Ross (1980) have summarized evidence showing that people tend to selectively search for and attend to data that confirms rather than corrects their existing theories and beliefs (i.e., they often do not use feedback information effectively when feedforward information is already available). This same tendency has been described by Beck (1976) with regard to the cognitive maintenance of depression. Thus, although little effort has been made to explicitly relate susceptibility to this confirmatory bias to indices of social competence (Nisbett & Ross, 1980), it seems likely that people who are more open to new information might be better able to effectively regulate their social behavior (e.g., Brophy, 1982).

In contrast to the paucity of social competence research focusing on the use of social feedback, there has been a virtual explosion of evidence during the past decade documenting the central role that two types of feedforward information, perceptions of control and perceptions of competence, have in promoting social adaptation. Although it is beyond the scope of this article to review all of the studies linking effective social behavior with perceptions of self-determination and self-efficacy, three major patterns of results can be summarized (M. Ford, 1983). The first pattern shows that individuals who perceive themselves as competent, controlling agents are generally more effective on a wide range of criteria. For example, locus of control research shows that "internals" tend to make greater efforts to master and cope with their environments, are less susceptible to social influences, are better able to delay gratification, and are generally more active and independent (Lefcourt, 1976, 1981; Phares, 1976). Children with an internal locus of control are also less likely to show passivity, withdrawal, and depressive symptomatology (Rothbaum, Wolfer, & Visintainer, 1979). Phares (1976) remarks that "internals seem to be more disposed toward behavior that will enhance their personal efficacy, even in the sense of rectifying inadequacies" (p. 66).

Research on social self-efficacy also confirms and contributes to this pattern of findings. Wheeler and Ladd (1982) obtained significant correlations ranging from .21 to .67 between children's self-efficacy for social interactions with peers and three peer- and teacher-rated measures of social competence. Ford and Tisak (1982) obtained a correlation of .39 ($p < .01$) between adolescents' social self-esteem and a composite measure of their ability to behave effectively in challenging or stressful social situations. Moe and Zeiss (1982) also found consistent relationships between self-efficacy strength and the Social Avoidance and Distress Scale. Finally, Kazdin (1979) found that self-efficacy reliably predicted the degree of clients' improvement in assertive behavior in a covert modeling treatment study. Of course, negative perceptions of social self-efficacy would not necessarily be problematic if they accurately reflected individuals' behavioral capabilities. However, French (1982) has shown that at least for lonely college students, the association between self-derogation of social abilities and poor social problem solving tends to disappear with practice, suggesting that perceptions of social inefficacy may often be more of a self-fulfilling prophecy than a realistic estimate of future behavioral possibilities.

The second and third patterns of results linking social behavioral effectiveness with perceptions of control and competence are frequently confounded. In one case, perceptions of control are weak, but self-efficacy tends to remain at moderately high levels. This pattern is typically associated with environments in which powerful others are in control. In the other case, perceptions of both competence and control are at low levels. This pattern is typically associated with environments that are consistently unresponsive and in which it is more difficult to exercise "secondary control" strategies such as vicarious or predictive control (Rothbaum, Weisz, & Snyder, 1982). Deci (1980) refers to these two patterns as the extrinsic and amotivational systems, respectively, while others have referred to them as the reactance and learned helplessness models (e.g., Wortman & Brehm, 1975).

These two patterns of regulatory functioning have only recently been conceptually and empirically separated (Bandura, 1982; Ford, 1983; Levenson, 1981; Rothbaum, 1980; Wortman & Brehm, 1975). This advance has made it possible to observe that the amotivational pattern is much more likely to be associated with generalized social ineffectiveness. Although Rothbaum (1980) has linked these patterns to the two major clinical syndromes in children (antisocial aggression and passive withdrawal), Levenson (1981) notes that "a powerful other orientation may, under some circumstances, involve realistic perceptions that are associated with purposeful action" (p. 31). Thus, interventions to promote increased perceptions of control and competence should be sensitive to the constraints imposed by limited personal resources and environmental opportunities (Bandura, 1982; Rothbaum et al., 1982).

This caution is appropriate since an increasing number of clinical studies are focusing on the need to increase clients' perceptions of self-determination and self-efficacy. In general, this research shows that "negative self-referent ideation contributes to inadequate performance in a variety of situations" (Meichenbaum, Butler, & Gruson, 1981, p. 40). Although much of this work has focused on nonsocial tasks, there is sufficient evidence to suggest that this generalization holds for social situations as well. For example, Thorpe (1974) found that altering beliefs and self-statements about assertion was as effective as skill-training procedures in promoting assertive behavior. In a similar study, Glass, Gottman, and Shmurak (1976) obtained results that actually favored a self-statement modification approach to enhancing dating skills. Moreover, Glass, Merluzzi, Biever, and Larsen (1982) have provided validity results for a self-statement questionnaire that directly link these cognitions to measures of social behavioral effectiveness. Finally, Fiedler and Beach (1978) have concluded that expectations about the consequences of a proposed action predict unassertiveness and social incompetence better than the subjects' behavioral repertoire.

There is consistent evidence that the behavioral inadequacies apparently caused by these self-regulatory deficits are primarily a function of negative rather than positive self-statements (Kendall & Korgeski, 1979). Schwartz and Gottman (1976) found that medium- and high-assertive subjects tended to have many positive but very few negative self-statements, while low-assertive subjects had moderate amounts of both. Similarly, Cacioppo, Glass, and Merluzzi (1979) observed that men high in heterosocial anxiety were especially likely to generate negative self-evaluative statements. An experimental study by Mandel and Shrauger (1980) is also consistent with these results; they found that subjects asked to concentrate on self-critical statements took longer to initiate conversation and spent less time conversing than those subjects asked to concentrate on self-enhancing thoughts. One may speculate that since humans appear to be intrinsically motivated to engage their environments to produce desired effects (Deci, 1980; White, 1959), the major concern with regard to the use of self-referent feedforward should be to promote people's natural inclination to actively pursue their social goals by helping them "unlearn" patterns of negative self-evaluation.

3. *Emotional Responsiveness to Goal*
   Attainment Failures

This requirement for effective regulatory functioning can be illustrated by again referring to the three patterns of self-referent perceptions described above. Except in extreme cases of generalized environmental unresponsiveness, it is adaptive to respond to goal attainment failures with activating rather than inhibiting emotions. This may involve increased efforts to attain the goal as a consequence of frustration or anger (the extrinsic pattern), or it may involve a redirection of interest and pleasure in alternative goals (the intrinsic pattern). These generally adaptive patterns stand in sharp contrast to the amotivational pattern, which is associated with emotions such as depression, apathy, and helplessness. As noted earlier, this third pattern of functioning is strongly linked to socially ineffective behavior.

Another type of emotion that is often aroused in problematic social situations is empathy. However, empathy is unique in that its function appears to be to activate responses intended to help other people overcome obstacles to goal attainment (Clarke, 1980; Hoffman, 1977; Estrada, 1982). Thus, the degree to which evaluations of social distress arouse empathic emotions may be a crucial factor in an often underrated type of social competence, prosocial behavior (Wine, 1981; M. Ford, 1981).

Evidence supporting the hypothesized association between empathy and prosocial behavior has been slow to accumulate because of fundamental disagreements about what empathy is and how one should assess it (Estrada, 1982). Despite these problems, there are indications that empathic responsiveness may be an exceptionally good predictor of integrative social achievements. M. Ford (1982) found very strong correlations in two adolescent samples between a behaviorally validated measure of empathy (Hogan's Empathy Scale) and a measure of social competence heavily weighted with prosocial content (r = .31–.50). Feshbach (1978) has obtained impressive results demonstrating the effectiveness of an empathy training program in reducing aggressive behavior in inner-city children. Experimental research in this area has also consistently supported the relation between empathic arousal and prosocial behavior (Hoffman, 1977).

These exciting results appear to confirm the prediction made earlier that the regulatory process may play a key role in social accomplishments that have a strong motivational basis. However, prosocial behavior may also have a significant "skill" component, as indicated by the need to view these results from a developmental perspective. Whereas research with adolescents and adults consistently supports the hypothesized link between empathy and prosocial behavior, there are about as many studies with children that show no such relationship as there are those that do (e.g., Eisenberg-Berg & Lennon, 1980; Strayer, 1980). Hoffman (1977) concludes that "very young children typically respond empathically to another's distress but often do nothing or act inappropriately, probably because of their cognitive limitations" (p. 202). Hoffman also argues that females are generally somewhat more empathic than males, which may explain the apparent tendency for women to be more prosocial than men (Estrada, 1982).

D. Representation Construction Control Processes and Effective Social Behavior

For many researchers the processes involved in constructing cognitive representations of social objects and events are what is meant by "social cognition." Consequently, there has been more theorizing and more research on this category of social-cognitive processes than on all of the others combined. This is certainly appropriate if one considers the goal of social cognition to be an increased understanding of social phenomena. However, if social-cognitive understanding is viewed primarily as a means to the goal of behaving more effectively, then other social-cognitive processes that might contribute to effective social behavior should be receiving more attention, unless of course, there is a uniquely strong relationship between representation construction skills and social competence. In fact, although there is not yet enough comparison data to draw firm conclusions, it appears that, if anything, representation construction skills may have less impact on behavior than other social-cognitive processes. This conclusion will be illustrated using research conducted under two broad rubrics, role taking and belief formulation.

1. Role Taking

Most studies conducted with normal populations have found low, equivocal relationships between role-taking skills and effective social behavior (Kurdek, 1978; Shantz, 1975, 1983). For example, in a study by Deutsch (1974), preschoolers' communicative role-taking ability was related to positive social behavior but not to popularity. Rubin (1972) also found no relationship between egocentric communication and popularity. Rothenberg (1970) has reported correlations between "social sensitivity" and peer, teacher, and self-ratings of social competence in third- and fifth-graders that are positive but inconsistent in terms of statistical significance. Complex, inconsistent results were also obtained with normal children in a study relating "interpersonal awareness" to a sociometric index and several teacher-rated measures of behavioral problems and competencies (Selman, Jaquette, & Lavin, 1977).

Training studies provide a similar, although somewhat more positive picture of the relationship between role taking and social competence. However, in each case it seems very likely that other skills besides role-taking ability were trained. For example, the partially successful use of role-playing techniques reported by Staub (1971) and Iannotti (1978) to enhance children's prosocial behavior may have worked primarily by teaching prosocial "scripts." This interpretation is consistent with Iannotti's data showing that some experimental subjects did not improve in role-taking ability and that the effects of treatment did not extend to a measure of aggression. Similarly, in Chandler's often cited studies demonstrating the effectiveness of a film-making intervention in promoting social competence, it seems likely that both empathic arousal and social problem-solving skills may have been influenced by the enactment of problematic social situations and the subsequent discussion of the videotapes (Chandler, 1973; Chandler, Greenspan, & Barenboim, 1974). Thus, although role-taking skills did improve following the film-making intervention, it is not clear whether this produced the observed improvements in social adjustment. Moreover, a replication of these studies conducted by Little (reported in Urbain & Kendall, 1980) found role-taking improvements that were not significantly greater than an attention control group and no apparent effects on social behavior.

Another interpretation of the Chandler (1973) and Chandler et al. (1974) results is that they were successful primarily because they involved clinical populations. As Little and Kendall (1979) note, "role-taking deficits are common among nonnormal groups of children" (p. 96). Affleck (1975a,b, 1976) has consistently found significant differences in role-taking ability between mentally retarded and nonretarded samples and between children varying in the extent of their retardation. Selman (1976) has also reported highly significant and developmentally increasing deficits in clinic children's interpersonal awareness skills compared to matched controls. And in the previously cited study by Selman et al. (1977), results for clinic children were much more consistent with expectations regarding social behavioral effectiveness than those involving normal children.

Perhaps the strongest evidence for the hypothesis that role taking plays a secondary role in promoting socially competent behavior comes from studies that directly compare the predictive power of representation construction control processes with behavioral planning control processes. These studies consistently show that the ability to cognize specific plans for resolving interpersonal difficulties is more strongly related to effective social behavior than the ability to infer or understand other people's thoughts and feelings. These results have been obtained in studies with preschoolers (Shure, 1979), with school-aged children (Pellegrini, 1980; Shure, 1980b), and with adolescents (Ford & Tisak, 1982). Other studies support these data by showing that role-taking processes have little impact on prosocial behavior unless they arouse empathic emotions (Coke, Batson, & McDavis, 1978). Of course, this does not mean that representation construction processes are unimportant. For example, Pellegrini (1980) found that the lowest levels of peer-rated social competence were associated with children who had deficits in both means–ends thinking and interpersonal awareness skills. Nevertheless, these results suggest that interventions to enhance representation construction skills are likely to be most appropriate for individuals with relatively large deficits in social competence.

2. Belief Formulation

In contrast to research on role-taking skills, most of which has been done by developmental psychologists, work in the area of belief formulation has been done primarily by social psychologists interested in causal attributions and theory-testing processes. As with role taking, little of the extensive research in this area has been directed toward the goal of exploring links between cognition and behavior (Nisbett & Ross, 1980). In fact, the available evidence is not really all that relevant to the hypothesis that skill in constructing rational beliefs contributes to effective social behavior. Instead, most of this research has focused on the regulatory function of beliefs (i.e., the use of beliefs as feedforward information in guiding behavior). For example, Ames, Ames, and Garrison (1977) have observed that high social status children tend to make causal attributions that protect their perceptions of competence and control, namely, external attributions for negative interpersonal outcomes and internal attributions for positive interpersonal outcomes.

One study that speaks indirectly to the question of whether the formulation of rational beliefs is important for social behavioral effectiveness is a study by Lewinsohn, Larson, and Muñoz (1982) on the cognitions of depressed individuals regarding depression-related events and general world events. They found that compared to nondepressed individuals, depressed people were more pessimistic about themselves but not about the world in general, and subscribed to more depression-related irrational beliefs but not more irrational beliefs in general. Thus, although the validity of depression as an index of social competence may be limited, these results suggest that belief formulation skills may be rather task specific and therefore unlikely to have consistent or generalizable effects on social adjustment. However, if a particular irrational belief is being frequently used as a behavioral guide (i.e., if it serves an important regulatory function), then the consequences for behavioral effectiveness could be rather dramatic.

A study congruent with these descriptions has been reported by Dodge (1980), who presents evidence suggesting that aggressive school-aged children interpret victimizing actions differently than nonaggressive children. In this study both groups reacted aggressively to clearly hostile actions and inhibited aggressive behavior when the victimization was clearly unintentional. However, when the intent was ambiguous, aggressive children reacted as if there was hostile intent while the nonaggressive children reacted as if the act was unintentional. This tendency to systematically make distorted attributions about frustrating social events appears to be a factor in maintaining aggressive behavior patterns. However, this attributional bias does not extend to victimizing actions involving other people, and it appears to have some basis in fact in that aggressive children are frequently targets of aggression (Dodge & Frame, 1982). Thus, the attributional bias of aggressive children does not appear to be interpretable as a general lack of skill in formulating accurate beliefs.

E. Behavioral Planning Control Processes and Effective Social Behavior

Planning skills have only recently been incorporated under the rubric of social-cognitive skills and treated as a theoretically important topic for study (Forbes & Greenberg, 1982). Consequently, we know relatively little about precisely how planning influences behavior and even less about the development of planning skills, even though "planning is so fundamental to the fabric of everyday experience that understanding its origins, components, and ways of developing is essential" (Pea, 1982, p. 5). However, one thing that does seem clear is that there is a strong relationship between behavioral planning skills and effective social behavior. Three relevant research topics will be used to support this conclusion: social problem-solving skills, self-control strategies, and social scripts.

1. Social Problem Solving

The taxonomy of "interpersonal cognitive problem-solving" (ICPS) skills developed by Spivack, Platt, and Shure has been the major stimulus for research in this area (Spivack et al., 1976; Spivack & Shure, 1974; Shure & Spivack, 1978). This taxonomy includes five skills: sensitivity to interpersonal problems, alternative thinking, means–ends thinking, consequential thinking, and causal thinking. The first skill is rarely studied, perhaps because it is operationalized as a simple information retrieval task. Alternative thinking, the ability to generate alternative plans of action, and means–ends thinking, the ability to specify step-by-step solutions to interpersonal problems, are the most frequently studied ICPS skills, the ones most uniquely associated with the control process, and the ones most strongly related to social competence. Causal thinking appears to be closely related to means–ends thinking in that the subject must specify a series of events that leads to a given outcome, although in this case the outcome has already occurred and is not necessarily positive. Finally, consequential thinking seems to be less a measure of the control process than of the regulatory process in that its function is to provide accurate feedforward information so that the effectiveness of proposed plans can be evaluated before they are implemented.

Spivack, Platt, and Shure have obtained results documenting the importance of social problem-solving skills for social adjustment with remarkable regularity. Many of the studies conducted during the early years of their research program concentrated on showing that psychiatric patients and emotionally disturbed individuals are deficient in means–ends thinking and other ICPS skills compared to normal control samples (e.g., Platt & Spivack, 1972a, 1973, 1974; Platt, Spivack, Altman, Altman, & Peizer, 1974; Shure & Spivack, 1972; Siegel, Platt, & Peizer, 1976). Some of these studies also successfully linked means–ends thinking with degree of impairment within groups of psychiatric patients (e.g., Platt & Spivack, 1972b). A number of other studies with preschool and school-aged children convincingly demonstrated that the relationship between ICPS skills and social adjustment could be extended to normal samples as well (Spivack et al., 1976; Spivack & Shure, 1974).

It appears that different ICPS skills are associated with social competence at different ages, presumably because their cognitive developmental requirements vary to a considerable degree (Spivack et al., 1976). In early childhood alternative thinking is by far the best predictor of social behavioral effectiveness, with consequential thinking a distant second. Means–ends thinking and causal thinking, which both require more detailed planning skills, are apparently too difficult for this age group. Middle childhood marks the emergence of means–ends thinking as an important predictor of social competence (e.g., Pel-

legrini, 1980), and by adolescence both causal and consequential thinking begin to show some predictive power (M. Ford, 1982; Ford & Tisak,
1982). However, alternative thinking is no longer significantly associated with effective social behavior in adolescence and adulthood
(Spivack et al., 1976; Ford & Tisak, 1982).

Recent work by Shure and Spivack has advanced this data base yet
one step further by demonstrating that training in ICPS skills is associated with increased social competence (Shure & Spivack, 1978, 1980).
The significance of these results is increased by several additional findings: (1) the best results of training occur when the trainers are themselves high in ICPS skills (Shure & Spivack, 1978), (2) children whose
ICPS skills do not increase as a result of training do not improve behaviorally (Shure & Spivack, 1980), and (3) improvements in social adjustment are maintained for at least a year or more (Shure, 1980). Moreover,
as Spivack, Platt, and Shure have shown throughout their research
program, these results cannot simply be attributed to the influence of
general intelligence.

This review glosses over some important issues in the conceptualization, measurement, and training of social problem-solving skills (see
Butler & Meichenbaum, 1981; Kendall et al., 1981; and Urbain & Kendall, 1980, for reviews and critiques of this literature). Nevertheless,
one cannot help but be impressed at the consistency and strength of the
data, not all of which have come from the Spivack, Platt, and Shure
research program. Correlations in the .30s and .40s between means–
ends thinking and various indices of social competence have been obtained in a number of independent studies (M. Ford, 1982; Pellegrini,
1980; Ford & Tisak, 1982). Only slightly lower correlations have been
reported for other social problem-solving skills (Enright & Sutterfield,
1980; M. Ford, 1982; Ford & Tisak, 1982). In addition, group comparison studies have shown significant deficiencies in means–ends thinking in lonely people (French, 1982), depressed university students
(Gotlib & Asarnow, 1979), and pregnant teenagers (Steinlauf, 1979).
Finally, a number of intervention studies have provided encouraging
results linking social problem-solving skills with decreases in aggression and increases in prosocial behavior and communication skills
(Camp & Bash, 1980; Sarason, 1981; Urbain & Kendall, 1980; Zahavi &
Asher, 1978).

2. Self-Control Strategies

Self-control competencies are frequently equated with self-regulatory skills; however, from a living systems theoretical perspective they
each refer to rather distinct functional capabilities. Self-regulation refers to one's ability to evaluate an act as "good" or "bad" and to use this

evaluation to initiate efforts to activate or inhibit such action, as appropriate. Alternatively, self-control refers to one's ability to actually create and implement an effective plan of action. Although the distinction is sometimes fuzzy due to the organized nature of a person's functioning, the distinction is a theoretically important one.

Self-control capabilities appear to make very important contributions to effective social behavior. This is most clearly demonstrated in the research programs of Mischel, Patterson, and Moore on the development of strategies for resisting temptations and waiting for delayed rewards (Mischel, 1981; Mischel & Patterson, 1976, 1979; Moore, 1977; Patterson & Mischel, 1975, 1976). These researchers have shown that even preschoolers can behave competently in these situations if they are provided with an effective plan (e.g., a self-distraction or cognitive transformation strategy). However, at this early age there is little spontaneous use of self-control strategies (Pressley, 1979). This suggests that developmental improvements in social competence may be attributable in part to children's increasing ability to create or use effective strategies for controlling their own behavior (Mischel, 1981), especially since knowledge of an effective strategy is a good predictor of self-control behavior (Mischel, 1981; Mischel & Patterson, 1976, 1979; Pressley, 1979).

Two recent studies involving much more general assessments of social competence than those used in the experimental studies cited above support the hypothesized importance of self-control strategies for effective social behavior. Humphrey and Kirschenbaum (1981) found a significant relationship between preschoolers' ability to tolerate noxious stimulation and teacher ratings of social competence. Even more impressive are longitudinal findings reported by Mischel (1983) showing strong and consistent correlations between a laboratory measure of the ability to delay gratification in preschool and parent ratings of social competence at adolescence. Parents of preschoolers who were able to delay gratification for longer periods considered their children (as adolescents) to be, among other things, more resourceful in initiating activities, more likely to be admired and sought out by other children, more self-assertive, more dependable, and better able to handle stress. These results suggest that children with good self-control skills early in life may profit from this resource throughout their development.

3. Social Scripts

Scripts can be construed as habituated or well-rehearsed plans of action, the availability of which should help free cognitive and attentional resources for other concerns. Because scripts would presumably not be created if they did not usually work, script accuracy may not be a particularly salient issue. However, one might expect script availability to be an important factor in producing socially effective behavior. Unfortunately, there is little evidence that can be directly brought to bear on this hypothesis. However, its plausibility is enhanced by developmental studies that show that despite the fact that "young children do not appear to be very skilled negotiators of uncharted social territory" (Nelson, 1981, p. 112), they are surprisingly competent in their everyday social interactions. Nelson (1981) suggests that this is due to the availability of learned scripts that effectively guide behavior in more familiar social situations. Thus, even though young children are not cognitively capable of generating detailed plans for goal attainment (recall the developmental evidence regarding means–ends thinking described above), they do appear to be capable of gradually building up fairly complex plans that enable them to behave effectively. Nelson (1981) concludes that

> it seems clear that children's knowledge of the social world is script based and may remain at that level for many years . . . this level enables the child to enter competently into social relationships. . . . Indeed, it seems a fair speculation that most of us operate at this level much of the time. (p. 116)

It is important to note that because living systems theory regards attention or consciousness as an arousal process rather than a part of the governing subsystems, script retrieval is considered to be every bit as "cognitive" in functional terms as creative planning. Thus, even though we often do not need to "think" (in terms of conscious awareness) before we act (Thorngate, 1978), effective social behavior always depends on the capable functioning of the control process. Whether one wishes to use the term *planning* to describe social script retrieval is fairly arbitrary—for example, school-aged children distinguish between "ritual" and "creative" plans and often regard only the latter as a "genuine" plan (Pea, 1982). What is important is that effective social behavior appears to be closely associated with the availability of relevant, workable plans, whether they be "new" or "used."

F. Information-Processing and Information Storage Capabilities and Effective Social Behavior

As noted earlier, these processes are so intimately linked with the other governing subsystems that it is difficult to sensibly evaluate their unique contributions to social adaptation. Needless to say, some foundation of information manipulation skills is needed to carry out any of the other cognitive functions. Nevertheless, it appears that developmental improvement in the efficiency of these skills reduces their importance in terms of accounting for social competence variance soon after early childhood, as planning and decision-making skills begin to carry more of the explanatory weight. This is similar to competence in other domains. For example, information retrieval efficiency loses its power to predict verbal ability by adulthood (Ford & Keating, 1981). Athletic competence operates in the same way; once you get to the big leagues, most of the variance in performance is accounted for by mental factors and highly technical skills rather than basic motor competencies.

1. Information Processing

In addition to the probable importance of these capabilities for young children's social competence (Chapman, 1981; M. Ford, 1979), there is evidence that this category of skills may be important for older individuals with gross deficits in social adjustment. Argyle (1981) nicely summarizes this research:

> Mental patients and people with inadequate social skills are often deficient in person perception. . . . Schizophrenics have been found to be poor at decoding nonverbal signals. . . . Manic and paranoid patients are notorious for the inaccuracy of their perception of events, and delinquents have been found to be very insensitive—failing to recognize either approval or annoyance in others. (p. 266)

2. Information Storage

It seems clear that socially incompetent behavior can occur even for the most skilled individuals when they lack knowledge of the goals and rules that apply in a given social situation (Argyle et al., 1979; Graham et al., 1980). However, this is probably not the main problem in most cases of generalized social ineffectiveness. For example, Schwartz and Gottman (1976) found that individuals low in assertive skills were just as knowledgeable about appropriate social behavior in assertive situations as those high in assertive skills. Hogan (1973; Hogan, Johnson, & Emler, 1978) has gone so far as to drop knowledge of moral rules as an explanatory dimension in his theory of moral development. Probably more important to the development of social competence than acquisition of content is the increased complexity of social planning and decision making that is made possible by developmental gains in memory capacity. For example, Forbes, Katz, Paul, and Lubin (1982) note that "children may only gradually acquire the ability to store plans that are organized on multiple levels" (p. 62).

IV. IMPLICATIONS FOR RESEARCH AND THERAPY

Although a number of implications and conclusions have been mentioned throughout this article, several key ideas are worthy of reemphasis. Each of these points follows from the premise that people are complexly organized systems with multiple components that function both semiindependently and interdependently to help create desired consequences for the person.

1. *Social behavioral effectiveness and ineffectiveness cannot be explained by any single social-cognitive process.* It seems clear that simplistic, unidimensional approaches to social-cognitive research and therapy are likely to be less effective than multidimensional approaches. This does not mean that one must embrace an incoherent eclecticism, but it does require that one adopt something like the living systems approach described here. Even though this framework does not specify all of the details of a person's functioning (that would clearly be beyond the scope of any theory), it does help one keep in mind all of the major functional attributes of the person (D. Ford, 1984). This is an especially important point for psychotherapists, who unlike researchers cannot choose to deal with something other than the person as the unit of functioning. However, it also suggests the need for multivariate research strategies, since one cannot fully understand the functioning of a system component without understanding the contexts in which it functions.

2. *Different types of social-cognitive interventions can be effective in promoting social competence; there is no one "right" method.* Because the person is a complexly organized unit, one could potentially create the same effects by intervening at a variety of different points in the system (the "equifinality" principle). This does not mean that all treatments will be equally effective for each type of social competence problem (see points 3–5 below), but it does suggest that artificial theoretical and therapeutic competitions that seek generalized "winners" and "losers" should be avoided. In fact, a multidimensional therapeutic repertoire may be essential for treating people with widespread deficits in social skills.

3. *Social-cognitive processes that are closely linked to behavior should be given special emphasis.* This of course assumes that one's objective is to promote effective social behavior. Given this premise, both living systems theory and the available evidence support the conclusion that social-cognitive processes that are directly concerned with behavioral output, especially those related to behavioral regulation and control, should be prime targets for social competence research and

practice. Social-cognitive researchers have overemphasized and perhaps overestimated the role of social inferencing processes in the development of social competence. They are not unimportant; however, therapies that teach social goal-setting, decision-making, and planning skills may have stronger and more consistent effects on behavior.

4. *Social-cognitive interventions must be sensitive to developmental processes.* Young children and people with severe deficits in social competence appear to have limited capabilities for understanding their social world. Since a minimum level of skill in perceiving, remembering, and interpreting social objects and events is needed to effectively engage situations requiring some degree of self-direction, self-regulation, and/or self-control, very different types of interventions may be appropriate for these groups. Basic component skills should be firmly in place before attempting to train more complex social-cognitive capabilities.

5. *Social-cognitive therapies should be prescriptive.* The previous point illustrates the need for a prescriptive approach. However, even more specific efforts to identify optimal targets for intervention may be needed when a person's skill deficits are limited to relatively specific kinds of situations or problems. For example, immoral or noncompliant behavior may require empathy training or practice in rule usage. Aggressive behavior may be more directly influenced by teaching social problem-solving or self-control skills. Unassertive behavior may be primarily attributable to low perceptions of control or competence. In any case, it seems evident that "as yet none of our treatments can be sufficiently powerful to help all or almost all types of people" (Goldstein, Sparfkin, Gershaw, & Klein, 1980, p. 7).

These conclusions underline both the "main effects" and the "interactions" in social-cognitive research and therapy. Some processes are probably better for producing effective social behavior, but there are several important exceptions, and the details always depend on the individual client. Nevertheless, it appears that one can be confident that effective social behavior will depend in large part on the adequacy of a person's social-cognitive processes. Indeed, we have only barely begun to understand some of the most exciting linkages between social cognition and social behavior.

ACKNOWLEDGMENT

The author wishes to thank Donald Ford for giving his permission to publish in this article a short abstract of his remarkable conceptual framework, which will be published elsewhere in book form in its entirety.

REFERENCES

Abelson, R. P. Script processing in attitude formation and decision making. In J. S. Carroll & J. W. Payne (Eds.), Cognition and social behavior. Hillsdale, NJ: Erlbaum, 1976.

Affleck, G. G. Role-taking ability and interpersonal conflict resolution among retarded young adults. American Journal of Mental Deficiency, 1975, **80,** 233–236. (a)

Affleck, G. G. Role-taking ability and the interpersonal competencies of retarded children. American Journal of Mental Deficiency, 1975, **80,** 312–316. (b)

Affleck, G. G. Role-taking ability and the interpersonal tactics of retarded children. American Journal of Mental Deficiency, 1976, **80,** 667–670.

Albee, G. W. A competency model must replace the defect model. In L. A. Bond & J. C. Rosen (Eds.), Competence and coping during adulthood. Hanover, NH: Univ. Press of New England, 1980.

Allport, G. W. The open system in personality theory. Journal of Abnormal and Social Psychology, 1960, **61,** 301–311.

Ames, R., Ames, C., & Garrison, W. Children's causal ascriptions for positive and negative interpersonal outcomes. Psychological Reports, 1977, **41,** 595–602.

Argyle, M. The contribution of social interaction research to social skills training. In J. D. Wine & M. D. Smye (Eds.), Social competence. New York: Guilford, 1981.

Argyle, M., Graham, J. A., Campbell, A., & White, P. The rules of different situations. New Zealand Psychologist, 1979, **8,** 13–22.

Baltes, P. B. Life-span development psychology: Some converging observations on history and theory. In P. B. Baltes & O. G. Brim, Jr. (Eds.), Life-span development and behavior (Vol. 2). New York: Academic Press, 1979.

Baltes, P. B., Reese, H. W., & Lipsitt, L. P. Life-span developmental psychology. Annual Review of Psychology, 1980, **31,** 65–110.

Bandura, A. Self-efficacy: Toward a unifying theory of behavior change. Psychological Review, 1977, **84,** 191–215.

Bandura, A. Self-efficacy mechanism in human agency. American Psychologist, 1982, **37,** 122–147.

Beck, A. T. Cognitive therapy and emotional disorders. New York: Int. Univ. Press, 1976.

Blasi, A. Bridging moral cognition and moral action: A critical review of the literature. Psychological Bulletin, 1980, **88,** 1–45.

Bronfenbrenner, U. Toward an experimental ecology of human development. American Psychologist, 1977, **32,** 513–531.

Bronfenbrenner, U. The ecology of human development: Experiments by nature and design. Cambridge, MA: Harvard Univ. Press, 1979.

Brophy, J. Research on the self-fulfilling prophecy and teacher expectations. Paper presented at the annual meetings of the American Educational Research Association, New York, March 1982.

Butler, L., & Meichenbaum, D. The assessment of interpersonal problem-solving skills. In P. C. Kendall & S. D. Hollon (Eds.), Assessment strategies for cognitive-behavioral interventions. New York: Academic Press, 1981.

Cacioppo, J. T., Glass, C. R., & Merluzzi, T. V. Self-statements and self-evaluations: A cognitive-response analysis of heterosocial anxiety. Cognitive Therapy and Research, 1979, **3,** 249–262.

Camp, B., & Bash, M. A. Developing self-control through training in problem solving: The "Think Aloud" program. In D. P. Rathjen & J. P. Foreyt (Eds.), Social competence: Interventions for children and adults. Oxford: Pergamon, 1980.

Chandler, M. J. Egocentrism and antisocial behavior: The assessment and training of social perspective-taking skills. *Developmental Psychology*, 1973, **9**, 326–332.

Chandler, M. J., Greenspan, S., & Barenboim, C. Assessment and training of role-taking and referential communication skills in institutionalized emotionally disturbed children. *Developmental Psychology*, 1974, **10**, 546–553.

Chapman, M. Egocentrism and mental capacity: A NeoPiagetian analysis. In J. A. Meacham & N. R. Santilli (Eds.), *Social development in youth: Structure and content.* Basel: Karger, 1981.

Clarke, K. B. Empathy: A neglected topic in psychological research. *American Psychologist*, 1980, **35**, 187–190.

Coke, J. S., Batson, C. D., & McDavis, K. Empathic mediation of helping: A two-stage model. *Journal of Personality and Social Psychology*, 1978, **36**, 753–766.

Colby, A. Evolution of a moral-developmental theory. In W. Damon (Ed.), *New directions for child development: Moral development.* San Francisco: Jossey-Bass, 1978.

Deci, E. L. *The psychology of self-determination.* Lexington, MA: Lexington Books, 1980.

Deutsch, F. Observational and sociometric measures of peer popularity and their relationship to egocentric communication in female preschoolers. *Developmental Psychology*, 1974, **10**, 745–747.

Dodge, K. A. Social cognition and children's aggressive behavior. *Child Development*, 1980, **51**, 162–170.

Dodge, K. A., & Frame, C. L. Social cognitive biases and deficits in aggressive boys. *Child Development*, 1982, **53**, 620–635.

Eisenberg-Berg, N., & Lennon, R. Altruism and the assessment of empathy in the preschool years. *Child Development*, 1980, **51**, 552–557.

Enright, R. D., & Sutterfield, S. J. An ecological validation of social cognitive development. *Child Development*, 1980, **51**, 156–161.

Estrada, P. *Empathy and prosocial behavior in adolescence.* Unpublished manuscript, Stanford University, School of Education, June 1982.

Feshbach, N. D. *Empathy training: A field study in affective education.* Paper presented at the annual meetings of the American Educational Research Association, Toronto, March 1978.

Fiedler, D., & Beach, L. R. On the decision to be assertive. *Journal of Consulting and Clinical Psychology*, 1978, **46**, 537–546.

Flavell, J. H. The development of inferences about others. In T. Mischel (Ed.), *Understanding other persons.* Oxford: Blackwell, 1974.

Flavell, J. H., & Ross, L. Concluding remarks. In J. H. Flavell & L. Ross (Eds.), *Social cognitive development: Frontiers and possible futures.* London and New York: Cambridge Univ. Press, 1981.

Flavell, J. H., Speer, J. R., Green, F. L., & August, D. L. The development of comprehension monitoring and knowledge about communication. *Monographs of the Society for Research in Child Development*, 1981, **46**(5, Serial No. 192).

Forbes, D. L., & Greenberg, M. T. (Eds.). *New directions for child development: Children's planning strategies.* San Francisco: Jossey-Bass, 1982.

Forbes, D. L., Katz, M. M., Paul, B., & Lubin, D. Children's plans for joining play: An analysis of structure and function. In D. L. Forbes & M. T. Greenberg (Eds.), *New directions for child development: Children's planning strategies.* San Francisco: Jossey-Bass, 1982.

Ford, D. H. *The organization and development of human behavior: A living systems perspective.* Book in preparation, Pennsylvania State University, College of Human Development, 1984.

Ford, M. E. The construct validity of egocentrism. *Psychological Bulletin,* 1979, **86,** 1169–1188.

Ford, M. E. *Androgyny as self-assertion and integration: Implications for psychological and social competence.* Unpublished manuscript, Stanford University, School of Education, 1981.

Ford, M. E. Social cognition and social competence in adolescence. *Developmental Psychology,* 1982, **18,** 323–340.

Ford, M. E. Competence: Current conceptual and empirical status and implications for mental health. State-of-the-science paper appearing in *Behavioral Sciences Research in Mental Health* (Vol. 2). Washington, DC: National Institute of Mental Health, 1983.

Ford, M. E., Burt, R., & Bergin, C. *Social-cognitive antecedents of adolescent self-assertive and integrative accomplishments: Directive social cognitions.* Unpublished manuscript, Stanford University, School of Education, 1984.

Ford, M. E., & Keating, D. P. Developmental and individual differences in long-term memory retrieval: Process and organization. *Child Development,* 1981, **52,** 234–241.

Ford, M. E., & Tisak, M. S. *Evaluation of an educational intervention to enhance social-cognitive skills.* Paper presented at the annual meetings of the American Educational Research Association, New York, March 1982.

Ford, D. H., & Urban, H. *Systems of psychotherapy.* New York: Wiley, 1963.

French, R. *Interpersonal problem solving skill in lonely people.* Unpublished doctoral dissertation, Stanford University, 1982.

Gerson, R. P., & Damon, W. Moral understanding and children's conduct. In W. Damon (Ed.), *New directions for child development: Moral development.* San Francisco: Jossey-Bass, 1978.

Glass, C. R., Gottman, J. M., & Shmurak, S. H. Response acquisition and cognitive self-statement modification approaches to dating skills training. *Journal of Counseling Psychology,* 1976, **23,** 520–526.

Glass, C. R., Merluzzi, T. V., Biever, J. L., & Larsen, K. H. Cognitive assessment of social anxiety: Development and validation of a self-statement questionnaire. *Cognitive Therapy and Research,* 1982, **6,** 37–55.

Goldstein, A. P., Sprafkin, R. P., Gershaw, N. J., & Klein, P. *Skillstreaming the adolescent: A structured learning approach to teaching prosocial skills.* Champaign, IL: Research Press, 1980.

Gotlib, I., & Asarnow, R. F. Interpersonal and impersonal problem-solving skills in mildly and clinically depressed university students. *Journal of Consulting and Clinical Psychology,* 1979, **47,** 86–95.

Graham, J. A., Argyle, M., & Furnham, A. The goal structure of situations. *European Journal of Social Psychology,* 1980, **10,** 345–366.

Harrison, E. F. *The managerial decision-making process.* Boston: Houghton, 1975.

Hoffman, M. L. Empathy, its development and prosocial implications. In C. B. Keasey (Ed.), *Nebraska Symposium on Motivation* (Vol. 25). Lincoln: Univ. of Nebraska Press, 1977.

Hogan, R. Moral conduct and moral character: A psychological perspective. *Psychological Bulletin,* 1973, **79,** 217–232.

Hogan, R., Johnson, J. A., & Emler, N. P. A socioanalytic theory of moral development. In W. Damon (Ed.), *New directions for child development: Moral development.* San Francisco: Jossey-Bass, 1978.

Holland, J. L. *Making vocational choices: A theory of careers*. New York: Prentice-Hall, 1973.

Humphrey, L. L., & Kirschenbaum, D. S. Self-control and perceived social competence in preschool children. *Cognitive Therapy and Research*, 1981, **5**, 373–379.

Iannotti, R. J. Effect of role-taking experiences on role taking, empathy, altruism, and aggression. *Developmental Psychology*, 1978, **14**, 119–124.

Jantch, E. *The self-organizing universe: Scientific and human implications of the emerging paradigm of evolution*. Oxford: Pergamon, 1980.

Jennings, K. D. People versus object orientation, social behavior, and intellectual abilities in preschool children. *Developmental Psychology*, 1975, **11**, 511–519.

Kazdin, A. E. Imagery elaboration and self-efficacy in the covert modeling treatment of unassertive behavior. *Journal of Consulting and Clinical Psychology*, 1979, **47**, 725–733.

Kendall, P. C., & Hollon, S. D. Cognitive-behavioral interventions: Overview and current status. In P. C. Kendall & S. D. Hollon (Eds.), *Cognitive-behavioral interventions: Theory, research, and procedures*. New York: Academic Press, 1979.

Kendall, P. C., & Korgeski, G. P. Assessment and cognitive-behavioral interventions. *Cognitive Therapy and Research*, 1979, **3**, 1–21.

Kendall, P. C., Pellegrini, D. S., & Urbain, E. S. Approaches to assessment for cognitive-behavioral interventions with children. In P. C. Kendall & S. D. Hollon (Eds.), *Assessment strategies for cognitive-behavioral interventions*. New York: Academic Press, 1981.

Klass, E. T. Cognitive appraisal of transgression among sociopaths and normals. *Cognitive Therapy and Research*, 1980, **4**, 353–367.

Klinger, E. Consequences of commitment to and disengagement from incentives. *Psychological Review*, 1975, **82**, 1–25.

Klinger, E. *Meaning and void: Inner experience and the incentives in people's lives*. Minneapolis: Univ. of Minnesota Press, 1977.

Koestler, A. *The ghost in the machine*. New York: Macmillan, 1967.

Kurdek, L. A. Perspective taking as the cognitive basis of children's moral development: A review of the literature. *Merrill-Palmer Quarterly*, 1978, **24**, 1–28.

Langer, E., Blank, A., & Chanowitz, B. The mindlessness of ostensibly thoughtful action: The role of "placebic" information in interpersonal interaction. *Journal of Personality and Social Psychology*, 1978, **36**, 635–642.

Lefcourt, H. M. *Locus of control: Current trends in theory and research*. Hillsdale, NJ: Erlbaum, 1976.

Lefcourt, H. M. (Ed.). *Research with the locus of control construct: Vol. 1. Assessment methods*. New York: Academic Press, 1981.

Lerner, R. M. Nature, nurture, and dynamic interactionism. *Human Development*, 1978, **21**, 1–20.

Levenson, H. Differentiating among internality, powerful others, and chance. In H. M. Lefcourt (Ed.), *Research with the locus of control construct: Vol. 1. Assessment methods*. New York: Academic Press, 1981.

Lewinsohn, P. M., Larson, D. W., & Muñoz, R. F. The measurement of expectancies and other cognitions in depressed individuals. *Cognitive Therapy and Research*, 1982, **6**, 437–446.

Little, V. L., & Kendall, P. C. Cognitive-behavioral interventions with delinquents: Problem solving, role-taking, and self-control. In P. C. Kendall & S. D. Hollon (Eds.), *Cognitive-behavioral interventions: Theory, research, and procedures*. New York: Academic Press, 1979.

Locke, E. A., Shaw, K. N., Saari, L. M., & Latham, G. P. Goal setting and task performance: 1969–1980. *Psychological Bulletin*, 1981, **90**, 125–152.

Mandel, N. M., & Shrauger, J. S. The effects of self-evaluative statements on heterosocial approach in shy and nonshy males. *Cognitive Therapy and Research*, 1980, **4**, 369–381.

Maslow, A. A theory of human motivation. *Psychological Review*, 1943, **50**, 370–396.

Maturana, H. R. The organization of the living: A theory of the living organization. *International Journal of Man-Machine Studies*, 1975, **7**, 313–332.

McDevitt, T. M., & Ford, M. E. *Children's speech adjustments to listeners: Communicative egocentrism or communicative competence?* Unpublished manuscript, Stanford University School of Education, 1983.

Meichenbaum, D. *Cognitive-behavior modification: An integrative approach.* New York: Plenum, 1977.

Meichenbaum, D., Butler, L., & Gruson, L. Toward a conceptual model of social competence. In J. D. Wine & M. D. Smye (Eds.), *Social competence.* New York: Guilford, 1981.

Miller, J. G. *Living systems.* New York: McGraw-Hill, 1978.

Mischel, W. Toward a cognitive social learning reconceptualization of personality. *Psychological Review*, 1973, **70**, 252–282.

Mischel, W. Metacognition and the rules of delay. In J. H. Flavell & L. Ross (Eds.), *Social cognitive development: Frontiers and possible futures.* London and New York: Cambridge Univ. Press, 1981.

Mischel, W. Delay of gratification as process and as person variable in development. In D. Magnusson & V. P. Allen (Eds.), *Human development: An interactional perspective.* New York: Academic Press, 1983.

Mischel, W., & Patterson, C. J. Substantive and structural elements of effective plans for self-control. *Journal of Personality and Social Psychology*, 1976, **34**, 942–950.

Mischel, W., & Patterson, C. J. Effective plans for self-control in children. In W. A. Collins (Ed.), *Minnesota symposium on child psychology* (Vol. 13). Minneapolis: Univ. of Minnesota Press, 1979.

Moe, K. O., & Zeiss, A. M. Measuring self-efficacy expectations for social skills: A methodological inquiry. *Cognitive Therapy and Research*, 1982, **6**, 191–205.

Monahan, J., & O'Leary, K. D. Effects of self-instruction on rule-breaking behavior. *Psychological Reports*, 1971, **29**, 1059–1066.

Moore, B. S. Cognitive representation of rewards in delay of gratification. *Cognitive Therapy and Research*, 1977, **1**, 73–83.

Nelson, K. Social cognition in a script framework. In J. H. Flavell & L. Ross (Eds.), *Social cognitive development: Frontiers and possible futures.* London and New York: Cambridge Univ. Press, 1981.

Nisbett, R. E., & Ross, L. *Human inference: Strategies and shortcomings of social judgment.* New York: Prentice-Hall, 1980.

O'Leary, K. D. The effects of self-instruction on immoral behavior. *Journal of Experimental Child Psychology*, 1968, **6**, 297–301.

Patterson, C. J., & Mischel, W. Plans to resist distraction. *Developmental Psychology*, 1975, **11**, 369–378.

Patterson, C. J., & Mischel, W. Effects of temptation-inhibiting and task-facilitating plans on self-control. *Journal of Personality and Social Psychology*, 1976, **33**, 209–217.

Pea, R. D. What is planning development the development of? In D. L. Forbes & M. T. Greenberg (Eds.), *New directions for child development: Children's planning strategies.* San Francisco: Jossey-Bass, 1982.

Pellegrini, D. S. *The social-cognitive qualities of stress-resistant children*. Unpublished doctoral dissertation, University of Minnesota, 1980.

Phares, E. J. *Locus of control in personality*. Morristown, NJ: General Learning Press, 1976.

Platt, J. J., & Spivack, G. Problem-solving thinking of psychiatric patients. *Journal of Consulting and Clinical Psychology*, 1972, **39**, 148–151. (a)

Platt, J. J., & Spivack, G. Social competence and effective problem-solving thinking in psychiatric patients. *Journal of Clinical Psychology*, 1972, **28**, 3–5. (b)

Platt, J. J., & Spivack, G. Studies in problem-solving thinking of psychiatric patients: Patient-control differences and factorial structure of problem-solving thinking. *Proceedings of the 81st Annual Convention of the American Psychological Association*, 1973, **8**, 461–462.

Platt, J. J., & Spivack, G. Means of solving real-life problems: I. Psychiatric patients versus controls, and cross-cultural comparisons of normal females. *Journal of Community Psychology*, 1974, **2**, 45–58.

Platt, J. J., Spivack, G., Altman, N., Altman, D., & Peizer, S. B. Adolescent problem-solving thinking. *Journal of Consulting and Clinical Psychology*, 1974, **42**, 787–793.

Powers, W. T. *Behavior: The control of perception*. Chicago: Aldine, 1973.

Powers, W. T. Quantitative analysis of purposive systems: Some spadework at the foundations of scientific psychology. *Psychological Review*, 1978, **85**, 417–435.

Pressley, M. Increasing children's self-control through cognitive interventions. *Review of Educational Research*, 1979, **49**, 319–370.

Riegel, K. F. The dialectics of human development. *American Psychologist*, 1976, **31**, 689–700.

Rokeach, M. *Beliefs, attitudes, and values*. San Francisco: Jossey-Bass, 1968.

Rothbaum, F. Children's clinical syndromes and generalized expectations of control. In H. W. Reese & L. P. Lipsitt (Eds.), *Advances in child development and behavior* (Vol. 15). New York: Academic Press, 1980.

Rothbaum, F., Weisz, J. R., & Snyder, S. Changing the world and changing the self: A two-process model of perceived control. *Journal of Personality and Social Psychology*, 1982, **42**, 5–37.

Rothbaum, F., Wolfer, J., & Visintainer, M. Coping behavior and locus of control in children. *Journal of Personality*, 1979, **47**, 118–135.

Rothenberg, B. B. Children's social sensitivity and the relationship to interpersonal competence, intrapersonal comfort, and intellectual level. *Developmental Psychology*, 1970, **2**, 335–350.

Rubin, K. H. Relationship between egocentric communication and popularity among peers. *Developmental Psychology*, 1972, **7**, 364.

Sarason, B. The dimensions of social competence: Contributions from a variety of research areas. In J. D. Wine & M. D. Smye (Eds.), *Social competence*. New York: Guilford, 1981.

Schwartz, R., & Gottman, J. Toward a task analysis of assertive behavior. *Journal of Consulting and Clinical Psychology*, 1976, **44**, 910–920.

Selman, R. L. A structural approach to the study of developing interpersonal relationship concepts. In A. Pick (Ed.), *10th annual Minnesota symposium on child psychology*. Minneapolis: Univ. of Minnesota Press, 1976.

Selman, R. L., Jaquette, D., & Lavin, D. R. Interpersonal awareness in children: Toward an integration of developmental and clinical child psychology. *American Journal of Orthopsychiatry*, 1977, **47**, 264–274.

Shantz, C. U. The development of social cognition. In E. M. Hetherington (Ed.), *Review of child development research* (Vol. 5). Chicago: Univ. of Chicago Press, 1975.

Shantz, C. U. Social cognition. In J. H. Flavell & E. M. Markman (Eds.), *Cognitive development*, in P. H. Mussen (Ed.), *Carmichael's manual of child psychology* (4th ed.). New York: Wiley, 1983.

Shure, M. B. *The problem-solving approach to social development.* Paper presented at the biennial meetings of the Society for Research in Child Development, San Francisco, March 1979.

Shure, M. Real-life problem solving for parents and children: An approach to social competence. In D. P. Rathjen & J. P. Foreyt (Eds.), *Social competence: Interventions for children and adults.* Oxford: Pergamon, 1980. (a)

Shure, M. B. *Interpersonal problem solving in ten-year-olds.* Final report to the National Institute of Mental Health, 1980. (b)

Shure, M. B., & Spivack, G. Means-ends thinking, adjustment and social class among elementary school-aged children. *Journal of Consulting and Clinical Psychology,* 1972, **38**, 348–353.

Shure, M. B., & Spivack, G. *Problem-solving techniques in childrearing.* San Francisco: Jossey-Bass, 1978.

Shure, M. B., & Spivack, G. Interpersonal problem solving as a mediator of behavioral adjustment in preschool and kindergarten children. *Journal of Applied Developmental Psychology,* 1980, **1**, 29–43.

Siegel, J. M., Platt, J. J., & Peizer, S. B. Emotional and social real-life problem-solving thinking in adolescent and adult psychiatric patients. *Journal of Clinical Psychology,* 1976, **32**, 230–232.

Smetana, J. G. Reasoning in the personal and moral domains: Adolescent and young adult women's decision-making regarding abortion. *Journal of Applied Developmental Psychology,* 1981, **2**, 211–226.

Spivack, G., Platt, J. J., & Shure, M. B. *The problem-solving approach to adjustment.* San Francisco: Jossey-Bass, 1976.

Spivack, G., & Shure, M. B. *Social adjustment of young children.* San Francisco: Jossey-Bass, 1974.

Staub, E. The use of role playing and induction in children's learning of helping and sharing behavior. *Child Development,* 1971, **42**, 805–816.

Steinlauf, B. Problem-solving skills, locus of control, and the contraceptive effectiveness of young women. *Child Development,* 1979, **50**, 268–271.

Strayer, J. A naturalistic study of empathic behaviors and their relation to affective states and perspective-taking skills in preschool children. *Child Development,* 1980, **51**, 815–822.

Strong, E. K., Jr. *Vocational interests of men and women.* Stanford, CA: Stanford Univ. Press, 1943.

Thoresen, C. E., & Mahoney, M. J. *Behavioral self-control.* New York: Holt, 1974.

Thorngate, W. Must we always think before we act? *Personality and Social Psychology Bulletin,* 1978, **2**, 31–35.

Thorpe, G. L. Desensitization, behavior rehearsal, self-instructional training, and placebo effects on assertive-refusal behavior. *European Journal of Behavioral Analysis and Modification,* 1974, **1**, 30–44.

Turiel, E. *The development of social knowledge: Morality and convention.* London and New York: Cambridge Univ. Press, 1983.

Urbain, E. S., & Kendall, P. C. Review of social-cognitive problem-solving interventions with children. *Psychological Bulletin,* 1980, **88**, 109–143.

vonBertalanffy, L. *General system theory: Foundations, development, applications.* New York: Braziller, 1968.

Wadsworth, M. W. *The measurement of personal goal hierarchies.* Unpublished manuscript, Pennsylvania State University, College of Human Development, 1982.

Wadsworth, M. W., & Ford, D. *Self-direction: A concept finding its way.* Unpublished manuscript, Pennsylvania State University, College of Human Development, 1982.

Weiner, B. A theory of motivation for some classroom experiences. *Journal of Educational Psychology,* 1979, **71,** 3–25.

Wheeler, V. A., & Ladd, G. W. Assessment of children's self-efficacy for social interactions with peers. *Developmental Psychology,* 1982, **18,** 795–805.

White, R. W. Motivation reconsidered: The concept of competence. *Psychological Review,* 1959, **66,** 297–333.

Wine, J. D. From defect to competence models. In J. D. Wine & M. D. Smye (Eds.), *Social competence.* New York: Guilford, 1981.

Wortman, C. B., & Brehm, J. W. Responses to uncontrollable outcomes: An integration of reactance theory and the learned helplessness model. In L. Berkowitz (Ed.), *Advances in experimental social psychology* (Vol. 8). New York: Academic Press, 1975.

Zahavi, S., & Asher, S. R. The effect of verbal instructions on preschool children's aggressive behavior. *Journal of School Psychology,* 1978, **16,** 146–153.

Childhood Emotion and
Cognitive Behavior Therapy:
A Rational–Emotive
Perspective[1,2]

MICHAEL E. BERNARD

Department of Education
University of Melbourne
Parkville, Victoria, Australia

[1]Portions of this chapter were adapted from *Rational-Emotive Therapy with Children and Adolescents: Theory, Treatment Strategies, Preventative Methods* (Bernard & Joyce, 1984) and *Rational-Emotive Approaches to the Problems of Childhood* (Ellis & Bernard, 1983).

[2]The general idea for this paper arose from a discussion this author had with Phil Kendall during the summer of 1981 at the Center for Advanced Study in the Behavioral Sciences, Palo Alto, California. A concern expressed by this author was that the name cognitive behavior therapy omitted reference to an all too important aspect of human experience: EMOTION. This omission appeared to derive from some but not all leading cognitive–behavioral therapists and researchers allegances to methodological behaviorism as well as metaphysical behaviorism, the latter having been modified to a mediational stimulus–response view of human behavior (see Mahoney, 1974). Emotions have

ADVANCES IN COGNITIVE–BEHAVIORAL RESEARCH
AND THERAPY, VOLUME 3

The purpose of this article is to both bring emotions into the forefront of child-oriented cognitive behavior therapy (CBT) consciousness as well as present an up-to-date rational–emotive (RET) conceptualization of childhood emotion and emotional disturbance. For some peculiar reason, RET has been omitted in recent discussions on the use of cognitive–behavioral interventions with children (e.g., Kendall, 1981). This oversight has been in part due to the lack of empirical work published that examines the clinical utility of RET with younger populations. Also up until recently there has been relatively little written by RET theorists concerning children and youth. The work that has appeared has not received sufficient exposure. This situation has changed today. An increasing number of books, chapters, articles, and research projects examine the question of how RET can be simplified for use with younger populations, and an extended review of theory and research has been published (Bernard & Joyce, 1984).

It is important to indicate right from the beginning that the descriptions of the irrational underpinnings of childhood emotions and behavior have not been empirically validated and documented. The theory presented in this article derives from extensive clinical work conducted by this author and other RET therapists with children as well as the extensive clinical literature on the use of RET with adults. The ideas presented in this article can be considered hypotheses to be tested by cognitively oriented researchers who are becoming increasingly interested in childhood emotions. This article does not review the research literature that is available on emotions in children, but rather describes what RET therapists consider the underlying irrationality to be in several types of emotional problems in children.

In this article, a brief summary of the RET position concerning cognition, emotion, and behavior is followed by a discussion of childhood maladjustment. The main portion of this article contains a RET analysis of emotions and emotional problems in children and adolescents. It is

---

never enjoyed great popularity in behavioral psychology due to problems inherent in achieving operational definitions. This author took exception with Phil Kendall's (1981) position that "the cognitive problems that are related to maladjustment (in children) . . . are cognitive *absences*" (p. 54). Although this comment referred to problems of impulsivity, it reflects a different emphasis. This author stated that almost all disorders of childhood had an emotional component and that affect in children was created and maintained by inappropriate and at times excessive negative self-talk as well as irrational ideas and beliefs—hence an argument for the treatment of excesses, not only deficits. As a consequence of that meeting, Phil Kendall extended an invitation to this author to submit his views in this volume.

hoped that this presentation will provide theoretical foundations for advances in cognitive behavior therapy and research.

I. RET CONCEPTION OF COGNITION, EMOTION, AND BEHAVIOR

While RET is renowned for its emphasis on the cognitive origins of psychological maladjustment and for the use of verbally based cognitive change procedures (scientific method of reasoning, cognitive disputation), Albert Ellis for over 20 years has indicated that the three modes of human experience (cognitions, emotions, behaviors) are often inseparable and that all three interact and reciprocally influence one another:

> A central thesis of rational-emotive therapy (RET) and cognitive behavior therapy (CBT) is that the terms "cognition", "emotion" and "behavior" are not disparate or separate aspects of human functioning, but that they are overlapping and interacting processes. Probably, no such thing as "pure" or "absolute" thought, feeling, or action exists. Thoughts or evaluations . . . are almost invariably accompanied by and interact with feeling . . . and are also accompanied by and interact with actions. . . . Similarly, feelings . . . lead to thoughts . . . and to actions. . . . And actions . . . lead to thoughts . . . and to feelings. (Ellis, 1984)

There is no doubt that while Ellis accepts the interrelationship of cognition, emotion, and behavior, cognition is of paramount importance in understanding why people manifest psychological maladjustment and how they can be helped to change. So while Ellis (1962) recognizes that emotions can be activated through sensorimotor processes and biological stimulation mediated through tissues of the automatic nervous system (subcortical ones), cognition and thinking processes have the greatest influence.

A. RET as Emotional Problem Solving

It is important to emphasize that RET considers one of its main therapeutic goals as helping clients overcome disabling emotions. Rational thinking skills and philosophies are taught as a means to enable clients to modify their own emotional states. When a client of any age presents for therapy, the RET practitioner seeks to establish as an initial priority what the client is feeling, the intensity of emotion experienced, and the extent to which the state of emotional arousal of the client is interfering with the client attaining his or her short-term and long-term goals. Does the client's emotions facilitate or inhibit the client engaging in goal-directed behaviors? If the client's emotions are inappropriate and are interfering with the client achieving what he or she wants from life, then (and only then) does the practitioner probe the beliefs, thoughts, and overall evaluations and philosophy of life to determine the cognitive origins of emotional disturbance and dysfunctional behavior. Therapy is geared towards emotional change (e.g., from extreme anger to irritation, depression to disappointment). While RET accepts that behavioral skill deficiencies and excesses such as encountered in some socially withdrawn and aggressive clients, respectively, are not always accompanied by inappropriate levels of emotionality (anxiety, anger), it also views such instances as exceptions rather than the rule. In these cases, the RET therapist engages in a cognitive functional analysis of those behaviors that are lacking in the client's repertoire and provides instruction in the use of verbal self-statements combined with behavioral rehearsal to bring the behavior under self-control. The point to be made is that while RET offers solutions to the practical problems encountered by clients, its distinctive contribution is as an emotional problem-solving therapy. RET theory describes the cognitive origins of different emotions and how different clusters of irrational ideas and beliefs lead to different types of feelings. One of the main purposes of this article is to present the RET theory of childhood emotion.

B. The Emotional Episode

Ellis has elaborated an ABC theory of emotional disturbance which describes how a person of any age becomes upset. RET starts with an emotional and behavioral consequence (C) and seeks to identify the activating event (A) that appears to have precipitated C. While the commonly accepted viewpoint is that A caused C, RET steadfastly maintains that it is the individual's beliefs (B) which are evaluations about what happened at A that determine C. For example, take 11-year-old Paul, a sixth grader, who screams in anger and thumps down hard on his desk because his teacher failed to call on him when he had his hand raised. The common misconception is that A, the activating event of being ignored, caused Paul to feel angry, to scream and bang his desk (Cs). However, if just at the moment Paul is being ignored and before he gets angry, one could somehow get him to forget and erase completely from his mind the memory trace of being ignored, one would observe a boy who was neither angry nor screaming. According to RET, it is Paul's thoughts and evaluations (Bs) about the incident that created or caused C.

Ellis has extended his alphabetical notional symbol system for representing his theory by adding a DE link to his ABCs. Disputation (D) is one of the cornerstones of the RET method of therapeutic change and employs where possible the scientific method of challenging and questioning shaky or untenable hypotheses and imperative and absolutistic assumptions that individuals may hold about themselves, about others, and about the world. With younger and less intelligent clients, disputation may examine the rationality of irrational self-statements that occur in specific situations ("How awful is it not to be called on in math class?") whereas with more capable adolescent clients disputation of the beliefs themselves can occur ("It's awful when things do not go my way"). With children less than 7 years of age or so, disputation is replaced by the use of instruction in rational self-statements ("This isn't so bad"). When clients begin to challenge their unsound assumptions and beliefs and to reformulate them into more empirically valid statements and when they really and strongly believe in their validity, they produce a new cognitive, emotive, and behavioral effect (E). When clients arrive at a new philosophic effect by giving up unsound beliefs, they begin to experience less severe emotional reactions and to behave differently, so as to be able, if they can, improve and change the situation at A.

In the example of Paul, we can see that if Paul evaluated the activating event of being ignored rationally and sensibly, he would have said to himself something such as "I don't like it when I'm not called on; I wish my teacher would pay more attention to me." He would have felt moderately annoyed, irritated, and disgruntled, but he would not have thrown a temper tantrum and he would have in all likelihood tried to answer his teacher's next question. And if he stopped his evaluation of the situations with these rational self-statements, all would be fine. But children as well as adults who are emotionally upset and whose behavior is dysfunctional follow up their rational statements with irrational and absolute demands about how things should be. So when Paul said to himself that his teacher should not ignore him, that he can't stand being treated awfully and horribly, and that his teacher is an awful person who deserves to be punished, he felt incredibly furious and irate and behaved in an aggressive fashion, which no doubt would lead to unfavorable consequences for Paul in the future.

RET theorists Wessler and Wessler (1980) have recently expanded the ABC model to help therapists more fully understand the complex psychological events that create emotional disturbances. Every emotional event starts out with a stimulus being presented to the child (adapted with permission from DiGiuseppe & Bernard, 1983):

Step 1: Stimuli are then sensed by the person's eyes, ears, sense of smell, touch, etc.
Step 2: Sensory neurons process the stimuli and transmit them to the central nervous system.
Step 3: Not all sensations enter consciousness. Some are filtered out and others perceived. Perception is step 3. Perception, however, is not an exact replication of reality; perceptions consist of equal parts of information provided by the senses and information provided by the brain (Neisser, 1971). At this point all information is organized, categorized, and defined. It is as much a peripheral as a central nervous system function.
Step 4: People usually do not stop thinking after they have perceived information. Most likely they attempt to extract more information than is present in the perception. So some interpretations or inferences are likely to follow perceptions.
Step 5: Humans are not just passive processors of information. Inferences and conclusions usually have some further meaning associated to them. Conclusions and inferences may vary in their importance to an individual. Almost all inferences are evaluated either positively or negatively in relation to the person's life. This appraisal or evaluation is step 5.
Step 6: Affect or emotion follows appraisal according to rational–emotive therapy. We feel happy or sad or mad at step 6 after we have appraised something as being beneficial, threatening, etc.
Step 7: Emotional states are not separate psychological phenomena. Emotions have evolved as part of the flight–fight mechanism and exist primarily to motivate adaptive behavior. Therefore, emotions usually include not only the autonomic nervous system reactions and the phenomenological sensations, but also action tendencies or behavioral response sets that are learned.
Step 8: Responses once they are made usually have some impact upon the external world. This effect can be desirable or undesirable, and feedback of our action tendencies serves as reward functions to strengthen or extinguish a response set.

In this model, emotional disturbance develops because of one or two types of cognitive errors: empirical distortions of reality which occur at step 4 (inferences), and exaggerated and distorted appraisal of inferences at step 5. According to traditional rational–emotive theory, it is primarily the appraisal that is necessary for emotional disturbance. This is the B in Ellis' ABCs. Ellis has noted, however, that many times the appraisals are of distortions of reality. Faulty inferences usually do accompany exaggerated appraisal, but the appraisal alone is sufficient to arouse disturbed affect.

Let's take a hypothetical clinical example to explain how these two cognitions operate. George, a 10 year old, moved to a new neighborhood and has not met new friends. He is sitting quietly in the neighborhood playground while the other children are running about. He feels frightened and his associated action potential is withdrawal. He sits alone, leaning up against a wall and reading a book. As he sees the other children coming, George thinks, "They'll never like me, they'll think I'm not very good at these games, and they won't play with me no matter what I do." George has drawn these inferences about the other children's behavior. In fact, they are predictions about what might happen, but which actually never has. Inferences alone are not sufficient to arouse fear. Some children, although not George, might be perfectly happy to sit by themselves and read books, but George appraises this situation quite negatively and catastrophizes. "It's awful that I don't have anyone to play with." "I must be a jerk if they won't play with me." Such catastrophizing leads to feelings of anxiety and low self-esteem.

A major question that arises from this discussion is whether all affect in children is preceded by cognition or whether emotions as some have suggested (e.g., Zajonc, 1981) may occur without the presence of antecedent cognitions. The RET position is that *most* emotions in children are cognitively motivated, although a small proportion may be activated subcortically. CBT theorists have argued that in some cases, such as hyperactivity and impulsivity, children are engaging in action without forethought and, therefore, any emotional component comes after the fact (Kendall, personal communication). While RET accepts that nonreflective behavior derives from a lack of verbal mediation, it also asserts that emotions that frequently accompany or immediately follow such behavior result from cognitive errors.

C. The Dual Functions of Inner Speech

It has been written elsewhere (Bernard, 1981; Bernard & Joyce, 1983) that one conception of cognition that is important for considering the role of cognition in human emotion and behavior is that of *inner speech* (also called inner dialogue, private dialogue, private speech, automatic thoughts, covert self-instructions, covert self-verbalizations, self-talk, primal whispers). Inner speech can be said to serve two distinct functions. When people are using their inner speech to think about, plan, and carry out a course of action, we can say that inner speech is serving an instrumental and problem-solving self-guiding function. When people talk to themselves and interpret and evaluate what they are planning and/or doing, we designate inner speech as serving an affective function. These two functions or dimensions of inner speech often run in parallel. As people describe to themselves a plan of action, they also wonder how they will perform, and as they engage in a series of behaviors, they constantly both judge their performance and themselves as reflected in the quality of their performance. It would appear that these functions begin to operate together in children as soon as children learn to use their own speech to regulate their own behavior. It certainly would appear that by the age of 7 or 8 when external speech has gone underground in inner speech and as the child enters the concrete operational period that the instrumental and affective functions of speech are fully operational. It is important that CBT considers both these functions in their analysis of childhood maladjustment.

D. Introspection and Awareness of Cognition

A number of fundamental questions have been raised when the role of introspection and self-analysis in the practice of RET has been examined (Bernard, 1981). These questions are especially relevant in considering the role of cognition in childhood emotion. What is the relationship between thoughts a client is aware of and can verbalize and thoughts that a client is not aware of immediately? How and why do thoughts that a client experiences but cannot immediately identify or verbalize to a practitioner activate emotional responses? How can thoughts that a client may describe in compound sentence form appear to occur in a fractional time period between an activating event and an emotional consequence? Ellis (1984) has indicated that people are largely unaware or unconscious of the cognitions they use to make themselves feel and act:

> Occasionally, they are ashamed of these thoughts and therefore suppress or repress them—as when they say that they love their parents but actually punish them because they are unconsciously saying to themselves, "My goddamned parents *should* have treated me better when I was a child and they therefore now *deserve* to be punished!" But most of the time, people can easily make themselves aware of their emotion-creating thoughts but do not bother to do so and unawarely or automatically think them without *observing* that they exist and contribute to their feelings. Thus, people who are enjoying ice cream do not notice that their enjoyment partly comes from such thoughts as, "Oh, how nice and cool this is! And so sweet! I just love this taste! I could eat ice cream like this forever!"

In addressing the above questions, this author has in a 1981 article entitled "Private Thought in Rational-Emotive Psychotherapy" proposed a model for representing thoughts that vary in client awareness and therapeutic accessibility. The model represents thoughts on a continuum from those that a person is immediately aware of and whose form corresponds quite closely to the words and speech structures of the language system of the person (covert verbalizations), to those having abbreviated and elliptical form and in which word structures and meanings are extremely idiosyncratic. This latter form of thinking occurs when people have no immediate intention of communicating their thoughts to another person and are not engaging in mental rehearsal. In this model thoughts vary in the time in which they are generated and, indeed, both single-word thoughts and more elaborated thoughts can occur in a brief time interval. It would appear that this model applies across the life span and is useful for considering the role of cognition in emotion.

II. A RET MODEL OF CHILDHOOD MALADJUSTMENT

In this section a brief overview of factors that occasion emotions in children and that lead to emotional disturbance in children and adolescents is presented. Rational–emotive theory holds that childhood maladjustment can be best understood from an examination of the thinking processes and thought content of a child who is manifesting a problem. More specifically, emotional distress even in a very young child appears to derive from a variety of cognitive errors and irrational ideas that are very much a part of the child's cognitive and personality make-up. It is the operation of faulty information processes and the presence of negative ideation that are paramountly responsible for the emotional upheavals of childhood. It is interesting to recall that psychoanalytic theory has always explained emotional distress and behavioral dysfunctions in adults in terms of faulty thinking processes and irrational beliefs that can be considered either characteristic of or a regression to earlier and more primitive stages of thinking. Writes Kessler (1966),

> For in general, abnormal psychological processes are drawn from psychological processes which are appropriate to younger ages. Abnormal behavior may appear as the inability to master the next higher level of learning, or as a regression to an earlier stage. (p. 18)

Freud has distinguished between primary mental processes that operate according to the pleasure principle and secondary mental processes that operate according to the reality principle, and he indicated that both principles operate side by side across the life span. In terms of Freud's formulations, Kessler (1966) has indicated that emotional disturbance can be considered a product of primary processes: "A symptom originates from affective needs rather than logic, and it usually contains within it a kernal of irrational thinking" (p. 37).

A RET conception of childhood maladjustment takes into account three major dimensions: cognitive–affective developmental status, psychological conditions, and environmental conditions. This analysis is a preliminary one in that while these three influences are seen as central to any cognitive model of abnormal child behavior and child psychopathology, the ways in which these three dimensions interact with one another are not fully understood (for a more detailed consideration of this area, see Bernard & Joyce, 1984).

A. Cognitive–Affective Developmental Status

Emotional disorders of children and adolescents can be explained by the manner in which the young person interprets and evaluates experience. In general, proponents of many different models of childhood psychopathology accept the principle that there is a reciprocal relationship between mental and emotional development. When children are very young the quality of their subjective emotional experience is very much limited by their capacity to think about and understand the meaning of experience. The cognitive limitations of the early childhood period can often result in children acquiring beliefs about themselves and their surrounding world that are untrue and irrational and that if not corrected can have an extremely deleterious effect on their future well-being. That is, children construct their own theories and arrive at their own conclusions based on inferences from what they have observed. The child's conception of the world is organized idiosyncratically and derives from the child's limited capacity to make observations and draw logical conclusions. An example of the influence of irrational beliefs can be seen in young children below the age of 7 who may make the observation that "bad children get punished" and conclude that because they are frequently being punished, they must be bad. By the age of 7, many children appear to have acquired a sense of their goodness and badness based on a faulty reasoning process and a primitive set of moral values which also derive from their limited reasoning capacities. If children believe that they are bad whenever they are disciplined for misbehavior, then no doubt there will be a strong emotional component to their behavior. Moreover, a child's misbehavior is frequently prompted by feelings of worthlessness which accompany the child's self-concept.

In working with children, the pervasive influence that their ideas and beliefs have on their emotions and behavior is apparent. These beliefs are often implicit and frequently result from the child having formed a conclusion based on limited evidence and having used the conclusion as an unquestioned rule for grading subsequent behavior. These rules (be they rational or irrational) that are formed early on become firmly fixed and represent part of the basic phenomenological framework of children, providing the basis for self-evaluation, for the demands they place on others, and for the interpretations they make of the behavior of others. Children's capacity for rational and logical thought limits the types of ideas they acquire and frequently reinforces a variety of irrational beliefs which often take many years to overcome.

A cognitive analysis of maladjustment in adolescents frequently reveals beliefs about themselves, others, and the world, as well as logical reasoning processes which appear to be either a holdover from or a regression to more immature levels of thinking and primitive belief systems. The adolescent also acquires a new set of beliefs—some rational, some irrational—which accompany the onset of adolescent egocentrism and the availability of more complex reasoning and thought processes characteristic of Piaget's formal level of development. This awareness may help the cognitively oriented practitioner to understand the problems of younger clients from a context different from the one which is frequently used, that is, a downward extension of an adult model of psychopathology. From this perspective, the child psychologist and practitioner employs concepts that characterize earlier levels of thinking as basic units of analysis in seeking to understand a given disorder. Adopting a developmental perspective may provide the practitioner with additional wisdom to determine whether certain behaviors and thoughts of children are manifestations of broader psychological problems (e.g., anxiety and stress), or whether they can be interpreted as symptomatic of a developmental phase in normal intellectual growth.

Moreover, it is not completely possible to determine the effects of an environmental event on a given child without knowing about the child's level of intellectual organization (Cowan, 1977). As RET and other forms of cognitive behavior therapy have for many years been successful in treating a variety of childhood problems without formally taking into account the cognitive–affective developmental status of the individual, such knowledge while being important may not be necessarily a prerequisite for applying cognitive approaches with younger clients.

A thorough reading of Piaget and secondary Piagetian sources is necessary to be able to identify the role of cognitive development in limiting and determining the affectivity of children. There are a number of interesting overlaps of Piagetian and RET theory, the first of which is their equal emphasis on constructivism. According to Piaget, there are no facts independent of the observer; all statements about reality are interpretations or constructions that represent outcomes of the interaction between the figurative aspects of external stimuli (no inherent meaning) and operative conceptualizations (what the learner already knows) (Cowan, 1977). A second interesting overlap between Piaget and Ellis is the faith they place in the scientific method of investigation and in the power of formal logical reasoning. According to Piaget, the most advanced level of intelligence is one that permits the individual to advance and systematically test propositions and hypotheses about the world by considering the full range of possible and potential outcomes. Ellis' therapy can be seen when practiced in its most elegant fashion (use of disputation, hedonic calculus) as an attempt to teach clients to apply principles of formal logic and reason to areas of their personal lives in which they are experiencing difficulty. Piaget and Ellis also appear in agreement concerning the importance of cognition in the experience and expression of emotions. Piaget has written in 1954 that "it is, in fact, only a romantic prejudice that makes us suppose that affective phenomena constitute immediate givens or innate and ready-made feelings similar to Rousseau's 'conscience'" (1981). He believed that emotions depend on the individual's cognitive capacity to construct meaning from experience. A major difference, however, between RET and Piagetian theory is that Piaget postulates four levels of intelligence which each individual sequentially passes through, each defined by its own set of logical rules. So whereas Ellis might consider the logic employed by young children as unscientific, Piaget views these earlier forms of thought as normal and characteristic of the logic that operates at developmentally earlier levels of intelligence.

The description of the thinking of children from a RET point of view is in many ways similar to the Piagetian view although RET concentrates more on explaining psychopathology. Consider the following RET perspectives concerning the self-defeating characteristics of childhood thought.

Emotional problems of children result from innate as well as acquired tendencies to think crookedly, to be grandiosely demanding, and to refuse to accept hassle-filled reality. (Ellis, 1971, p. 3)

Tendencies toward short-range hedonism, oversuggestibility, grandiosity, overviligance, extremism, overgeneralization, wishful thinking, inertia, ineffective focusing, and discrimination difficulties . . . innate vulnerability to criticism, and damnation of others long after his original tormenter's barbs have ceased. (Ellis, 1973, p. 33)

[Childhood neurosis] . . . is an unrealistic, immature, and unusually self-immolating way of looking at oneself and the world. It is a perfectionistic or grandiose demand (rather than a reasonable enough preference) that things occur and people act in a certain way; it is over-concern about and an over-reactivity to the things that may or do happen in life; and it is usually a determined, pigheaded refusal to accept

oneself and the world as they are and an asinine insistence that things *should*, or
ought, or *must* be different from the way they are. . . . The true neurotic is a Jeho-
vian or Hitlerian moralist who usually believes right is right and wrong is wrong
and there are no two ways about it. (Ellis, Wolfe, & Moseley, 1966, pp. 19–20)

The point I wish to make is that many children and adolescents who
have psychological problems hold on to and construct irrational beliefs
and continue the tendency to think "crookedly." The inability to let go
of their cognitive distortions is fundamental to their problems.

RET locates the origins of a great deal of psychopathology in the
thinking processes of children who are less than 6, because this group
has not as yet acquired the capacity for rational and logical thought. As
Piaget indicates, children of less than 6 or 7 appear to be extremely
selective in what they attend to in their environment. Their perceptions
are very much dominated by concrete and immediate stimulus salience. Their egocentrism and inability to decenter and view things from
another perspective may make them appear extremely self-interested
and antisocial in behavior. They also tend to see themselves and others
in black and white and can only make good–bad evaluative judgments
of people and events around them. The conclusions that they make
about the world around them and that help create their emotional and
behavioral upsets are determined on the basis of arbitrary and imaginary associations and evidence that is only available in their own perceptual field. They tend to interpret the meaning of events when the
evidence is lacking, they make outlandish overgeneralizations about
themselves and others solely on the basis of a single event, and they
tend to believe that everything they can observe happening around
them is related to them.

Young children's motivational systems appear dominated by self-
defined needs and pleasure seeking. Rather than saying to themselves
they would like something, they carry on in a way such that we infer
they believe they must have certain things to be happy. Believing that
the world revolves around them, many children make extraordinary
demands upon others and believe that the world should always treat
them fairly and justly and grant them their every wish when called
upon. Many children of this age are the greatest of "awfulizers" and
their tendencies to think in all-or-none categories exacerbates mild
frustration into catastrophic reactions.

Children frequently appear to be born "people raters" for they are
constantly making comparative judgments about themselves, their parents, and peers. Unfortunately, because children find it difficult to
logically and objectively evaluate themselves and their surroundings,

they almost invariably accept the castigating attitudes of their parents, internalize them, and make them their own for the rest of their lives (Ellis, 1973). One of the most pernicious attitudes that many children acquire early on is that of perfectionism and self-blame, in which they feel their self-worth depends upon the realization of unrealistically high standards and in which they continuously put themselves down for mistake making and blundering.

According to RET, most if not all children have low frustration tolerance. When their wills are thwarted they appear to experience large amounts of emotional stress and demonstrate low frustration tolerance in a variety of maladaptive behaviors. As a result of both their inborn propensities as well as the reactions of significant others, children acquire different styles of and skills for handling frustration. RET holds that the way children resolve frustration over the course of time is a telltale hallmark of their overall adjustment. What determines whether children are at risk for future emotional and behavioral problems is largely the product of how they cope with frustration. Bard (1980) appears to be in agreement in locating the origins of psychopathology in the irrationality of childhood thought.

> It is very clear that some children have much more difficulty overcoming the universal irrationality of early childhood than others do. It appears that all children believe the world *should* be the way they want it. Some give up that idea after a while; others do not. It appears that all children are born condemners; some get over a lot of that and some do not. It appears that all children are born catastrophizers; some get over it and some do not. (pp. 99–100)

B. Psychological Conditions

Psychological conditions can be conceived of as internal personality and cognitive factors that exert a direct and contemporaneous influence on the emotions and behavior of the individual. While they may vary in terms of the degree to which they are removed from observable data, they are considered as conditions that serve as the basis for mediation and self-control. As such, they are in principle capable of being modified and are seen to have a controlling influence. An analysis of psychological conditions involves determining those conditions within the organism that are related to the manifestation of maladjustment.

Whereas the cognitive–affective developmental status of children and adolescents describes the types of thinking and emotional experience they are capable of as a consequence of the interaction between internal maturational and learning factors, psychological conditions describe the type of mental operations that are actually employed or brought to bear by them in problematic situations. The point to be made again is that it would appear that the thinking processes that underlie psychological problems in both older children, adolescents, and adults appear quite similar to the thinking characteristics of children at a very early stage of cognitive–affective development.

A variety of psychological concepts can be employed to conceptualize internal conditions that influence emotions and behaviors. Those that are of most interest can be defined cognitively and can be seen to have a direct link to emotions and behavior. There are at least five reasonably distinct psychological conditions that provide some understanding into the dysfunctional cognitive activity of the young person (pp. 4–37 and 4–48, Bernard & Joyce, © 1984. Reprinted by permission of John Wiley & Sons, Inc.):

1. *Attention processes* refer to children's patterns of selective attention to certain aspects of both their external and internal worlds (Mahoney, 1974).

2. *Mediational* processes which are frequently but not always verbal range from the store of concepts the child has available for representing and understanding experience (Klausmeier, Ghatala, & Frayer, 1974) to those processes which aid basic learning such as attention and memory (Kendler & Kendler, 1959). The covert verbalizations (Vygotsky, 1962) and images (Lazarus, 1972) of children which play an important role in controlling affective and instrumental responses can also be subsumed within this category.

3. *Logical-reasoning* processes characterize both the manner in which children interpret and draw generalizations and conclusions from personal observation as well as employ the premises, assumptions, and beliefs deductively to arrive at conclusions (Beck, Rush, Shaw, & Emery, 1979).

4. *Beliefs* are the understandings and assumptions children hold of themselves and of the world around them. There appear to be at least two different types of beliefs children evolve: (a) beliefs concerning their individual needs, how others and themselves should behave, the manner in which they characterize the qualities of events and experience (e.g., "awfulize") and the rules they apply and the conclusions they draw in judging the worth of themselves and others (Ellis & Grieger, 1977); and (b) beliefs children hold concerning the extent to which they view themselves as being the cause of events which occur in their lives (internal locus of control) or whether they consider outside environmental factors as responsible for their successes and fortunes (external locus of control) (Rotter, 1966).

5. *Cognitive strategies* are broad constructs which describe the capacity of children to generate plans and solutions to novel problems (Gagne, 1977) and can be seen, for example, in the variety of ways they employ the scientific method of problem solving (D'Zurilla & Goldfried, 1971) for dealing with impersonal and interpersonal problems (Spivack & Shure, 1974).

C. Environmental Conditions

This third category refers to those aspects of the immediate environment of children that provide stimulation and enrichment. Stimulation of different kinds and intensities is seen as facilitative of the cognitive–affective development of children. There appear to be critical periods in the years of infancy and early childhood in which the child requires both nurturance and proper intellectual and linguistic stimulation to grow emotionally and mentally. Moreover, there are various points during the early development of children at which they are especially vulnerable to improper stimulation (i.e., inadequate enrichment, desertion, exposure to conflict and criticism) that may serve to delay and inhibit development as well as promote dysfunctional cognitive thought processes and beliefs.

The environment of the child not only creates the conditions for normal cognitive–affective develpment, it also provides the basis for the child learning situation-specific adaptive behavior as well as acquiring mediational control of emotions. An examination of antecedent stimuli and reinforcing consequences which surround children's emotional and behavioral reactions provides extensive insights into the role the environment plays in either creating or maintaining maladjustment. Antecedent stimuli can be analyzed to determine why they are not occasioning adaptive behavior as can the density, quality, and consistency of the rewards and punishments that operate.

The delimitation of the importance of environmental conditions in childhood disorders is obviously not a distinctive contribution to RET. It is hoped that practitioners working with younger populations have a thorough grasp of behavioral principles. The distinctive role proponents of RET have played in describing environmental conditions is in their description of styles of parenting and child management that may have a deleterious influence on their children. Irrational parental beliefs often create inappropriate levels of emotionality which manifests itself in poor parent–child interaction.

Parents as role models and reinforcing–punishing agents may play a major part in preventing, minimizing, or exacerbating emotional and behavioral problems in their children. This is not to say that poor parenting is the only cause of psychological maladjustment in children. It is often the case that children who experience emotional strife have parents who appear to be reasonably well-adjusted, who hold positive attitudes toward their child, and whose child-rearing practices appear to be sound. Additionally, mental health practitioners do not receive referrals for well-adjusted children whose parents because of their problems would seem likely to produce disturbed offspring. There appear to be temperamentally difficult children who as a result of their frustrating behavior literally induce emotional problems in their parents.

Ellis (1962) has consistently maintained that the worst care parents can provide for their children is that of blaming them for their mistake making and wrongdoing. Such blaming encourages children to continue to blame themselves for their wrongs, which inevitably leads to chronic feelings of anxiety, guilt, and low self-esteem for some children and hostility and bigotry in others.

Hauck (1967, 1977, 1983) is the RET practitioner who has written most extensively regarding irrational parenting styles. Through his work with children and families he has identified the following erroneous parental beliefs concerning child management which are irrational not only because they are inaccurate and empirically insupportable, but also because they appear to lead to destructive emotions and self-defeating behavior in themselves as well as their children (from Hauck, 1967).

1. Children must not question or disagree with their superiors.
2. A child and his behavior are the same.
3. Children can upset their superiors.
4. Punishment, guilt, and blame are effective methods of child management.
5. Children learn more from what their superiors say than from what they do.
6. Praise spoils a child.
7. Children must not be frustrated.
8. Heavy penalties work best if applied first.
9. A child must earn his parent's love.
10. Children should be calmed first, adults second.

For a more detailed consideration of parental influences on childhood emotion and adjustment, a number of recent RET publications are recommended (Bard, 1980; Hauck, 1983; McInerney, 1983; Woulff, 1983).

III. A RET ANALYSIS OF CHILDHOOD EMOTION

The seeds of emotional disturbance in children and adolescents are the ideas, assumptions, and beliefs they have acquired as a result of the interaction of their developing cognitive–affective characteristics with social, cultural, and familial influences. Most children and adolescents discard many of their irrational ideas as they grow older. Some, however, tenaciously hold on to them. And it is the group of children who have a propensity for reality distortion and irrational thinking who populate the offices of mental health practitioners.

Over the past 20 years, RET practitioners have written about their experiences in working with younger populations. More particularly, they have begun to speculate about the antiempirical assumptions, irrational ideas, and beliefs that appear to underlie a wide variety of problems in childhood. This material is invaluable for the practitioner in assessing dysfunctional cognitions, in that he/she is in a good position to know what to look for when questioning a child concerning a specific problem.

What follows then is an account of the irrational thinking and thought processes that are proposed to underlie much of the emotional maladjustment that occurs in children and adolescents and that quite often persists into adulthood. A discussion of the general irrational beliefs of childhood precedes a discussion of specific childhood emotional and behavioral problems.

A. Irrational Beliefs of Childhood

The delimitation of the irrational beliefs of children by RET theorists is based largely on clinical experience rather than empirical work. As such, the material to be reported is better viewed as hypotheses rather than facts. Additionally, the RET working assumption that the irrationalities of children have similarities with those of adults should be investigated experimentally. The lack of a research base for validating the manifestations and consequences of the irrational beliefs of children is recognized.

There are two scales available for the assessment of the irrational beliefs of children. Knaus (1974) developed two forms of the Children's Survey of Rational Beliefs (Form B, ages 7–10; Form C, ages 10–13). While these scales have been used extensively as dependent measures by RET researchers in seeking to confirm the effects of rational–emotive interventions on school-age populations, it is unfortunately the case that no normative, reliability, and validity test data are available. In seeking to measure developmental trends in rational thinking, Kassinove, Crisci, and Tiegerman (1977) developed the Idea Inventory. This scale assesses the degree of endorsement of a number of irrational ideas and can be administered to students in grades 4–12. Limited reliability and validity data are reported. In the Kassinove et al. study, results indicated irrationality decreases with age although the relation between individual irrational ideas and grade was variable. In investigating grade, race, and sex differences in rational thinking, Briley (1980) found a high correlation between the Idea Inventory and the Children's Survey of Rational Beliefs (Form C). In general, data from these studies have not been directly employed in the following discussion.

The determination of whether a given belief will lead to one or more emotional problems in children depends on, among other things, (1) the number of irrational beliefs the child holds, (2) the range of situations in which the child applies his or her ideas (school, home, peers, adults, work, play), (3) the strength of the child's belief, and (4) the extent to which the child tends to distort reality as observed in errors of inference about what has happened or what will happen.

There appears to be three major clusters of irrational beliefs in childhood (a detailed discussion of these beliefs can be found in Ellis et al., 1966; Ellis, 1973; Ellis & Bernard, 1983; Bernard & Joyce, 1984). There are two major beliefs that surround the child's developing sense of personal identity of self-worth: "It is a dire necessity for me to be loved by everyone for everything I do" and "I should be thoroughly competent, intelligent, and achieving in all possible respects." Children who hold these beliefs doubtless experience feelings of inferiority, worthlessness, guilt, and anxiety, tend to engage in excessive approval-seeking behaviors, and either work assiduously to avoid social and task situations in which they believe they will fail or work compulsively to succeed in everything they do.

A second cluster of irrational beliefs that underlies a variety of problems includes "I should always get what I want" and "It is horrible when things are not the way I would like them to be." The "demandingness" observed in many children leads to feelings of anger, hostility, and jealousy, and can be revealed in antisocial behavior, underachievement, and aggression.

A third set of pernicious ideas of the childhood period surrounds Ellis' recent formulations concerning "discomfort anxiety." Children and adolescents who believe "I cannot stand feeling uncomfortable," "It is horrible to be frustrated," and "Life should be easy and comfortable at all times" are at risk for a variety of emotional difficulties. Certain children escalate mild upsets into huge emotional disturbances because they are "sensation sensitive" and as a consequence find that they cannot stand even the mildest degree of emotional unpleasantness. Children who avoid schoolwork and domestic chores often find it impossible to tolerate or endure the initial feelings of discomfort they experience when confronted with a task.

These three clusters of general irrational ideas can be briefly summarized as follows: (1) I must do well and be approved of. (2) I must get what I want. (3) I cannot tolerate discomfort.

Waters (1982) has provided a more detailed list of the irrational beliefs of children as follows: (1) It's awful if others don't like me. (2) I'm bad if I make a mistake. (3) Everything should go my way; I should always get what I want. (4) Things should come easy to me. (5) The world should be fair and bad people must be punished. (6) I shouldn't show my feelings. (7) Adults should be perfect. (8) There's only one right answer. (9) I must win. (10) I shouldn't have to wait for anything.

For adolescents, the following irrational beliefs have been identified by Waters: (1) It would be awful if peers didn't like me. It would be awful to be a social loser. (2) I shouldn't make mistakes, especially social mistakes. (3) It's my parent's fault I'm so miserable. (4) I can't help it; that's just the way I am and I guess I'll always be this way. (5) The world should be fair and just. (6) It's awful when things do not go my way. (7) It's better to avoid challenges than to risk failure. (8) I must conform to my peers. (9) I can't stand to be criticized. (10) Others should always be responsible.

B. Emotional Problems

RET does not consider that all children who emotionally over- or underreact to situations are prime candidates for the "loony bin" and, therefore, for RET. Obviously, most if not all children exhibit from time to time and from situation to situation emotional and behavioral reactions that do not serve their best interests. This is because others do not like to be around children who throw temper tantrums or who are sulking. Of course, emotional reactions can be used as primary offensive weapons in a child's power struggle with others and often, because of their aversiveness, act as negative reinforcers. Children turn on the tears, whines, or screams when they want something and turn them off when they get it. RET identifies children who *tend to consistently demonstrate inappropriate emotional reactions that occur with a high degree of intensity and that often last for long periods of time* as in need of some form of help.

As indicated earlier, RET adopts a cognitive model to explain the origins of emotional problems in children. The model identifies two sources of cognitive distortion that lead to emotional upset. The first type of cognitive error occurs at the interpretation stage in which the child may distort reality through several illogical reasoning processes such as arbitrary inference, overgeneralization, selective abstraction, minimization, and magnification of what they experience (see Beck, 1976; Beck et al., 1979). This type of error has been referred to as an error of inference (DiGiuseppe, 1981) in that the child goes beyond the information present in his immediate sphere and draws false conclusions or predictions. Faulty appraisals are the second type of cognitive distortion that exacerbates emotional upset. Grieger and Boyd (1983) have suggested that faulty appraisals can be considered errors of evaluation (i.e., irrational attitudes, ideas, or beliefs) about what has occurred or will occur. RET maintains that the tendency to make errors of inference or faulty appraisals of our interpretation is supported by the irrational beliefs a child holds. For example, a child who believes that everything should go his way is likely to misinterpret situations as being unfair and is equally likely to appraise the "unfairness" as something truly awful.

Many of the inferences concerning the origins of different emotions in children derive from the extensive clinical observations made with adult clients. Given the proclivity of overly upset adults to employ reasoning processes characteristic of younger children, the types of cognitive errors, distortions, irrational and antiempirical ideas that are observed in children may share many things in common with those of adults. This as previously stated remains an empirical question. Granted that adult concerns are far different from those of children, we find both upset children and adults to be equally demanding, to build mountains out of molehills, to experience equal degrees of low frustration tolerance, and to continuously rate the worth of themselves and others in terms of the "goodness" or "badness" of their behavior. In our discussion of childhood emotions we refer both to RET theorizing and observation of adults and of children. It will be seen that there is a relatively small number of child and adolescent beliefs that underlie different childhood emotions. The extent of overlap between the irrational thinking processes of children and adults is also a largely unexamined area of scientific inquiry.

1. Depression and Low Self-Esteem

Feelings of worthlessness, inadequacy, and inferiority are not exactly the same as their use in common parlance would have us believe. When someone says, "I feel depressed," it may well be they are feeling inadequate because of some self-perceived rejection or failure. However, depression is a broader and more complicated state than is feeling badly about oneself. While depression does encompass an affective component that involves feelings of low self-esteem, it tends to be considered as a clinical syndrome that involves other areas of cognitive, behavioral, and emotive functioning. The following discussion of low self-esteem leads to a general consideration of depression, with specific attention directed towards childhood depression.

It is important to distinguish between self-concept and self-esteem. Self-concept can be considered as the picture one holds of oneself. It is a general idea we have of our skills, abilities, and characteristics, which we derive from personal experience. One's self-concept—one's personal identity—can be conceived of as involving three general areas of self-appraisal: social (skills in relating to people), intellectual (academic and cognitive abilities), and physical (characteristics of body) (Samuels, 1977). Self-concept is an idea, a cognition of oneself which does not involve any attitudinal or emotional judgments of what one sees. Self-esteem involves how individuals judge and evaluate the different aspects of their self-concept, that is, does the individual like or dislike, approve or disapprove of the things she sees in herself. The self-evaluations we make of our performances in our different roles (school, family, work, religion) across the three dimensions of our self-concept determine our feelings about ourselves. We tend to rate ourselves in terms of our performances in different activities. There are a number of standards we use in making these judgments. The criteria we employ to make our self-ratings involve our comparing our performance with our past performance, the performance of others around us, or some societally defined ideal. In those roles and for those activities we value and care about, we evaluate our behavior in terms of its success or failure on the basis of the previously mentioned criteria which, in turn, determines our feelings about ourselves. If we perform poorly, we feel badly about ourselves (low self-esteem). As the distance between the standards we set for ourselves and our performances becomes greater, our self-esteem diminishes. The greater the mismatch between a person's ideal self and his or her self-concept, the greater the likelihood will be of low self-esteem. Cognitive judgments or our success and failure experiences are a crucial element of our self-esteem. Our self-esteem can be considered a composite of all our self-evaluations and resultant feelings we have of ourselves.

To feel somewhat upset when we perform poorly (fail, get rejected) is a normal human emotion. And even though RET views low self-esteem as central to most human disturbance, not all people who play the game of ego rating are disturbed, for most people do not overly upset themselves when they fail to live up to some standard or goal they have set for themselves. And even when they put themselves down for failing, the resultant feelings of sadness and worthlessness do not last for very long and do not interfere with the individual's pursuit of goals. It is only those persons who frequently put themselves down and who experience prolonged and self-sabotaging periods of low self-esteem leading to other behavioral and somatic effects who manifest a depressive disorder.

There are a number of faulty beliefs that lead to feelings of worthlessness. The two main irrational beliefs appear to be "I must be loved and approved of by every significant person in my life and if I'm not it's awful" and "I am not worthwhile unless I am thoroughly competent, adequate, achieving, and attractive at all times." People who frequently experience low self-esteem tend to make the cognitive distortion of selective abstraction (they only view the negative aspects of their behavior), dichotomous thinking (they tend to see themselves in terms of bad and good), and overgeneralization (they view one instance of failure as proof of their basic inferiority). People with chronic low self-esteem often set overly ambitious and unrealistic performance standards for themselves. Perfectionism almost inevitably leads to feelings of low self-esteem. This is frequently the case for depression prone children.

Young children occasionally experience bad feelings about themselves as a consequence of failure or rejection. Because of their cognitive tendency to view themselves and others in all-or-none unidimensional dimensions, they may think to themselves that they are bad because of some mistake and as a result temporarily feel lousy about themselves. When, however, their teacher smiles at them, or they get a spelling word correct, or make a good catch on the field, they are sublimely happy with themselves. There seems to be a small percentage of children and adolescents who almost seem to search for failure, home in on it like a bee to honey, and sting themselves when they find what they are looking for. The tunnel vision of these children resembles the compulsive, selective focusing witnessed in adult depressives. Chronic low self-esteem appears to be one of the prime symptoms of learned helplessness and depression in children. Self-talk that leads to low self-esteem is illustrated in the following example:

Antecedent event:	Mary is asked to spell a word and gives the wrong answer.
Rational thoughts:	"I failed to spell correctly and this is unpleasant. I hope this does not happen often. I had better study harder so I get it right the next time."
Consequences:	Disappointment, mild shame, and embarrassment. Better preparation.
Irrational thoughts:	"I failed to spell correctly and this is the worst thing that could ever happen to me; I am a hopeless failure."
Consequences:	Low self-esteem. Repeated failures.

By far the greatest amount of work into the cognitive dynamics of depression has been conducted by Aaron T. Beck and his associates.

Beck (1976) has proposed the following three cognitive components (the "cognitive triad") as being central to understanding the development and maintenance of depression.

> 1. *A negative view of self.* The depressed individual shows a marked tendency to view himself as deficient, inadequate, or unworthy, and to attribute his unpleasant experiences to a physical, mental, or moral defect in himself. Furthermore, he regards himself as undesirable and worthless because of his presumed defect and tends to reject himself (and to believe others will reject him) because of it.
>
> 2. *A negative view of the world.* His interactions with the environment are interpreted as representing defeat, deprivation, or disparagement. He views the world as making exorbitant demands on him and presenting obstacles which interfere with the achievement of his life goals.
>
> 3. *A negative view of the future.* The future is seen from a negative perspective and revolves around a series of negative expectations. The depressed patient anticipates that his current problems and experiences will continue indefinitely and that he will increasingly burden significant others in his life. (p. 121)

Hauck (1971, 1973) offers a cognitive view of depression that departs from Beck's on the issue of the cognitive triad and, instead, proposes his own three-factor theory of depression. Hauck argues that if people see the world according to Beck's triad, they need not be depressed at all. In fact, asserts Hauck, such a view may demonstrate good reality testing (he cites the example of a victim of a concentration camp). It is not the pessimism itself that causes the depression he argues, "but the additional act of blaming ourselves, or feeling sorry for others over the accurately and inaccurately assessed self, world, or future" (Hauck, 1977, pp. 117–118). It is these three elements that account for Hauck's three-factory theory: self-blame, self-pity, and other pity. According to Hauck (1971), underlying each factor are the following irrational beliefs that are the central causes of depression.

1. Self-blame: (a) "There are such things as bad and evil people in the world (he or she being one) and that they must be punished in order to assure the future avoidance of that heinous behavior."

2. Self-pity: (a) "It is not merely sad, regrettable, and unfortunate when events do not pass as one hoped for, but that it is literally horrible, earth shaking and catastrophic;" (b) "That emotional pain is inflicted upon us from without rather than from within."

3. Pitying others: (a) "One should be upset over other people's disturbances and difficulties;" (b) "That it is vitally important to our existence what other people do, and that we should make great efforts to change them in the direction we would like them to be." (p. 33)

Ellis *et al.* (1966) indicated that there are two general activating events for depression: failure and being rejected by someone whose approval you definitely want to have. According to Ellis, feelings of rejection and failure do not produce depression; rather, depression derives from putting yourself down, blaming, punishing and, finally, pitying yourself for the failure or rejection. Rational thoughts after rejection and failure might be, "I don't like failing. I wish I had succeeded and been accepted by that person. How unfortunate for me to fail and get rejected." Irrational beliefs are revealed in the following declarative self-statements: "How awful to have failed and been rejected. I'll never get what I really want. This reveals me as a rotten person. How hopeless. I'll never get what I really want. I'll go on forever, never really getting what I most desire."

Wessler and Wessler (1980) synthesize the work of Beck, Ellis, and Hauck and indicate that depression involve the ideational components of self-pity, self-downing, helplessness, and hopelessness. They propose that depression can arise from guilt or shame, self-pity, and low frustration tolerance and associated discomfort anxiety. When guilty or shameful depression exists, the individual feels guilty or ashamed of something she has done and, as a consequence, feels helpless and hopeless about achieving self-worth. They are in accord with Beck's position that some forms of depression stem from self-pity that results from the loss of something or someone highly valued. The third form of depression they identify arises from the need for comfort and involves people who are unwilling to take the risks and experience the discomfort involved in removing themselves from problematic situations. They feel trapped and can see little they can do about it because of their unwillingness to "gain through pain."

There is increasing empirical evidence to suggest that depression in children and adults have a number of similarities, although there are a number of features that are thought to be unique to children (e.g., Lefkowitz & Tesiny, 1980). There is another point of view that suggests that childhood depression is quite distinct from the disorder in adults, and that depression in children is expressed in masked symptoms (behavioral equivalents) such as accident proneness, impulsivity, psychosomatic disturbance, and school avoidance. Children who demonstrate a wide variety of the following behaviors with some degree of frequency may be diagnosed as depressed: sadness, unhappiness, apprehension, weepiness, aggression, apathy, withdrawal, listlessness, self-deprecation, poor schoolwork, and some somatic complaints such as headaches and stomachaches. Lefkowitz and Tesiny (1980) characterize childhood depression as a state marked by a reduction in ebullience and in the capacity for pleasurable experience. Four areas of functioning may be involved: (a) affective, by manifestations of dysphoria, (b) cognitive, by manifestations of self-depreciation, (c) motivational, by decreased performance and withdrawal, and (d) vegetative, by fatigue, sleep problems, and loss of appetite. (p. 44)

It would appear that depression in children is extremely hard to assess due to the transitory developmental nature of many of the behaviors thought symptomatic of depression in normal children as well as the unavailability of psychometrically sound measurements.

Attributional theory suggests that the attributions and beliefs that people hold concerning the causes of events in their lives influence their sense of helplessness, depression, and self-esteem (Metalsky & Abramson, 1981). Research conducted mostly with college-age students indicates that people who attribute negative events in their lives to internal factors such as lack of ability are more likely to be high in depression and low self-esteem (e.g., Ickes & Layden, 1978). It appears sensible to assert that children who sense a lack of personal control over their environment for positive outcomes and who hold themselves responsible for negative outcomes (joint negative cognitive appraisals) would be prime candidates for depression. A number of studies (Dweck, 1975; Dweck & Rippucci, 1973) have found that children who manifest chronic learned helplessness attribute their failures to their own stable and enduring characteristics.

Ellis (1973) has provided his view on the cognitive basis of depression in children. He distinguishes between depression and displeasure and indicates,

Depression, however, includes a much stronger feeling than that of displeasure: the feeling that the unpleasant event *should not* have existed: that it probably will *always* exist; and that it will lead to unbearable, horrible, results. (p. 118)

Ellis disagrees with the traditional analytic notion that all depression consists in children (and adults) of anger turned inward and that all anger is depression turned outward. Occasionally (but not regularly) we get angry at ourselves for pitying ourselves and being depressed and turn our anger against others who have caused the events we believe we cannot tolerate.

2. Anxiety, Fear, and Phobia

There are a number of ways in which RET distinguishes among the related emotions of anxiety, fear, and phobia. There appears to be the greatest confusion between anxiety and fear. Hauck (1975) defines fear and distinguishes it from anxiety on the basis of the extent to which the emoting individual is conscious of the cause of the emotion. He argues that an individual who feels threatened in a situation without knowing exactly why and what it is she is afraid of is experiencing anxiety. Fear, on the other hand, is defined as a feeling of threat from a cause of which one is aware. Hauck makes the additional point that anxiety generally invites no clear-cut evasive action whereas fear can be controlled simply by avoiding the feared stimulus. According to Hauck, the three most common fears are the fear of rejection, fear of failure, and the fear of being afraid.

Ellis *et al.* (1966) suggest that there are two major kinds of fears in children, fears of external things and events (animals, dark, moving objects) and fears of one's own basic inadequacies. The latter he redefines as anxiety. Specifically, Ellis (1973) differentiates the fear of being physically hurt from the fear of being socioemotionally hurt. He provides the following description of an anxious individual.

> He finds dangers when there are none; or he exaggerates them when they do exist; or he thinks the penalties that risks involve are much too great; or he keeps worrying, worrying about what may occur in the future, though there is less likelihood that the event he fears will actually occur, and still less that it will be truly catastrophic if and when it does. (p. 36)

According to Ellis (1973), fear is a self-preserving emotion because it encourages persons to be cautious and vigilant towards the world around them. "Fear, in other words, is prophylactic, and includes the notions: (a) something or someone is dangerous to me: (b) therefore I'd better *do something* to protect myself against this dangerous thing or person" (p. 148). Anxiety differs from fear in that it includes the idea that because the person is basically incompetent and has experienced some difficulty coping with threats and dangers, he will *never* be able to cope with dangerous people or things, that he will *never* be able to come up with solutions to problems that entail dangerous aspects, and that he is *blameworthy* for being so incompetent. Whereas fear is based on an objective appraisal of a dangerous circumstance and leads to the individual trying to find effective solutions, anxiety, which is based on the individual's negative self-appraisal and self-perceived ineptness, leads to ineffective performance which in turn stimulates additional anxiety.

Ellis (1979, 1980) has illuminated and separated two forms of anxiety that have origins in different irrational ideas. *Discomfort anxiety* stems from the idea that one must be comfortable and without pain at all times, that one cannot stand troublesome events, and that one cannot stand to feel distress. As a consequence of this irrational belief, people spend inordinate amounts of time worrying about and avoiding events and people because they anticipate feeling uncomfortable and miserable, which they mistakenly believe they would not be able to tolerate. *Ego anxiety* results from the same irrational ideas concerning self-worth and the need for love and approval that underlie low self-esteem. The main difference is that ego anxiety stems from individuals anticipating events in which they perform badly (commit a moral indiscretion) or poorly (failure and rejection) which results in either others or themselves (or both) putting themselves down.

Fears and anxieties are somewhat more distinguishable from phobias. Whereas fear is a relatively normal and healthy adaptive living emotional response to objects and events that may cause harm, phobias are irrational and disabling fears that are generally specific to one object or situation (Ross, 1980). Hauck (1975) indicates that a phobia is a combination of a fear and anxiety. "It occurs when you do not know what it is you are afraid of *but you think you know.* Furthermore, the object that you fear must symbolically represent the fear you actually have" (p. 22). Children who have a school phobia have a general idea what they fear (school, teachers, classmates, tests) but they cannot clearly articulate what it is they are specifically worried about. Their worry and uneasiness stems from a variety of sources at school which remain largely unclear in the mind of the child. Ellis (1973) asserts that people who have a phobia cling to two major irrational beliefs: "(a) The world is much too difficult and dangerous a place to live in and *should* be made much easier, and (b) They cannot single-handedly cope with it and therefore they desperately and absolutely *need* the acceptance, love, and support of others in order to accept themselves and to perform even minimally well" (p. 218). In addition, they blame and condemn themselves for not being able to cope with their problems.

Traditionally, RET theorists have considered three major kinds of anxiety that are commonly observed in school-age children: interpersonal anxiety (fear of rejection), and test and speech anxiety (fear of failure). All three stem from the young person's cognitions that tend to catastrophize the personal consequences of failing at some activity. The younger client tends to overestimate the probability and personal cost of some undesirable event as well as underestimating his/her resources to cope with the perceived threat in an adaptive fashion (McFall & Wollersteim, 1979). Many students who experience high levels of anxiety in competitive situations appear to have at the core of their anxiety a poor self-concept and quite often low self-esteem. They view their performances as public (and private) signs of their self-worth. Hauck

(1975) indicates that fear of rejection is more prevalent because children and adolescents are "often afraid to fail for the very reason they might be rejected if they do" (p. 16).

Students who obsessively ruminate about their performance have "double trouble" for not only do they experience the unpleasant and painful sensations associated with anxiety, their anxiety-producing thoughts distract them from and interfere with effective task performance, thereby increasing the likelihood of the impending doom they have been worrying about. Children and adolescents do make mountains out of molehills and talk themselves into believing that social rejection and academic failure would be horrible and awful. Children who experience frequent episodes of anxiety subscribe to a number of self-defeating ideas including (1) "I must at all times be loved and win the approval of others. Unless others love and approve of me I am not a worthwhile person," (2) "I must succeed at all times and if I fall short of my standard or if I fail that would be awful for it would prove I am a failure," (3) "I cannot tolerate any sort of public embarrassment or humiliation," (4) "It is impossible for me to face up and handle any situation successfully," and (5) "I must worry and stew about the uncertainties of the future."

Children by nature are afraid and scared of many more things than are older adolescents and adults. The content of children's fears change with age. Fears of young children are concerned with physical harm whereas older children show fears associated with psychological harm including rejection and failure. Because of the range and intensity of fears of children, it is not always possible to recognize when fears become irrational and phobic. A fear can be viewed as being rational if a disinterested observer would label the situation as realistically dangerous. A fear can be labeled irrational if it is based on imaginary and fallacious assumptions or on faulty reasoning. Childrens' fears, then, are better assessed in terms of the reality of their perception of danger as well as the degree to which they exaggerate the awfulness of the feared event and underestimate their coping resources. The cognitive steps underlying irrational fears in children may be considered as follows: "Something is dangerous and will hurt me. I must avoid being near it at all costs. Being near it is awful; I can't even bear to think about it. I can't cope. I can't cope with the thought of being hurt." It should be kept in mind that as children begin to be able to distinguish imagination from reality, a number of their fears being to evaporate. Fears that persist after the age at which they would normally appear and that significantly impair the functioning of the child are of concern to the RET practitioner.

When children's fears become intense, persistent, and self-defeating, they can be termed phobias. Their fears can either be of physical dangers or psychosocial danger such as dog phobia, dental phobia (generally called dental anxiety), school phobia, and test, speech, and social phobia (commonly referred to as anxieties). The RET view of childhood phobias is that children are more afraid of the consequences of confronting the feared stimulus than they are of the stimulus itself. Ellis *et al.* (1966) indicate that children who experience phobic reactions often have a general fearful attitude to their environment. They tend to be more afraid of physical dangers, of making mistakes, of being laughed at, and of being left alone. "Certain children are enormous catastrophizers who actually seek out conditions to worry and fret about" (p. 38). Some of their ideas which create phobias include "I cannot stand being around scary things." "I am unable to cope with things I am afraid of." "I will be overwhelmed by scary things and that would be unbearable." In the case of school phobia, schools contain elements of physical and psychosocial danger. Children who exhibit school phobic reactions are often overstimulated by the number and severity of the physical dangers and social threats they imagine and anticipate, and they view themselves as largely incapable of coping with each and every one. The cognitions of these children are often those that create anxiety, including a sense that they are basically no good and that they cannot handle situations effectively.

Grieger and Boyd, RET theorists (1983), have examined childhood anxieties in terms of Ellis' newer conceptions of ego and discomfort anxiety. Ego anxiety in children results from the belief that "she/he must do well and be approved for it or else she/he is worthless, bad, and an unworthy person whom no one could ever care for again" (Grieger & Boyd, 1983). Grieger and Boyd have identified four classes of problems which are related to ego anxiety in children: avoidance/ withdrawal from people, attention-seeking, avoidance/withdrawal from tasks, and perfectionism.

Discomfort anxiety in children has a number of irrational beliefs and assumptions at its core including the idea that "it is *horrible, terrible,* and *awful* when things go wrong or when something difficult or dangerous is confronted" (Grieger & Boyd, 1979). Discomfort anxiety may or may not begin with a child making a faulty inference about perceived reality.

The child who makes a faulty inference (e.g., "Because the neighbor kid was pushed down on the playground, I'll be hurt if I go to school") will be afraid; the child with only discomfort anxiety will be highly fearful; and children with both are usually terrified about many things, and their terror prompts them to continually create more faulty inferences and irrational evaluations (Grieger & Boyd, 1983).

Children who experience discomfort anxiety tend to exaggerate and "awfulize" about unpleasantness and they strongly believe and demand that things should always go the way they desire, quickly and easily. Problems associated with discomfort anxiety include school phobia, procrastination of school work and home chores, obsessional worrying about an event or activity, and childhood obesity.

3. Anger

As with all other emotions, RET views anger and hostility as arising from anger-creating philosophies rather than directly from stressful or frustrating events. RET takes the position that although there is a large physiological component to anger, angry feelings become physiological only after they are created cognitively. Ellis and Harper (1975) indicate that Miller and Dollard's frustration–aggression hypothesis (Dollard & Miller, 1950) stems from the irrational idea that you have to view things as awful, terrible, horrible, and catastrophic when you get seriously frustrated, treated unfairly, or rejected. Whereas many kinds of frustration do lead to feelings of anger, it is often the case that frustration may lead to other feelings such as self-pity, low self-esteem, or even exhilaration ("I really like a challenge"), or to no feelings at all if the person elects not to view the frustration as all that awful or if the frustrating agent appears to be justified, nonarbitrary, or reasonable (Beck, 1976).

Ellis (1977) draws an important distinction between healthy and unhealthy anger. Healthy anger is an emotion of moderate intensity (it does not overly upset the individual) that helps individual attain goals, and is based on a nonabsolutistic view of self and others that is consistent with reality. Unhealthy anger is an extremely upsetting emotion which because of the turmoil it creates does not permit the attainment of person goals and is based on a demanding, condemning, blaming, and punishing philosophy that causes individuals to misinterpret and distort reality. Synonyms for healthy anger include the moderate emotions of irritation, disappointment, and displeasure whereas synonyms for unhealthy anger are rage, hate, and bitterness. The main RET idea is that when you are thwarted from obtaining what you desire or when someone else mistreats you or violates some personal rule or value that you feel strongly about, it is perfectly normal, rational, and appropriate to be moderately upset and irritated, because such feelings will no doubt help motivate you to act constructively to change the situation so that you obtain what you want or so your rights are not violated in the future. However, if you become extremely angry and hostile after being frustrated, it is quite likely that not only will you not be able to perform in a way that will rectify the situation, your behavior which will most likely be viewed as provocative and aggressive will tend to exacerbate the situation for the worse. Extreme anger results in effects that are not conducive to individual survival and general fitness.

At this point it may be useful to distinguish between the emotion of anger and the physical act of aggression. It is not always the case that anger leads to aggressive and conduct-disordered behavior. Many people including children who experience episodes of intense hostility and anger toward others have learned to control or hide their feelings. They may refrain from "hitting out" when they are upset because they have been firmly and consistently punished when younger for aggressive behavior or because they have been socialized away from the expression of anger. Equally, there are a significant number of children who demonstrate conduct-disordered behavior (vandalism, stealing, bullying) who are not particularly upset at the time they are being destructive. They appear to behave impulsively without thinking and therefore may lack the cognitive means for creating the feeling of anger. These persons do not suffer from irrational beliefs but rather from the absence of inappropriate verbal mediators for behavioral self-control. Or alternatively, they may believe that their aggressive behavior is appropriate and adaptive in which case their antiempirical ideas and conclusions need to be challenged.

Ellis and Harper (1975) specify two basic irrational beliefs that create the conditions for anger. The first is the idea that when people act obnoxiously and unfairly, you should blame and condemn them, and see them as bad, wicked or rotten individuals. They describe the process of becoming angry in these cognitive steps: (1) "I do not like Joe's behavior." and (2) "Because I do not like it, he shouldn't have acted that way." The second irrational idea that leads to anger is that one must view things as awful, terrible, horrible, and catastrophic when one gets seriously frustrated, treated unfairly, or rejected. Essentially one says "I don't like this situation. I can't stand it. It drives me crazy. It shouldn't exist this way. It simply has to change otherwise I can't possibly feel happy" (Ellis & Harper, 1975, p. 126).

Angry feelings result from low frustration tolerance and discomfort anxiety according to Wessler and Wessler (1980). Anger is one major emotional consequence of the irrational belief they indicate underlies low frustration tolerance, "Life should be easy and go the way I want. If not, it's awful and I can't stand it." In accordance with Ellis, they believe that "anger derives from demandingness and awfulizing directed toward perceived frustration. We experience frustration when we do not get what we want; we experience anger when we do not get what we want *and* believe we *should have* and therefore it is *awful*" (p. 98). If people thwart themselves because of some inability or imperfection (procrastination), anger can be directed at themselves ("I should have worked harder!"). Otherwise, anger can be turned against others of the world, depending on where the individual appraises the source of frustration to be. They make an important distinction between feeling annoyed, which results from rationally preferring that other people not break personal rules and violate personal rights, and anger, which stems from grandiosely demanding that others behave differently.

In relation to anger in children, a number of further comments can be made. Because younger children have difficulty controlling their anger once it starts, and because it seems to be triggered so easily especially in impulsive children, it sometimes appears that anger is under the control of external events and internal physiological rather than psychological processes. It seems that this picture is misleading in that underlying most unhealthy anger in neurologically intact children are a number of egocentric views concerning their importance. Discussing the anger-creating view of a 9-year-old boy of average intelligence whom he was seeing, Ellis *et al.* (1966) wrote

> He believed that practically everyone in the world existed solely for the purpose of doing his bidding and making things easy for him and that when anyone acted otherwise, this person deserved instantly to be put in his place and made to feel miserable. (p. 101)

Ellis *et al.* (1966) also made the point that most children resent others for their undesired behavior and that this should not be viewed as a sign of abnormal aggression. There are, however, some children who are "not only angry when they are seriously frustrated, but they are also resentful when they are only mildly thwarted; or they are resentful out of all proportion to the frequency or degree of their frustration; or they find severe frustrations when there are actually few or none" (p. 47). Anger often serves to protect these children against their own feelings of worthlessness. "By being angry at others, one can demean them, then by comparison, make oneself feel enormously superior to others. Children compensate for inadequacy feelings and their relentless frustration by seeing others as miserable worms and themselves as would-be saviors" (p. 45).

An underlying irrational belief of children who have overly hostile reactions is that "Everything should be made exceptionally easy for me and I should not have to put up with any kind of frustration." Angry children frequently have low frustration tolerance. Their demandingness derives from their rigidly held belief that things are unfair and should not exist. Consider Jeff who pushes in front of Jason and Mark to get into class first. Mark might think to himself, "I'm annoyed with Jeff for moving in front of me. I wish he wouldn't do it. I'm going to ask him to get back." Such rational thoughts would lead to irritation and the use of an adaptive problem-solving skill. Jason, on the other extreme, might think to himself the irrational, unrealistic, and anger-creating thoughts, "He can't get away with doing that. He has no right. The teacher will like him more than she'll like me and that's awful. He's really gone too far this time. It's not fair and I'm going to get him!" One can predict what Jason's ensuing emotions and behavior would be.

In his innovative approach to the understanding and treatment of conduct disorders in children, DiGiuseppe (1983) has described the cognitive origins of a variety of children's misbehavior including teasing, temper tantrums, impulsivity, hitting, stealing, and verbal aggression. According to DiGiuseppe, there are two main cognitive–emotive clusters that appear in children who manifest disorders in their conduct.

> As with adults, children usually get angry when they demand that the world be the way they want it to be (Ellis, 1977). Significant others in the lives of children may very early treat them like they are special and should have unlimited rewards. These children are not hard to convince that they should always have their way. Their children's disturbance comes from the belief that since their parents believed that they should always have what they wanted, the rest of the world should do the same. The second emotional-cognitive state which appears in children who manifest disorders in their conduct is discomfort anxiety and the corresponding irrational beliefs associated with low frustration tolerance. . . . These are, first, that any discomfort, pain, or anxiety is terrible, awful, and intolerable; and second, that denial of a desire is unbearable and intolerable. (p. 117)

A third less frequently seen cognitive–affective cluster that underlies aggression in children is, according to DiGiuseppe, connected to the belief that they are worthless and will never be able to succeed in life.

> Some antisocial children behave aggressively because of a combination of depression and anger. . . . These children are usually seen in residential centers for adolescents and usually have a history of parental abandonment or obvious and sustained parental rejection. They have had a history of relaxed controls and thus failed to learn many appropriate behaviors and cognitive control skills similar to other children who misbehave. In addition, they condemn themselves for being unlovable. This group of children appears to experience no fear of negative consequences for their misbehavior and have no concern that they will negatively impact

their life by misbehavior. There is an absence of hope and a sense of helplessness. All the bad things have already happened. For some, life is viewed as externally controlling and all the payoffs are negative, so they might as well do as they please. (p. 118)

4. Guilt

RET distinguishes between guilt and feelings of guilt (Bard, 1980). The former refers to someone having violated a societal standard of acceptable behavior, which is defined as a wrong act because it interferes with a person pursuing and obtaining the long-term goals of social acceptance and survival in a community, getting along reasonably well with others, and forming and maintaining intimate relations with a few significant others. Guilt feelings stand somewhere between anger and anxiety and derive from persons putting themselves down, blaming, condemning, and punishing themselves because of their having committed a wrong (Bard, 1980). Knaus (1974) provides the following definition of the affect guilt:

An unpleasant cognitive-emotion stimulated by the belief that one has transgressed against one's own, or against normative codes of conduct, and has acted wrongly against another, and therefore deserving of blame. This awareness is followed by self-condemning thoughts, and frequently the belief that one is obligated to act justly and fairly under any and all circumstances. Related affects: anger, self-blame. Behavioral manifestations include attempting to undo the damage, contriteness, withdrawal, high-pitched agitated voice, subdued voice, apologetic language. Sometimes this reaction is followed by resentment. (p. 82)

Guilty feelings originate in guilty cognitions. Walen, DiGiuseppe, and Wessler (1980) indicate two cognitive steps to guilt. People believe that they are doing, will do, or have done something wrong and condemn themselves for doing the wrong thing. The first step may be a correct interpretation or inference by the person based on a particular system of ethics and values (which the RET practitioner will no doubt have a sense of, from having conducted a RET assessment). The irrationality associated with the second element involves the concept of self-worth and self-rating which leads to dysfunctional emotional and behavioral reactions. The RET view is that while it is certainly desirable for people to internalize a system of morality so that they know both what is adaptive behavior (self-helping and other accepting) and what is wrong (self-sabotaging and antisocial) and so they do the self- and socially approved thing, it is certainly not desirable and appropriate to be moralistic and condemn and punish themselves and others for being mistaken and immoral.

Guilt in children cannot be experienced as an emotion before the age of 4 or 5 because it is not until that age that children begin to internalize a socially accepted standard of behavior. Before that age, children's good behavior is motivated by a fear of punishment and a desire for reward, rather than by guilt feelings associated with violations of social standards. When children younger than this age commit some impropriety, their ensuing feelings are not of guilt but rather of fear stimulated by the anticipated consequences of discovery. Beginning around the fourth or fifth year, children begin to develop a rudimentary sense of right and wrong based on ethical principles, and they strongly adhere to the belief that wrongdoers (including themselves) must be punished and should repent for their "sins." Through an internalization of their parents' value system and "conscience structure" children begin to be aware of the importance of considering others. They "learn that their interests are best served by a spirit of cooperation and application of the golden rule 'Do unto others as you would be done by'" (Kessler, 1966, p. 58). Unfortunately, as children begin to internalize the values of their parents, they do not have the intellectual equipment to judge whether parental proscriptions of "dos" and "don'ts" serve their own best interests let alone the welfare of their parents. As a consequence, children acquire an abundance of moral commandments that they never have the opportunity to empirically test to determine whether they serve to enhance their well-being and the attainment of happiness and pleasure. By the time children are old enough to make such judgments, their absolutistic moral beliefs and values are so firmly entrenched in, and serve to define, their cognitive structures that they often operate at a preconscious level and lead to self-defeating self- and other-appraisals. Simply stated, what parents view as morally wrong may not work for their children. One problem for the children of parents who endorse a set of perfectionistic beliefs is that these parents often encourage their children's feelings of guilt by overreacting to and labeling their children's behavior as awful and criminal. "These children cannot escape the feeling of guilt no matter how exemplary their behavior" (Kessler, 1966, p. 59).

According to RET, two of the irrational beliefs underlying excessive guilt feelings in children appear to be "There are certain things that I do that are wrong and when I do them I am a bad and sinful person who deserves to be punished" and "I deserve whatever I get because I have done such a bad thing and I'm such a horrible person." Ellis *et al.* (1966) illustrate the cognitive psychology of guilt in children.

> Once, however, he performs an unmitigatedly heinous antisocial act he also knows that he may repeat a similar act anytime in the future; and this knowledge of his

past and possible future immorality may keep him conceiving of himself as an arrant failure or sinner who is *hopelessly* immersed in failure (or inquity). . . . He tends to denigrate himself morally, to feel that his entire being is worthless, and, therefore feels guilty or sinful. (pp. 40–41)

5. Jealousy

Jealousy is an emotion that most people seem to understand and that most people admit to having experienced at some time in their lives. It is also an emotion that has escaped the concentrated focus other emotions have received. Jealousy overlaps significantly with, appears to derive from as well as lead to, other feelings such as fear and anxiety, anger and rage, and worthlessness. Jealousy, when used to describe the feelings of adults, derives largely and commonly from a person suspecting the unfaithfulness of an intimate other, being apprehensive about the loss of another's exclusive attention, and being hostile toward and intolerant of the rival suspected of enjoying an advantage.

The irrational beliefs that underlie jealousy relate to the need for approval, to notions of self-worth, to the awfulness of being frustrated, to the false idea that human misery is externally caused, and to the irrational belief that one needs someone to depend and rely on. People who feel insecure rely on others to define their self-worth. Thus, if something causes an insecure person to question whether or not their spouse cares for them, a jealous reaction may develop. The general cognitive steps that lead to debilitating and irrational jealousy can be described as follows: (1) I need everybody's approval. To have this I must be better than everybody else. (2) If I'm not more successful, I will be compared and won't be as good. People won't like me. That would be horrible. (3) It's their fault that I'm unhappy. He has no right to be better than me. (4) I should have tried harder, I'm a failure. An alternate formulation of the cognitive steps that lead to jealousy is as follows (Walen et al., 1980): (1) I need your love and all your attention. (2) If you are with someone else, or not attending to me, it's not fair to me and is horrible for me. (3) I can't stand that situation. I hate you for doing this to me. I'll get back at you.

As would be expected, jealousy derives from different external sources in children than in adults and is expressed differently. The underlying belief system, however, appears similar. The feelings of jealousy and envy though different are often indistinguishable in children. Whereas jealousy stems from one's intolerance of a rival for possessing what one regards as being one's own possession or due, envy stresses a coveting of something that belongs to another or something (success, luck) that has come to another. Envy, then, is a painful awareness that someone else is enjoying an advantage and that you would like to possess or experience the same advantage.

Ellis et al. (1966) indicate that one of the main causes of anger in children is jealousy and envy. "They see some child with more toys, more money, or more abilities than they possess. They become terribly frustrated because he has more and that makes themselves angry about their frustration" (p. 119). According to Ellis, jealousy stems from children believing they amount to very little as people because another child of whom they are jealous has certain things they want. Envy derives from children's belief that the world is horribly unfair for depriving them of its benefits.

The general cognitive steps to jealousy in children appear to be (1) When I compare myself with you (on the basis of some measure of success such as size of present, winning a contest, number of friends), I do not seem very worthwhile and loved and that is awful. ("I'm a failure," "I'm unlovable," "I should have tried harder.") (2) Because you are more successful and loved than I am (and because others can see this to be the case), I feel embarrassed, I might lose my friends, people will hate me, and that is intolerable. (3) You are to blame for all my problems. You have no right to do that. You are an ass and I hate you. The first two steps lead to progressively greater amounts of anxiety and low self-esteem, whereas the third adds the affective component of anger. Two central irrational beliefs appear to be underlying jealousy and envy in children: (1) "To be happy, I need other people to approve of me and to show their approval," and (2) "I should not be deprived, disadvantaged, and do without."

The destructive effects of jealousy in children can be observed in severe instances of sibling rivalry. The irrational belief underlying sibling rivalry appears to be "I must be better than my sibling in all respects to show that I am not inferior." The variety of competitions that siblings play who endorse this belief are tests of each other's self-worth. Other deleterious effects of intersibling rivalry are that the siblings are constantly vying for the love and attention of their parents, which serves to create a stressful and tense environment at home. They sometimes develop profound hate for each other, sabotage each others' efforts, compulsively play games not for enjoyment but to take each other apart, and avoid areas of endeavor in which the other sibling does very well and in which he or she believes they cannot do better (Ellis et al., 1966).

IV. CONCLUSION

This review hopefully provides cognitive–behavioral mental health practitioners with a fuller understanding of the emotions of children, and furthers their insight into the relationships among cognition, emotion, and behavior in children and adolescents. Practitioners may do a disservice if a child's behavioral problems (e.g., social withdrawal, conduct disorder) are discussed without asking the question, "How is this child feeling?"

Recent experimental research supports the proposition that children's thoughts play a central role in the treatment of maladjustment.

> It has been clearly demonstrated that induced affective states resulting from cognitive processes affect patterns of behavior and cognition including self-gratification and altruism . . . resistance to temptation . . . expectancies for future outcomes . . . memory . . . productive cognition (problem solving) . . . facial expressive behavior . . . and even the learning process itself. (Masters, Felleman, & Barden, 1981, p. 95)

There is, however, a clear need for further development and refinement of assessment instruments to empirically validate the hypotheses concerning the cognitive origins of childhood emotion advanced in this article. Such instrumentation employed within a behaviorally oriented research methodology will help to confirm or disconfirm the utility of RET in both understanding and resolving the problems of childhood.

REFERENCES

Bard, J. A. Rational-emotive therapy in practice. Champaign, IL: Research Press, 1980.

Beck, A. T. Cognitive therapy and the emotional disorders. New York: Int. Univ. Press, 1976.

Beck, A. T., Rush, A. J., Shaw, B. F., & Emery, G. Cognitive therapy of depression. New York: Guilford, 1979.

Bernard, M. E. Private thought in rational-emotive psychotherapy. Cognitive Therapy and Research, 1981, 5, 125–142.

Bernard, M. E., & Joyce, M. R. Rational-emotive therapy with children and adolescents: Theory, treatment strategies, preventative methods. New York: Wiley, 1984.

Briley, C. M. Grade, race, and sex differences in students' rational-irrational thinking: The rational-emotive model. Ann Arbor, MI: Univ. Microfilms Int., 1980.

Cowan, P. Piaget: With feeling. New York: Holt, 1977.

DiGiuseppe, R. A. Cognitive therapy with children. In G. Emery, S. D. Hollon, & R. C. Bedrosian (Eds.), New directions in cognitive therapy. New York: Guilford, 1981.

DiGiuseppe, R. A. Rational-emotive therapy and conduct disorders. In A. Ellis & M. E. Bernard (Eds.), Rational-emotive approaches to the problems of childhood. New York: Plenum, 1983.

DiGiuseppe, R. A., & Bernard, M. E. Principles of assessment and methods of treatment with children. In A. Ellis & M. E. Bernard (Eds.), *Rational-emotive approaches to problems of childhood.* New York: Plenum, 1983.

Dollard, J., & Miller, N. E. *Personality and psychotherapy.* New York: McGraw-Hill, 1950.

Dweck, C. The role of expectations and attributions in the alleviation of learned helplessness. *Journal of Personality and Social Psychology,* 1975, **31,** 674–685.

Dweck, C., & Repucci, N. Learned helplessness and reinforcement responsibility in children. *Journal of Personality and Social Psychology,* 1973, **25,** 109–116.

D'Zurilla, T. J., & Goldfried, M. R. Problem solving and behavior modification. *Journal of Abnormal Psychology,* 1971, **78,** 107–126.

Ellis, A. *Reason and emotion in psychotherapy.* New York: Stuart, 1962.

Ellis, A. *Rational-emotive therapy and its application to emotional education.* New York: Institute for Rational Living, 1971.

Ellis, A. *Humanistic psychotherapy: The rational-emotive approach.* New York: McGraw-Hill, 1973.

Ellis, A. *How to live with and without anger.* New York: Readers Digest Press, 1977.

Ellis, A. Discomfort anxiety: A new cognitive behavioral construct. Part 1. *Rational Living,* 1979, **14,** 3–7.

Ellis, A. Discomfort anxiety: A new cognitive behavioral construct. Part 2. *Rational Living,* 1980, **15,** 25–30.

Ellis, A. *Rational-emotive therapy and cognitive behavior therapy.* New York: Springer Publ., 1984.

Ellis, A., & Bernard, M. E. *Rational-emotive approaches to the problems of childhood.* New York: Plenum, 1983, in press.

Ellis, A., & Grieger, R. *Handbook of rational-emotive therapy.* New York: Springer Publ., 1977.

Ellis, A., & Harper, R. A. *A new guide to rational living.* North Hollywood, CA: Wilshire, 1975.

Ellis, A., Wolfe, J. L., & Moseley, S. *How to raise an emotionally healthy, happy child.* Hollywood, CA: Wilshire, 1966.

Gagne, R. M. *The conditions of learning* (3rd ed.) New York: Holt, 1977.

Grieger, R. M., & Boyd, J. D. *Rational-emotive therapy: A skills-based approach.* New York: Van Nostrand-Reinhold, 1979.

Grieger, R. M., & Boyd, J. D. Childhood anxieties, fears, and phobia: A cognitive-behavioral psychosituational approach. In A. Ellis & M. E. Bernard (Eds.), *Rational-emotive approaches to the problems of childhood.* New York: Plenum, 1983.

Hauck, P. A. *The rational management of children.* New York: Libra Publ., 1967.

Hauck, P. A. An RET theory of depression. *Rational Living,* 1971, **6,** 32–35.

Hauck, P. A. *Overcoming depression.* Philadelphia: Westminster Press, 1973.

Hauck, P. A. *Overcoming worry and fear.* Philadelphia: Westminster Press, 1975.

Hauck, P. A. Irrational parenting styles. In A. Ellis & R. Grieger (Eds.), *Handbook of rational-emotive therapy.* New York: Springer Publ., 1977.

Hauck, P. A. Working with parents. In A. Ellis & M. E. Bernard (Eds.), *Rational-emotive approaches to the problems of childhood.* New York: Plenum, 1983.

Ickes, W., & Layden, M. A. Attributional styles. In J. Harvey, W. Ickes, & R. Kidd (Eds.), *New directions in attribution research* (Vol. 2). Hillsdale, NJ: Erlbaum, 1978.

Kassinove, H., Crisci, R., & Tiegerman, S. Developmental trends in rational thinking: Implications for rational-emotive school mental health programs. *Journal of Community Psychology,* 1977, **5,** 266–274.

Kendall, P. C. Cognitive-behavioral interventions with children. In B. Lahey & A. Kazdin (Eds.), *Advances in clinical child psychology,* (Vol. 4). New York: Plenum, 1981.

Kendall, P. C., & Hollon, S. D. (Eds.). *Cognitive behavioral interventions: theory, research and procedures.* New York: Academic Press, 1979.

Kendler, T. S., & Kendler, H. H. Reversal and nonreversal shifts in kindergarten. *Journal of Experimental Psychology,* 1959, **58,** 56–60.

Kessler, J. *Psychopathology of childhood.* New York: Prentice-Hall, 1966.

Klausmeier, H. J., Ghatala, E. S., & Frayer, D. A. *Conceptual learning and development.* New York: Academic Press, 1974.

Knaus, W. J. *Rational-emotive education. A manual for elementary school teachers.* New York: Institute for Rational Living, 1974.

Lazarus, A. *Behavior therapy and beyond.* New York: McGraw-Hill, 1972.

Lefkowitz, M. M., & Tesiny, E. P. Assessment of childhood depression. *Journal of Consulting and Clinical Psychology,* 1980, **48,** 43–50.

Lehman, P. Practical applications of RET: Group techniques. *Rational Living,* 1973, **8,** 33–36.

Mahoney, M. J. *Cognition and behavior modification.* Cambridge, MA: Ballinger, 1974.

Masters, J. C., Felleman, E. S., & Barden, R. C. Experimental studies of affective states in children. In B. Lahey & A. Kazdin (Eds.), *Advances in clinical child psychology* (Vol. 4). New York: Plenum, 1981.

McFall, M. E., & Wollersteim, J. P. Obsessive-compulsive neurosis: A cognitive-behavioral formulation and approach to treatment. *Cognitive Therapy and Research,* 1979, **3,** 333–348.

McInerney, J. F. Working with the parents and teachers of exceptional children. In A. Ellis & M. E. Bernard (Eds.), *Rational-emotive approaches to the problems of childhood.* New York: Plenum, 1983.

Metalsky, G. I., & Abramson, L. Y. Attributional styles: Towards a framework for conceptualization and assessment. In P. C. Kendall & S. D. Hollon (Eds.), *Assessment strategies for cognitive-behavioral interventions.* New York: Academic Press, 1981.

Piaget, J. Intelligence and affectivity: Their relationship during child development. In M. R. Rozenzwerg (Ed.), *Annual Reviews Monograph.* Palo Alto, CA: Annual Reviews, 1981.

Ross, A. O. *Psychological disorders of children* (2nd ed.). New York: McGraw-Hill, 1980.

Rotter, J. B. Generalized expectancies for internal versus external control of reinforcement. *Psychological Monographs,* 1966, **80,** (whole).

Samuels, S. *Enhancing self-concept in early childhood.* New York: Hyman Sciences Press, 1977.

Spivack, G., & Shure, M. B. *Social adjustment of young children: A cognitive approach to solving real-life problems.* San Francisco: Jossey-Bass, 1974.

Walen, S. R., DiGiuseppe, R., & Wessler, R. L. *A practitioner's guide to rational-emotive therapy.* London and New York: Oxford Univ. Press, 1980.

Waters, V. Therapies for children: Rational-emotive therapy. In C. Reynolds (Ed.), *Handbook of School psychology.* New York: Wiley, 1982.

Vygotsky, L. *Thought and language.* New York: Wiley, 1962.

Wessler, R. A., & Wessler, R. L. *The principles and practice of rational-emotive therapy* San Francisco: Jossey-Bass, 1980.

Woulff, N. Involving the family in the treatment of the child: A model for rational-emotive therapists. In A. Ellis & M. E. Bernard (Eds.), *Rational-emotive approaches to the problems of childhood.* New York: Plenum, 1983.

Zajonc, R. B. Feeling and thinking. *American Psychologist,* 1981, **35,** 151–175.

Index

A

ABC theory of emotional disturbance, 216–219
Abnormal behavior, dimensions of, 221–222
Academic performance, 145–146
Affect modification, 43–46
Aggression, 139–142
ALSCAL, 81, 88
Alternative thinking, 197
ANAVA, 80
Anger, 243–247
ANOVA, 80
Anxiety, 238–243
Arousal functions, 172, 173
Assertion training, 106–108
Attentional problems, 136–139
Attention processes, 227
Attribute ratings, bipolar
  analysis of, 89–90
  collection of, 83–84
Attribution, causal, in intimate dyads, 13–22
Attribution theory, 7–13
Attributional categories
  employed by actors and observers, 12–13
  employed by married couples, 20–21
  employed by nonstranger dyads, 22–31
Attributional schemes, 9–11

B

Behavioral enactment, 38–43
Behavioral marital therapy, 3–7, 54
Belief, 227
  irrational, in childhood, 230–232
Belief formulation, 195–196
Bender–Gestalt test, 138
Biological functions, 171, 173

C

Causal schema, 9
Causal thinking, 197
CBMT, see Cognitive–behavioral marital therapy
Challenge of myths, expectations, and beliefs, 35–37
Childhood emotion, cognitive behavior therapy and, 215–253
Childhood maladjustment
  cognitive–affective developmental status and, 222–226
  environmental conditions and, 227–229
  psychological conditions and, 226–227
  RET model of, 221–229
Cognition, awareness of, 220–221
Cognitive–affective developmental status, abnormal behavior and, 222–226
Cognitive–behavioral intervention in educational settings, 131–165
  history, 132–135
  outcome research, 147–148, 151–158
  setting, 150–151
  weaknesses, 158–161
Cognitive–behavioral marital therapy, 3–7, see also Attribution theory
  application, 31–53
  attributional themes, 33–34
  cognitive skills in, 34–35
  considerations and risks, 52–53
  eroticizing, 51–52
  specific interventions, 35–51
  theoretical basis, 7–31
Cognitive skills, in CBMT, 34–35
Cognitive strategies, 227
Cognitive triad, 236
Communal exchange, 29–30
Connors Teacher-Rating Scale, 138
Consequential thinking, 197

Life in a Rock Shelter

Life in a Rock Shelter

Prehistoric Indians of the Lower Pecos

By G. Elaine Acker

Hendrick-Long Publishing Co.

Library of Congress Cataloging-in-Publication Data

Acker, G. Elaine.
Life in a rock shelter: prehistoric Indians of the Lower Pecos
G. Elaine Acker.
p.cm.
Includes bibliographical references and index.
ISBN 0-937460-84-2 (softcover)
1. Indians of North America — Texas — Antiquities. 2. Indians of
North America — Pecos River Valley (N.M. And Tex.) — Antiquities.
3. Texas — Antiquities. 4. Pecos River Valley (N.M. and Tex.) — Antiquities.
I. Title.
E78.T4A18 1995
976.4'901 — dc20
95-17291
CIP

Design and Page Composition: Dianne Borneman, Shadow Canyon Graphics, Evergreen, Colorado

Printed in the United States of America

Hendrick-Long Publishing Company
Dallas, Texas

Contents

To Joe Albright,
With Thanks

Acknowledgements

Many archeologists and other professionals generously contributed their time and expertise as I researched the Lower Pecos region: Pancho Brotherton, Vaughn Bryant, Betty Pat. Gatliff, Joe Labadie, Nola Montgomery, David Robinson, Harry Shafer, and Solveig Turpin.

I owe an extra-special thank-you to Mary-Love Bigony, Tom Hester, and Roberta McGregor.

I also want to thank my friends and family for their love, support and encouragement, especially Warner Williams, for the patience to read my early drafts and the faith to push me forward; my sisters Becky and Sherry, and my Aunt Dorothy for believing in me and my dreams; and my mother, Katherine, for teaching me that dreams can come true.

A hiking trail at Seminole Canyon State Park ends at a bluff where the Rio Grande backs up into Seminole Canyon. The bluff overlooks Panther Cave.

Introduction

In the fall of 1991, I camped at Seminole Canyon State Historical Park. One afternoon, I hiked to a bluff overlooking Panther Cave and the Rio Grande. Situated just above the water line where the river backs up into the mouth of Seminole Canyon, Panther Cave was the site of many ancient Indian rituals. Its walls are covered with rock art paintings called pictographs. The sun sank slowly into the water behind me, chasing the shadows from the shallow rock shelter's back wall, and lighting the mural of mystical shaman figures, animal drawings, and weaponry.

I focused my binoculars on the pictographs, then stared across the Rio Grande at the land the Spanish called the *despoblado* (unpopulated). These remote areas of Mexico appeared wild and untamed — no houses or roads in sight. I pondered the broad expanse of dry, rocky terrain — a landscape that must have mirrored the Texas side before railroads brought the settlers west. My imagination wandered back in time. If I were an Indian in this rugged environment, what would it take to survive? What would I eat and where would I sleep?

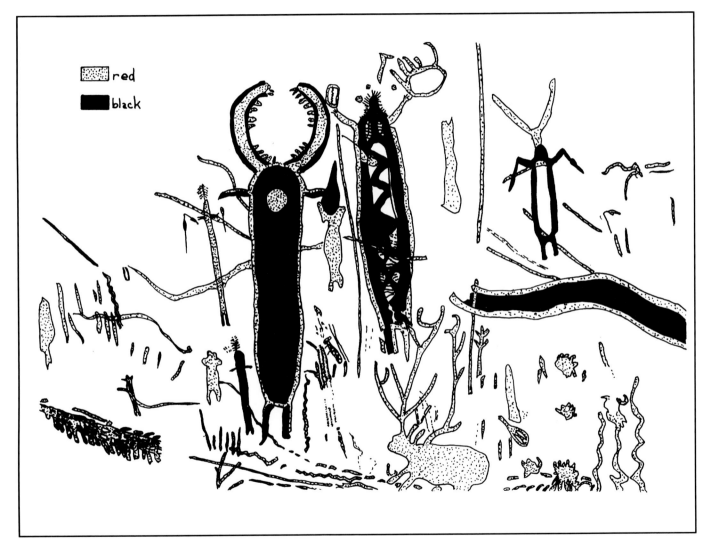

Shaman figures were often shown with antlers, which signified their association with animal or spirit "familiars."

For answers, I turned to archeologists who have spent many years studying the Lower Pecos region and the Indians who lived there thousands of years ago. With their help, I discovered the secrets of *Life in a Rock Shelter.*

In the upper right-hand corner of this pictograph, a bird shaman is drawn, depicting the flight of the soul as it rises through a cloud of spirit birds.

Fate-Bell Shelter once provided a home for native populations.

The terrain above Fate Bell Shelter is typical of the rugged canyon country of the Lower Pecos region.

Texas' Lower Pecos Region

When ancient storytellers sat beside a glowing fire and shared the tales of their people, the story came to life. Wise old men shared legends, not only with words, but with the light in their eyes, the lines on their faces, and the resonance in their voices. Texas' Lower Pecos region is like an immortal storyteller. Vast canyons were etched into Cretaceous limestone rock, which formed over 70 million years ago after a time when warm, shallow seas covered the area. These canyons remember 11,000 years of human habitation, and reveal a series of geological and climatic changes that shaped the future of the region.

Located in southwest Texas, northwest of Del Rio, the Lower Pecos region encompasses all of Val Verde and Terrell counties, as well as portions of Crockett, Pecos, and Sutton counties. The region also extends at least 100 miles into northern Coahuila, Mexico. Three rivers: the Pecos, to the west; the Rio Grande, to the south; and the Devils, to the east; slice through the rocky terrain and roughly define Texas' Lower Pecos boundaries. *Los Tres Rios* — the three rivers — probably attracted the region's earliest inhabitants.

The first people who came to the North American Continent arrived at the end of the

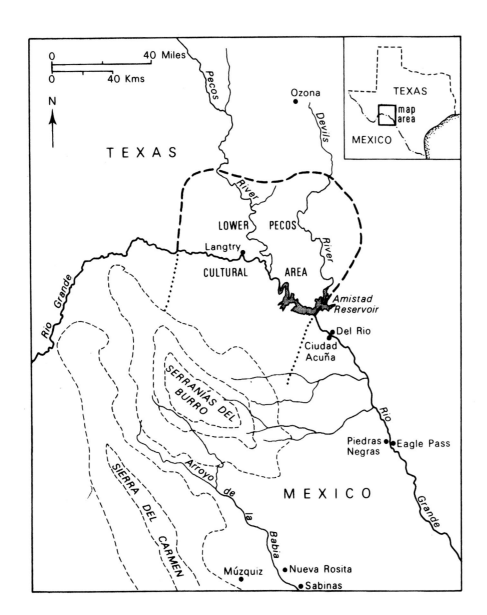

Map of the Lower Pecos Cultural Area

last Ice Age, some 11,000 years ago, by crossing a land bridge that joined Siberia and Alaska. During the glacial period, ice had covered the northern half of North America, and the climates south of the glacier were cool and moist. About 10,500 years ago, nomadic big-game hunters (Paleo-Indians) entered the Lower Pecos region. At that time, the area was a grassland with pine trees, oaks, and junipers. The people enjoyed abundant food resources, and hunted several species of megafauna — Pleistocene mammals of massive proportions such as mammoth and bison that were still present during this period. Herds of camels, horses, and elephants all roamed the fertile land.

As the glaciers melted, the weather patterns changed, and the climate gradually became warmer and drier. By approximately 10,000 years ago, most of the megafauna had become extinct, and other species had migrated to moister environments. Some plant species, whose survival depended upon the cool, moist climate, also disappeared from the

Prickly pear cactus is now one of the most abundant plant species present in the Lower Pecos.

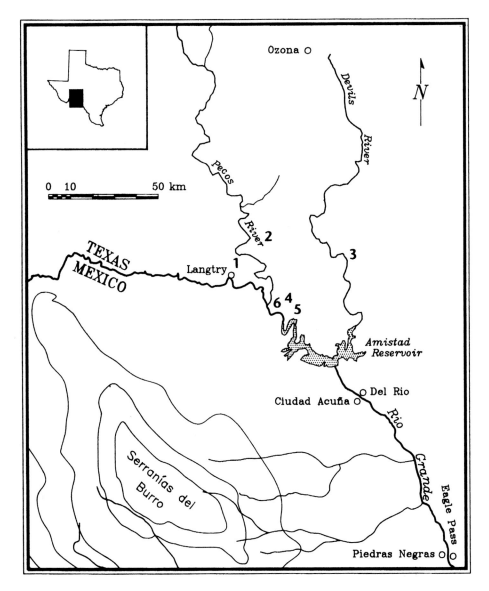

(1) *Bonfire Shelter*
(2) *Hinds Cave*
(3) *Baker Cave*
(4) *Fate Bell Shelter*
(5) *Painted Caves*
(6) *Panther Cave*

region, but other arid-adapted species gradually took their places. Pinion pines, oaks, and junipers retreated to the higher elevations, and sotol, yucca, lechuguilla, and prickly pear appeared along the canyons and arroyos.

These climatic changes were slow, occurring over a period of 4,000 to 5,000 years, and would have gone unnoticed by the region's inhabitants. By the end of this transition period, small bands of prehistoric Indians had replaced the big-game hunters, and the emphasis shifted from hunting to gathering. These bands of Indians would occupy the region for the next 9,000 years.

The Indians continued to hunt smaller animals such as deer and rabbit, but more frequently they foraged the river terraces for pecans, walnuts, and wildflowers. They also collected sotol, lechuguilla, and prickly pear along the canyons. Housing was readily available in natural rock shelters that the rivers had eroded into the sides of the canyon walls. These Indian bands lived on what nature provided and continually adapted to their environment.

The root bulbs of sotol plants were a popular food source.

Ocotillo grows upward in long tendrils throughout the region.

The drying trend continued throughout the centuries with only two significant shifts: one, approximately 2,500 years ago, and another, approximately 700 years ago, which lasted into historical times. In both instances, the climate temporarily became cooler and wetter, and attracted herds of bison. A site named Bonfire Shelter contains the bones of many bison from the period dating 2,500 years ago. Archeologists describe the site as a "bison jump," because the animals were stampeded off a cliff above the shelter, and then processed at the site. [Spanish explorers encountered bison as recently as 300 years ago in the 1680s as noted in the journals of the expedition.]

Unusually cold Arctic weather may have temporarily pushed the bison herds southward, but the drying trend returned and continues today. The canyons now lie at the eastern edge of the Chihuahuan Desert where annual temperatures range from 11 to 111 degrees Fahrenheit. Scrub brush and cactus sprout from the hard, rocky terrain, and the landscape resembles a scene from a classic Western movie.

The Spaniards first explored the area in the early 1500s, marking the beginning of the historic era. By the late 1800s, settlers began claiming the land. Modern man has exerted more pressure on the land in the last 125 years than any other group previously inhabiting the region.

The bison were eliminated in 1874, and in 1875, the remaining Native American populations were removed. In 1882, the Southern Pacific railroad completed a bridge across the Pecos River, and on January 12, 1883, railroad crews witnessed the completion of the first southern transcontinental railroad. The east and west sections were joined with a silver spike at Dead Man's Gulch, about one mile north of the mouth of the Pecos at the Rio Grande.

In the late 1800s, Painted Caves Station was one stop along the southern transcontinental railroad route.

The railroad opened the area to settlers, who brought cattle, sheep, and goats. Unlike the bison, which had roamed free, grazing and fertilizing the open plains, the livestock grazed within fenced ranches, and soon the grasslands disappeared. The cycle of erosion began. [The Lower Pecos receives less than 18 inches of annual rainfall, and much of this occurs as torrential downpours during the summer.] When the summer rains came, the soil washed away, and woody scrub plants, thorny brushes, and other desert-adapted plants gradually replaced the grasslands.

The last significant change man effected in the region occurred in 1968, when Amistad Reservoir was completed. The impoundment created a water reserve, and offered many recreational opportunities. But it flooded stretches of the Rio Grande, Pecos and Devils rivers, and destroyed many significant archeological sites, which now lie below the waterline. The waters also increased the regional humidity, accelerating the deterioration of the remaining rock art sites.

Thorny bushes such as this acacia plant became more prevalent in the region when overgrazing began a cycle of erosion.

The stories of the Lower Pecos are written in archeological language. The canyons share the mysteries of their past through modern archeologists who study the geological and climatic records, and excavate archeological sites in the Lower Pecos. Archeologists interpret these stories as they explore the region and reveal the prehistoric lifeways of Texas' Lower Pecos Indians.

SEMINOLE CANYON

Seminole Indians never resided in the Lower Pecos. The canyon was named for the Seminole-Negro army scouts stationed at Fort Clark (present-day Brackettville located east of Del Rio) during the 1870s. Seminole Canyon is located 45 miles west of Del Rio, in Val Verde County. To visit the park, travel west from Del Rio on U.S. 90 to Comstock. The park entrance is nine miles west of Comstock, just east of the Pecos River High Bridge.

Campsites and shelters accommodate up to eight persons, with two motor vehicles. Camping facilities include eight tent campsites with water, electricity, and sanitary dump stations available; picnic facilities with tables, grills, and drinking water.

Hikers will find eight miles of trails within the park's boundaries, and cyclists will enjoy area routes that begin and end in the park. Fishermen and boaters can use the boat ramp at the Pecos High Bridge and cruise the Pecos and Rio Grande arms of Amistad Reservoir.

Guided tours of Fate Bell Shelter are offered twice daily, Wednesday through Sunday, at 10 A.M. and 3 P.M. Because some moderately strenuous hiking is involved, persons planning to go on the tour should be in good physical condition. Tours may be canceled during inclement weather.

January's average low is 46.2 degrees, while July's average is 89.1 degrees. The park is open seven days a week, year around, with a busy season from March to June. Reservations should be made at least four weeks in advance, and can be made up to a year in advance. For more information, see Chapter 8, *Traveling the Lower Pecos*.

Texas state law makes it illegal for anyone to disturb in any way any historic or prehistoric archeological or paleontological site, or any historic marker, situated on lands owned or controlled by the State of Texas.

During the 1930s, archeologists began excavating sites in the Lower Pecos, including Fate Bell Shelter.

Daily Life in a Rock Shelter

In the early 1930s, archeologists began excavating ancient Indian campsites in the Lower Pecos region and analyzing artifacts and other materials deposited by prehistoric groups for 11,000 years. Harry Shafer, Ph.D., a professor at Texas A&M University, has worked in the region for three decades, putting together the pieces of the archeological puzzle.

"I'm interested in any aspect of archeology that tells us a little more about the people," Shafer said. "Archeologists are particularly interested in the Lower Pecos region because the climate and protected rock shelters have preserved artifacts that are normally lost to deterioration."

In addition to artifact analysis, archeologists make assumptions about the people of the Lower Pecos by reading historical accounts of Spanish explorers who first observed Indian cultures residing in northern Mexico, and southern and southwestern Texas in the 1500s. These Indian groups are referred to as "hunter-gatherers," modern versions of which still exist in some countries world wide. These modern hunter-gatherers offer an opportunity to study behavioral patterns and

Spaniards first explored the region in the early 1500s.

make inferences regarding the possible life-ways of the people of the Lower Pecos.

"Throughout the culture history of the Lower Pecos region, the people were hunters and gatherers," Shafer said. "We're dealing with groups who were semi-nomadic. They lived for periods of time in one locality and foraged out from their camp. In season, they moved to another area."

The Indians of the Lower Pecos roamed the area in small bands of 25 to 30 people — probably part of an extended family of mothers, fathers, children, aunts, uncles, and other close relatives. These groups may have gathered for annual feasts and celebrations, which gave them opportunities to visit relatives, share stories, participate in group hunts, and arrange marriages between members of neighboring bands.

The Indians' mobile lifestyle resulted in the rich archeological deposits discovered in the region. "A mobile group would carry only essential possessions such as weapons, digging sticks, carrying baskets, and tool bags," Shafer said. "The other items were left at the habitation sites since they could be replaced quickly at the next campsite."

The rock shelters were natural choices for living sites, and the overhangs that protected the Indians from the rains and winds now protect the remaining traces of their culture. Stone tools, mat fragments, rabbit skin robes, cradle boards, and painted pebbles lie buried in the earth. Pictographs (ancient rock paintings) are preserved on the limestone walls.

"The rock shelters were houses," Shafer said. "You've got to look at a cave (rock shelter) as a house. We don't use the space in our house randomly. We have it very highly structured. They did too." The floor space was divided by households. Sleeping areas were situated along the back wall. The Indians dug shallow pits in the cave floor, and filled them them with a layer of green twigs covered by a thick layer of grass. They topped the grass with another layer of flat objects such as discarded sandals or prickly pear pads (with spines removed), and finally covered this

Dioramas at Seminole Canyon State Park depict family scenes such as this one with a woman grinding beans and a child asleep nearby on a mat.

"mattress" with a woven mat. The bathroom areas were located near the outer edges of the shelter at the far end of the living space.

Fire hearths were located throughout the shelter. "These fires may have had different functions," Shafer said. "Some would serve as basic sources for light, heat, and quick open-flame cooking, while others would be used for oven baking and as heaters on cold nights." Warming fires were often located near the sleeping areas, while the cooking areas were located near the front of the shelter.

Cooking and gathering were the women's responsibilities, while hunting was the men's responsibility. "The division of labor was based on sex and age," Shafer said. "Men performed the more dangerous chores, while women assumed those chores that kept them closer to the camp because of their role in caring for the children. The women's activities were often no less strenuous than those of the men."

Tools were typically made by whichever sex used them. The women constructed woven baskets for collecting, cooking, and serving food, and the men crafted stone spear points or fishing nets.

Although routine hunting and gathering was a part of daily life, the Indians also found time to paint. Archeologists have found a few examples of painted pebbles buried along with other artifacts at sites in the Lower Pecos. The smooth, flat, limestone rocks were decorated with geometrical designs and human-like

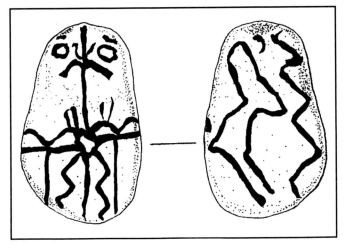

Painted pebbles were frequently decorated on both sides, as shown in this example.

faces. Although researchers suggest that the pebbles represent human beings, their actual purpose is unknown.

The Indians expressed a very sophisticated world view through their pictographs, which are abundant in the region. "I've always been fascinated with the rock art and the humanistic aspects of archeology," Shafer said. "We would miss an awful lot about these people if we failed to explore their thought world, or their symbolic world."

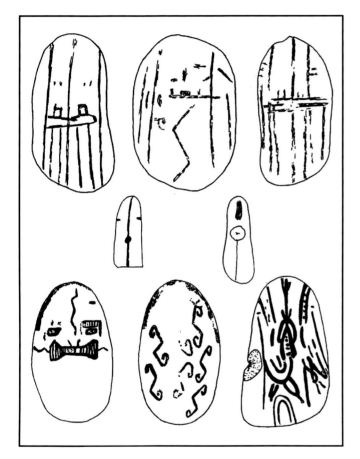

Painted pebbles

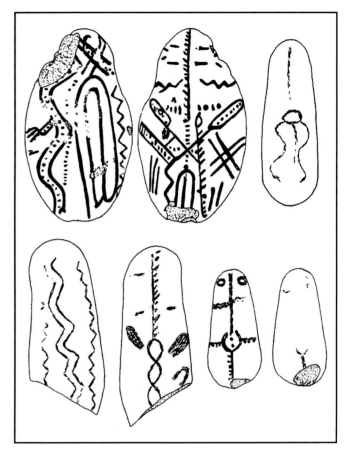

Painted pebbles

Several distinctive styles of pictographs can be found in the region. The murals often feature human-like figures and animals such as mountain lions and deer. The human figures depicted are described as "shaman," medicine men or religious leaders, and the paintings reflect religious rituals.

"We know that these were shamanistic societies," Shafer said. "In hunting and gathering societies, views about existence and the world tend to be strongly supernaturalistic. Everything in their world has supernatural explanations." The shaman offered explanations for the sun, moon, stars, wind, and rain, and by using trance-inducing plants or by fasting, they took trips to the Otherworld — the world of the dead — to commune with spirits.

The shaman also presided over healing rituals, births, deaths, marriages, and puberty rites. "They had nothing equivalent to our teenage years," Shafer said. "When the girls and boys were old enough to go through puberty rites, they went from childhood to adulthood."

By the time children entered adulthood, probably at 12 or 13 years of age, they had learned the skills to participate as an adult in their group. Boys had learned to track game, to make and set traps, and to manufacture stone tools. Girls had learned to identify, gather, and cook plants; to weave mats and baskets; and to care for younger children. Both boys and girls married soon after they entered adulthood and began families of their own.

"We know from the skeletal records that not a lot of people lived to be very old," Shafer said. "You did have people who lived to be 60 or 70 years old, but they were a very small minority of the overall population." At death, following the shaman's ritual, the bodies were most often wrapped with a mat or rabbit skin robe in a flexed or semi-flexed position, and buried in a shallow pit resembling a sleeping pit. The grave was then piled with stones. Other methods of burial included cremating bodies before burial or dropping bodies down vertical shaft sinkholes. The bodies were

A park ranger conducts a tour of Fate Bell Shelter.
Some of the group members look up at the smoke-darkened ceiling.

sometimes buried with personal possessions such as net bags or baskets.

"The Lower Pecos region was occupied for more than 9,000 years by populations that followed essentially the same way of life," Shafer said. "You cannot help but be impressed by the simplicity and durability of these ancient people." These people of the Lower Pecos disappeared from the region in the early 1700s. Archeologists theorize that some may have joined Apache tribes; some may have been drawn into the Spanish missions; and others may have migrated into northern Mexico. Studies in the region have allowed archeologists to better understand the environment surrounding the Indians and their ability to adapt to life in this harsh, arid climate, but the unanswered questions motivate them to continue their quest.

Archeologists typically establish a grid pattern prior to excavating a site to help them map the site more accurately.

Tools for Survival

Thomas R. Hester, Ph.D., professor of anthropology at the University of Texas at Austin and director of the Texas Archeological Research Laboratory (TARL), divides his time among the classroom, the lab, and the field. Archeology has been a lifetime passion. "I started out at seven years old, following my grandmother around as she picked up Indian artifacts on our farm in south Texas," Hester said. "After that, I was always going to be an archeologist."

Over the years, much of Hester's work has focused on stone tools, and in 1985, he and co-author Ellen Sue Turner published the first edition of the popular *Field Guide to Stone Artifacts of Texas Indians*. The book provides both amateur and professional archeologists with a reliable source for identifying stone artifacts and dating archeological sites.

During the initial archeological excavations in the Lower Pecos region, archeologists studied projectile points, such as spear points, and examined how the points changed through time. They then used radiocarbon dating, analyzing organic materials associated with the points at the sites, to confirm the time period of each different type of point. "Once they could get radiocarbon dates that marked

SITES	ESTIMATE DATES	POINT TYPES	TIME PERIODS	CULTURE TYPES
DEVILS MOUTH CENTIPEDE 41VV7	1,000 A.D. —0— 1,000 B.C.	ARROW POINTS FIGUEROA MONTELL ENSOR FRIO	LATE	ARCHAIC
DEVILS MOUTH CENTIPEDE 41VV7	2,000 B.C. 3,000 B.C.	LANGTRY SHUMLA	MIDDLE	ARCHAIC
DEVILS MOUTH	4,000 B.C. 5,000 B.C.	EARLY BARBED PANDALE	EARLY	ARCHAIC
DEVILS MOUTH	6,000 B.C.	SOLONDRINA	LATE	PALEO-INDIAN

Provisional point sequence for the Amistad Reservoir area Archeologists frequently use projectile points found at a site to help determine the age of a particular site and identify the Indian tribes who may have occupied the area.

those changes, then the projectile points became very important to archeologists for determining what period they were digging in," Hester said.

Radiocarbon dating was developed by an American chemist, Willard F. Libby, in the 1940s. By examining the amount of radiocarbon remaining in organic samples, the process can be used to determine the age of an artifact, and subsequently, the age of an archeological site. Since they are composed of stone, the projectile points themselves cannot be dated. But, they can be examined for clues to how the tools were used. "One of the neat things about the Lower Pecos rock shelters is that if a stone tool were used to cut up plants or to butcher an animal and then immediately discarded, the blood or plant residues are still on the edges of some of the tools," Hester said. Other organic materials associated with the excavation such as charcoal from fire pits, wooden implements, baskets woven from plant fibers, and hair and bone fragments from burials can also be used in radiocarbon dating.

Tom Hester displays a rabbit stick from a collection of artifacts housed at the Texas Archeological Research Laboratory.

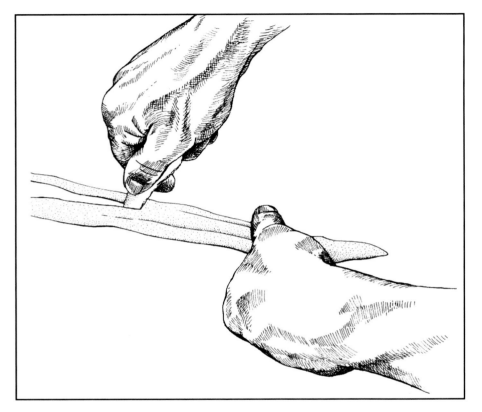

Cutting a plant leaf with a flint knife

"A second area in the study of stone tool technology has been the study of how stone tools were made," he continued. "The earliest archeologists that dug in the Lower Pecos threw away all of the stone artifacts except for the finished, recognizable points, and so all of the flakes and unfinished points went into the trash heap." Contemporary archeologists gather and analyze the flake debris for information on the methods of manufacturing stone tools, and how they were reshaped or resharpened when they were worn and dulled.

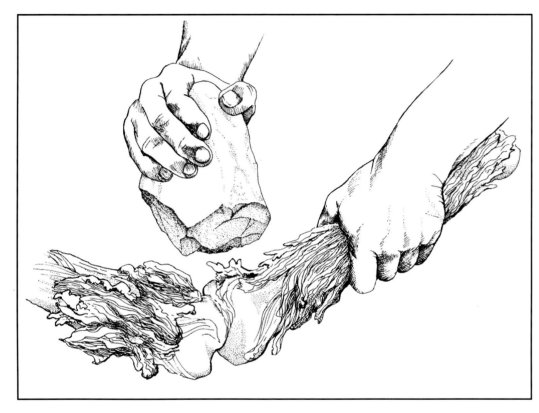

Chopping a bone joint

The Indians were accomplished flintknappers who created stone tools from rough blocks of chert or "flint." Chert is a brown to dark gray stone formed in limestone by the chemical action of minerals containing silica. Like other Stone Age cultures, the Indians crafted spear points, knives, and awls, along with other tools used for specialized scraping.

Modern flintknappers preserve this 12,000-year-old tradition by crafting replicas of stone tools using ancient techniques. Six-inch spear points may begin with blocks of

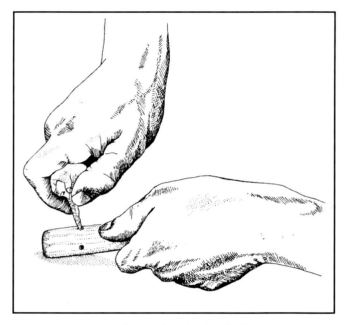

Drilling wood with a flint drill

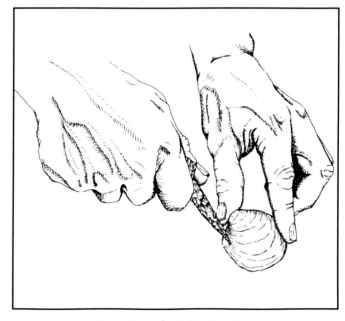

Drilling a hole in a shell with a flint drill

chert approximately 10 inches long and two inches thick. Holding hammerstones, such as palm-sized river rocks, flintknappers work the chert using percussion strokes, striking the chert and removing flakes until they reduce the blocks to smaller cores. Then, using the base of an antler, they thin and shape the spear using soft-hammer percussion strokes.

(The pieces that flake off using the antler will be finer than those removed by striking the chert with the rock.) Pressure flaking with the antler tip refines the point and edges. Flintknapping is the process of reduction. Much like sculptors, flintknappers are artists who unlock the potential of each raw block of chert. Experienced flintknappers can complete

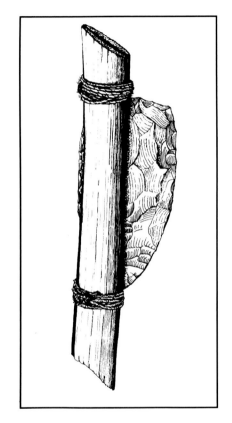

Hafted axe, sometimes called a "sotol knife"

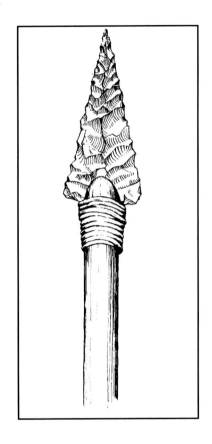

Hafted spear point

the entire process of creating a spear point in less than an hour.

"The third category of study is stone tool function," Hester said. There are two broad categories of stone tools, "uniface," and "biface." "A unifacial tool is a stone tool that's chipped only on one side, or face," he explained. "We usually call those scrapers, but we don't really know what they were used to scrape, or even *if* they were used for a scraper. A bifacial tool is anything that's chipped on both sides. A projectile point is a biface, and

FLINTKNAPPING PROCESS

Left and Above: Percussion flaking with a hammerstone

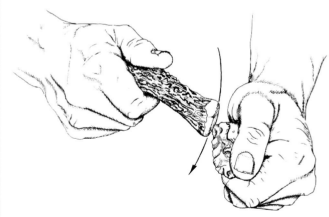

Soft-hammer percussion flaking with the base of an antler

A flintknapper often uses an antler or animal bone to shape and refine the edges of a stone tool.

FLINTKNAPPING PROCESS

Pecking

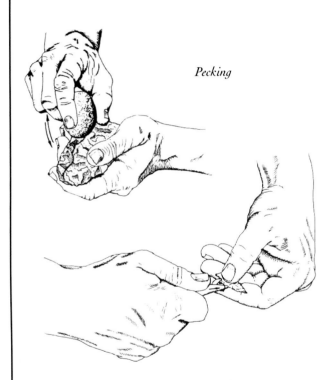

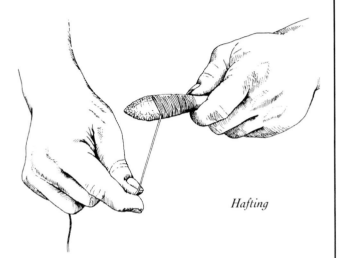

Hafting

Pressure flaking with an antler tip

Right: A flintknapper uses an antler tip to create the scalloped edges and to shape the base of the spear point.

*Unifacial tools — tools chipped only on one side —
are often called scrapers.*

the function of projectile points was primarily to tip the atlatl spears for hunting."

Atlatl is the Aztec word for spear thrower. The spear throwers used by prehistoric Indians were approximately 18 inches long and were made with a handle on one end and a hook·on the other. The butt of the spear fitted into the hook, and when thrown, the spear flew much farther and faster than when thrown by hand.

The fourth area of stone tool study is the distribution of tools across the space within the cave. "Things are plotted, recorded on a grid map, as the excavation progresses — not just vertically but also horizontally," Hester said. "If you look at these grids, theoretically you should be able to isolate an area of the cave where at a certain time, plant processing went on using certain kinds of stone tools; or an area where someone butchered an animal or processed a skin and discarded the stone tool."

These four areas make up the bulk of modern archeological research: point shapes and the use of those points in dating sites; how the tools were made; the evidence of use and function; and the identification of activity areas within the rock shelter. Hester, however, also conducts research in a fifth area, tracing obsidian artifacts to their natural source. "Obsidian is a volcanic glass that doesn't occur in artifact quality anywhere in Texas," Hester said. "Yet, at a few of the rock shelters in the Lower Pecos, flakes of obsidian have

USING THE ATLATL

A vertical trench dug in Fate Bell Shelter shows the cross-section of different soil strata and evidence of human occupation over a long period of time.

been found. We take an obsidian flake and use a non-destructive technique called x-ray fluorescence. Using that, you can come up with a chemical characterization, or a 'fingerprint,' for the obsidian and can then link that back to the geologic outcrop where the obsidian first formed in a volcanic event."

Each obsidian flow from volcanic activity is chemically different, and flakes found in the Lower Pecos have been traced back to geologic sources in the mountains north of Santa

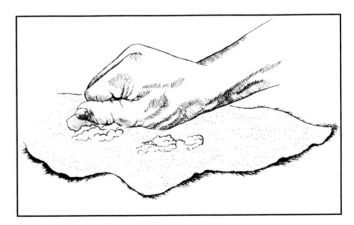

Scraping a hide with a flint scraper

Fe, New Mexico. "I think the presence of this obsidian, so many hundreds of miles from its original source in these sites, is really important, because it does indicate that these hunters and gatherers were not isolated out there in this harsh environment. They did have contact with other people and acquired trade items from great distances."

Other tools that played important roles in the Indian's survival were *manos* or grinding stones, rabbit sticks, digging sticks, and fire-making tools. Manos were rounded stones that fit easily into the palm of the hand, and

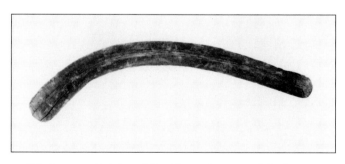

Wooden, curved clubs called rabbit sticks were used for hunting

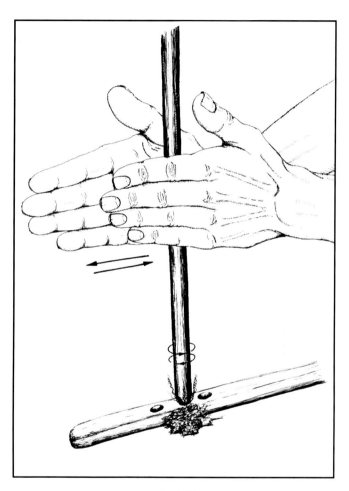

Fire drill

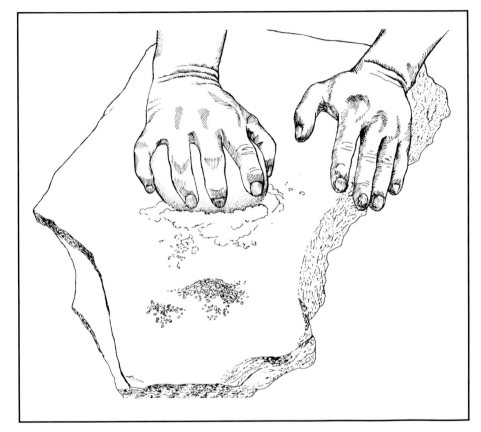

Grinding with a mano and metate

were used to process nuts and seeds. Women usually would crush the food against grinding stones, converting the nuts or seeds into a fine flour or meal. Rabbit sticks were wooden, curved clubs, most often used by men. They were used in hunting rabbits and other small game, as well as a multi-purpose tool for clearing a way through thick brush, raking coals, or digging. Women carried pointed digging sticks that enabled them to gather other foods

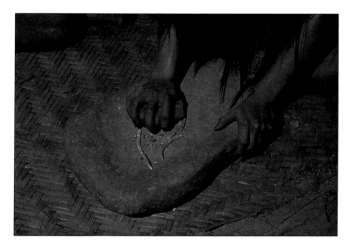

Another diorama depicts a mano and metate used to grind mesquite beans.

such as plants and roots. Fire-making tools included a hardwood fire drill, tinder, and a stalk such as a sotol stalk, which was split and dried. The drill was inserted into a small cup, or hole, in the stalk and rotated between the palms. The friction created heat, and embers dropped onto the tinder below. Blowing on the embers soon resulted in flames.

Hester's excavations of Baker Cave have provided examples of many of these artifacts. "The earliest habitation is radiocarbon dated to 7,000 B.C., and is known as the Golondrina Complex," Hester said. The Golondrina Complex material was deposited on the bottom of the cave, followed by deposits from Early Archaic hunters and gatherers between 6,000 B.C. and 3,500 B.C. Middle and Late Archaic deposits complete the time span, dating from 3,000 B.C. to the early centuries A.D.

"Baker Cave is remarkable for its preservation of more than 9,000 years of human occupation," Hester said. "While this span can be divided into periods by examining stylistic differences in the various artifacts, there seem to have been few major changes in the Lower Pecos way of life."

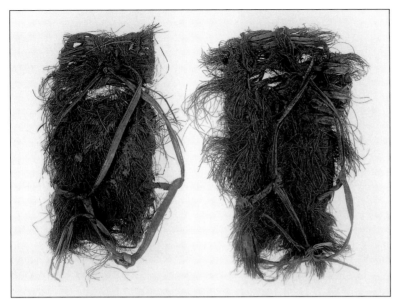

The fibers of lechuguilla plants were used to create sandals.

*Woven artifacts such as these basket fragments demonstrate
the Indians' ability to adapt to the region.*

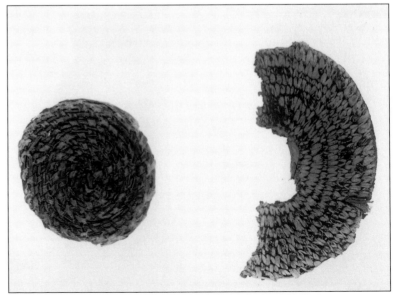

Woven Artifacts

Roberta McGregor steps inside the vast store-room of San Antonio's Witte Museum and browses the rows of artifacts. In a room larger than the average house, 12-foot shelves contain Filipino shields, African sculpture, and Native American beadwork, as well as artifacts from many other cultures. Near the back, McGregor stops at a cabinet where each drawer contains woven mats, sandals, and remnants of carrying baskets — relics from the people of the Lower Pecos.

McGregor, associate curator of anthropology for the Witte Museum, specializes in the study of basketry. "I don't think I originally preferred baskets over other artifacts, but being surrounded by them every day and handling them gave me a new appreciation for their workmanship and beauty," McGregor said. "More than that, I was struck by the fact that no two peoples or cultures make baskets exactly the same way."

Because they tend to decompose quickly in most environments, fibrous artifacts are not usually preserved in the archeological record. But the Lower Pecos region's arid climate and the protective rock shelters have preserved samples of fragments and complete mats and sandals for study.

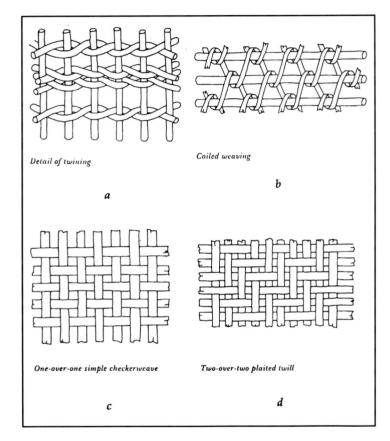

Detail of twining

Coiled weaving

a

b

One-over-one simple checkerweave

Two-over-two plaited twill

c

d

Basketry techniques
(a) Open and close simple twining
(b) Close coiling, interlocking stitch
(c) Simple plaiting
(d) Plaited twill

"All baskets are either handwoven, using one or two primary techniques called plaiting and twining, or they are sewn using a third method generally referred to as coiling," McGregor said. "Coiling is the most complex, requires the greatest skill, and offers the widest variety of forms. Twined baskets, on the other hand, avoid many of the mechanical complexities of coiled work. Plaiting is the simplest basketmaking technique." Archeologists

Coiled basketry

Simple, checkerweave mats may have been used as mattress covers.

analyze basketry by examining the way the baskets are constructed and dividing the baskets into these three sub-classes according to the type of weaving demonstrated.

For the people of the Lower Pecos, the basketry served many of the functions of modern purses, grocery bags, mattress covers, storage containers, and backpacks, and by studying the shapes of baskets, archeologists attempt to determine their specific uses. "The most common woven objects in the Lower Pecos are mats," McGregor said. They were almost always plaited and were used to sleep on, to sit on, and as wrappings for the dead. I think the Lower Pecos basketry is so important because, more than any other class of artifact, it epitomizes the cultural adaptation of that prehistoric population."

Adaptation to the region required that the Indians take advantage of what nature offered and learn to live efficiently in that environment. One thing nature offered in abundance was fibers. The plentiful fibers of the sotol and yucca provided valuable raw materials for

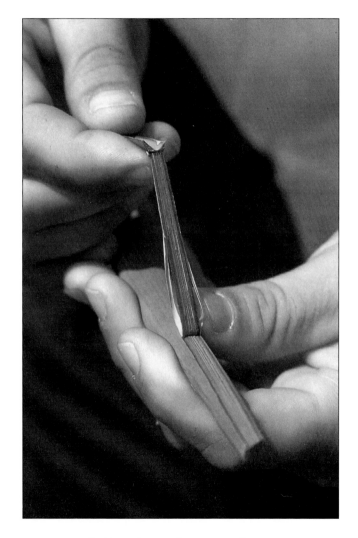

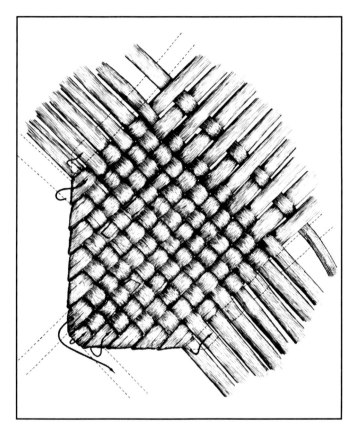

How a mat is woven

*The fibers of many plants were used to create
sandals, baskets, and twine.*

weaving baskets used to collect, transport, and store food. The pads of prickly pear cactus could be sewn together to form carrying pouches. Likewise, sandals were constructed from the leaves of lechuguilla plants, and the long fibers from the lechuguilla leaves could be twisted into strands of cordage. Cordage was essential for net bags, and fishing and trapping nets.

Fibers from lechuguilla leaves may be separated by placing the leaf against a hard surface and scouring it with lengthwise movements using an antler or a piece of bone. Scouring causes the fibers to separate from the leaf's inner pulp. By separating the fibers into two smaller portions and anchoring with a knot at one end, the fibers can then be twisted together to form a length of cordage.

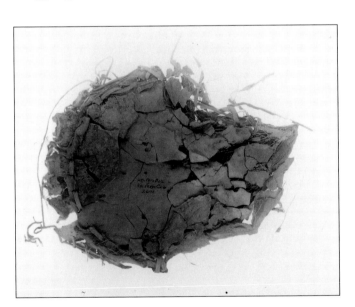

Prickly pear pads could be sewn together to create a carrying pouch.

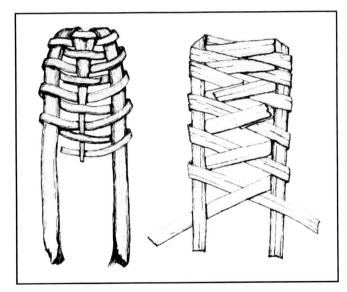

Foundations for sandals

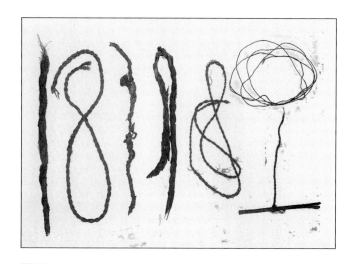

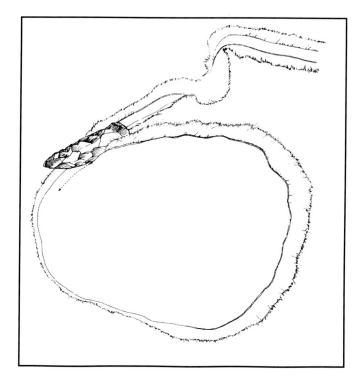

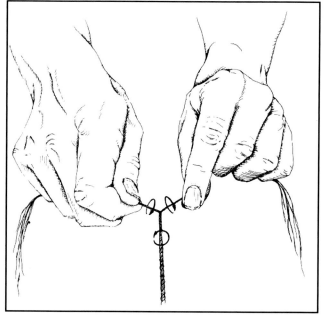

Above, Left: Cordage created from plant fibers

Above: Cutting skin into a long strip

Left: Twisting technique for making cordage

The Indians used this cordage to create rabbit skin robes, sandals, and knotted or knotless bags and nets. Although they probably wore as little as possible during the summer months, they wore rabbit skin robes during the winter. The skins were cut into long strips and twined together with lengths of cordage for winter garments. They wore few adornments such as necklaces or bracelets, although uncommon artifacts such as bone beads, shell beads made from land snails, or stone pendants have been found.

"Women, with few exceptions, were the basketmakers," McGregor said. While the men most certainly twisted cordage and constructed fishing and hunting nets, the majority of the basketry was used in gathering and preparing foods, which was the female's responsibility. Flat trays could have been used for serving foods, in addition to other household uses; small-mouthed containers may have held insects.

Carrying baskets, used like backpacks when gathering plants, were constructed with

Plaited tumplines or headbands supported carrying baskets.

Artifacts such as this bone necklace are uncommon in the region.

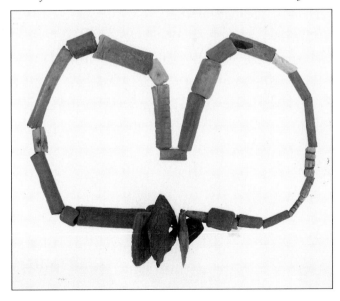

a wide mouth and a smaller base. Wooden sticks shaped the frame and the cone-shaped basket could be made from netting. Carrying baskets were worn by extending a plaited tumpline, similar to a head band, across the forehead, which helped to distribute and support the load.

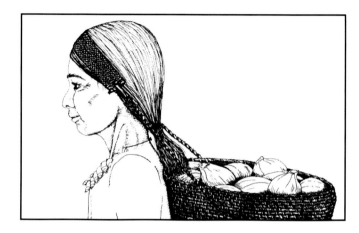

Tumplines were plaited bands worn across the forehead to help distribute the weight of heavy loads.

"All three of the major sub-classes of basketry — twining, coiling and plaiting — are represented in the Lower Pecos," McGregor said. "The bowls are often heavily worn and patched, indicating the value placed on these utilitarian objects. Most mats have straight selvages (edges or borders), neatly turned corners, and evenly split fibers — evidence of the considerable pride these weavers took in their work."

MUSEUMS OF RELATED INTEREST

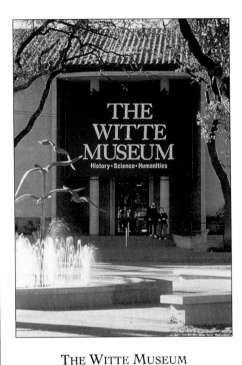

THE WITTE MUSEUM
3801 Broadway
San Antonio, Texas 78209
(210) 820-2111
Hours: 10-6 Mon. through Sat.
(Open Tues. until 9) and Sun. 12-6.
Closed major holidays

Seminole Canyon State Historical Park features a comprehensive exhibit relating to the Lower Pecos. Other museums with exhibits are:

TEXAS MEMORIAL MUSEUM
The University of Texas at Austin
2400 Trinity
Austin, Texas 78705
(512) 471-1604
Hours: 9-5 weekdays, 10-5 Sat., 1-5 Sun.. Closed major holidays
Call for updated information

CROCKETT COUNTY MUSEUM
404 11th Street
Ozona, Texas 76943
(915) 392-2837
Hours: 9-5 weekdays.
Closed most weekends and major holidays.
Call for updated information.

Archeologist Vaughn Bryant inspects an excavation in Hinds Cave.

Foraging for Food

Vaughn Bryant, Ph.D., uses a paintbrush and removes layers of sand and dirt from hardened, cow-patty-shaped clumps of material buried near the outer edge of Hinds Cave. The clumps are coprolites — dried, prehistoric feces. "Human coprolites reveal some of the most important insights about ancient cultures because they represent material that actually passed through the digestive tracts of prehistoric humans," Bryant said. "What you have to do is find one of their toilet areas and excavate it." The bacteria and germs died long ago, leaving only undigested materials such as tough fibers, bone fragments, hair, and traces of pollen. Bryant returns to his laboratory with several samples for further analysis.

As head of the department of anthropology at Texas A&M University, Bryant conducts extensive coprolite research. Each sample is measured, weighed, and placed in trisodium phosphate, a very strong detergent. After a few days, this solution will reconstitute the coprolite, softening it and making it easier to work with. "Unfortunately, when returned to their original state, coprolites also return to their original smell," Bryant said.

Despite the malodorous hazards of his work, Bryant has used his research to determine

SOTOL

Hafted flint axe or "sotol knife" used to collect sotol bulbs

*Bryant constructed pits similar to those found
in Hinds Cave and experimented
with roasting sotol.*

what the people of the Lower Pecos ate, and how they prepared and cooked their food. The Indian women commonly harvested sotol, lechuguilla, and prickly pear cactus. "We suspect that 75 to 80 percent of what they ate was plant food," Bryant said. "There is a great misconception that prehistoric man went out each day and brought home a deer for dinner. In reality, only occasionally were they able to get rabbit or deer. The men probably went out hunting each day, but I don't think they contributed much to the caloric intake." Small fish, rodents, birds, reptiles,

Nutritious meals included insects such as grasshoppers.

The fruit of the prickly pear cactus, called tunas, *ripen in the fall.*

freshwater clams, land snails, and insects — most often collected by the women — were more frequent sources of meat protein.

Using digging sticks and stone knives, the women unearthed the sotol and lechuguilla bulbs. "We think they prepared their food two or three different ways," Bryant said. "They probably barbecued food directly over the fire, roasted food in the earthen ovens, or boiled it. They also ate many foods raw." Although most meats would have been barbecued over the flames, the sotol and lechuguilla bulbs were roasted by placing them inside a large earthen oven. The oven was constructed by digging a pit, lining the pit with limestone rocks, and building a fire to heat the rocks. When the fire burned down to hot coals, the bulbs were placed on the coals and the pit was filled with soil. The bulbs were left to cook for two or more days. "When cooked, the bulbs were eaten very much like artichokes," Bryant said. The cooked bulbs could also be sun-dried, ground into powder, and later mixed with water and baked into cakes.

Acorns could be pounded into a fine flour to make cakes.

Prickly pear cactus may have been boiled, using a boiling device constructed by fastening a piece of hide to a tripod of sticks. The bowl-shaped hide could be filled with water, which was brought to a boil by adding hot rocks.

Other foods were eaten seasonally. Yucca flowers were eaten fresh or cooked, and the fresh yucca fruits tasted like applesauce. The ripe, reddish fruits of the prickly pear, called *tunas*, were often eaten raw. Mesquite pods may have been eaten in the spring, when they were young and tender, but were more often eaten in the fall after they matured. The mesquite beans could then be ground into meal and prepared as cakes. In the fall, walnuts and pecans were plentiful in some areas. Elsewhere, acorns would be gathered, cracked, shelled, and leached (filtered) with water to remove the tannic acid. The acorns were then pounded into a fine flour and mixed with water, forming a mush or gruel. The mush could also be formed into cakes and cooked in a basket placed over hot rocks.

The land provided all the nourishment the Indians needed. Plants such as cactus and sotol provided carbohydrates; fruit, flowers, and berries provided vitamins and minerals; nuts, seeds, and meat provided protein. "These people ate what to some people might look like a gruesome diet — cactus pads, yucca roots, lizards," Bryant said. "But, in terms of nutrition, they probably ate a wonderfully balanced diet, rich in potassium, and low in fat, sugar, and sodium."

Another dietary clue found in coprolites is pollen. Pollen studies are especially interesting to Bryant, who is director of Texas A&M's palynology laboratory. Palynologists study individual grains of pollen, visible only through powerful microscopes. "Many plants produce great quantities of pollen or spores, which are dispersed and carried by wind or water currents, or are transported by insects and animals," Bryant said.

The coprolite samples excavated at Hinds Cave often contained ancient pollen, which offered clues to the time of year a given meal was eaten. "When a coprolite is full of pollen from plants that bloom in the spring, we can assume that it contains the remains of a meal that was eaten during the springtime," Bryant said. Archeologists also use pollen to determine the time of year a site was occupied, the environment surrounding the Indians at the time a meal was eaten, and the functional use of some types of artifacts including grinding stones and stone knives.

During the summer of 1976, while conducting field studies in the Lower Pecos, Bryant and his students decided to try an

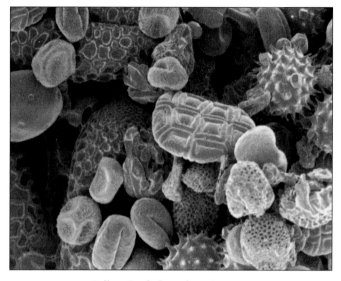

Pollen viewed through a microscope

Indian-style diet. "The foods the prehistoric people ate — the cactus, the agave, the wild onions, nuts and berries — are still abundant in the area," Bryant said. "We'd get up about five o'clock every morning and walk the four miles to the site — there were no roads. Instead of eating breakfast before setting out, we'd forage. I'd pass a persimmon tree and eat four or five persimmons. I'd pick a cactus fruit, a bunch of wild grapes, or a couple of

Vaughn Bryant

In contrast with common American ailments, prehistoric people lived relatively healthy lives. "Their teeth had few cavities, and their skeletons show few of the deformities that would indicate nutritional stress or deficiencies," Bryant said. "And although they lived shorter life spans (an average of 35-50 years) than ours today (70+ years), their early deaths were not due to their diets. They got plenty of exercise and did not have a problem with obesity. Undoubtedly they did not have a problem with hypertension (high blood pressure), heart disease, or cancer. These may have existed as isolated examples in some people in the past, but have only reached epidemic levels in our modern society."

Bryant theorizes that the rigorous, physical labor associated with the Indians' lifestyle caused their bodies to wear out more quickly than today. "A vehicle that is driven 10 miles a day will last many more years than one driven 100 miles a day," Bryant explained. There was also a greater risk of injury from falls or other wounds while hiking across the steep, rocky

wild onions. When hackberries were ripe, we snacked on them throughout the day. We cooked cactus and sotol at night. We didn't eat any pack rats, but we did eat fish, chicken in place of native birds, and once, even a rattlesnake."

After returning to "civilization," Bryant started to wonder about his standard American diet, which was full of salt, sugar, fats and processed foods.

terrain. Since antibiotics were not readily available, bacterial or viral infections from wounds may have claimed many victims.

As a result of his coprolite research, Bryant developed the Caveman Diet. Because it was not practical to forage in the wild, he began "foraging" in the supermarket, choosing fresh vegetables over canned ones, eliminating most high-fat dairy products, substituting fish, poultry, and lean meats for fatty meat, and eating pita bread and whole wheat crackers instead of pies and cakes. Creating the diet was a way for Bryant to share his discoveries with others, and he wrote about his findings in *Prevention* magazine. He enjoys his position as an archeologist and palynologist because it involves this challenging sort of detective work. "Most archeologists like to be out of doors digging holes in the ground," Bryant said. "But given the choice, I'd rather look through a microscope and think of myself as a modern Sherlock Holmes, trying to use tiny clues to answer questions about the past."

Nopalitos

When gathered in the wild, *nopalitos*, the tender, new pads of the prickly pear cactus, are harvested by using tongs to hold the pad, and slicing the cactus at the stem joint. The pads are then held over a flame to remove the *glochids*, tiny hairlike spines, which are just beginning to form. After singeing, the pads should be scraped and rinsed to remove any additional spines before using them to prepare any dish.

Fortunately, prickly pear pads, minus their spines, are available in the produce section of many Texas grocery stores. While there are many recipes that include cactus, they can also be sliced, boiled, and eaten alone as a substitute for green beans, squash, bell peppers, or okra.

Pack Rat Stew

Bryant created a dish he calls, "Pack Rat Stew," which calls for prepared nopalitos and other fresh vegetables. He uses lean beef (such as stew meat) or rabbit and common dry spices replace the Indians' fresh herbs. This recipe is adapted from Bryant's list of ingredients, most of which are available in Texas grocery stores.

Ingredients:
2 nopalitos (small to medium sized pads)
1 jicama (a root plant found in Mexico that looks and tastes similar to a potato)
1 lb. cubed, lean beef stew meat or rabbit
2 stalks celery
2 carrots
2 onions (small to medium sized)
1/2 cup dry pinto beans

1/2 teaspoon thyme
1/2 teaspoon oregano
2 teaspoons coriander
2 teaspoons cumin
1/4 teaspoon garlic powder
salt and pepper to taste
2-3 tablespoons corn starch

Nopalitos — young prickly pear pads

Pack Rat Stew (continued)

Place the meat, spices, and pinto beans into a quart-sized pot. Fill pot to halfway point with water. Turn heat to medium setting and bring to a boil. Reduce heat, and boil covered for approximately one hour.

Cut the nopalitos into strips, then cut each strip into bite-sized pieces. Boil the nopalitos in a separate pot for about 10 minutes, or until tender. Drain, rinse, and set aside.

Peel the jicama and cut into small squares. Wash and chop the carrot into bite sized pieces, and cut the onions into quarters. Add nopalitos and other vegetables to the meat and beans. If necessary, add enough water to cover vegetables. Return to boil. Reduce heat and simmer covered on low heat approximately one hour or until vegetables are tender.

Add corn starch to thicken the mixture. Blend 2-3 tablespoons corn starch with a small amount of cool water before adding to liquid.

Salt and pepper to taste.

The red shaman figures in Panther Cave are some of the most dramatic pictographs found in the Lower Pecos.

Pictographs

Solveig Turpin, Ph.D., first studied the Lower Pecos when she was sent by the Texas Parks and Wildlife Department to document the rock art in Seminole Canyon in 1979 before it became a state park. Although Seminole Canyon had already been the subject of extensive archeological activity, Turpin's team discovered 37 additional sites that had not been previously recorded. "I wondered, if it's like this in a place where everybody's hung out for 50 years doing archeological research, what's it like in the rest of the region?" Turpin said. She began surveying the region, working with area landowners, and has spent up to 100 days each year hiking the vast canyons. "When we started, there were 107 recorded rock art sites out there," she said. "Now we're up to 300.

"I think rock art is of critical importance, because it interjects that human element into archeology," she continued. "But you can't take this art out of its context. I'm an archeologist first and foremost, and I just happen to work someplace where there's a lot of art." The rock art, viewed in the context of what archeologists know of the hunter-gatherer culture, their technology,

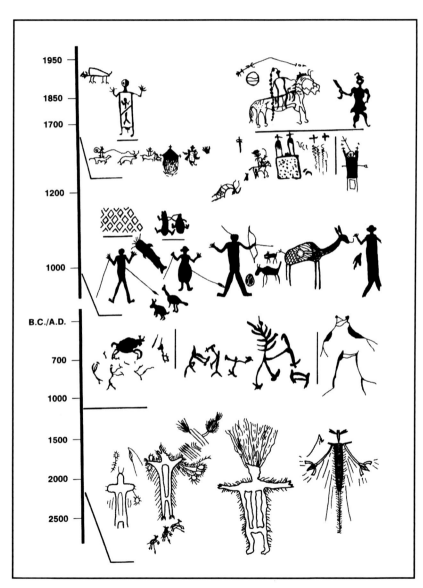

This rock art sequence shows the approximate time periods in which rock art was produced, and the differences in styles.

2500 B.C. – 1100 B.C. — *Pecos River*
1100 B.C. – A.D. 100 — *Red Linear*
A.D. 100 – A.D. 1100 — *Red Monochrome*
A.D. 1100 – A.D. 1300 — *Bold Line Geometric*
A.D. 1500 – A.D. 1950 — *Early to Late Historic*

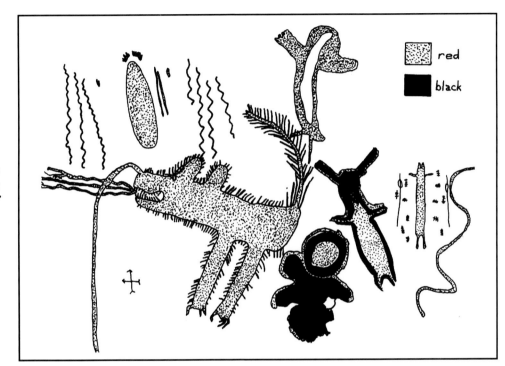

Lines from this Pecos River style panther's mouth represent the power of this animal "familiar."

and their environment, adds another dimension to what we know of the people of the Lower Pecos, because it reflects what was important in their world.

Rock art paintings, also known as pictographs, were painted over a period of 4,000 to 6,000 years, and archeologists divide the art into five separate styles: Pecos River, Red Linear, Red Monochrome, Bold Line Geometric, and Historical. "Each one of these styles is distinctly different and shows a distinctly different reason why people painted rock art," Turpin said. "The Lower Pecos is one of the few places where we can look at what Indians thought about, what their ideas and beliefs were, and what was important in their lives."

In *Pecos River Rock Art: A Photographic Essay*, co-produced with photographer Jim Zintgraff, Turpin wrote:

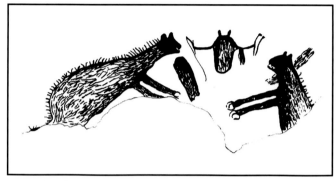

A panther shaman (note the ears) is drawn between two leaping panthers who are his spirit guides.

We can only imagine the preparations involved in the production of a major pictograph composition, some of which are over 30 feet across and as much as 12 feet high. These more elaborate paintings must have been drawn from scaffolds or ladders erected for that purpose, perhaps by the group responsible for organizing the festivities. . . . Bedrock mortars, pestles, portable grinding slabs, and grinding stones were used to turn colored pebbles into paint. Iron oxides provided the reds and yellows, manganese dioxide the blacks, and calcite nodules, the white. Blood red, the favorite color, could be produced by heating yellow hematite nodules until they darkened. Molded lumps of red and yellow pigment recovered from

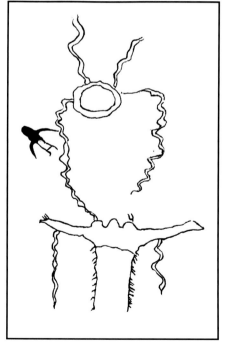

The spirit animal, a bird, flies from the shaman, and is perhaps his guide to the Otherworld.

dry rock shelter deposits show how the ground minerals were collected and stored. The paints were mixed to the desired shade and consistency in mussel shell palettes and applied through a variety of techniques, including spattering, finger-painting, crayon, or with brushes manufactured from the leaves of desert succulents.

Turpin believes that the oldest style, the Pecos River style, is the oldest religious art form in Texas and North America (and possibly in the Americas). It exhibits elements of religious art because of the repetitive themes that portray certain dominating principles. "I recognize certain elements and themes that run through it," Turpin said. "We cannot interpret them as though we were reading them. They're not a written language. They have a lot of symbols that are supernatural and mythological.

"I think it was an animistic religion where there isn't a dividing line between people and nature," Turpin continued. "They're trying to

Pecos River style animal procession

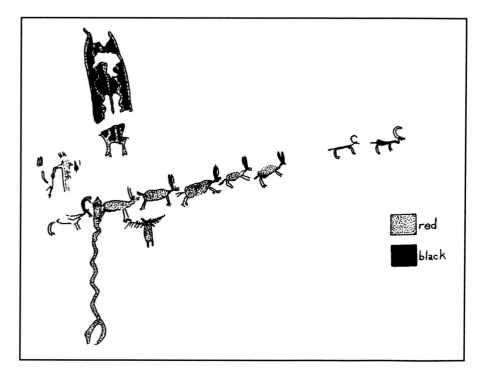

This Pecos River style animal procession depicts minor shaman who holds sticks and appears to herd the animals.

red

black

show you the way people could move back and forth in the animal world and take on animal characteristics." The most dominant theme is the shaman, or religious leader, who possesses the power to change his form into that of an animal "familiar," a spirit constantly at the command of the shaman. Pictographs show the shaman as a bird, flying upward into the sky, as a fish, swimming the rivers, and as a panther, prowling the desert.

The role of the shaman in the hunter-gatherer society was that of a historian, who traced the group's history; a scientist, who explained the mysteries of natural world; and a healer, who performed miracles and battled forces of evil.

Pictographs in northern Mexico, such as this drawing of a powerful shaman, are found near the southern limits of the Pecos River region.

Turpin has added her work and interpretations to that of other archeologists who preceded her in the region. In 1958, T.N. Campbell, Ph.D., suggested that the paintings represented visions experienced while in a trance induced by consuming mescal beans. Mescal beans are the red seed of the mountain laurel, and are potentially fatal when consumed.

Later, in 1967, W.W. Newcomb Jr., Ph.D., first identified the central rock art characters as shaman, also suggesting that the art was their way of communicating what they had encountered while in the trance state. Turpin, in turn, has further defined the time periods in which these pictographs were produced, and has constructed a framework for their interpretation.

The limestone canvasses in the Lower Pecos' outdoor exhibit depict tall shaman figures, dressed in multi-colored robes. They often carry prickly pear pouches, spear throwers and darts, and stand with animals such as deer, birds, and panthers. The most dramatic examples of these figures are in

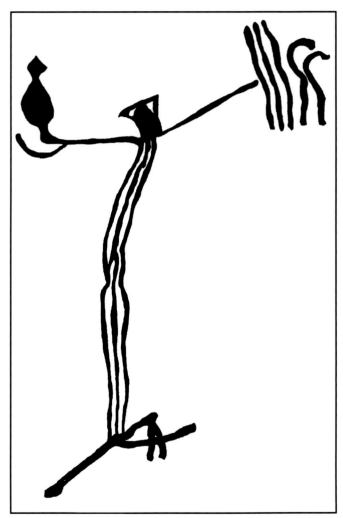

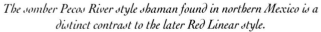

The somber Pecos River style shaman found in northern Mexico is a distinct contrast to the later Red Linear style.

The Red Linear style shaman appears almost whimsical compared to the Pecos River style.

These pregnant dancers of the Red Linear style are a rare depiction of female sexuality and fertility.

Panther Cave, located in Seminole Canyon State Historical Park.

"Panther Cave was the scene of many rituals," Turpin said. "And they painted over and over and over again in the same place. Obviously the place is what's important." Turpin believes this ritual site was associated with annual gatherings, where the separate groups of Indians met and exchanged information, chose marriage partners, traded goods, visited with their families, and performed sacred ceremonies.

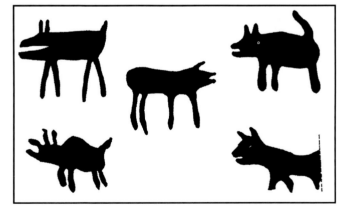

Red Monochrome composite of a dog motif found in various sites across the region.

a   11.1 cm

b   11 cm

c   No Scale

d   10 cm

e   5 cm

f   4 cm

Bold Line Geometric designs include zig zags and other angular patterns.

Bold line Geometrics

The Red Linear style followed the Pecos River style. "This is a miniature, stick-figure art form that deals mostly with warfare, ceremonies, ritual processions, and human reproduction," Turpin said. While the figures appear almost comical, the recurring themes are more serious, reflecting the Indians' everyday activities and their concern for basic survival. For Turpin, the art expresses another reason for painting. "In the Pecos River style, you have a very rich, elaborate, supernaturally oriented religious system. In the next, the Red Linear style, you have more personal depictions of individual rites of passage, where probably children were introduced into an adult world."

A third style, the Red Monochrome, portrays more realistic human and animal figures as they might have appeared to the artist in their natural environment. The figures are often drawn standing side by side. Human figures are drawn facing the artist, and often are armed with bows and arrows. Animals are drawn in profile.

Bold Lne Geometrics

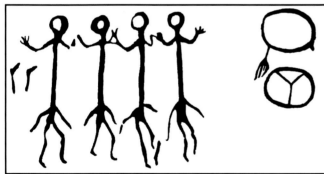

The dancing figures found in Bailando Shelter are generally believed to be Red Monochrome drawings, and one of the first depictions of groups.

A fourth style, the Bold Line Geometric style, is more abstract. The artists used intersecting straight lines to form geometrical patterns. The pictographs, including zig zag lines, blocks, and insect-like figures, exist in only a few known sites.

The region's written history begins with Spanish expeditions beginning in 1590. The fifth and final category of pictographs, Historical pictographs, are not characterized by a particular style as much as subject matter. Artists painted accounts of their travels, creat-

Caballero Shelter, Early Historic Period

ing drawings of Spanish missions and men on horseback, as well as accounts of hunts and warfare.

"In my work, the most important thing is making a record of these for posterity," Turpin said, "because they're going to deteriorate. I also want to put their interpretations in a secure, intellectual framework that isn't rampant speculation. You can use rock art, like any other class of archeology, to gather information about the people who produced it, and I'm putting out ideas that other people can either argue with or improve upon."

Man with bison or bison dancer,
Dolan Falls, Historic Period

HUSSIE MEYERS SITE, LATE HISTORIC PERIOD

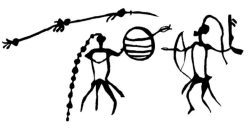

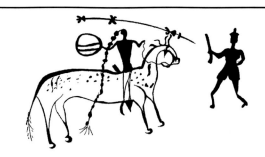

This Late Historic pictograph series recreates a Native American encounter with an armed soldier. The heroic warrior is depicted with identifying markings on his lance and shield, and onion braids in his hair. The weaponry includes bows, arrows, and guns. The soldier wears a Prussian style spiked helmet adopted by the U.S. Army in the late 1870s.

As Turpin continues to hike the canyons, prospecting for pictographs like a miner with an eye for gold, she savors the memories from her work in the region. "I remember finding one site in particular," Turpin said. "We'd been walking all day, and we were hot and tired — ready to turn back — but we decided to explore one more canyon. When we walked up, we saw the paint from 500 yards away and started running. That's what archeology is all about. Discovery."

Solveig Turpin

The Rio Grande flows past a bluff overlooking Panther Cave in Seminole Canyon State Park and divides Texas and Mexico.

Preserving the Past

Betty Pat. Gatliff examines the skull of an Archaic child, then attaches the mandible (lower jaw) firmly to the cranium (main part of the skull) replacing cartilage with clay and cotton. Using a chart of established tissue thicknesses, she then glues rubber markers directly onto the skull to indicate the thickness of the facial tissues, including muscles, fatty tissues, and skin. With layers of modeling clay, she fills the open spaces between the markers, forming the shape of the face before adding the eyes, mouth, nose, ears, and hair.

The Witte Museum, located in San Antonio, invited Gatliff to create two such sculptures for their permanent exhibit entitled, *Ancient Texans: Rock Art and Lifeways Along the Lower Pecos*. Roberta McGregor, associate curator of anthropology for the museum, discussed the museum's interest in the region. "The Witte Museum was one of the first institutions to become actively involved in the archeology of the Lower Pecos region," McGregor said. "In 1931, the Witte sent a small scouting expedition to investigate a number of rock shelters near Langtry. In 1933, the museum excavated Shumla Caves, a series of nine rock shelters, and volunteer teams recovered 14 burials."

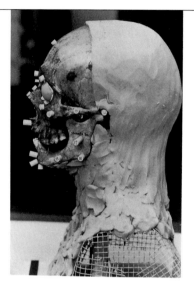

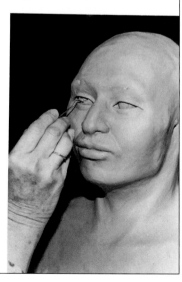

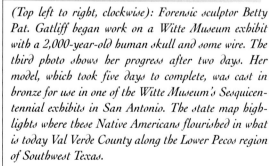

(Top left to right, clockwise): Forensic sculptor Betty Pat. Gatliff began work on a Witte Museum exhibit with a 2,000-year-old human skull and some wire. The third photo shows her progress after two days. Her model, which took five days to complete, was cast in bronze for use in one of the Witte Museum's Sesquicentennial exhibits in San Antonio. The state map highlights where these Native Americans flourished in what is today Val Verde County along the Lower Pecos region of Southwest Texas.

Three of the skulls recovered in the 1930s excavation were selected for facial sculptures. One sculpture recreates the face of a man, while the other portrays a mother and child. Gatliff, a medical illustrator and forensic sculptor, brought impressive credentials to the project: consultant for Universal Studios' production of the television series "Quincy," consultant for Orion Pictures' production of the movie, *Gorky Park*, and advisor for the U.S. House of Representatives, Select Committee on Assassinations, President John F. Kennedy, 1978.

Gatliff performed her first facial reconstruction as a medical illustrator at the Federal Aviation Administration in Oklahoma City. There she developed the sculpting technique for use in identifying airplane crash victims.

The process is synonymous with facial reconstruction, and Gatliff worked closely with anthropologists who examined each skull and provided information regarding the individual's gender, estimated age at death, and other relevant information. The finished sculptures

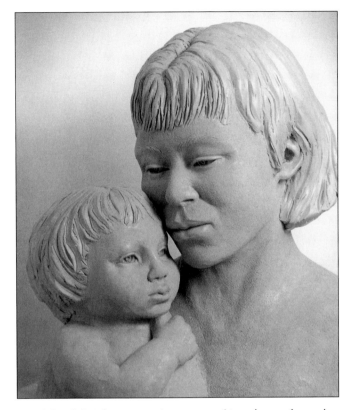

Gatliff used facial reconstruction to create this sculpture of a mother and her child.

bring the people of the Lower Pecos back to life, reminding museum visitors that artifacts and rock art are traces of people from another culture — another time.

The skull of a man, recovered in the 1930s, was also selected for facial reconstruction.

The *Ancient Texans* exhibit opened in January 1987, and includes Gatliff's sculptures, along with videos and photographs of the Lower Pecos region by well-known San Antonio photographer Jim Zintgraff, and an extensive artifact collection. A realistic diorama, a life-sized display, illustrates life in the Lower Pecos. The exhibit has earned several awards of merit and distinction from museum associations and historical commissions.

While artifacts and sculptures can be displayed and preserved in museums, the vast collection of pictographs can be seen only on the walls of rock shelters in the Lower Pecos. Forrest and Lula Kirkland were among the first to recognize the enormous cultural value of the Lower Pecos rock art. They worked together during the 1930s to preserve the pictograph images, spending their vacations traveling throughout West Texas and making watercolor copies of the pictographs. Many of their paintings are the only record of sites that have since been destroyed by erosion or vandalism.

Rattlesnake Canyon, Shelter 1
Watercolor painting by Forrest Kirkland

Pecos River, Site 14
Watercolor painting by Forrest Kirkland

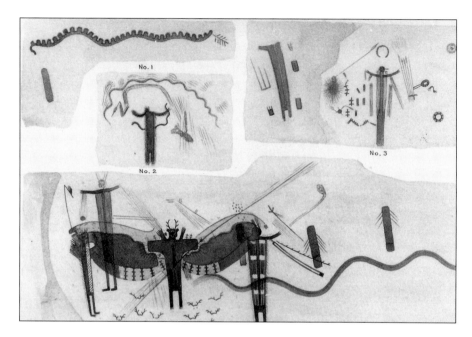

Seminole Canyon, Shelter 4
Watercolor painting by Forrest Kirkland

Seminole Canyon, Panther Cave
Watercolor painting by Forrest Kirkland

Today, the Interpretation and Exhibits Branch of the Texas Parks and Wildlife Department continues the Kirklands' efforts. Their professional artists work with Texas Archeological Society volunteers as part of the department's on-going archeological site protection and preservation efforts.

Artist Nola Montgomery paints murals and works with a sculptor and other artists in the Interpretation and Exhibits Branch to create the intricate dioramas that appear in many state parks. She also uses her talents to document the rock art of the Lower Pecos and other areas of Texas, joining volunteer rock art recording teams who compile permanent records of rock art sites, complete with maps, drawings, and photographic records.

The teams record the rock art site by first examining existing documentation. They then establish a one-square-meter grid of the rock surface to be inventoried, and draw shelter profiles and floor plans. "Most artists are assigned to a panel and do scaled drawings, but the process also involves photographers

Artist Nola Montgomery documents rock art in the region and creates paintings and sketches that illustrate the Indians' way of life.

and writers," Montgomery said. "The drawings are done very carefully to scale, and when transferred to watercolor paper, are very accurate. We take photographs panel by panel, including a card displaying all the site data. The writers do descriptions of the shelter and inventory the rock art from observation."

The written documentation includes descriptions of the art forms and motifs, dimensions and colors, and the level of deterioration. Photography includes black and white or color photographs for panel-by-panel documentation, close-ups of individual elements or deteriorating surfaces, and wide angle views of the entire site. The team is very careful to avoid damaging the rock art while recording it. They do not touch the art with their hands or equipment, and often put protective putty on the metal ends of measuring tapes to avoid damage from accidental contact.

A small shelter can be recorded in one or two days, but larger shelters may require up to four days. All of the Texas Parks and Wildlife volunteers are members of the Texas Archeological Society. "We've had up to 150 people involved in the project, although each recording trip is limited to 35 people," Montgomery said. "There are always new people, but about 70 people work on a regular basis, are well trained, and can assist newcomers. We try to select sites that are newly discovered or that are endangered by vandalism."

One of the group's goals is to record sites on private lands. "This is important because there's no other way to preserve the art," Montgomery said. "It's painted on a rock and it's going to decay with the elements, even without the vandalism. The region's climate changed with the construction of the Amistad Reservoir, raising the humidity level and accelerating the decay. Unfortunately, vandalism could increase as the population grows and more people visit the area."

When completed, one copy of the rock art recording team's file is retained by the department as a working copy, and a second copy is filed with the Texas Archeological Research Laboratory (TARL). Directed by Thomas R.

Hester, Ph.D., TARL is a part of the University of Texas at Austin and houses Texas' central library of archeological information. "This lab is the largest repository in the state," Hester said. "We have collections from over 8,000 sites in the state of Texas, both prehistoric and historic, and we have records on more than 47,000 sites. We add to these all the time."

The lab is organized into three different units: collections, records, and sponsored projects, which does contract archeology. TARL issues new site numbers for excavations and maintains excavation records. "Our main goal is to have the collections kept in the best possible shape, so that they're accessible for research by students, faculty, staff, and people from other universities," Hester said. With this in mind, TARL constructed a state-of-the-art stainless steel facility within their existing building, approximately 1,700 square feet of storage space, which has self-contained systems for temperature and humidity control, fire suppression, and security. These high-tech measures help to ensure that all of the artifact

analysis, documentation and research completed by the archeologists of today will be preserved for future generations.

Preservation is a growing concern for archeologists. Valuable sites are now threatened by population growth, mining, reservoir construction, and real estate development. Federal laws protect archeological sites on public lands or in areas of publicly funded projects. This includes projects such as highway construction. According to law, the construction must avoid significant sites whenever possible. But when it is impossible to avoid the site(s), as in the construction of the Amistad Reservoir, archeologists complete a survey, record or map the site(s), and excavate any significant sites that are to be destroyed.

However, only a limited number of Texas' archeological resources lie on public lands or in areas where public projects will protect them from destruction. The rest are on private property, where they are sometimes destroyed by relic collectors who disregard the value of the site in terms of archeological information. Once removed from a site without proper notations about the location, depth, and surrounding materials, the basket, sandal, or spear point is reduced to the status of an interesting object. Without detailed information within the context of the site, the artifact no longer offers clues about the culture that created it.

Amateur archeologists are welcomed in several archeological groups that excavate sites within their communities and benefit from working with trained archeologists. These groups encourage landowners to protect their land and archeological resources by checking the credentials of anyone claiming to be an archeologist or requesting permission to excavate sites on their property.

Professional archeologists hope to work with the state and private landowners to preserve unexcavated archeological sites. National parks and state natural areas are protected from destruction and development, and archeologists believe that both prehistorical and historical sites should be preserved untouched for future generations. Many sites are damaged each year as acid rain, floods, sun exposure, wind, and burrowing insects take their toll, but man remains the greatest enemy. Many rock shelters once occupied by Indians are now beneath the waters of the Pecos River and the Rio Grande. Vandals, wielding aerosol paint cans, can destroy a 4,000-year-old painting in five minutes. Looters, digging indiscriminately in caves, plow through 7,000-year-old artifacts, removing valuable pieces of puzzles that will never be complete.

Joe Labadie, National Park Service archeologist assigned to the Pecos River, works to generate a greater awareness of the value of these fragile sites. "We try to get people to look at the parks as outdoor museums," Labadie said. "The parks were paid for with money that came out of our pockets as taxpayers. We should always be able to go and see this land, or these pictographs, where no amount of a developer's money is going to make them go away." Man has affected the

National Park archeologist Joe Labadie identifies a dagger leaf yucca plant, useful for food and basket-making materials.

Lower Pecos' environment more in the last 150 years than the Indians did in 11,000 years of prehistoric occupation. The stone tools, mat fragments, and fading pictographs are our only records of their culture. In 11,000 more years, what will be left of ours?

For more information, write:

The Witte Museum
3801 Broadway
San Antonio, Texas 78209

Texas Archeological Society
c/o Center for Archeological Research
The University of Texas at San Antonio
San Antonio, Texas 78285

Texas Archeological Research Laboratory
The University of Texas at Austin
Balcones Research Center, 5
Austin, Texas 78712-1100

Texas Parks and Wildlife Department
Interpretation and Exhibits Branch
4200 Smith School Road
Austin, Texas 78744

Dioramas at Seminole Canyon State Park depict tool-making scenes.

Traveling the Lower Pecos

The thunderstorm gathered over the Chihuahuan Desert and pushed its way through Mexico. Fingers of lightning, projecting bright, jagged streaks against darkening clouds, reached across the Texas border into the Lower Pecos region. Soon the smell of rainsoaked creosote bushes permeated the air, and for a few intense moments, rain pounded the dusty ground. As the brooding storm rolled away across the plains, nature welcomed the evening, painting a strawberry-colored sunset on the horizon.

Both the Amistad National Recreation Area just outside Del Rio, and Seminole Canyon State Park, 45 miles west of Del Rio, offer opportunities to study the lands and lifeways of Texas' prehistoric Indians.

Small bands of hunter-gatherers traveled the region on foot, and it's still the best way to explore the area. Off the roadway, you see, feel and hear nature as they knew it thousands of years ago. Seminole Canyon's three hiking trails guide visitors through the Indians' culture. Pictographs grace the walls of their rock shelter homes, and artifacts, preserved by the dry environment, provide clues to their lifeways. An extensive interpretive center, located inside the park's headquarters, offers exhibits

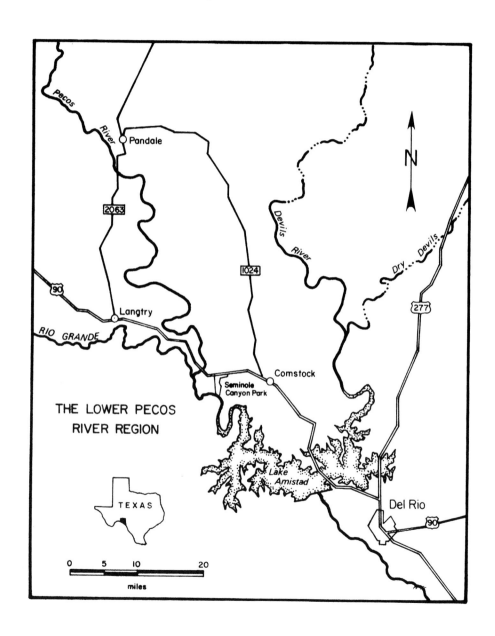

THE LOWER PECOS
RIVER REGION

(based upon artifacts and pictographs) chronicling the area's rich history.

The walk to Fate Bell Shelter is a moderately strenuous, one and one-half-hour guided tour that departs from the park headquarters. Steep, uneven steps lead you down into the canyon and into a more protected ecosystem. Stands of green live oaks and mesquite trees sprout from the canyon floor and water fills natural cisterns sculpted by erosion. Plovers, tiny "rain birds," dance in and out of the glistening reservoirs, and families of cliff swallows emerge from their mud nests, built high along the canyon's sheer walls.

When the powerful, driving rains echoed through the canyon, the people of the Lower Pecos sought refuge in natural rock shelters carved deep within the layered limestone walls. Named for Fate Bell, a rancher and the last owner of the land, the shelter is a 450-foot-long, cave-like hollow set into the side of the canyon.

Indian fires burned in small pits inside the shelter for thousands of years, blackening the ceiling with soot. Near the ledge, a large flat rock served as a workbench where Indians worked leather, prepared plant fibers, and shaped tools. Centuries of use have worn and smoothed its surface, except for the scars left by flint tools. The fats and oils of plants and animals have polished it to a glossy sheen. The blackened ceiling and timeless rock seem almost eerie, as though the shelter waits for the Indians' return.

Fate Bell Shelter contains some of North America's oldest pictographs, believed to have been painted 4,000 years ago. The Indians crushed ochre, colored iron ores, and mixed them with a binder, possibly animal fats, to create paints. If you contemplate the bold, angular pictographs, the deep red, orange, yellow and black hues fuel your imagination, but the meanings of the paintings are forever locked into the past, along with the artists who created them. The mystical shaman figures, animal drawings, and darts and atlatls are spectres from a vanished culture.

The longest trail in the park is a three-mile hike over flat, natural terrain that leads

Mystical shaman figures were painted with colored iron ores.

you to a remote bluff overlooking the Rio Grande and Panther Cave. The Rio Grande flows 200 feet below the cliff, and its emerald green waters cut through the barren landscape, dividing Texas from Mexico. As the afternoon sun lights the shadowy rock shelter, several vivid pictographs are visible with binoculars. The most impressive image is a 15-foot-long panther, an ancestor of the mountain lions that still roam the area. Because of the rich colors and extensive overpainting, researchers believe that Panther Cave was the site of ancient ceremonies and rituals.

Near the interpretive center, the Windmill Nature Trail is a short, relaxing walk through the Gatherers' garden. Along the path, you discover *agarita* with its bright red berries that make excellent wines and jellies. The *cenizo*'s pink to lavender flowers bloom after summer showers, and the leaves can be brewed for tea to treat chills and fever. Vibrant yellow to orange flowers characterize the most abundant and versatile plant, the prickly pear cactus. *Nopalitos*, young prickly pear joints, are still a popular regional food.

At the halfway point, the skeleton of a windmill dating back to the 1890s stands against the rough escarpment. Large oaks shade the deep, clear watering hole, and in the early morning or late evening cool, the spring-fed pool is a popular place to observe wildlife.

You may also choose to explore the region by boat. The Amistad National Recreation Area, administered by the National Park Service, includes portions of the Rio Grande, and Pecos and Devils rivers, in addition to the 540 miles of shoreline surrounding the reservoir. Pictograph sites are recorded throughout the area, but the most notable ones can be found by touring the Pecos River District.

A park brochure provides a map and details of both historical and prehistoric sites along the self-guided tour of the Pecos River and Rio Grande. On the Pecos, the remnants of old trails and river crossings used by settlers are contrasted with the new Pecos River High Bridge, Highway 90, which stands 321

Visitors can stand at the bluff overlooking the Rio Grande and Panther Cave and see the rugged Mexican despoblado *across the border.*

Panther Cave is named for the large red panther, or mountain lion, sketched onto the wall.

feet above the river. Along the Rio Grande, old railroad tunnels, blasted from the solid rock walls, arch above the waterline. These were the first railroad tunnels in Texas, completed in the early 1800s by the Southern Pacific Railroad.

Farther downstream, boaters may dock at Parida and Panther caves, and view extensive pictographs. Archeologists from the University of Texas excavated Parida Cave in the 1960s, and found that the site was first occupied about 5,000 years ago and remained occupied until about 500 years ago. The cave was also a stop along the railroad, known as Painted Caves Station. Archeologists estimate the pictographs in Panther Cave are between 3,000 - 4,000 years old.

All of the archeological sites are protected by state and federal laws, and activities such as digging, removal of artifacts, defacement, or disturbance of the sites are illegal. Park officials remind visitors that the archeological sites are our only link to these early Indian cultures, and that today's visitors must preserve the history of the Lower Pecos for future generations. They frequently quote the old saying, "take only pictures, leave only footprints."

The Lower Pecos region is your portal to the past. The area's people, plants, and animals have learned to weather nature's moods and wait for rare stormy afternoons to fade into legendary Texas sunsets. Here, 20th century travelers trace the footsteps of prehistoric Indians who called the rugged country "home."

For brochures, maps, and information, write or call:

Amistad Recreation District
P.O. Box 420367
Del Rio, Texas 78842-0367
(210) 775-7491

Seminole Canyon State Historical Park
Box 820
Comstock, Texas 78837
(915) 292-4464

DESERT POOLS

Indians and other early travelers followed careful routes through Texas' Lower Pecos region. They traveled from river to spring to desert pool to stay alive. Called *tinajas* in Spanish, these pools occur in canyons and dry arroyos leading to the Rio Grande. Some of the pools are spring-fed, filled with cool water all year. Others occur only when heavy summer rains or flash floods wash through the canyon, filling natural cisterns sculpted by erosion.

When the flood waters recede, a new population of insects, frogs and crayfish inhabit the tinajas. Bright green aquatic plants grow upward toward the light from the bottom of spring-fed pools, and leopard frogs croak along the water's edge. Crayfish seek out comfortable crevices between the rocks. The smooth, glassy surface is disturbed only by whirligig beetles, swirling in confusion like bumper cars at the county fair.

Above the water, sulphur butterflies flit through the willow trees, along with blue damselflies that mate and deposit their eggs near the water. The damselfly larvae, or nymphs, then feed and mature underwater. After several months, the nymphs crawl from the water onto a rock where their shells split down the back, and another generation of damselflies tries their wings.

During the early morning hours or evening dusk, a variety of wildlife drinks from the pools. White-tailed deer and porcupines depend on the water for survival.

The isolated oases add an unexpected touch of color to the landscape, reflecting an azure sky and offering refuge from the parched earth waiting only 200 feet above the canyon floor.

Tinajas — *pools of water collected in natural cisterns — were important sources of water for animals and early travelers.*

Bibliography

Brunnemann, Eric Jackson. *An Artifact Analysis of the Prickly Pouch: A Museum Studies — Archaeological Analysis in the Lower Pecos River Region of Southwest Texas*. Unpublished MA thesis. The University of Texas at Austin, 1988.

Bryant, Vaughn. "I Put Myself on a Caveman Diet — Permanently." *Prevention*, September 1979, pages 128–137.

Bryant, Vaughn M. "Ethnobotany of Hinds Cave." *National Geographic Society Research Reports*, 1975, pages 127–129.

Bryant, Vaughn M. "Pollen Grains: The Tiniest Clues in Archaeology." *Environment Southwest*. Autumn, 1987, pages 10–13.

Chadderdon, Mary Frances. *Baker Cave, Val Verde County, Texas: The 1976 Excavations*. Center for Archaeological Research, The University of Texas at San Antonio, Special Report, No. 13, 1983.

Gatliff, Betty Pat. "Forensic Sculpture Adapts to Museum Use." *Scientific Illustration*. Selected papers from the 7th Annual Conference of the Guild of Natural Science Illustrators. Washington, D.C., 1986.

Glassman, David M., Betty Pat. Gatliff, and Roberta McGregor. "Applications of Facial Sculpturing to the Biological Study of an Archaeological Population." *Plains Anthropologist*. Journal of the Plains Anthropological Society. Vol. 34-125: 1989, pages 223–231.

Hester, Thomas R. "A Chronological Framework for Lower Pecos Prehistory." *Bulletin of the Texas Archeological Society.* Vol. 59: 1988, pages 53–64.

Hester, Thomas R. and others. *From the Gulf to the Rio Grande: Human Adaptation in Central, South, and Lower Pecos, Texas.* Arkansas Archeological Survey Research Series No. 33, 1989.

Hester, Thomas R. *Hunters and Gatherers of the Rio Grande Plain and the Lower Coast of Texas.* Center for Archaeological Research, The University of Texas at San Antonio, 1976.

Hester, Thomas R. "Late Paleo-Indian Occupations at Baker Cave Southwestern Texas." *Bulletin of the Texas Archeological Society.* Vol. 53: 1983, pages 101–120.

Lampe, David. "Reader of the Invisible Dust." *The World and I.* November, 1990, pages 316–323.

McGregor, Roberta. "Threaded and Twined Matting: A Late Introduction Into The Lower Pecos." *Papers on Lower Pecos Prehistory.* ed. by Solveig A. Turpin. Texas Archeological Research Laboratory. Studies in Archeology 8, The University of Texas at Austin, 1991, pages 141–148.

McGregor, Roberta. *Prehistoric Basketry of the Lower Pecos, Texas.* Madison, Wisconsin: Prehistory Press, 1992.

Montgomery, Nola. *Rock Art Recording Manual.* ed. by Georg Zappler. Texas Parks and Wildlife Department, 1992.

Newcomb, W.W. Jr., *The Indians of Texas.* Austin: University of Texas Press, 1961.

Nunley, Parker. *A Field Guide to Archeological Sites of Texas.* Houston, Texas: Gulf Publishing, 1989.

Office of the State Archeologist. *You are the Guardian of the Past.* Texas Historical Commission. Austin, Texas: 1990.

Roberts, John R. and James P. Nash. *The Geology of Val Verde County.* Austin, Texas: University of Texas Bulletin No. 1803, 1918.

Shafer, Harry J. *Ancient Texans.* Houston, Texas: Gulf Publishing, 1993.

Shafer, Harry J. "The Prehistoric Legacy of the Lower Pecos Region of Texas." *Bulletin of the Texas Archeological Society.* No. 59, 1988, pages 23–52.

Turner, Ellen Sue and Thomas R. Hester. *A Field Guide to Stone Artifacts.* 2nd ed. Houston, Texas: Gulf Publishing, 1993.

Turpin, Solveig A. and Jim Zintgraff. *Pecos River Rock Art.* San Antonio, Texas: Macpherson Publishing Co., 1992.

Turpin, Solveig A. "Rock Art and Hunter-gatherer Archaeology: A Case Study from SW Texas and Northern Mexico." *Journal of Field Archaeology.* Vol. 17, 1990, pages 263–281.

Turpin, Solveig A. "Speculations on the Age and Origin of the Pecos River Style, Southwest Texas." Keynote address for the International Rock Art Congress and 16th Annual ARARA meeting. The Witte Museum, San Antonio, Texas: 1989.

Turpin, Solveig A. "The Iconography of Contact: Spanish Influences in the Rock Art of the Middle Rio Grande." *Columbian Consequences.* ed. by David Hurst Thomas. Volume 1, Smithsonian Institution Press: 1989, pages 277–299.

Turpin, Solveig A. "New Perspectives on the Red Linear Style Pictographs of the Lower Pecos River Region, Texas." *Plains Anthropologist.* Journal of the Plains Anthropological Society. Vol. 35-132, 1990, pages 375–381.

Turpin, Solveig A. "Sin Nombre and El Fortin: Pecos River Style Pictographs in Northern Mexico." *Bulletin of the Texas Archeological Society.* Vol. 60, 1989, pages 267–281.

Williams, John E. *Windmill Nature Trail: Seminole Canyon State Historical Park.* Texas Parks and Wildlife Department, 1991.

Photo/Illustration Credits

Page viii: Stephan Myers

Page x: David G. Robinson/Courtesy Texas Archeological Research Laboratory

Page xi (left): Stephan Myers

Page xi (right): David G. Robinson/Courtesy Texas Archeological Research Laboratory

Page xii: Stephan Myers

Page 2: Courtesy Texas Archeological Research Laboratory

Page 3: Stephan Myers

Page 4: Courtesy Texas Archeological Research Laboratory

Page 5: Stephan Myers

Page 6: Stephan Myers

Page 7: General 66, Texas Archeological Research Laboratory

Page 8: Stephan Myers

Page 10: 41VV74-101, Texas Archeological Research Laboratory

Page 12: Courtesy Interpretation and Exhibits Branch, Texas Parks and Wildlife

Page 13: Stephan Myers

Page 14: David G. Robinson/Courtesy Texas Archeological Research Laboratory

Page 15 (left): David G. Robinson/Courtesy Texas Archeological Research Laboratory

Page 15 (right): David G. Robinson/Courtesy Texas Archeological Research Laboratory

Page 17: Stephan Myers

Page 18: Courtesy Thomas R. Hester

Page 20: Courtesy Thomas R. Hester

Page 21: G. Elaine Acker

Page 22: Courtesy Interpretation and Exhibits Branch, Texas Parks and Wildlife Department

Page 23: Courtesy Interpretation and Exhibits Branch, Texas Parks and Wildlife Department

Page 24 (left): Courtesy Interpretation and Exhibits Branch, Texas Parks and Wildlife Department

Page 24 (right): Courtesy Interpretation and Exhibits Branch, Texas Parks and Wildlife Department

Page 25 (left): Courtesy Interpretation and Exhibits Branch, Texas Parks and Wildlife Department

Page 25 (right): Courtesy Interpretation and Exhibits Branch, Texas Parks and Wildlife Department

Page 26 (upper left): Courtesy Interpretation and Exhibits Branch, Texas Parks and Wildlife Department

Page 26 (upper right): Courtesy Interpretation and Exhibits Branch, Texas Parks and Wildlife Department

Page 26 (lower left): Courtesy Interpretation and Exhibits Branch, Texas Parks and Wildlife Department

Page 26 (lower right): Stephan Myers

Page 27 (lower right): Stephan Myers

Page 27 (upper leftand right): Courtesy Interpretation and Exhibits Branch, Texas Parks and Wildlife Department

Page 27 (lower left): Courtesy Interpretation and Exhibits Branch, Texas Parks and Wildlife Department

Page 28: 41VV74-162, Texas Archeological Research Laboratory

Page 29: Courtesy Interpretation and Exhibits Branch, Texas Parks and Wildlife Department

Page 30 (left): 41VV74-88, Texas Archeological Research Laboratory

Page 30 (right): Courtesy Interpretation and Exhibits Branch, Texas Parks and Wildlife Department

Page 31 (left): 41VV74-105, Texas Archeological Research Laboratory

Page 31 (right): Courtesy Interpretation and Exhibits Branch, Texas Parks and Wildlife Department

Page 32: Courtesy Interpretation and Exhibits Branch, Texas Parks and Wildlife Department

Page 33: Stephan Myers

Page 34 (top): 41VV74-158, Texas Archeological Research Laboratory

Page 34 (bottom): 41VV74-153, Texas Archeological Research Laboratory

Page 36: Courtesy the Witte Museum

Page 37 (top): Courtesy Interpretation and Exhibits Branch, Texas Parks and Wildlife Department

Page 37 (bottom): 41VV74-119, Texas Archeological Research Laboratory

Page 38 (left): Stephan Myers

Page 38 (right): Courtesy Interpretation and Exhibits Branch, Texas Parks and Wildlife Department

Page 39 (left): 41VV74-113, Texas Archeological Research Laboratory

Page 39 (right): Courtesy Interpretation and Exhibits Branch, Texas Parks and Wildlife Department

Page 40 (upper left): 41VV74-147, Texas Archeological Research Laboratory

Page 40 (lower left): Courtesy Interpretation and Exhibits Branch, Texas Parks and Wildlife Department

Page 40 (right): Courtesy Interpretation and Exhibits Branch, Texas Parks and Wildlife Department

Page 41 (bottom): 41VV74-111, Texas Archeological Research Laboratory

Page 41 (top): 41VV74-152, Texas Archeological Research Laboratory

Page 42: Courtesy Interpretation and Exhibits Branch, Texas Parks and Wildlife Department

Page 44: Courtesy Vaughn M. Bryant

Page 46 (top): General 17, J.C. Hudson Collection, Texas Archeological Research Laboratory

Page 46 (lower right): Stephan Myers

Page 46 (lower left): Courtesy Vaughn M. Bryant

Page 47: Stephan Myers

Page 48: Stephan Myers

Page 49: Courtesy Vaughn M. Bryant

Page 50: Courtesy Vaughn M. Bryant

Page 52: Stephan Myers

Page 54: Stephan Myers

Page 56: David G. Robinson/Courtesy Texas Archeological Research Laboratory

Page 57: David G. Robinson/Courtesy Texas Archeological Research Laboratory

Page 58 (top): David G. Robinson/Courtesy Texas Archeological Research Laboratory

Page 58 (bottom): David G. Robinson/Courtesy Texas Archeological Research Laboratory

Page 59: David G. Robinson/Courtesy Texas Archeological Research Laboratory

Page 60: David G. Robinson/Courtesy Texas Archeological Research Laboratory

Page 61: David G. Robinson/Courtesy Texas Archeological Research Laboratory

Page 62 (left): David G. Robinson/Courtesy Texas Archeological Research Laboratory

Page 62 (right): David G. Robinson/Courtesy Texas Archeological Research Laboratory

Page 63 (top): David G. Robinson/Courtesy Texas Archeological Research Laboratory

Page 63 (bottom): David G. Robinson/Courtesy Texas Archeological Research Laboratory

Page 64: David G. Robinson/Courtesy Texas Archeological Research Laboratory

Page 65: David G. Robinson/Courtesy Texas Archeological Research Laboratory

Page 66 (top): David G. Robinson/Courtesy Texas Archeological Research Laboratory

Page 66 (bottom): Abby C. Treece/Courtesy Texas Archeological Research Laboratory

Page 67 (right): David G. Robinson/Courtesy Texas Archeological Research Laboratory

Page 67 (left): David G. Robinson/Courtesy Texas Archeological Research Laboratory

Page 68: David G. Robinson/Courtesy Texas Archeological Research Laboratory

Page 69: Phelps/Gredell Photography, San Antonio, Texas

Page 70: Stephan Myers

Page 72: Courtesy the Witte Museum

Page 73: Courtesy the Witte Museum

Page 74: Courtesy the Witte Museum

Page 75 (top) Courtesy Texas Memorial Museum, acc. #2261-2

Page 75 (bottom): Courtesy Texas Memorial Museum, acc. #2261-8

Page 76 (top): Courtesy Texas Memorial Museum, acc. #2261-12

Page 76 (bottom) Courtesy Texas Memorial Museum, acc. #2261-160

Page 77: R.K. Florence/Courtesy Texas Parks and Wildlife Department.

Page 81: Stephan Myers

Page 82: Stephan Myers

Page 84: Courtesy Texas Archeological Research Laboratory

Page 86: 41VV74-224, Texas Archeological Research Laboratory

Page 88: Stephan Myers

Page 89: Stephan Myers

Page 91: Stephan Myers

Index

About the Author

G. Elaine Acker's interest in the lesser-known ancient Texas Indians stems from her research and preparation of articles on the Lower Pecos for *Texas Parks and Wildlife Magazine*. She is a native of Longview, Texas, but lives in Austin, where she now works for Texas Parks and Wildlife.

She recently completed a master's degree in English from the University of St. Thomas after earning a bachelor's degree in advertising from the University of Texas at Austin. Ms. Acker is a member of the Society of Children's Book Writers and the National Council of Teachers in English.

Renee Agee